ITALIAN RAILWAYS

LOCOMOTIVES & MULTIPLE UNITS

FOURTH EDITION

The complete guide to all Locomotives
and Multiple Units of the railways of Italy

David Haydock

Published by Platform 5 Publishing Ltd., 52 Broadfield Road, Sheffield S8 0XJ, England.

Printed in England by The Lavenham Press, Lavenham, Suffolk.

ISBN 978 1 909431 60 7

CONTENTS

Left: Up in the Dolomites: FLIRT EMU ETR.170.111, in the Trento province livery, waits to leave Merano with a train to Bolzano and Brennero on 13 September 2018. **David Haydock**

Front Cover: Trenitalia E.402.121, in the new Intercity livery, passes Mezzocorona whilst working train EXP 13421 from Krakow (Poland) to Firenze SMN on 24 January 2019. **Laurence Sly**

Back Cover Top: Old and new at Trento on 13 September 2018. A Trenitalia ETR.610 set arrives from Bolzano with a train to Roma, passing 1910 vintage 2-6-0 625.011 plinthed there. **David Haydock**

Back Cover Bottom: SAD FLIRT ETR.170.101 and Trento province "Jazz" EMU ETR.526.013 are seen at Fortezza/Franzenfeste on 9 June 2017. **Jan Lundstrøm**

INTRODUCTION

Welcome to the fourth edition of *Italian Railways*, which contains full details of all locomotives and multiple units of Italian Railways (passenger activity Trenitalia and freight activity Mercitalia), as well as all independent and private railways in Italy.

In the past few years the Trenitalia fleet has become far more standardised, whilst the independent railways have expanded and modernised their fleets. In many cases they are now operating passenger services on the RFI network, in many cases on behalf of Trenitalia. Some of these companies are also expanding into freight services on the main line too. The number of new companies operating freight continues to grow, and Italy has a unique phenomenon: NTV, a private company operating high speed passenger trains.

Most neighbouring railways have stopped cooperating with Trenitalia: SNCF operates its TGVs to Milano alone, while Trenitalia runs passenger trains to Paris and Marseille with subsidiary Thello. SBB operates alone to Milano, while Trenitalia runs to Zürich and Basel. ÖBB, with DB and FNM, operates EC trains from München and Innsbruck to Italy, and so on. Similar things have happened to freight, while Trenitalia operates into Austria and Switzerland through its German subsidiary TX Logistik. Details of railways based outside Italy can be found in other books in this series on the countries concerned.

Italy is a difficult country to document. Internet data is very patchy. Most railways do not reply to requests for information. Thus much of the information in this book has been obtained from the author's personal observations and from other contributors, especially **Today's Railways Europe** correspondent Marco Cacozza. The details of the Trenitalia fleet are likely to be the least accurate! This is because the company seems to consider the sort of data we publish as a "State secret" and does not reply to our queries.

Most livery information has been removed from this edition. Almost all trains in the Trenitalia fleet are now in the standard XMPR livery (not diesel locos) of white with green and blue relief and red visibility panels on the front end. Trains which differ considerably from this livery are indicated.

This book can be kept up-to-date by subscribing to the magazine **Today's Railways Europe** published monthly by Platform 5 which gives regular news and stock changes for Italy.

David Haydock, March 2019.

ABBREVIATIONS

The following abbreviations are used in this book:

de	diesel electric
dh	diesel hydraulic
dm	diesel mechanical
e	electric
km/h	kilometres per hour
kN	kilonewtons
kW	kilowatts
m	metres
ČD	Česke Dráhy (Czech Railways)
CFR	Compania Nationala de Cai Ferate (Romanian Railways)
DB	Deutsche Bahn (German Railways)
FSI	Ferrovie dello Stato Italiane (Italian State Railways)
HŽ	Hrvatske Željeznice (Croatian Railways)
MÁV	Magyar Állumvasutak (Hungarian State Railways)
NS	Nederlandse Spoorwegen (Netherlands Railways)
NSB	Norwegian State Railways
ÖBB	Österreichische Bundesbahnen (Austrian State Railways)
PKP	Polskie Koleje Panstwowe (Polish State Railways)
SBB	Schweizerische Bundesbahnen (Swiss Federal Railways)
SJ	Swedish State Railways
SNCB	Société Nationale des Chemins de Fer Belges (Belgian State Railways)
(S)	Stored serviceable
(U)	Stored unserviceable

A BRIEF HISTORY OF ITALY

Italy, or *Italia* in Italian, is formed mainly of a large peninsula plus the islands of *Sicilia* (Sicily) and *Sardegna* (Sardinia). The area has been a seat of civilisation for some 4000 years, most significantly as the centre of the Roman empire. Christianity became established during this period and Roma became the seat of the Christian church. After a brief Byzantine occupation, Carlo Magno (Charles the Great), king of the Lombards, became head of the Holy Roman Empire which spread across Europe.

Italy continued to be fought over from 1500 to 1800, particularly by the French, Spanish and Austrians. In 1814, the peninsula became a "geographical entity" albeit partly in foreign hands. In the middle of the 19th century, several revolts resulted in the northern areas of Piemonte and Lombardia becoming Italian but the Savoie and Nice areas were lost to France. In 1861, Italy became a united kingdom apart from the Roma area. In 1870, the Pope gave up government of the city which became the capital of Italy.

In 1918, the Italians won Trieste from Austria, the port was taken by the Yugoslavs in 1945 then restored to Italy in 1954. In 1919 the Treaty of St. Germain-en-Laye attributed the former Austrian areas of Trentino and Alto Adige (Südtirol) to Italy. The population here is still largely German speaking and communities have both German and Italian names, e.g. Bolzano/Bozen. In 1920 Italy annexed the Istrian peninsula and the port of Fiume (now Rijeka) but the area was returned to Yugoslavia after the Second World War and is now divided between Slovenia and Croatia. Electrification in this former Italian area is still mainly at 3000 V DC and with FS equipment. Sicilia, Sardegna and the Valle d'Aosta regions have special status, the last having belonged to the house of Savoie until 1945, and many inhabitants still speak French. In the early 1960s, Friuli Venezia-Giulia and Trentino-Alto Adige became regions with special statuses.

Today Italy is a member of the European Union with a population of around 60 million – similar to Britain and France. The north is considerably richer (industry and proximity to the rest of Europe) than the south (agriculture) and this leads to large flows of workers filling Trenitalia's day and overnight trains. This also means that most of Trenitalia's freight traffic is in the north.

As in other European countries, power has been transferred from central to regional government in recent years. Italy is divided into 20 regions (*regione*), many with local operators (in brackets) – Valle d'Aosta, Piemonte (GTT), Lombardia (FNM, SSIF), Trentino-Alto Adige (SAD, TT), Veneto (ST), Friuli-Venezia Giulia (FUC), Liguria (FGC), Emilia-Romagna (TPER), Toscana (TFT), Marche, Umbria (FCU), Lazio (ATAC), Abruzzo (FAS), Molise, Campania (EAV), Puglia (FAL, FG, FSE, FT), Basilicata, Calabria (FC), Sicilia (FCE) and Sardegna (ARST).

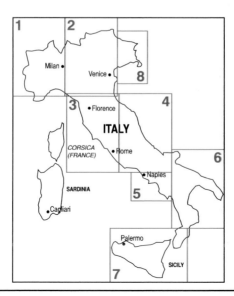

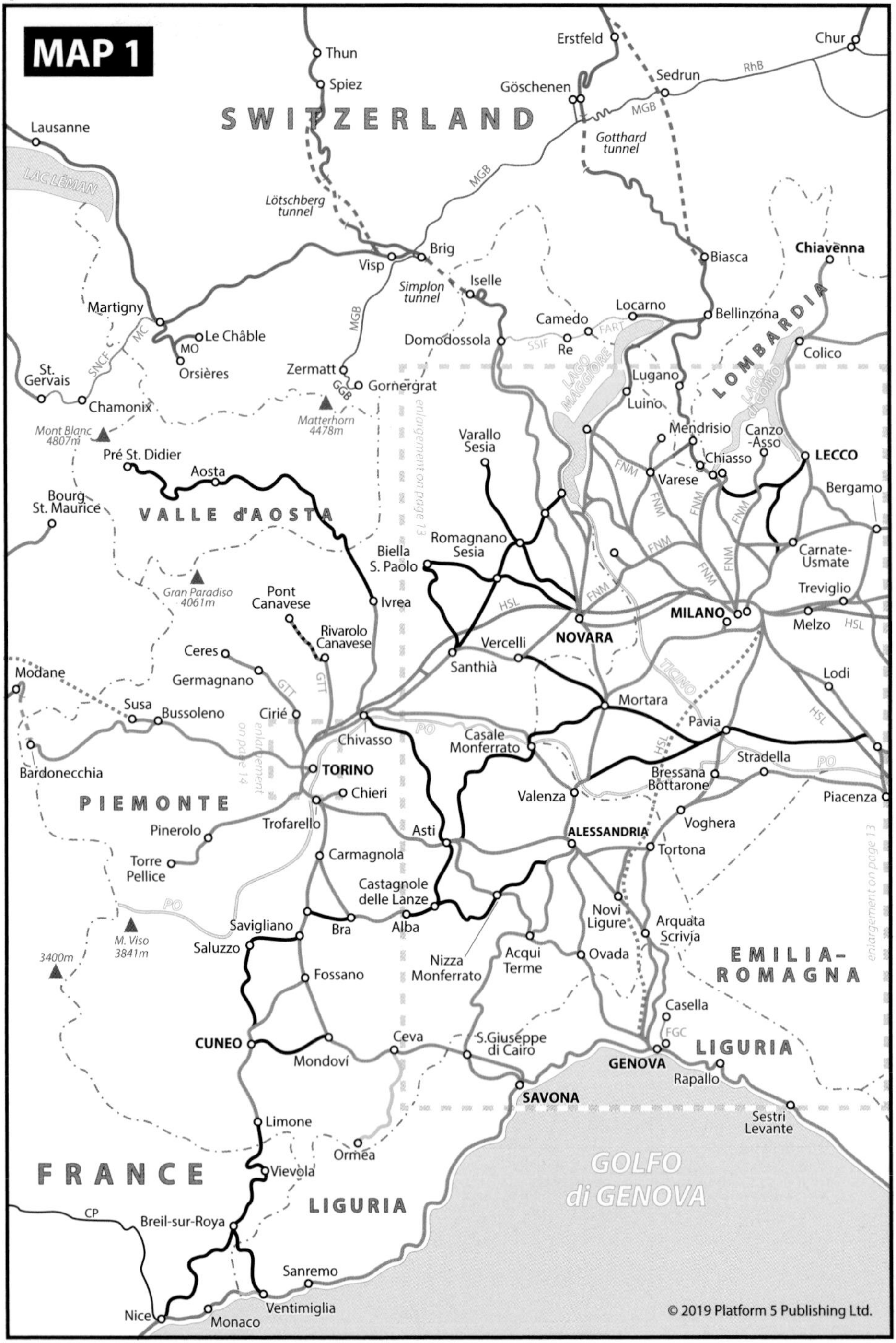

MAP 1

SWITZERLAND

Thun
Spiez
Erstfeld
Sedrun
Chur
Göschenen
RhB
Gotthard tunnel
MGB
Biasca
Chiavenna

Lausanne

Lötschberg tunnel

Brig
Simplon tunnel
Iselle
Visp
MGB
Domodossola
Camedo
Re
Locarno
Bellinzona
Colico

Martigny
MC
Le Châble
MO
SNCF
Zermatt
Gornergrat
SSIF
Lugano
Luino
LOMBARDIA
FART

St. Gervais
Orsières
GB
Chamonix
Matterhorn 4478m
Varallo Sesia
Mendrisio
Chiasso
Canzo -Asso
LECCO

Mont Blanc 4807m
Pré St. Didier
Aosta
enlargement on page 13
Varese
FNM
Bergamo

Bourg St. Maurice
VALLE d'AOSTA
Gran Paradiso 4061m
Pont Canavese
Ivrea
Biella S. Paolo
Romagnano Sesia
FNM
Carnate-Usmate

Modane
Ceres
Rivarolo Canavese
GTT
Vercelli
NOVARA
MILANO
Treviglio
Melzo
HSL

Susa
Germagnano
Bussoleno
Cirié
Santhià
Mortara
Pavia
Lodi

Bardonecchia
Chivasso
TORINO
Chieri
Casale Monferrato
Valenza
Bressana Bottarone
Stradella
Piacenza
PO

PIEMONTE
Trofarello
Asti
ALESSANDRIA
Voghera
Tortona
HSL

Pinerolo
Carmagnola
Castagnole delle Lanze
Novi Ligure
Arquata Scrivia
EMILIA-ROMAGNA

Torre Pellice
Savigliano
Bra
Alba
Nizza Monferrato
Acqui Terme
Ovada
enlargement on page 13

M. Viso 3841m
Saluzzo
Fossano
Casella
FGC
LIGURIA

3400m
CUNEO
Mondoví
Ceva
S.Giuseppe di Cairo
GENOVA
Rapallo

Limone
Ormea
SAVONA
Sestri Levante

FRANCE
Vievola
LIGURIA
GOLFO di GENOVA

CP
Breil-sur-Roya

Sanremo
Nice
Ventimiglia
Monaco

© 2019 Platform 5 Publishing Ltd.

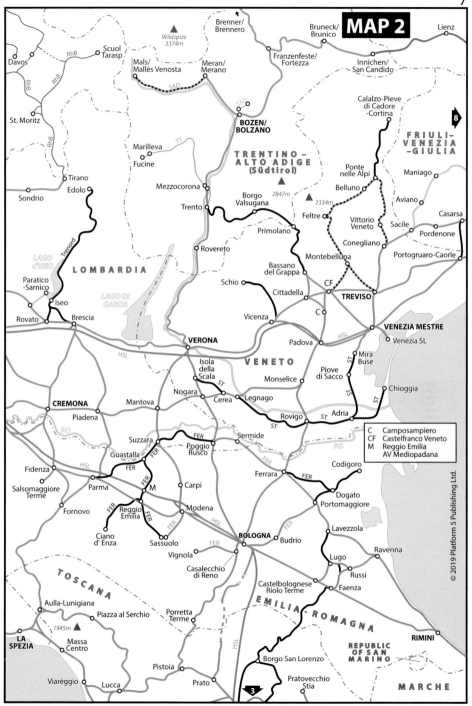

MAP 2

8

3

C   Camposampiero
CF Castelfranco Veneto
M   Reggio Emilia
    AV Mediopadana

© 2019 Platform 5 Publishing Ltd.

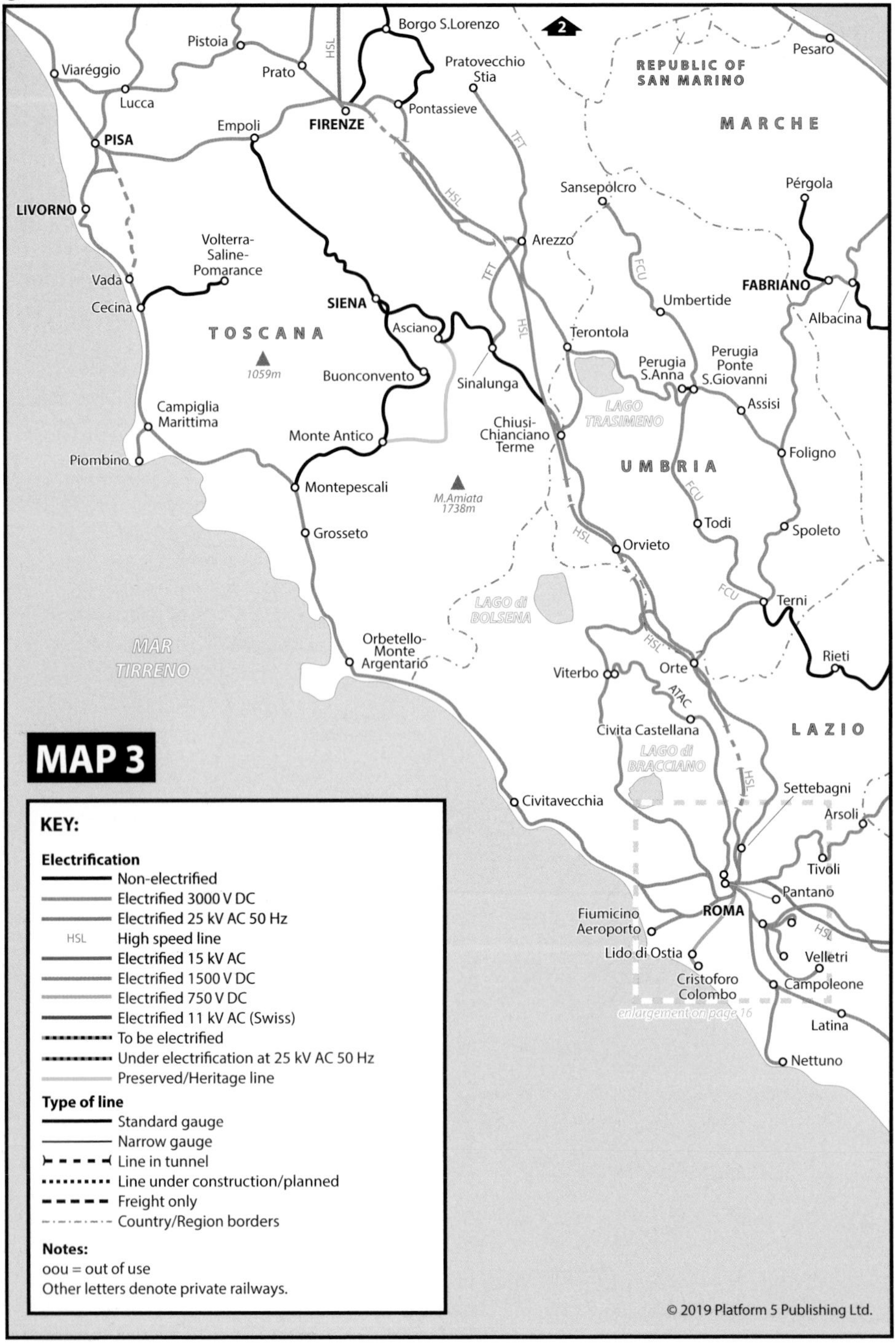

Pistoia
Viaréggio
Prato
Lucca
Empoli
FIRENZE
PISA

Borgo S.Lorenzo
Pratovecchio Stia
Pontassieve

REPUBLIC OF SAN MARINO
Pesaro

MARCHE

LIVORNO

Volterra-Saline-Pomarance

Vada
Cecina

SIENA

TOSCANA
1059m

Asciano

Buonconvento

Monte Antico

Campiglia Marittima

Piombino

Montepescali

Grosseto

M.Amiata 1738m

Sansepólcro

Arezzo

Umbertide

Terontola

Perugia S.Anna
Perugia Ponte S.Giovanni

Sinalunga

Chiusi-Chianciano Terme

Orvieto

UMBRIA

Todi

Pérgola

FABRIANO
Albacina

Assisi

Foligno

Spoleto

Terni

Rieti

LAGO TRASIMENO

LAGO di BOLSENA

MAR TIRRENO

Orbetello-Monte Argentario

Viterbo

Orte

LAGO di BRACCIANO

Civita Castellana

Civitavecchia

LAZIO

Settebagni
Arsoli

Fiumicino Aeroporto

ROMA

Lido di Ostia

Cristoforo Colombo

enlargement on page 16

Tivoli

Pantano

Velletri

Campoleone

Latina

Nettuno

MAP 3

KEY:

Electrification
——— Non-electrified
——— Electrified 3000 V DC
——— Electrified 25 kV AC 50 Hz
HSL High speed line
——— Electrified 15 kV AC
——— Electrified 1500 V DC
——— Electrified 750 V DC
——— Electrified 11 kV AC (Swiss)
••••••••• To be electrified
••••••••• Under electrification at 25 kV AC 50 Hz
——— Preserved/Heritage line

Type of line
——— Standard gauge
——— Narrow gauge
>– – – –< Line in tunnel
•••••••••• Line under construction/planned
– – – – Freight only
–··–··– Country/Region borders

Notes:
oou = out of use
Other letters denote private railways.

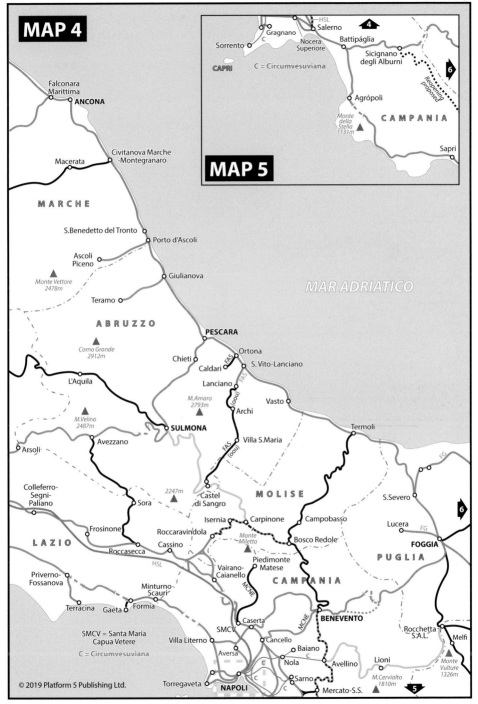

MAP 4

MAP 5

C = Circumvesuviana

CAPRI

Gragnano
Sorrento
Nocera Superiore
Salerno
HSL
Battipáglia
Sicignano degli Alburni
Agrópoli
Monte della Stella 1131m
CAMPANIA
Sapri
Reopening proposed

Falconara Marittima
ANCONA

Macerata
Civitanova Marche -Montegranaro

MARCHE

S.Benedetto del Tronto
Porto d'Ascoli

Ascoli Piceno
Giulianova

Monte Vettore 2478m

Teramo

ABRUZZO

Corno Grande 2912m

Chieti
Caldari
Lanciano
M.Amaro 2793m
Archi
M.Velino 2487m
SULMONA
Avezzano

PESCARA
Ortona
S. Vito-Lanciano
Vasto
Villa S.Maria
Termoli

MAR ADRIATICO

L'Aquila

Arsoli

Colleferro-Segni-Paliano
Sora
Frosinone
Roccaravindola
Roccasecca
Cassino
2247m
Castel di Sangro

Isernia
Carpinone
Campobasso
Bosco Redole

MOLISE

S.Severo
Lucera
FOGGIA

FG

PUGLIA

LAZIO

HSL

Priverno-Fossanova

Terracina
Gaeta
Formia
Minturno Scauri

SMCV = Santa Maria Capua Vetere
C = Circumvesuviana

© 2019 Platform 5 Publishing Ltd.

Vairano-Caianello
Piedimonte Matese
Monte Miletto
CAMPANIA

BENEVENTO

Caserta
SMCV
Villa Literno
Aversa
Cancello
Baiano
Nola
Sarno
Torregaveta
NAPOLI
Mercato-S.S.

Avellino
Lioni
M.Cervialto 1810m

Rocchetta S.A.L.
Melfi
Monte Vulture 1326m

FAS (100u)
FAS (100u)
MCNE
MCNE

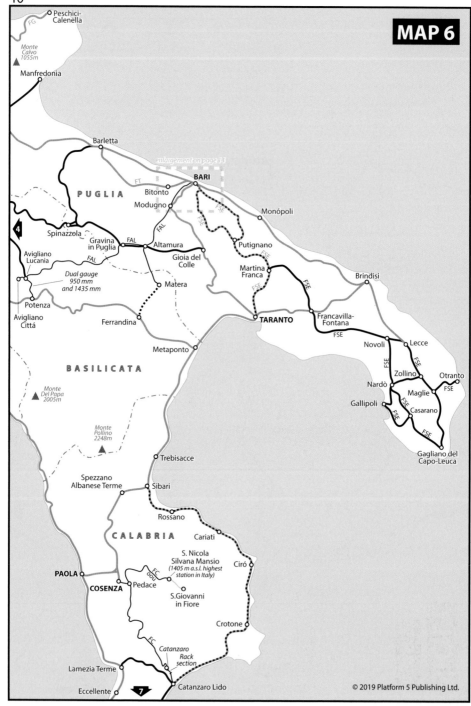

MAP 6

Peschici-Calenella

Monte Calvo 1055m

Manfredonia

Barletta

enlargement on page 13

BARI

PUGLIA

Bitonto

Modugno

Monópoli

Spinazzola

Gravina in Puglia

Altamura

Putignano

Avigliano Lucania

Gioia del Colle

Martina Franca

Brindisi

Dual gauge 950 mm and 1435 mm

Matera

Potenza

Avigliano Cittá

Ferrandina

TARANTO

Francavilla-Fontana

Metaponto

Novoli

Lecce

BASILICATA

Zollino

Otranto

Monte Del Papa 2005m

Nardò

Maglie

Gallipoli

Casarano

Monte Pollino 2248m

Gagliano del Capo-Leuca

Trebisacce

Spezzano Albanese Terme

Sibari

Rossano

CALABRIA

Cariati

S. Nicola Silvana Mansio (1405 m a.s.l. highest station in Italy)

Ciró

PAOLA

COSENZA

Pedace

S.Giovanni in Fiore

Crotone

Catanzaro Rack section

Lamezia Terme

Eccellente

Catanzaro Lido

© 2019 Platform 5 Publishing Ltd.

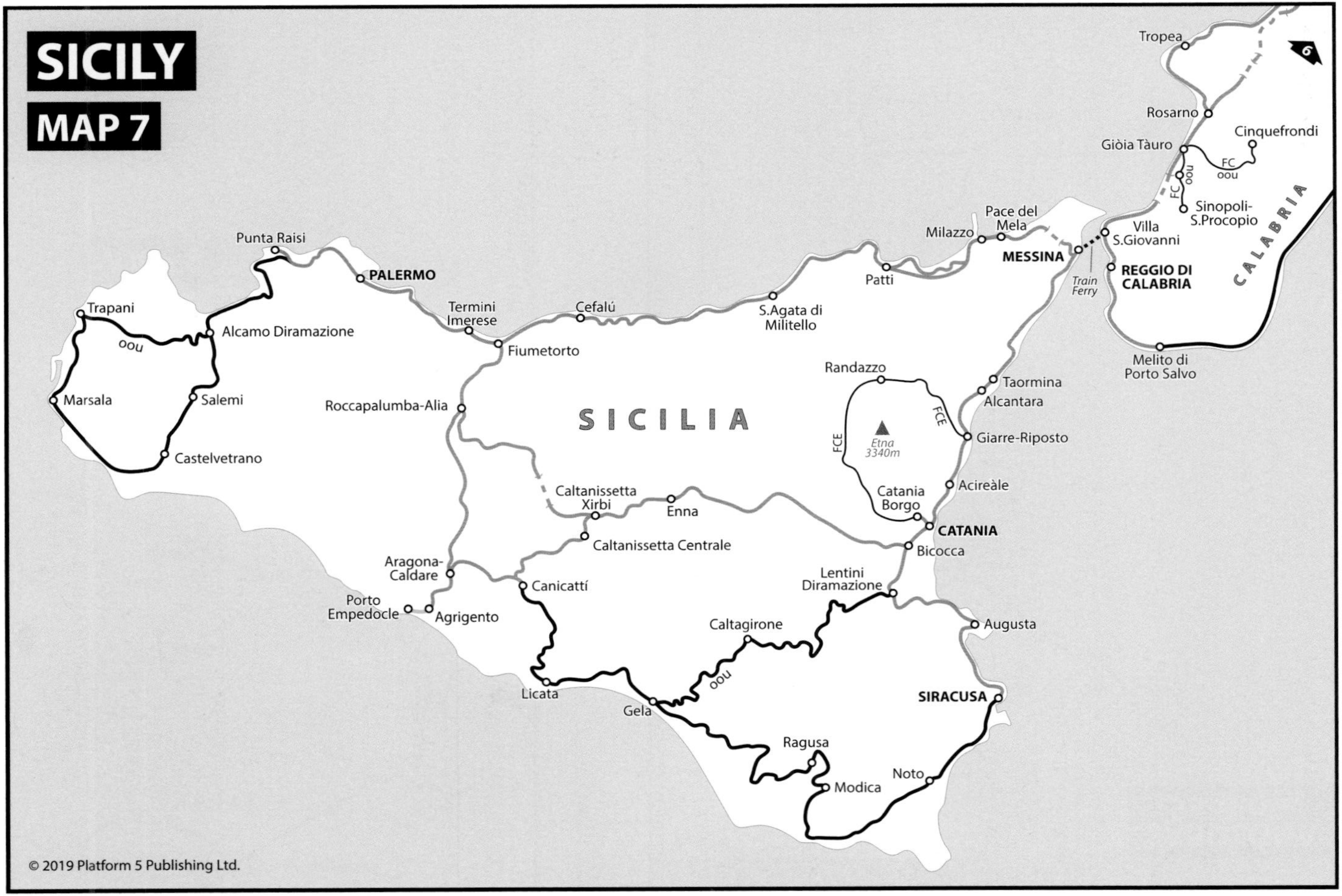

SICILY
MAP 7

CALABRIA

Cinquefrondi

Tropea

Rosarno

Gióia Tauro

FC
noo
FC

Sinopoli-
S.Procopio

Villa
S.Giovanni

REGGIO DI
CALABRIA

Melito di
Porto Salvo

Train
Ferry

MESSINA

Pace del
Mela

Milazzo

Patti

S.Agata di
Militello

Taormina

Alcantara

Giarre-Riposto

Acireale

CATANIA

Bicocca

Augusta

SIRACUSA

Noto

Modica

FCE

Etna
3340m

Catania
Borgo

Randazzo

FCE

Lentini
Diramazione

Ragusa

Caltagirone

noo

Gela

SICILIA

Cefalù

Fiumetorto

Termini
Imerese

PALERMO

Roccapalumba-Alia

Caltanissetta
Xirbi

Enna

Caltanissetta Centrale

Canicattì

Licata

Aragona-
Caldare

Agrigento

Porto
Empedocle

Punta Raisi

Alcamo Diramazione

Salemi

Castelvetrano

noo

Trapani

Marsala

© 2019 Platform 5 Publishing Ltd.

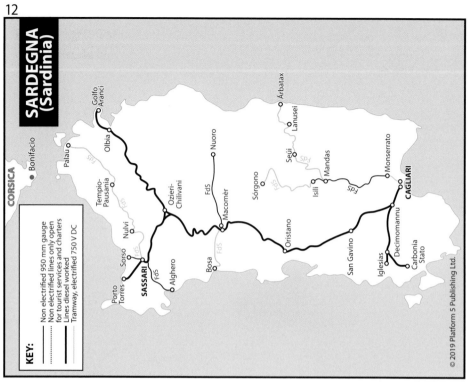

SARDEGNA (Sardinia)

KEY:

- Non electrified 950 mm gauge
- Non electrified lines only open for tourist services and charters
- Lines diesel worked
- Tramway, electrified 750 V DC

CORSICA

Bonifacio

Golfo Aranci, Olbia, Palau, Tempio-Pausania, Ozieri-Chilivani, Nulvi, Sorso, Porto Torres, SASSARI, Alghero, Bosa, Macomèr, Nuoro, Sórgono, Oristano, San Gavino, Iglesias, Decimomannu, Carbonia Stato, CAGLIARI, Monserrato, Isili, Mandas, Seùi, Lanusei, Árbatax, FdS, SP1

© 2019 Platform 5 Publishing Ltd.

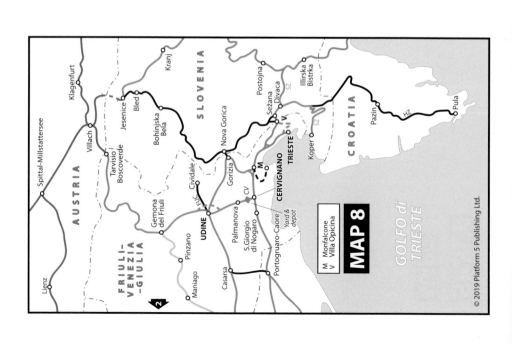

MAP 8

M Monfalcone
V Villa Opicina

AUSTRIA, FRIULI-VENEZIA-GIULIA, SLOVENIA, CROATIA

Lienz, Spittal-Millstättersee, Klagenfurt, Villach, Tarvisio Boscoverde, Jesenice, Bled, Bohinjska Bela, Kranj, Gemona del Friuli, Pinzano, Maniago, Casarsa, UDINE, Cividale, Nova Gorica, Gorizia, Palmanova, S.Giorgio di Nogaro, Portogruaro-Caore, CERVIGNANO, Monfalcone, TRIESTE, Sežana, Divača, Postojna, Illirska Bistrka, Koper, Pazin, Pula, FUC, CV, Yard & depot, SŽ, HZ

GOLFO di TRIESTE

© 2019 Platform 5 Publishing Ltd.

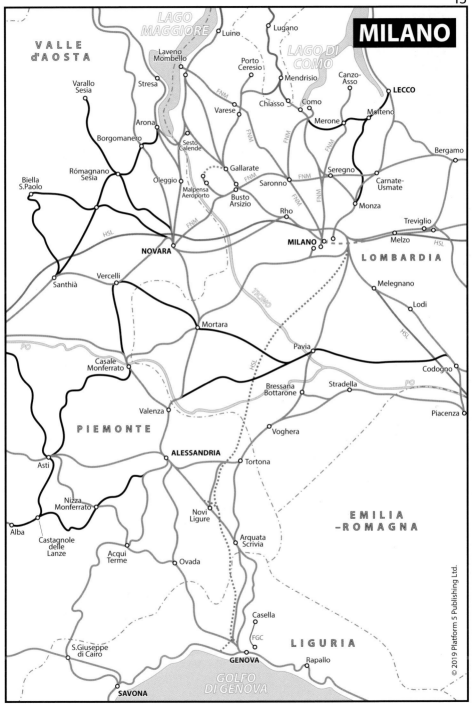

MILANO

VALLE d'AOSTA

LAGO MAGGIORE

LAGO DI COMO

Luino

Lugano

Laveno Mombello

Porto Ceresio

Mendrisio

Canzo-Asso

LECCO

Varallo Sesia

Stresa

Chiasso

Como

Molteno

Arona

Varese

Merone

Bergamo

Borgomanero

Sesto Calende

Gallarate

Seregno

Carnate-Usmate

Rómagnano Sesia

Oleggio

Malpensa Aeroporto

Saronno

Biella S.Paolo

Busto Arsizio

Monza

Treviglio

Rho

Melzo

NOVARA

MILANO

LOMBARDIA

Vercelli

Melegnano

Santhià

Lodi

PO

Mortara

Pavia

HSL

Casale Monferrato

Codogno

Valenza

Bressana Bottarone

Stradella

PO

Piacenza

PIEMONTE

Voghera

ALESSANDRIA

Tortona

Asti

EMILIA -ROMAGNA

Nizza Monferrato

Novi Ligure

Alba

Castagnole delle Lanze

Arquata Scrivia

Acqui Terme

Ovada

Casella

FGC

LIGURIA

S.Giuseppe di Cairo

GENOVA

Rapallo

SAVONA

GOLFO DI GENOVA

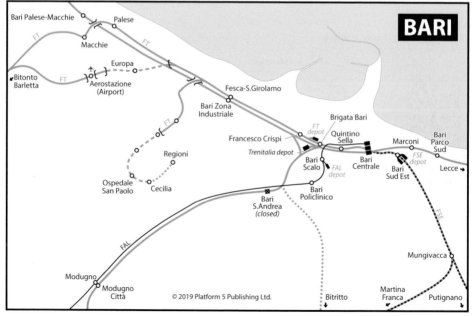

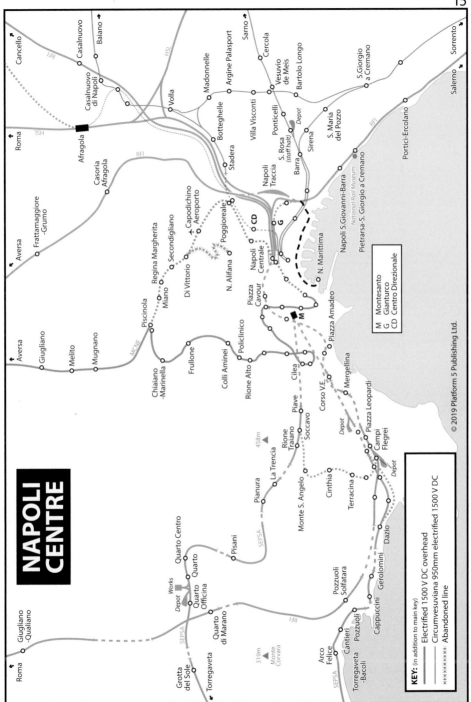

NAPOLI CENTRE

KEY: (in addition to main key)
— Electrified 1500 V DC overhead
— Circumvesuviana 950mm electrified 1500 V DC
······ Abandoned line

M Montesanto
G Gianturco
CD Centro Direzionale

© 2019 Platform 5 Publishing Ltd.

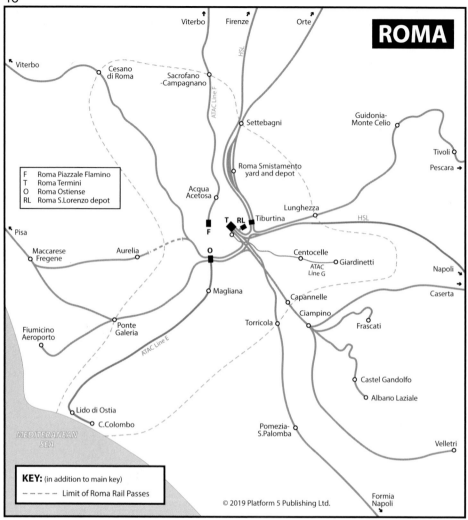

ROMA

Viterbo ↑ Firenze ↗ Orte ↗

Viterbo ↖

Cesano di Roma

Sacrofano-Campagnano

Settebagni

Guidonia-Monte Celio

Tivoli

Pescara →

Roma Smistamento yard and depot

F	Roma Piazzale Flamino
T	Roma Termini
O	Roma Ostiense
RL	Roma S.Lorenzo depot

Acqua Acetosa

Lunghezza

Pisa ↖

T RL Tiburtina

F

HSL

Maccarese Fregene

Aurelia

Centocelle

Giardinetti

ATAC Line G

Napoli →

O

Magliana

Capannelle

Caserta →

Ciampino

Torricola

Frascati

Fiumicino Aeroporto

Ponte Galeria

ATAC Line E

Castel Gandolfo

Albano Laziale

Lido di Ostia

C.Colombo

MEDITERANEAN SEA

Pomezia-S.Palomba

Velletri

KEY: (in addition to main key)

– – – – Limit of Roma Rail Passes

© 2019 Platform 5 Publishing Ltd.

Formia Napoli ↓

THE RAILWAYS OF ITALY

Italy is a country of great contrasts, from the Alps in the north, to the flat plain of the river Po and the central Apennine mountain chain which made building railways very difficult. Many lines through the mountains and along the coast are very scenic. One of the difficulties Italy has faced is the number of single track lines which make operations difficult. The busiest of these are being doubled, in many cases through the construction of completely new sections of line. In the 21st century, Italy has completed the north–south section of a T-shaped high speed network from Torino via Milano to Venezia and from Milano to Napoli via Bologna, Firenze and Roma, plus a line from Milano to Genova.

The first railway line in Italy was from Napoli to Portici which opened on 3 October 1839. At the time, each part of Italy was a kingdom or Grand Duchy, each one having its own railway company. The country was unified in 1861, by which time the network totalled 2371 km, operated by seven companies. In May 1865 the government forced these to merge into four large companies:

- Società' delle Strade Ferrate dell'Alta Italia (SFAI), which was given all the northern Italian lines;
- Società' Generale delle Strade Ferrate Romane (SGSFR), which took over the lines along the Campania, Lazio and Toscana coasts plus a small part of Liguria and the former Papal State;
- Società' Italiana per le Strade Ferrate Meridionali (SFM), to operate lines in Emilia, Marche, Abruzzo, Molise and Puglia – the Bologna–Ancona–Bari–Otranto route;
- Società' Strade Ferrate Calabro-Sicule (SFCS), which took over Sicily and southern Italy (the Palermo–Trabia line was the only one built by then).

This proved unsatisfactory and four new railway networks were then formed. The four largest railway stations (Milano, Firenze, Roma and Napoli) and some minor stations were jointly managed by them. The companies were:

- Società Italiana per le Strade Ferrate Meridionali was responsible for the lines down the Adriatic coast in Lombardia, Veneto, Emilia and central Italy and the Roma–Firenze line, totalling 4303 km.
- Società per le Strade Ferrate del Mediterraneo, running the Rete Mediterranea (RM), was given 4250 km of lines partly in Lombardia, Piemonte and Liguria, and the long Ventimiglia–Genova–Roma–Napoli–Salerno and Battipaglia–Potenza–Metaponto–Taranto lines, as well as Cosenza–Sibari and the Taranto–Sibari–Reggio Calabria line around the Ionic coast.
- Società Strade Ferrate della Sicilia was given 597 km of lines in Sicily to manage, mainly comprising the Messina–Catania–Siracusa, Catania–Caltanissetta–Palermo and Palermo–Trapani lines.
- Società delle Strade Ferrate Sarde was formed to run the Cagliari–Decimomannu–Iglesias, Decimomannu–Ozieri–Golfo Aranci and Ozieri–Porto Torres lines, opened from 1871 to 1883.

Italy's railways were nationalised in 1905 as Ferrovie dello Stato (FS) but many local railway companies have remained. These are now coming under the control of local regions, merging, being renamed and expanding into new activities and areas. The regions are increasingly financing new trains. This may end the charming tendency for local railways to buy second-hand stock from far afield.

Italy has metro and tram networks in Torino, Milano, Genova, Roma and Napoli and tramways in Torino, Milano, Bergamo, Firenze, Roma, Napoli, Messina, Cagliari and Sassari with new tram networks to come. These are not generally dealt with in this book.

Open access freight operators are expanding fast, especially in northern Italy, and NTV was the first open access passenger operator with high speed trains in the world.

LOCOMOTIVE & RAILCAR NUMBERING SYSTEM

Locomotive numbers have the prefix E for electric and D for diesel. High speed EMUs are prefixed ETR, EMUs are prefixed ALe and DMUs ALn. EMU trailers are Le and DMU trailers Ln. Steam locomotives do not have a prefix. In recent years ETR has started to be used for non-high speed EMUs and ATR for DMUs. Local railways sometimes have similar systems but often use their own, often idiosyncratic, systems although the advent of the pan-European Vehicle Numbering system (EVN) is leading to more standardisation.

In the past locomotive class numbers usually distinguished the number of axles – E.405 is Bo-Bo, E.656 Bo-Bo-Bo, D.445 B-B. EMU and DMU class numbers usually reflect capacity – Ale 582 has 58 seats, Le 682 has 68 seats and so on. But there are exceptions to these rules.

In this fourth edition, all locomotives and multiple units operated by local railways over national lines have been incorporated into the "main lists" as there is now much increased interworking. Locomotives and multiple units restricted to local networks can be found under their local operators in Section 2.

1. FERROVIE DELLO STATO ITALIANE (FSI)

FSI ORGANISATION

Originally FS (*Ferrovie dello Stato*, Italian State Railways), the company later became FSI. In 2001 FS was split up according to EU directives into the FSI Holding infrastructure manager *Rete Ferroviaria Italiana* (RFI) and operating company *Trenitalia*. Trenitalia is itself divided into activities – the *Passeggeri* (long-distance passenger), *Regionale* (regional passenger) and *Mercitalia* (freight) activities now have their own dedicated fleets. Other locomotives, mainly shunters, are allocated to *Mercitalia Shunting & Terminals*, *Infrastruttura* (RFI) and *Direzione Manutenzione Approvvigionamenti e Logistica* (DML, rolling stock).

RFI is also charged with some shunting activities, particularly at international borders. DML is divided geographically, the division increasingly coinciding with the borders of regional government – the regions expect stock partially financed by them to be maintained locally. Increasingly, maintenance depots concentrate on trains for one division only.

In 2017 FSI completely reorganised its freight division. *Trenitalia Cargo* became *Mercitalia Rail*, while the shunting subsidiary Ser.Fer became *Mercitalia Shunting & Terminals*. The latter has now taken over direct responsibility for maintenance of about 200 shunting locomotives as well as being "Entity in Charge of Maintenance" for about 250 other shunters, although work will still be carried out close to the loco's area of use.

DEPOTS AND WORKSHOPS

A list of depots and workshops and codes is given in Appendix III on page 207.

TRENITALIA TRAIN SERVICES

These are classified as follows, in descending order of importance/price:

FR	*Frecciarossa Alta Velocità*. ETR.500 high speed trains.
FA	*Frecciargento Alta Velocità*. Pendolino high speed trains.
FB	*Frecciabianca*. Highest quality intercity trains (Pendolino and hauled).
EC	*EuroCity*. Quality international services.
EN	*EuroNight*. Quality international overnight services.
ICN	*Inter City Notte*. Quality national overnight trains.
IC	*InterCity*. Quality domestic services.
RV	*Regionale Veloce*. Limited stop inter-regional train.
R	*Regionale*. Regional stopping services.
S	*Suburbano*. Suburban train.
M	*Metropolitano*. Suburban train in largest conurbations.

FSI ACTIVITY CODES

These codes are used throughout the book to indicate to which department of Trenitalia a locomotive is allocated. Codes are not used for high speed train sets which are all *Passeggeri*.

C   *Mercitalia Rail*, freight.
D   DML – traction and rolling stock management.
H   Historic fleet, owned by FSI.
I   RFI, infrastructure manager.
M   *Mercitalia Shunting & Terminals*
P   *Divisione Passeggeri Long Haul*, long distance passenger.
R   *Divisione Passeggeri Regionale*, regional passenger.
TR   Trenord (Trenitalia/FNM joint company)

ROLLING STOCK CHANGES

The *Passeggeri* division is currently revising operation of high speed trains, as it is receiving "new" ETR.700 trains and may order more ETR.400s. *Passeggeri*'s ageing E.444 and E.656 locomotives are to be replaced by Class E.464 locos transferred from *Regionale*.

Regionale is now receiving large numbers of DMUs and EMUs. The latter will free some Class E.464 (see above) and replace all the oldest stock.

Mercitalia Rail is receiving new locomotives which will replace Class E.655/656.

Keeping track of FSI stock is difficult because of the secrecy surrounding data, but also because many trains are taken out of service and stored for several years before being officially withdrawn.

LIVERIES

Most Trenitalia locomotives are now in the XMPR livery of white, blue and green. Almost all *Passeggeri* trains have been reliveried in the past five years as the FA, FB and FR brands have been introduced. From 2017 a new intercity livery was introduced.

Other than the XMPR livery, the following liveries exist (all trains have a red flash on the front end, in theory to improve visibility).

The following codes are used to denote specific liveries throughout this book:

FA   **Frecciargento:** Silver and red with black window band.
FB   **Frecciabianca**: White with dark grey chassis and red bands.
FR   **Frecciarossa:** Silver and red with black window band.
I   **Intercity:** White with dark grey roof, front ends and side panel, lined in red.
L   **Leonardo Express (Roma–Fiumicino airport):** White with red roof and front end plus green chassis.
M   **Mercitalia Rail:** Silver grey and red.
N   **Trenord:** White with dark green front end and roof.
R   **Regional:** Livery for regional trains introduced in 2014 – silver grey with dark grey window band, blue roof and front end, apple green doors, plus blue and yellow lines.
T   **TILO:** White with dark grey, red and green stripes.
V   **Vivalto:** White with green bands.

Old electric loco livery: Pale blue, lined in dark blue.
Old diesel loco livery: Green with brown lower body and roof.
1980s heavy shunters: Orange line in yellow. Classes D.145.1000 and D.145.2000.
Old shunting locomotives: Dark green lined in yellow. All small shunters.
RFI shunters: Some small, old shunters "owned" by RFI have been repainted in all over yellow.
Class 255: All over dark red.
Recent shunting locomotives: Green with some blue, lined in red with yellow safety rails. Classes D.146 and D.147.

Many preserved electric locos and railcars are in Isabella brown livery. This is brown, sometimes two-tone, with red lining in the case of railcars.

EUROPEAN VEHICLE NUMBER & VEHICLE KEEPER MARKING

A 21st century development has been the European Vehicle Number (EVN). This is a refinement of the former UIC full identification number. Because of open access in Europe it is essential that all traction (and indeed all rolling stock) has a European number. The Vehicle Keeper Marking (VKM) has been deemed necessary because of the large number of railway operators in a country following open access and follows the country code. This has helped to simplify matters in some countries as many private operators had duplicate numbers. Now they have a unique EVN as well!

Taking electric loco E.656.431 as an example its full EVN is 91 83 2656 431-0 I-IT which breaks down as follows:

The first digit is a code for a traction unit with the second digit giving the type of traction. The types are:

90. Miscellaneous traction – mostly used for steam locomotives, but also hybrid locomotives.
91. Electric Locomotives faster than 99 km/h.
92. Diesel locomotives faster than 99 km/h.
93. High speed Electric Multiple Units.
94. Electric Multiple Units.
95. Diesel Multiple Units
96. Loose trailers.
97. Electric shunting locomotives or electric locomotives with maximum speed less than 100 km/h.
98. Diesel shunting locomotives or diesel locomotives with maximum speed less than 100 km/h.
99. Departmental self powered vehicles.

The third and fourth digits indicate the country; 83 in the case of Italy. The railway concerned is indicated at the end as the vehicle keeper. In some cases this might not be a railway but a leasing company.

It will be seen that the old classification, e.g. 656, forms part of the new number. But in years to come there could be a 3656, 4656 etc. The running number and check digit are next followed by a country code and the VKM; in the example quoted, I for Italy and IT for Trenitalia.

The full EVN/VKM is shown on the sides of locomotives and vehicles and can be very small as it is a rather long piece of information. For this same reason numbers on the front of locomotives and units usually only show the basic number, with or without a check digit. Check digits are not shown in the lists in this book.

PASSENGER ACCOMMODATION IN RAILCARS AND MULTIPLE UNITS

Seating capacity of railcars and multiple units given in class headings and sub-headings is in the form F/S nT (or TD) nW. For example 12/54 1T 1W denotes 12 First Class and 54 Second Class seats, one toilet and one space for a wheelchair. A number in brackets (ie (2)) denotes tip-up seats (in addition to the fixed seats). TD denotes a universal access toilet suitable for use by a disabled person.

1.1. DIESEL LOCOMOTIVES

Trenitalia diesel locomotives fall into three groups. First, bogie locomotives used for shunting, empty coaching stock movements and local freight which are numbered in the D.100 series. Then tractor-style shunters which are numbered in the 200 series, inexplicably without the D prefix. Finally, real main line diesels, numbered in the D.300 and D.400 series.

There have been many changes to the Trenitalia fleet since the third edition of this book was published. The Mercitalia Rail (formerly Trenitalia Cargo) fleet has shrunk significantly due to the fall in wagonload freight traffic; some locomotives were transferred during 2018 to FS subsidiary Mercitalia Shunting and Terminals, formerly known as Ser.Fer. RFI also has a fleet of locos for shunting freight yards as well as those for shunting and hauling infrastructure maintenance trains.

Since the last edition, all Class D.141, D.143, 245.6000, 250, 255.2100 and D.443 have been withdrawn. In this new edition, we have added classes owned by other operators which operate over the national network to this section. Those locos restricted to local networks can be found under their local operators (see Section 2).

CLASS D.100   VOSSLOH TYPE G 1000 BB   B-B

A small number of Vossloh G 1000 diesels are used in Italy. Hired locos do not change users very often.

Built: 2005–10.
Builder: Vossloh.
Engine: MTU 8V 4000 R41L of 1100 kW.
Transmission: Hydraulic. Voith L4r4.
Maximum Tractive Effort: 259 kN.
EVN: 92 83 2100 001-c and so on.

Wheel Diameter: 1000 mm.
Weight: 80 tonnes.
Length over Buffers: 14.13 m.
Maximum Speed: 100 km/h.

Number	Owner	Built	Works no.	User
D.100.001	Alpha Trains	2005	5001612	Inrail
D.100.002	Alpha Trains	2005	5001613	InRail/Adriafer
D.100.003	Alpha Trains	2007	5001736	InRail/DP
D.100.004	InRail	2009	5001854	
D.100.051	HUPAC	2006	5001614	
D.100.052	HUPAC	2007	5001675	Captrain IT
D.100.100	HUPAC	2007	5001737	Captrain IT
D.100.101	Akiem	2009	5001671	Captrain IT
D.100.102	Akiem	2009	5001850	Captrain IT
D.100.103	Akiem	2009	5001853	Captrain IT
D.100.104	Akiem	2010	5001678	Captrain IT/Adriafer
D.100.105	Akiem	2010	5001788	Captrain IT

CLASS D.145.1000   Bo-Bo

These centre-cab heavy shunters were highly advanced when introduced, having inverter drive to their traction motors. They are used on heavy yard shunting, trip freights and station pilot duties. Rheostatic braking. The locos equipped for rescue duties have now been replaced by Vossloh G 2000s.

Built: 1982–89.
Builder: Savigliano.
Engine: 2 x Fiat 8297.22 of 425 kW.
Transmission: Electric via Parizzi/AEG inverter.
Continuous Rating: 620 kW.
EVN: 98 83 2145 101-c and so on.

Wheel Diameter: 1040 mm.
Weight: 72 tonnes.
Length over Buffers: 15.20 m.
Maximum Speed: 100 km/h.

m   Multiple working fitted.

▲ InRail D.100.004 is seen in Udine with E.190.313 on 12 September 2018. **David Haydock**

▼ D.145 1025 shunts wagons in the yard at Terni on 8 November 2012. **Laurence Sly**

No.		m		No.		m		No.		m	
D.145.1001	C		CV	D.145.1014	M		BS	D.145.1027	I		CV
D.145.1002	M		TO	D.145.1015	I		MS	D.145.1028	I		MS
D.145.1003	I		LV	D.145.1016	I		BC	D.145.1029	I		CV
D.145.1004	M		TO	D.145.1017	I		BC	D.145.1030	I		CV
D.145.1005	M		MS	D.145.1018	I		BC	D.145.1031	I		TO
D.145.1006	I		VR	D.145.1019	I		BC	D.145.1032	C		MS
D.145.1007	M		MA	D.145.1020	I		BC	D.145.1033	C		CV
D.145.1008	C		CV	D.145.1021	C		CV	D.145.1034	I		CV
D.145.1009	I		TO	D.145.1022	I	m	CV	D.145.1035	C	m	MS
D.145.1010	C		CV	D.145.1023	I		MS	D.145.1036	I	m	CV
D.145.1011	I		VR	D.145.1024	C		MS	D.145.1037	C	m	MS
D.145.1012	C		CV	D.145.1025	I		LV	D.145.1038	I		RS
D.145.1013	C		MA	D.145.1026	C		MS				

CLASS D.145.2000 — Bo-Bo

Similar to Class D.145.1000 but with a curious stepped bonnet and only one engine instead of two. Used for heavy yard shunting and station pilot duties. Messina locos shunt the train ferry on both sides of the Messina straits.

Built: 1983/84; 1987–89.
Builder: TIBB.
Engine: BRIF ID 36 SS12V of 840 kW.
Transmission: Electric via TIBB inverter.
Continuous Rating: 680 kW.
EVN: 98 83 2145 201-c and so on.

Wheel Diameter: 1040 mm.
Weight: 72 tonnes.
Length over Buffers: 15.50 m.
Maximum Speed: 100 km/h.
Maximum Tractive Effort: 205kW.

No.			No.			No.		
D.145.2001	C	CV	D.145.2023	I	ME	D.145.2043	I	CV
D.145.2002	C	CV	D.145.2024	I	ME	D.145.2044	I	ME
D.145.2003	C	CV	D.145.2025	I	ME	D.145.2045	I	ME
D.145.2004	C	MS	D.145.2026	I	ME	D.145.2046	I	MA
D.145.2005	C	CV	D.145.2027	I	ME	D.145.2047	I	MS
D.145.2006	I	CV	D.145.2028	I	MS	D.145.2048	C	MS
D.145.2007	I	MS	D.145.2029	I	MA	D.145.2049	C	MS
D.145.2008	C	CV	D.145.2030	I	MS	D.145.2050	C	LV
D.145.2009	C	CV	D.145.2031	I	MA	D.145.2051	I	LV
D.145.2010	C	CV	D.145.2032	C	LV	D.145.2052	C	MA
D.145.2011	C	CV	D.145.2033	I	ME	D.145.2053	C	MS
D.145.2012	C	CV	D.145.2034	I	ME	D.145.2054	C	LV
D.145.2013	C	LV	D.145.2035	I	LV	D.145.2055	C	MS
D.145.2014	C	MS	D.145.2036	I	ME	D.145.2056	C	LV
D.145.2015	C	LV	D.145.2037	I	ME	D.145.2057	C	LV
D.145.2016	I	MA	D.145.2038	C	MS	D.145.2058	C	MS
D.145.2017	C	MS	D.145.2039	I	ME	D.145.2059	C	MS
D.145.2018	C	MS	D.145.2040	I	ME	D.145.2060	C	MS
D.145.2020	I	CV	D.145.2041	C	MA	D.145.2061	C	MA
D.145.2021	I	ME	D.145.2042	C	LV	D.145.2062	C	MS
D.145.2022	I	ME						

CLASSES D.146 & D.147 — B-B

A class of diesel locomotive used for heavy shunting and trip freights. The hydraulic transmission gives two outputs – low speed/high tractive effort or higher speed/lower tractive effort. The last of the class was turned out with a Caterpillar engine as a trial, is numbered as Class D.147 and is officially still owned by the builder. The loco operates around Trieste.

Built: 2002–05.
Builder: FIREMA.
Engine: Isotta Fraschini V1712 T2F of 1260 kW (* Caterpillar 3513 DITA SCAC of 1260 kW).
Transmission: Hydraulic. Voith L5 r4zse U2.
Power at Rail: 920 kW.
EVN: 98 83 2146 201-c and so on.

Wheel Diameter: 1000 mm.
Weight: 72 tonnes.
Length over Buffers: 14.43 m.
Maximum Speed: 60/120 km/h.

Class D.146

Number			Number			Number		
D.146.2001	C	MS	D.146.2012	C	MS	D.146.2023	C	MS
D.146.2002	C	MS	D.146.2013	C	MS	D.146.2024	C	MA
D.146.2003	C	MA	D.146.2014	C	MA	D.146.2025	C	TO
D.146.2004	P	MS	D.146.2015	C	TO	D.146.2026	P	RL
D.146.2005	C	TO	D.146.2016	C	TO	D.146.2027	P	MS
D.146.2006	C	MS	D.146.2017	C	TO	D.146.2028	P	RL
D.146.2007	C	TO	D.146.2018	C	MA	D.146.2029	P	MS
D.146.2008	C	TO	D.146.2019	C	MS	D.146.2030	P	RL
D.146.2009	C	TO	D.146.2020	C	TO	D.146.2031	P	RL
D.146.2010	C	TO	D.146.2021	C	TO	D.146.2032	P	MS
D.146.2011	C	MS	D.146.2022	C	TO			

Class D.147

D.147.001	C	*	CV

CLASS D.200 or G2000   VOSSLOH TYPE G 2000   B-B

The G 2000 is a standard Vossloh design which is used across Europe. Those used in Italy are the G 2000-2 BB, with left hand drive. G2000.14–19 were originally G2000.01–06. G2000.32–34 were originally G2000.08–10. G2000.51 and 52 were originally owned by Del Fungo Giera then IFI. DP locos are also known as 200.014 to 200.024. Some DP locos are hired by Trenitalia as rescue locos.

Built: 2003–06.
Builder: Vossloh (Type G2000-2 BB).
Engine: Caterpillar 3516B-HD of 2240 kW.
Transmission: Hydraulic. Voith L620 re U2.
Maximum Tractive Effort: 283 kN.
EVN: 92 83 2200 001-c and so on.

Wheel Diameter: 1000 mm.
Weight: 87 tonnes
Length over Buffers: 17.40 m.
Maximum Speed: 120 km/h.

Number	Owner	Built	Works no.	User/Notes
G2000.01	MIST	2003	1001340	Also known as L 001
G2000.02	MIST	2003	1001341	Also known as L 002
G2000.03	DB Cargo IT	2003	1001044	
G2000.08	Alpha Trains	2004	5001523	DB Cargo IT
G2000.14	DP	2003	1001045	
G2000.15	DP	2003	1001046	
G2000.16	DP	2003	1001047	
G2000.17	DP	2003	1001450	
G2000.18	DP	2003	1001451	
G2000.19	DP	2003	1001452	
G2000.20	DP	2004	5001519	
G2000.21	DP	2005	5001590	
G2000.22	DP	2005	5001597	
G2000.23	DP	2005	5001598	
G2000.24	DP	2005	5001599	
G2000.27	Alpha Trains	2004	5001524	DB Cargo IT
G2000 L03	MIR S&T	2004	5001525	Ex G2000.28
G2000 L04	MIR S&T	2004	5001526	Ex G2000.29
G2000.30	Alpha Trains	2004	5001575	DB Cargo IT
G2000.31	Alpha Trains	2004	5001576	DP
G2000.32	Alpha Trains	2004	5001520	DB Cargo IT
G2000.33	Alpha Trains	2004	5001521	DP
G2000.34	Alpha Trains	2004	5001522	DP
G2000.35	Alpha Trains	2005	5001527	Captrain IT
G2000.36	Alpha Trains	2005	5001528	DB Cargo IT
G2000.51	CFI	2005	5001589	
G2000.52	Salcef	2006	5001600	

▲ D.146.2011 is seen at Milano Smistamento depot on 6 April 2018, with a Class D.145.2000 in the background. **David Haydock**

▼ Dinazzano Po 200.022 (G2000.22) and another of the class are seen at Reggio Emilia station on 23 May 2013. **David Haydock**

CLASS 214.1000 B

Small shunting tractors fitted with the same Fiat engine as Class ALn 668 DMUs; found on minor duties all over Italy. Those owned by the infrastructure department are receiving yellow liveries and "industrial loco" numbers.

Built: 1970–79.
Builder: CNR, 1001–1020; Aerosicula, 1021–1040, 1092–1102; Badoni, 1041–1060, 1104–1128; Greco, 1061–1091, 1103, 1129–1156.
Engine: Fiat 8217 of 95 kW.
Transmission: Hydraulic. Voith L 33 U.
Power at Rail: 67 kW.
EVN: 98 83 2214 106-c to 256-c.

Wheel Diameter: 910 mm.
Weight: 22 tonnes.
Length over Buffers: 7.158 m.
Maximum Speed: 35 km/h.

*   Modified for use in tunnels.
Y   Yellow livery.

No.				No.				No.			
214.1006	*I*		BC	214.1055	*I*		BC	214.1104	*R*		CG
214.1012	*M*		VR	214.1057	*M*		VR	214.1108	*I*	**Y**	BC
214.1013	*R*		BS	214.1062	*I*	**Y**	BC	214.1110	*M*		MA
214.1015	*D*		BW	214.1066	*I*	**Y**	BC	214.1112	*I*		BC
214.1018	*I*	**Y**	BC	214.1071	*D*	*	FO	214.1120	*I*	**Y**	BC
214.1021	*P*		NS	214.1073	*I*		BC	214.1129	*I*	**Y**	BC
214.1030	*M*		MA	214.1074	*I*	**Y***	BC	214.1130	*I*	**Y***	BC
214.1031	*I*		BC	214.1075	*I*		BC	214.1135	*M*		MA
214.1032	*P*		NS	214.1076	*I*		BC	214.1136	*R*		CG
214.1034	*P*		NS	214.1078	*I*	**Y**	BC	214.1137	*I*		BC
214.1035	*M*		MA	214.1083	*I*	**Y**	BC	214.1142	*I*		BC
214.1040	*D*		RW	214.1085	*I*	**Y**	BC	214.1143	*I*	**Y**	BC
214.1041	*D*		FW	214.1086	*I*	**Y**	BC	214.1148	*M*		MA
214.1042	*I*	**Y***	BC	214.1088	*M*		VR	214.1152	*M*		MA
214.1049	*I*		BC	214.1090	*I*	**Y**	BC	214.1156	*P*		BC
214.1052	*I*		BC	214.1092	*R*		BC				

CLASS 214.4000 B

Another small shunting tractor found all over Italy.

Built: 1979–88.
Builder: SOCIMI/Badoni/Greco/San Giorgio/FIPEM.
Engine: VM 1308 V of 130 kW.
Transmission: Hydraulic. Voith L 33 U.
Power at Rail: 75 kW.
EVN: 98 83 2214 301-c to 617-c (214.4001 = 2214 301 etc).

Wheel Diameter: 910 mm.
Weight: 22 tonnes.
Length over Buffers: 7.168 m.
Maximum Speed: 30 km/h.

Y   Yellow livery.

No.				No.				No.			
214.4001	*R*		TS	214.4044	*R*		MC	214.4081	*M*		CV
214.4003	*M*		MS	214.4047	*R*		FI	214.4082	*M*		MS
214.4007	*R*		FI	214.4048	*I*		VR	214.4083	*I*		MS
214.4011	*M*		TO	214.4053	*D*		VW	214.4088	*R*		TC
214.4013	*I*		MS	214.4055	*M*		CV	214.4089	*R*		TC
214.4018	*M*		MS	214.4059	*I*		MS	214.4091	*R*		TC
214.4021	*R*		FI	214.4060	*I*		MS	214.4096	*R*		AL
214.4022	*R*		SU	214.4061	*I*		MS	214.4099	*R*		VR
214.4023	*R*		BZ	214.4062	*I*		MS	214.4100	*M*		VR
214.4024	*R*		FI	214.4064	*I*		MS	214.4101	*R*		VR
214.4025	*I*	**Y**	FI	214.4067	*R*		GB	214.4102	*I*	**Y**	FI
214.4027	*I*		MS	214.4069	*I*		MS	214.4105	*R*		FI
214.4029	*M*		CV	214.4071	*D*		VW	214.4108	*R*		GR
214.4031	*D*		VR	214.4074	*P*		MS	214.4109	*I*		VR
214.4032	*I*	**Y**	FI	214.4075	*M*		VR	214.4110	*M*		MS
214.4036	*R*		BZ	214.4077	*R*		GR	214.4113	*R*		GR
214.4037	*R*		BZ	214.4078	*I*		MS	214.4117	*R*		MS
214.4039	*M*		MS	214.4079	*R*		GR	214.4118	*TR*		MS
214.4041	*M*		VR	214.4080	*I*		FI	214.4119	*R*		CU

28

No.		Y	Code	No.		Y	Code	No.		Y	Code
214.4121	D		VR	214.4182	I	Y	RL	214.4254	R		PA
214.4124	R		TC	214.4184	I	Y	FI	214.4255	I		PA
214.4126	R		TC	214.4189	P		RL	214.4256	R		PA
214.4127	R		AL	214.4193	I		RL	214.4257	P		PA
214.4130	R		TV	214.4194	P		PA	214.4258	R		PA
214.4133	R		VR	214.4195	I		PA	214.4259	I		PA
214.4135	R		FI	214.4197	I		RL	214.4260	R		PA
214.4136	I		VR	214.4198	R		CZ	214.4262	M		LV
214.4137	M		VR	214.4200	M		VR	214.4263	I	Y	FI
214.4140	I		VR	214.4201	I		PA	214.4264	I		PA
214.4142	I		VR	214.4202	P		PA	214.4266	I		FA
214.4145	M		MS	214.4203	R		RS	214.4267	M		MS
214.4147	I	Y	TC	214.4206	I	Y	PA	214.4269	I		MS
214.4149	I		MS	214.4208	M		MA	214.4271	R		VR
214.4150	D		ME	214.4209	P		RL	214.4272	R		AL
214.4151	I	Y	FI	214.4211	P		RL	214.4278	I		AN
214.4152	P		RL	214.4212	I	Y	FI	214.4279	R		FA
214.4153	R		SU	214.4213	M		LV	214.4281	I	Y	AN
214.4154	R		AL	214.4214	R		RS	214.4283	M		VR
214.4159	M		MA	214.4215	R		SU	214.4285	I		MS
214.4160	D		RL	214.4216	P		RL	214.4291	I	Y	AN
214.4162	M		MA	214.4219	I	Y	FI	214.4293	I		AN
214.4165	P		ME	214.4222	I		PA	214.4296	I	Y	AN
214.4166	P		PA	214.4225	R		PA	214.4301	P		MG
214.4167	M		VR	214.4229	R		PA	214.4304	R		AL
214.4168	I		VR	214.4231	I		PA	214.4305	R		AL
214.4169	I	Y	AN	214.4235	M		MA	214.4309	R		SV
214.4170	R		RC	214.4236	R		RL	214.4311	M		VR
214.4174	M		MS	214.4241	D		GR	214.4312	I		FI
214.4178	M		MS	214.4242	D		CW	214.4313	I		GR
214.4180	M		MS	214.4245	R		CT	214.4315	R		TS
214.4181	D		MS	214.4249	I		PA	214.4317	I		FI

▲ In RFI yellow livery, 214.1090 is seen at San Benedetto station between Prato and Bologna on 8 April 2018. **David Haydock**

CLASS 214.7000   B

A small class of shunter all based in Firenze. 214.7013 has been preserved.

Built: 1964/65.
Builder: Greco.
Engine: Deutz A8L 714 of 103 kW.
Transmission: Hydraulic. Voith L 33 U.
Power at Rail: 74 kW.

Wheel Diameter: 910 mm.
Weight: 21 tonnes.
Length over Buffers: 6.958 m.
Maximum Speed: 35 km/h.

Y   Yellow livery.

| 214.7001 | / | Y | FI | 214.7007 | / | Y | FI | 214.7014 | / | Y | FI |
| 214.7006 | / | Y | FI | 214.7008 | / | Y | FI | 214.7020 | / | Y | FI |

CLASS 220   B-B

Former DB locomotives on which the British "Warship" class was modelled, ten of these locos were used by Dinazzano Po until recently; the company is now selling them. 220 041 came from a firm of contractors in 1993, 220 051 from SNFT in 1999 and 220 028, 029, and 060 were acquired in 2003 from contractor Salcef. They operated freight including steel coil from Ravenna to Mantova and to Brescia. Two have been sold to RTC and four to track contractor GCF. The DP locos are now mainly used to shunt in Ferrara and Ravenna. 220 006 (220 R01) was experimentally re-engined with Isotta Frachini engines but was quickly withdrawn by DP.

Built: 1956–59.
Builders: Krauss-Maffei (except 220 011 MaK).
Engine: Two Caterpillar 3508 B DIT SCAC of 810 kW each.
Transmission: Hydraulic. Voith LT 306r.
Maximum Tractive Effort: 189 kN.

Weight: 72–80 tonnes.
Length over Buffers: 18.47 m.

Maximum Speed: 140 km/h.

220 011	RTC	220 041	DP	220 049	RTC	220 060	GCF
220 028	GCF	220 045	GCF	220 051	DP	220 074	DP
220 029	GCF						

CLASS 225.2100   B

These shunters are significantly larger than previous classes and are often found on station pilot duties. The class is identical to Class 225.5000 except for the engine type. Locos have two speed ranges for shunting and for working on the main line.

Built: 1971–78.
Builder: SOFER.
Engine: BRIF D 26 N6L of 188 kW. * IVECO engine.
Transmission: Hydraulic. Voith L 24 U.
Power at Rail: 129 kW.

Wheel Diameter: 1040 mm.
Weight: 32 tonnes.

Length over Buffers: 7.68 m.
Maximum Speed: 30/50 km/h.

| 225.2104 | R | * | PI | 225.2111 | R | | LV | 225.2141 | R | NS |
| 225.2110 | R | | VR | 225.2127 | R | * | FI | | | |

CLASS 225.5000   B

Identical to Class 225.2100 except for the engine type.

Built: 1973–78.
Builder: CNR/Aerosicula/IMER.
Engine: Jenbach JW 400 of 188 kW.
Transmission: Hydraulic. Voith L 24 U.
Power at Rail: 129 kW.

Wheel Diameter: 1040 mm.
Weight: 32 tonnes.
Length over Buffers: 7.68 m.
Maximum Speed: 30/50 km/h.

▲ Former DB 220 074, owned by Dinazzano Po, is seen at Sermide depot on 23 May 2013.

David Haydock

▼ 225.5035 is seen with a double-deck coach at Foggia in March 2010.　　　**Marco Cacozza**

225.5002	I	PA	225.5020	C	MS	225.5033	R	TA
225.5004	P	NS	225.5022	R	TA	225.5034	P	BA
225.5006	P	BA	225.5023	R	TA	225.5035	P	NS
225.5007	P	NS	225.5027	R	TA	225.5038	P	BA
225.5008	C	MS	225.5030	P	NS	225.5039	R	FG
225.5009	R	FG	225.5031	P	BA	225.5042	R	TV
225.5013	P	NS	225.5032	P	NS	225.5044	P	MT
225.5014	P	NS						

CLASS 245.0000   C

A first attempt at a standard 0–6–0 shunter but superseded by the real standard Class 245.1000, 2000 and 6000 from 1965. This class has a much wider bonnet than the other Class 245. The original transmission was from Titan von Roll but was replaced by Voith equipment from 1975–80.

Built: 1964–68.
Builder: Badoni/SIMM.
Engine: OM (Saurer) SEV of 400 kW.
Transmission: Hydraulic. Voith L 24 U.
Power at Rail: 270 kW.
EVN: 98 83 2245 006-c.

Wheel Diameter: 1090 mm.
Weight: 41 tonnes.
Length over Buffers: 8.515 m.
Maximum Speed: 32/65 km/h.

245.0006	M	PE

CLASS 245   C

These standard shunters actually exist in three different versions with the same body but different engines. Originally, Class 245.1000 had OM-SRM transmission and 245.2000 had BRIF D 26 N12V engines: Both types were modified from 1982.

Built: 1965–69.
Builder: OM, 245.1000; Reggiane, 245.2000; CNR, 245.6010.
Engine: BRIF V1712 NF of 370 kW, 245.1000 & 245.6010; BRIF ID 36 N12V of 370 kW, 245.2000.
Transmission: Hydraulic. Voith L 24 U.
Power at Rail: 258 kW.
Maximum Speed: 32/65 km/h.

Wheel Diameter: 1040 mm.
Weight: 48 tonnes.
Length over Buffers: 9.24 m.

Class 245.1000. EVN: 98 83 2245 103-c and so on.

245.1003	M	LV	245.1005	M	TO	245.1019	M	LV
245.1004	M	TO	245.1011	M	LV			

Class 245.2000. EVN: 98 83 2245 204-c and so on. 245.2014 was converted to 250.2001, now preserved, in 1986.

245.2004	M	TO	245.2009	M	TO	245.2020	M	TO
245.2005	M	MA	245.2019	M	BA			

CLASS 245.2100   C

Although these are not supposed to be "standard" they are very similar to Class 245.2000. 186 examples were built; they can be found all over Italy, particularly on station pilot duties.

Built: 1976–87.
Builder: Badoni/Greco/Ferrosud/IMER/IMESI.
Engine: BRIF ID 36 N12V of 370 kW.
Transmission: Hydraulic. Voith L 24 U.
Power at Rail: 265 kW.
EVN: 98 83 2245 302-c to 486-c (245.2102 = 2245 302 etc).

Wheel Diameter: 1070 mm.
Weight: 46 tonnes.
Length over Buffers: 9.24 m.
Maximum Speed: 30/60 km/h.

245.2102	P	MS	245.2109	M	MS	245.2115	C	MS
245.2104	P	MS	245.2110	I	MS	245.2116	M	MS
245.2105	M	BA	245.2111	C	MS	245.2117	M	MS
245.2106	I	MS	245.2112		MS	245.2119	I	MS
245.2107	TR	MS	245.2113	M	MS	245.2121	C	MS
245.2108	I	MS	245.2114	R	FI	245.2122	TR	MS

No.			No.			No.		
245.2123	P	MS	245.2177	R	MS	245.2228	M	FI
245.2124	M	VR	245.2178	P	MT	245.2229		AL
245.2125	M	MS	245.2180	I	MS	245.2230	R	AL
245.2126		MS	245.2181	M	MS	245.2231	M	TO
245.2127	M	MS	245.2182	M	MS	245.2232	P	MT
245.2128	M	MS	245.2183	TR	MS	245.2233	M	GR
245.2131	R	BC	245.2184	I	VR	245.2234	M	LV
245.2132	M	MS	245.2185	I	SS	245.2235	M	VR
245.2133	M	MS	245.2186	M	MS	245.2236	P	MT
245.2134	M	BA	245.2187	M	TA	245.2237	M	MT
245.2135	I	MS	245.2188	P	BA	245.2238	R	GR
245.2136	D	MS	245.2189	I	PA	245.2239	M	MS
245.2137	M	MS	245.2190	P	BA	245.2242	R	TC
245.2138	R	MS	245.2191	P	BA	245.2243	M	LV
245.2139	I	BA	245.2192	I	BA	245.2244	M	TC
245.2140	P	BA	245.2193	R	NS	245.2245	M	GR
245.2141	P	MS	245.2194	P	NS	245.2246	M	LV
245.2142	M	MS	245.2195	P	NS	245.2247	I	LV
245.2143		MS	245.2196	R	NS	245.2248	TR	MS
245.2144		FA	245.2197	M	MA	245.2249	R	PI
245.2145	M	MS	245.2198	M	MA	245.2250	M	GR
245.2146	I	MT	245.2199	P	BA	245.2251	R	GR
245.2147	M	TO	245.2200	R	GR	245.2252	M	GR
245.2148	P	NS	245.2201	C	MA	245.2253	M	GR
245.2149	M	MS	245.2202	I	MS	245.2254	M	GR
245.2150	M	MS	245.2203	C	MA	245.2255	M	LV
245.2151	M	MS	245.2204	M	MA	245.2256	R	PI
245.2153	C	MS	245.2205	M	TA	245.2257	R	PI
245.2154	M	MS	245.2206	R	NS	245.2259	M	TO
245.2155	R	MS	245.2207	R	NS	245.2260	M	TO
245.2156	TR	MS	245.2208	M	MS	245.2261	M	TC
245.2157	M	VR	245.2210	M	MS	245.2263	M	TC
245.2158	M	MS	245.2211	P	MS	245.2265	M	TC
245.2159	M	MS	245.2212	C	MS	245.2266	M	TC
245.2160	M	MS	245.2213	M	MA	245.2268		TO
245.2161	C	MS	245.2214	P	NS	245.2270	M	TC
245.2162	M	MS	245.2215	M	BA	245.2272	M	MS
245.2163	I	MS	245.2216	M	MS	245.2273	M	TO
245.2165	P	MT	245.2217	M	TA	245.2274	M	TO
245.2166	M	MS	245.2218	R	FI	245.2275	M	MS
245.2167		MS	245.2219		MA	245.2277		VR
245.2169	I	MS	245.2220		LV	245.2278		TO
245.2170	M	BS	245.2221	C	LV	245.2280	M	CT
245.2171	M	MS	245.2222	M	GR	245.2281	M	MS
245.2172	P	MT	245.2223	C	LV	245.2282	R	AL
245.2173	I	MS	245.2224		FG	245.2283	M	VR
245.2174	M	TA	245.2225	M	LV	245.2284	R	AL
245.2175	M	LV	245.2226	R	GR	245.2286		TO
245.2176	P	MT	245.2227	R	GR			

▲ 245.6011 is seen at Udine station on 12 September 2018. **David Haydock**

▼ 255.2001 is seen at Ferrara on 29 January 2014. **Marco Cacozza**

CLASS 245 (continued)   C

For technical details see Class 245 above.

EVN: 98 83 2245 610-c to 724-c.

Class 245.6010.

245.6010	P	SU	245.6050		RL	245.6088	M	FI
245.6011	R	TV	245.6051	M	MS	245.6089		VR
245.6012	I	BZ	245.6052	I	CV	245.6090		VR
245.6013	M	MA	245.6053	I	TA(S)	245.6091	I	VR
245.6014	M	CV	245.6054	I	TA(S)	245.6092	M	RL
245.6015	I	CV	245.6055	R	VR	245.6093	M	TS
245.6016	M	MA	245.6056		CV	245.6094	R	VR
245.6017		CV	245.6057	I	PE	245.6095	I	CV
245.6018	I	SU	245.6058	M	CV	245.6096	M	VR
245.6019	R	MT	245.6059	R	VR	245.6097		RL
245.6020	I	BZ	245.6060	M	VR	245.6098	M	CV
245.6021	I	MS	245.6061	I	TA(S)	245.6099		GR
245.6022	I	CV	245.6062	M	MS	245.6100		CV
245.6023	P	RL	245.6063		TA(S)	245.6102	I	TA
245.6025	M	RL	245.6064	I	PE	245.6103	M	MS
245.6026	R	GB	245.6065		VR	245.6104	M	CV
245.6027	I	RL	245.6066	I	RL	245.6105	R	BZ
245.6028	R	TV	245.6067	M	CV	245.6106	I	CV
245.6029	P	RL	245.6068	M	VR	245.6107	M	VR
245.6031	M	GR	245.6070	M	MS	245.6109	C	VR
245.6032	M	GR	245.6071	C	BS	245.6110	I	RL
245.6033	P	BA	245.6072	M	LV	245.6111	I	RL
245.6034	I	RL	245.6073	M	VR	245.6112	R	RS
245.6035	I	CV	245.6074	R	SU	245.6113		TR
245.6037	M	LV	245.6075	M	MA	245.6114	R	PI
245.6038	R	TS	245.6076	R	VR	245.6115	I	CV
245.6039	M	VR	245.6077	I	LV	245.6116	M	MS
245.6040	M	VR	245.6078	M	MS	245.6117	R	GR
245.6041	P	RL	245.6079	M	MS	245.6118	R	RS
245.6043		BA	245.6080	M	MS	245.6119		RL
245.6044	M	CV	245.6081		CV	245.6120	I	TA
245.6045	M	CV	245.6083		VR	245.6121		GR
245.6046	M	CV	245.6084		RL	245.6122	M	RS
245.6047	I	BZ	245.6085	M	CV	245.6123		LV
245.6048	M	BS	245.6086		MA	245.6124	P	RL
245.6049	P	TC	245.6087	M	RL			

CLASS 255.2000   C

FS's most recent shunters; built to a quite different design to earlier locos. The off-centre cab affords excellent vision thanks to the sloping bonnets. The dark red livery is also a departure from previous practice. A large number of locos are used around Bologna Centrale station and in stations along the line towards Milano.

Built: 1991–93.	**Wheel Diameter:** 940 mm.
Builder: Greco/Badoni.	**Weight:** 53 tonnes.
Engine: BRIF ID 36 S8V of 450 kW.	**Length over Buffers:** 10.00 m.
Transmission: Hydraulic. Voith L3r4 U2.	**Maximum Speed:** 50 km/h.
Power at Rail: 325 kW.	**Livery:** Dark red.

EVN: 98 83 2255 001-c and so on.

255.2001	M	BS	255.2007	M	BS	255.2013	M	BS
255.2002	M	BS	255.2008	M	BS	255.2014	M	BS
255.2003	M	BS	255.2009		BS	255.2015	I	BC
255.2004	M	BS	225.2010	I	BC	255.2016	M	BS
255.2005	M	BS	255.2011	M	BS	255.2017	M	BS
255.2006	M	BS	255.2012	M	MS	255.2018	I	BC

255.2019	M	BS	255.2023	M	BS	255.2027	I	BC
255.2020		BS	255.2024	M	BS	255.2028	I	BC
255.2021	M	BS	255.2025	M	BS	255.2029	M	BS
255.2022	M	BS	255.2026	M	BS	255.2030	I	BC

CLASS D.284   VOSSLOH EUROLIGHT   Bo-Bo

This locomotive was bought by Dinazzano Po and was being used for freight on a circular route in Toscana from Reggio Emilia in May 2018.

Built: 2010.
Builder: Vossloh Espagna.
Engine: Caterpillar CAT C175-12.
Transmission: Electric. ABB.
Power at Rail: 2300 kW.
EVN: 92 83 2284 002-8.

Wheel Diameter: 1100 mm.
Weight: 79 tonnes.
Length over Buffers: 20.32 m.
Maximum Speed: 120 km/h.

D.284 002

CLASS D.343 & D.449   B-B

The first of a series of diesel locomotives that are very compact due to the use of monomotor bogies. The medium power versions are Classes D.343 and D.345 and the higher power versions D.445. All of these classes originally had wrap-round cab windows which were replaced with flat glass for safety reasons from 1980. Like other diesel classes, except D.445, locos have no train heating. D.343.2016 was re-engined by TVZ Gredelj of Croatia and received a new body in 2005 as a prototype for more rebuilds. D.343.2011 was later rebuilt by Fervet in 2010 as D.449.001 in a similar move. These eventually came to nothing, but in early 2014 RFI acquired both locos to haul diagnostic trains – both were still stored in mid-2018!

Built: 1967–70.
Builder: Breda/Pistoiesi.
Engine: Caterpillar 3512B of 1433 kW.
Transmission: Electric (Marelli Autoload).
Continuous Rating: 785 kW.
Train Heating: None.

Wheel Diameter: 1040 mm.
Weight: 72 tonnes.
Length over Buffers: 13.24 m; D.449 14.04 m.
Maximum Speed: 130 km/h; D.449 120 km/h.

Class D.343.2000.

D.343.2016   I   *

Class D.449.

D.449.001   I   *

▲ D345 1003 and D345 1107 pass Vrtojba whilst working a freight from Gorizia Centrale to Novara Gorica in Slovenia on 5 May 2017. **Laurence Sly**

▼ D.445.1125 leaves Castelfranco Veneto pushing a train from Padova to Montebelluno on 12 September 2018. **David Haydock**

CLASS D.345 B-B

A development of Class D.343 with the second generation of Fiat 218 SSF engine. A number of examples have been modified for push-pull or multiple operation. Many are now used as rescue locos or to haul breakdown trains.

Built: 1974–79.
Builder: Breda Pt, 1001–1040; Sofer, 1041–1070; Savigliano, 1071–1145.
Engine: Fiat 218 SSF of 990 kW.
Transmission: Electric (Marelli Autoload).
Continuous Rating: 785 kW.
Train Heating: None.
EVN: 92 83 2345 003-c and so on.

Wheel Diameter: 1040 mm.
Weight: 64 tonnes.
Length over Buffers: 13.24 m.
Maximum Speed: 130 km/h.

m   Equipped for multiple working.
p   Equipped for push-pull operation.

No.			Depot	No.			Depot	No.			Depot
D.345.1003	C	m	CV	D.345.1048	R		AN	D.345.1101	C		LV
D.345.1004	C	m	CT	D.345.1052	R		AL	D.345.1102	C	m	CV
D.345.1005	C	mp	MA	D.345.1053	R		AL	D.345.1103	C		LV
D.345.1008	R		PE	D.345.1060	H		TA	D.345.1106	C		MA
D.345.1009	R		AL	D.345.1061	C	m	VR	D.345.1107	C	m	CV
D.345.1010	R		BZ	D.345.1062	R		PA	D.345.1108	C	p	MA
D.345.1011	R		BC	D.345.1063	C	m	VR	D.345.1110	C		MA
D.345.1012	C		MA	D.345.1067	C		MA	D.345.1113	C		VR
D.345.1014	C	mp	MA	D.345.1071	C	m	VR	D.345.1115	P		TS
D.345.1016	P		ME	D.345.1073	C		LV	D.345.1116	R	m	GB
D.345.1019	C	p	LV	D.345.1078	C		MA	D.345.1119	C	p	MA
D.345.1021	R		RS	D.345.1080	C	m	MA	D.345.1120	C	m	LV
D.345.1024	P	p	FG	D.345.1082	C	m	CV	D.345.1121	C		CT
D.345.1025	C		MA	D.345.1086	C	m	CV	D.345.1126	C		CT
D.345.1031	C		CT	D.345.1087	R	p	SI	D.345.1127	C		LV
D.345.1032	C		MA	D.345.1090	C	p	CV	D.345.1136	C	m	LV
D.345.1041	C	p	VR	D.345.1091	C	p	MA	D.345.1138	C	m	MA
D.345.1044	C	mp	LV	D.345.1092	C		GR	D.345.1139	C		VR
D.345.1046	R		BE	D.345.1096	C		MA	D.345.1144	C		LV
D.345.1047	R		TS	D.345.1097	C		RL	D.345.1145	C		MA

CLASS D.445 B-B

The most recent FS main line diesel locomotives which were finally equipped with electric train heating; this means that they are in charge of most diesel-hauled passenger trains in Italy. After the first batch, it was decided to fit push-pull equipment as standard.

Built: 1974–76, 1001–35; 1981–88 1036–1150.
Builder: Savigliano, 1001–35; Reggiane/Omeca/Casertane, 1036–1150.
Engine: Fiat 2112 SSF of 1560 kW, 1001–35; Fiat A 210.12 SSF of 1560 kW, 1036–1150.
Transmission: Electric.
Continuous Rating: 1250 kW.
Train Heating: Electric.
EVN: 92 83 2445 001-c and so on.

Wheel Diameter: 1040 mm.
Weight: 72 tonnes (p 76 tonnes).
Length over Buffers: 14.10 m.
Maximum Speed: 130 km/h.

m   Equipped for multiple working.
p   Equipped for push-pull operation.
*   Equipped as HSL rescue locos.

No.			Depot	No.			Depot	No.			Depot
D.445.1001	R	p	RC	D.445.1018	C		TO	D.445.1027	P	p	TA
D.445.1003	R	p	PA	D.445.1019	C		TO	D.445.1029	R	p	RC
D.445.1005	P		RC	D.445.1020	C		TO	D.445.1030	C		MA
D.445.1012	R	p	SI	D.445.1021	P	p	RL	D.445.1031	H		ME
D.445.1014	R	p	SI	D.445.1022	P	p	TA	D.445.1033	C	p	MA
D.445.1015	C		TO	D.445.1024	C		TO	D.445.1035	R	p	RC
D.445.1016	C		MA	D.445.1025	R	p	SI	D.445.1036	R	p	TA
D.445.1017	C		TO	D.445.1026	C		TO	D.445.1038	R	p	CG

ID				ID				ID			
D.445.1040	R	p	SV	D.445.1081	I	mp*	MT	D.445.1118	R	p	SI
D.445.1043	R	p	TV	D.445.1083	R	p	TC	D.445.1119	R	p	CG (S)
D.445.1045	R	p	TV	D.445.1085	R	p	TV	D.445.1121	C	p	MA
D.445.1046	R	p	TV	D.445.1086	R	p	RC	D.445.1122	R	p	SI
D.445.1048	R	p	TV	D.445.1090	R	p	SI	D.445.1123	R	p	TV
D.445.1049	R	p	CG	D.445.1091	R	p	SI	D.445.1124	R	p	TV
D.445.1050	R	p	SI	D.445.1092	R	p	RC	D.445.1125	R	p	TV
D.445.1051	R	p	CG	D.445.1094	I	mp*	MA	D.445.1126	R	p	RC
D.445.1052	R	p	PA	D.445.1097	C	p	TO	D.445.1127	R	p	TV
D.445.1053	R	p	CG	D.445.1098	R	p	SI	D.445.1128	R	p	RC
D.445.1054	R	p	CG (S)	D.445.1100	R	p	RC	D.445.1129	R	p	CG
D.445.1055	R	p	CG	D.445.1101	R	p	PA	D.445.1132	R	p	SI
D.445.1056	R	p	RC	D.445.1102	C	p	MA	D.445.1134	R	p	RC
D.445.1060	R	mp*	SI	D.445.1103	R	p	CG	D.445.1136	TR	p	CR
D.445.1061	R	p	SI	D.445.1104	R	p	RC	D.445.1137	R	p	TV
D.445.1062	R	p	AL	D.445.1106	C	p	TO	D.445.1138	R	p	CG
D.445.1063	R	p	RC	D.445.1107	R	p	TA	D.445.1139	C	p	MA
D.445.1064	R	p	PA	D.445.1108	R	p	TC	D.445.1140	R	p	RC
D.445.1066	R	p	TC	D.445.1109	C	mp*	TO	D.445.1141	R	p	RC
D.445.1068	R	p	SI	D.445.1110	C	p	TO	D.445.1142	R	p	TV
D.445.1069	C	mp*	MA	D.445.1111	R	p	SI	D.445.1143	R	p	SI
D.445.1070	C	p	TO	D.445.1112	R	p	SI	D.445.1144	R	p	SI
D.445.1073	R	p	SI	D.445.1113	I	mp*	SI	D.445.1145	H	p	SU
D.445.1074	C	mp*	MA	D.445.1114	R	p	SI	D.445.1147	R	p	RC
D.445.1075	TR	p	CR	D.445.1115	R	p	SI	D.445.1148	R	p	SI
D.445.1076	R	p	CG	D.445.1116	R	p	SI	D.445.1149	C	p	MA
D.445.1077	R	p	TC	D.445.1117	R	p	SI	D.445.1150	C	mp*	MA
D.445.1078	R	p	RC								

▲ DE 520.016 stands outside Iseo depot on 5 April 2018. The loco is still in FNM Cargo livery but is owned by Trenord.   **David Haydock**

CLASSES DE 520, D.752 & D.753 — Bo-Bo

Former Czech Railways (ČD) Class 750/753; the previous ČD number is shown in brackets. These locos are commonly nicknamed "goggles" due to their curious cab windows. Class D.752 were purchased through Leon d'Oro of Marimorolo, and have been re-engined with power units from ČD Class 770/771. FNM bought 18 locos, numbering them DE 520.01 to 18. DE 520.01 to 10 were then sold or hired to Del Fungo Giera which numbered them DE.753.051 to 060, out of order. DFG then went bankrupt and the locos returned to FNM (later Nordcargo, then DB Cargo). They were then renumbered DE 520.001 upwards.

Built: 1973–76.
Builder: ČKD Type T478.3.
Engine: ČKD K6S310DR of 1213 kW, D.752 & DE 520; Caterpillar 3512 B DITA of 1455 kW, D.753.
Transmission: Electric.
Continuous Rating: 1325 kW.
Weight: 74 tonnes.
Length over Buffers: 16.50 m.
Maximum Speed: 100 km/h.

Class DE 520

Number	Former ČD No.	Operator	Number	Former ČD No.	Operator
DE.520.001	(753 172)	FUC/Inrail (ex D.753.051)	DE 520.010	(753 310)	DB Cargo IT
DE 520.002	(753 076)	DB Cargo IT	DE 520.011	(753 347)	DB Cargo IT
DE 520.003	(753 284)	FUC/Inrail (ex D.753.058)	DE 520.012	(753 099)	DB Cargo IT
DE 520.004	(753 087)	Trenord	DE 520.013	(753 359)	Trenord
DE 520.005	(753 134)	DB Cargo IT (S)	DE 520.014	(753 140)	Trenord
DE 520.006	(753 034)	FG (ex D.753.059)	DE 520.015	(753 179)	Trenord
DE 520.007	(753 045)	FG (ex D.753.060)	DE 520.016	(753 362)	Trenord
DE 520.008	(753 297)	Trenord	DE 520.017	(753 324)	DB Cargo IT
DE 520.009	(753 075)	DB Cargo IT	DE 520.018	(753 373)	DB Cargo IT

Class D.752. Rheostatic brakes

D.752.501	(750 081)	FAS	D.752.505	(753 295)	FAS
D.752.502	(753 304)	FAS	D.752.506	(753 355)	FAS
D.752.503	(753 316)	FAS	D.752.507	(753 262)	FAS
D.752.504	(753 090)	FAS	D.752.508	(753 137)	FAS

Class D.753

D.753.001	(753 321)	ST	D.753.701	(753 039)	FSE(S) (ex HUPAC)
D.753.002	(753 269)	ST (U)	D.753.702	(753 190)	FSE(S) (ex HUPAC)
D.753.003	(753 383)	ST	D.753.703	(753 315)	CLF
D.753.004	(753 360)	ST	D.753.704	(753 047)	CLF
D.753.005	(753 327)	Captrain IT	D.753.732	(753 394)	RTC
D.753.006	(753 385)	Captrain IT	D.753.733	(753 402)	RTC
D.753.007	(753 403)	ST (U)			

"CLASS 650" — VOSSLOH G6 — C

This is a heavy shunter type from Vossloh, many of which are used in Germany and France. All are leased from Vossloh Locomotives; heavy maintenance is carried out at Imateq in Arquata Scrivia. The DB Cargo locos are used at Domo 2 yard, Domodossola.

Built: 2012/15.
Builder: Vossloh, Kiel.
Engine: Cummins QSK23-L of 671 kW.
Transmission: Hydraulic. Voith L3r4zseU2.
Maximum Tractive Effort: 219 kN.
EVNs: 98 87 0650 003-6 and so on.
Driving Wheel Diameter: 1000 mm.
Weight: 60 tonnes.
Length over Buffers: 10.79 m.
Maximum Speed: 40/80 km/h.

Short EVN	Works no.	User	Short EVN	Works no.	User
650 003	5102194	ISC	650 007	5102219	DB Cargo IT
650 004	5102195	DB Cargo IT			

CLASSES 741.7 & 744   Bo-Bo

Class 741.7 locos are rebuilds of Czech Railways (ČD) Classes 740 or 742 by CZ LOKO which calls them Effishunter 1000. Class 744 is also an Effishunter 1000 but has a Caterpillar C32 engine of 895 kW. DP has ordered two more locos with an option for four more. RTC has ordered two with options for two more.

Built: 2012–
Builder: CZ LOKO.
Engine: Caterpillar CAT 3508C of 1000 kW.
Transmission: Electric.
Maximum Tractive Effort: 220 kN.
EVN: 92 54 2741 701-c and so on.

Weight: 80 tonnes.
Length: 16.30 m.
Maximum Speed: 100 km/h.

Class 741.7.

Number	Operator	Built		Number	Operator	Built
741.701	DP	2015		741.737	Terminali Italia	2016
741.707	DP	2015		741.738	Terminali Italia	2016
741.710	MIR S&T	2015		741.741	Ventura	2017
741.731	Terminali Italia	2011		741.742	Ventura	2017
741.733	DP	2012		741.745	Terminali Italia	2018
741.734	DP	2012		741.746	Terminali Italia	2018

Class 744. Delivered as 744.101 to 105, these were rapidly renumbered 744.001 to 005

Number	Operator	Built		Number	Operator	Built
744.001	MIST	2018		744.004	MIST	2018
744.002	MIST	2018		744.005	MIST	2018
744.003	MIST	2018				

▲ Snowplough S.244.001 has been hard at work at Fabriano in February 2012.   **Marco Cacozza**

SNOWPLOUGHS

Numbered in the same series as shunters but prefixed S (for *Spazzaneve* or *Sgombraneve* from *sgombrare* to remove and *neve* – snow), these are necessary in the northern Italian Alps but also in the Abruzzo mountains in central Italy.

CLASS S.224   B

Rolba Type RR 4.000 COPDS snowplough. Based at Tarvisio for the route to Villach, Austria.

Built: 1989.
Builder: Rolba.
Engine: BRIF ID 36 SS 8V of 685 kW.
Transmission: Hydrostatic.
Livery: Yellow.
EVN: 99 83 2224 001-c.

Wheel Diameter: 950 mm.
Weight: 36.6 tonnes.
Length over Buffers: 11.51 m.
Maximum Speed: 60 km/h.

S.224.001	CV

CLASS S.244   B-B

244.001 is a Beilhack Type HB 900 S and 244.002/003 Beilhack Type HB 1000 S. 001 is based at Sulmona for the Abruzzo region, 002 at Bolzano for the line to Brennero and Innsbruck, Austria and 003 at Torino for the line to Bardonecchia and Modane, France.

Built: 1981, 001; 1988, 002/003.
Builder: Beilhack.
Engine: Deutz BF 12L 513 of 335 kW.
Transmission: Hydraulic. Voith T 320 r.
Livery: Yellow.

Wheel Diameter: 850 mm.
Weight: 53 tonnes, 001; 58 tonnes, 002/003.
Length over Buffers: 13.06 m, 001; 13.40 m, 002/003.
Maximum Speed: 80 km/h.

S.244.001	SU	S.244.002	BZ	S.244.003	TC

1.2. ELECTRIC LOCOMOTIVES

All electric locomotives operate from 3000 V DC overhead only unless otherwise stated. Historically, electric locomotive numbering depends on the number of powered axles, those having four powered axles being in the E.400 series and those with six powered axles being in the E.600 series.

In this edition we have combined all classes of electric locomotive which can be seen on the main line in Italy, within this section. Previously locomotives were listed by operator, whereas now locomotives are listed in numerical order, with the owner/operator shown. Note that some owners are also the operators. Many locomotives now used in Italy are not numbered in the traditional Italian way, instead adopting the increasingly widespread German system. In general, Italian railways are adopting international loco types (TRAXX, Vectron, etc) and the "typical" Italian Bo-Bo-Bo locos are gradually disappearing.

CLASS EU43

See Class E.412 below.

CLASS 186   TRAXX   Bo-Bo

Bombardier TRAXX MS multi-voltage electric locomotives.

Built: See list.
Builder: Bombardier Transportation, Kassel.
Continuous Rating: 5600 kW (4000 kW under 1500 V DC).
Maximum Tractive Effort: 300 kN.   **Weight:** 86 tonnes.
Systems: 1500/3000 V DC, 15/25 kV AC.   **Length over Buffers:** 18.90 m.
Maximum Speed: 140 km/h.
EVN: All EVNs incorporate the same Class 186 number as shown below.

Version D A CH I NL

Number	Owner	Built	Works no.	Operator
186 101	Railpool	2006	34299	WRS (DE)
186 102	Railpool	2006	34300	LTE (AT)
186 103	Railpool	2007	34317	BLS Cargo (CH)
186 104	Railpool	2007	34318	BLS Cargo (CH)
186 105	Railpool	2007	34319	BLS Cargo (CH)
186 106	Railpool	2007	34320	BLS Cargo (CH)
186 107	Railpool	2007	34327	Kombiverkehr
186 108	Railpool	2007	34325	Captrain NL
186 109	Railpool	2007	34328	RTB (DE)
186 110	Railpool	2007	34330	LTE NL

Version D A CH I

186 251	Railpool	2008	34421	RCCI

Version D A CH I B NL

186 256	Railpool	2018	35405	DB Cargo NL
186 257	Railpool	2018	35406	DB Cargo NL
186 258	Railpool	2018	35408	LINEAS (BE)
186 259	Railpool	2018	35409	LINEAS (BE)

Version D A I

186 281	Railpool	2009	34460	RCC Italy
186 282	Railpool	2009	34468	Lokomotion (DE)
186 283	Railpool	2009	34488	RCC Italy
186 284	Railpool	2009	34756	RCC Italy
186 285	Railpool	2009	34476	RCC Italy
186 286	Railpool	2011	34827	Lokomotion (DE)
186 287	Railpool	2011	34828	RCC Italy
186 288	Railpool	2012	34837	RCC Italy
186 289	Railpool	2012	34841	Kombiverkehr

186 290	Railpool	2011	34839	RCC Italy
186 440	Lokomotion	2014	35174	
186 441	Lokomotion	2014	35175	
186 442	Lokomotion	2014	35124	
186 443	Lokomotion	2014	35152	
186 444	Lokomotion	2014	35178	

Version D A CH I B NL

186 445	Railpool	2016	35299	LINEAS (BE)
186 446	Railpool	2017	35405	LINEAS (BE)
186 447	Railpool	2017	35402	LINEAS (BE)
186 448	Railpool	2017	35403	LINEAS (BE)
186 449	Railpool	2017	35404	LINEAS (BE)
186 450	Railpool	2017	35305	LINEAS (BE)
186 451	Railpool	2017	35306	LINEAS (BE)
186 452	Railpool	2017	35307	LINEAS (BE)
186 453	Railpool	2017	35308	LINEAS (BE)
186 454	Railpool	2017	35351	LINEAS (BE)
186 491	Railpool	2018	35525	DB Cargo NL
186 492	Railpool	2018	35522	DB Cargo NL
186 493	Railpool	2018	35524	DB Cargo NL
186 494	Railpool	2018	35413	LINEAS (BE)
186 495	Railpool	2018	35533	DB Cargo NL
186 496	Railpool	2018	35539	DB Cargo NL
186 497	Railpool	2018	35540	LINEAS (BE)
186 498	Railpool	2018	35541	DB Cargo NL
186 499	Railpool	2018	35542	DB Cargo NL
186 500	Railpool	2018	35548	LINEAS (BE)
186 501	Railpool	2018	35559	DB Cargo NL

Version D A CH I

186 901	Macquarie	2007	34314	TXL
186 902	Macquarie	2007	34353	TXL
186 903	Macquarie	2007	34354	TXL
186 904	Macquarie	2007	34352	TXL
186 905	Macquarie	2007	34357	TXL
186 906	Macquarie	2008	34358	TXL
186 907	Macquarie	2008	34362	TXL
186 908	Macquarie	2008	34363	TXL
186 909	Macquarie	2008	34370	TXL
186 910	Macquarie	2008	34371	TXL

CLASS 189   ES64F4   Bo-Bo

Siemens Type ES64F4 multi-voltage electric locomotives.

Built: See list.
Builder: Siemens, München Allach.
Continuous Rating: 6400 kW.
Maximum Tractive Effort: 300 kN.
Systems: 1500/3000 V DC, 15/25 kV AC according to version.
EVN: All EVNs incorporate the same Class 189 number as shown below.

Wheel Diameter: 1250 mm.
Weight: 86 tonnes.
Length over Buffers: 19.58 m.
Maximum Speed: 140 km/h.

Version VE: D A CH I NL SI HK

Number	Owner	Built	Works no.	User
189 101	MRCE	2009	21501	RCC Italy
189 102	MRCE	2009	21502	SBB Cargo
189 103	MRCE	2009	21503	CFI
189 104	MRCE	2009	21505	Lokomotion
189 105	MRCE	2009	21506	Inrail
189 106	MRCE	2009	21508	SBB Cargo
189 107	MRCE	2009	21509	SBB Cargo
189 108	MRCE	2009	21511	SBB Cargo

189 109	MRCE	2009	21512	SBB Cargo
189 110	MRCE	2009	21514	ISC
189 111	MRCE	2009	21515	SBB Cargo
189 112	MRCE	2009	21517	SBB Cargo
189 113	MRCE	2009	21518	DB Cargo IT
189 114	MRCE	2009	21520	CFI
189 115	MRCE	2009	21521	SBB Cargo

Version VI: Italy only

189 400	MRCE	2006	21242	CFI
189 401	MRCE	2008	21472	DB Cargo IT
189 402	MRCE	2008	21473	DB Cargo IT
189 403	MRCE	2008	21474	ISC
189 404	MRCE	2008	21475	CFI
189 405	MRCE	2008	21476	ISC
189 406	MRCE	2008	21477	CFI
189 407	MRCE	2009	21494	CFI
189 408	MRCE	2009	21495	CFI
189 409	MRCE	2009	21496	CFI

Version VE: D A CH I NL SI HK

189 820	LOCON	2010	21613
189 821	LOCON/Railforceone	2010	21614
189 822	DB Cargo IT	2010	21617
189 823	DB Cargo IT	2011	21627

Version VD: D A H I SI HK

189 901	RTC	2003	20680
189 902	RTC	2003	20683
189 903	RTC	2002	20669
189 904	RTC	2002	20670
189 905	RTC	2002	20671

▲ Lokomotion 189 918 heads an intermodal service to Verona through Ala station on 13 September 2018. **David Haydock**

189 907	Lokomotion	2004	20727	
189 908	MRCE	2004	20731	TXL
189 909	MRCE	2004	20735	Lokomotion
189 910	MRCE	2004	20724	Lokomotion
189 912	Lokomotion	2005	20983	
189 914	Lokomotion	2005	20988	
189 915	MRCE	2005	20991	DB Cargo IT
189 916	MRCE	2005	20993	ISC
189 917	Lokomotion	2005	21060	
189 918	Lokomotion	2005	21062	
189 923	MRCE	2006	21236	Lokomotion
189 924	MRCE	2006	21237	Lokomotion
189 926	MRCE	2006	21239	Fuorimuro
189 927	MRCE	2006	21240	Lokomotion
189 930	MRCE	2006	21243	Lokomotion
189 931	MRCE	2006	21244	TXL
189 932	MRCE	2006	21245	Lokomotion
189 934	MRCE	2008	21478	BoxXpress
189 935	MRCE	2008	21479	TXL
189 936	MRCE	2008	21480	Lokomotion
189 937	MRCE	2008	21481	DB Cargo IT
189 938	MRCE	2010	21650	DB Cargo IT

Version VE: D A CH I NL SI HK

189 982	MRCE	2009	21635	SBB Cargo
189 983	MRCE	2009	21636	SBB Cargo
189 984	MRCE	2009	21637	SBB Cargo
189 985	MRCE	2009	21638	CFI
189 986	MRCE	2009	21639	TXL
189 987	MRCE	2009	21640	SBB Cargo
189 988	MRCE	2004	20732	RTB (DE)
189 989	MRCE	2004	20734	TXL
189 990	MRCE	2004	20736	SBB Cargo
189 991	MRCE	2004	20739	SBB Cargo
189 992	MRCE	2004	20721	TXL
189 993	MRCE	2004	20723	TXL
189 994	MRCE	2003	20695	SBB Cargo
189 995	MRCE	2003	20698	Rail Force One (NL)
189 996	MRCE	2003	20701	SBB Cargo
189 997	MRCE	2003	20704	Off lease
189 998	MRCE	2004	20707	TXL
189 999	MRCE	2004	20730	DB Cargo IT

CLASS E.190   TAURUS   Bo-Bo

Siemens Type ES64U4 multi-voltage electric locomotives which can operate in Italy, Austria, Germany and Slovenia. ÖBB also operates its Class 1216, known as Class E.190 in Italy. See "Austrian Railways" book for details.

Built: See list.
Builder: Siemens, München Allach.
Continuous Rating: 6400 kW.
Maximum Tractive Effort: 300 kN.
Systems: 1500/3000 V DC, 15/25 kV AC according to version.

Wheel Diameter: 1150 mm.
Weight: 87 tonnes.
Length over Buffers: 19.28 m.
Maximum Speed: 230 km/h.

Number	Owner	Built	Works no.	Operator
E.190.301	FUC	2008	21604	
E.190.302	FUC	2010	21463	
E.190.311	InRail	2008	21462	"Lia"
E.190.312	InRail	2010	21464	
E.190.313	InRail	2011	21678	FuoriMuro
E.190.314	InRail	2011	21679	FuoriMuro
E.190.321	CFI	2011	21673	
E.190.322	CFI	2011	21674	

CLASS E.191   VECTRON   Bo-Bo

Siemens Vectron DC capable of working from 3000 V DC supply in Italy only. CFI locomotives are fitted with auxiliary diesel engines for last mile operation. Leasing company Locoitalia has four on order, the first of which was E.191.103.

Details as Class E.190 except:

Continuous Rating: 5200 kW.   **Maximum Speed:** 160 km/h.
Maximum Tractive Effort:

Number	Owner	Built	Works no.	User
E.191.001	Siemens	2012	21823	InRail
E.191.002	Locoitalia	2013	21845	Fuorimuro
E.191.003	Locoitalia	2013	21846	Fuorimuro
E.191.009	CFI	2017	22181	
E.191.010	CFI	2017	22182	
E.191.011	CFI	2014	21906	
E.191.012	CFI	2014	21909	
E.191.013	Unicredit	2017	22057	DB Cargo IT
E.191.014	Unicredit	2017	22059	DB Cargo IT
E.191.015	Unicredit	2017	22060	DB Cargo IT
E.191.016	Unicredit	2017	22157	DB Cargo IT
E.191.017	Unicredit	2017	22158	DB Cargo IT
E.191.018	Unicredit	2017	22160	DB Cargo IT
E.191.019	Unicredit	2017	22161	DB Cargo IT
E.191.020	Unicredit	2017	22183	DB Cargo IT
E.191.021	MRCE	2010	21693	InRail (ex 191 951)
E.191.022	MRCE	2011	21698	InRail (ex 191 952)
E.191.023	MRCE	2013	21828	InRail
E.191.024	MRCE	2018	22468	
E.191.025	MRCE	2018	22469	CFI
E.191.026	MRCE	2018	22470	InRail
E.191.027	MRCE	2018	22488	CFI
E.191.028	MRCE	2018	22489	CFI
E.191.029	MRCE	2018	22434	

▲ CFI E.191.011 is seen at Codogno on 7 April 2018.   **David Haydock**

E.191.030	MRCE	2018	22435	
E.191.031	MRCE	2018	22436	
E.191.032	MRCE	2018	22437	
E.191.033	MRCE	2018	22438	
E.191.034	MRCE	2018	22512	
E.191.035	MRCE	2018	22513	
E.191.036	MRCE	2018	22514	
E.191.045	MRCE	2019	22494	
E.191.100	Inrail	2015	21910	(ex 191.004)
E.191.103	Locoitalia	2019	22495	
E.191.104	Locoitalia	2019		
E.191.105	Locoitalia	2019		
E.191.106	Locoitalia	2019		

CLASS 193   VECTRON   Bo-Bo

These are Siemens MS (multi-system) locos in various versions. ÖBB also has 30 identical which now operate into Italy. MRCE has a further 20 locos in order for Italy.

Built: 2017–
Builder: Siemens, München-Allach.
One Hour Rating: 6400 kW.   **Weight:** 88–96 tonnes.
Continuous Rating: 6400 kW.   **Length over Buffers:** 18.98 m.
Wheel Diameter: 1250 mm.   **Maximum Speed**: 200km/h.
Maximum Tractive Effort: 300 kN.   **Electric Brake:**

Version D A CH I NL

Number	Owner	Built	Works no.	Operator
193 256	ELL	2016	22152	SBB CI
193 257	ELL	2016	22153	SBB CI
193 258	ELL	2016	22154	SBB CI
193 259	ELL	2016	22155	SBB CI
193 260	ELL	2016	22159	SBB CI
193 278	ELL	2017	22279	TXL
193 280	ELL	2017	22265	LTE
193 281	ELL	2017	22271	TXL
193 282	ELL	2117	22276	TXL
193 283	ELL	2017	22277	TXL
193 299	ELL	2017	22357	CTI

193 300 to 193 359 are version D A CH I NL. Please see "German Railways Part 1" for details.

Version D A CH I

193 461	Lokroll	2017	22281	SBB CI
193 462	Lokroll	2017	22282	SBB CI
193 463	Lokroll	2017	22289	SBB CI
193 464	Lokroll	2017	22290	SBB CI
193 465	Lokroll	2017	22303	SBB CI
193 466	Lokroll	2017	22304	SBB CI
193 467	Lokroll	2017	22305	SBB CI
193 468	Lokroll	2017	22306	SBB CI
193 469	Lokroll	2017	22310	SBB CI
193 470	Lokroll	2017	22311	SBB CI
193 471	Lokroll	2018	22313	SBB CI
193 472	Lokroll	2018	22315	SBB CI
193 473	Lokroll	2018	22318	SBB CI
193 474	Lokroll	2018	22319	SBB CI
193 475	Lokroll	2018	22320	SBB CI
193 476	Lokroll	2018	22321	SBB CI
193 477	Lokroll	2018	22322	SBB CI
193 478	Lokroll	2018	22323	SBB CI

48

Version D A CH I NL

193 490	HUPAC/BLS	2017	22359
193 491	HUPAC/BLS	2018	22288
193 492	HUPAC/BLS	2018	22364
193 493	HUPAC/BLS	2018	22301
193 494	HUPAC/BLS	2018	22307
193 495	HUPAC/BLS	2018	22386
193 496	HUPAC/BLS	2018	22390
193 497	HUPAC/BLS	2018	22385

Version D A I

193 550	AT	2016	22184	TXL
193 551	AT	2016	22185	TXL
193 552	AT	2016	22189	TXL
193 553	AT	2016	22190	TXL
193 554	AT	2016	22194	TXL
193 555	AT	2016	22195	TXL
193 556	AT	2017	22216	TXL
193 557	AT	2017	22236	TXL
193 558	AT	2017	22241	TXL
193 559	AT	2017	22242	TXL
193 640	MRCE	2016	22164	TXL
193 641	MRCE	2016	22165	MIR
193 642	MRCE	2016	22166	MIR
193 643	MRCE	2016	22167	MIR
193 644	MRCE	2016	22168	MIR
193 645	MRCE	2017	22169	MIR
193 646	MRCE	2017	22170	MIR
193 647	MRCE	2017	22171	MIR
193 648	MRCE	2017	22172	MIR
193 649	MRCE	2017	22173	MIR
193 650	MRCE	2017	22174	MIR
193 651	MRCE	2016	22210	Lokomotion
193 652	MRCE	2016	22211	MIR
193 653	MRCE	2016	22156	Lokomotion
193 654	MRCE	2017	22196	CFI
193 655	MRCE	2017	22199	CTI
193 656	MRCE	2017	22201	InRail
193 657	MRCE	2017	22205	Lokomotion
193 658	MRCE	2017	22217	ecco-rail (AT)
193 659	MRCE	2017	22219	ecco-rail (AT)
193 660	MRCE	2017	22243	TXL
193 661	MRCE	2017	22237	Lokomotion
193 662	MRCE	2017	22238	Lokomotion
193 663	MRCE	2017	22240	Lokomotion
193 664	MRCE	2017	22244	Lokomotion
193 665	MRCE	2017	22245	
193 666	MRCE	2017	22223	Lokomotion
193 667	MRCE	2017	22226	TXL
193 668	MRCE	2017	22227	TXL
193 669	MRCE	2017	22228	TXL
193 670	MRCE	2017	22246	TXL
193 671	MRCE	2017	22230	TXL
193 672	MRCE	2017	22232	TXL
193 673	MRCE	2017	22233	TXL
193 674	MRCE	2017	22266	Adriafer
193 675	MRCE	2017	22270	Adriafer

Version D A CH I NL

193 700	MRCE	2018	22316	TXL
193 701	MRCE	2018	22366	Lokomotion
193 702	MRCE	2018	22367	Lokomotion
193 703	MRCE	2018	22381	LTE AT

193 704	MRCE	2018	22388	TXL
193 705	MRCE	2018	22389	
193 706	MRCE	2018	22392	MIR
193 707	MRCE	2018	22395	
193 708	MRCE	2018	22399	MIR
193 709	MRCE	2018	22400	MIR

Version D A I

193 770	Lokomotion	2016	22061	
193 771	Lokomotion	2016	22186	"Viola"
193 772	Lokomotion	2016	22187	
193 773	Lokomotion	2017	22197	
193 774	Lokomotion	2017	22204	
193 775	Lokomotion	2017	22212	
193 776	Lokomotion	2017	22213	
193 777	Lokomotion	2017	22218	

Version D A CH I NL

193 818	Siemens	2017	22300	LTE (AT)
193 819	Siemens	2017	22363	
193 829	Siemens	2017	22358	RTB Cargo
193 833	BoxXpress	2017	22263	
193 834	BoxXpress	2017	22264	
193 835	BoxXpress	2017	22273	
193 836	BoxXpress	2017	22275	

Version D A I

| 193 847 | InRail | 2017 | 22260 | |

BLS Cargo works into Italy with its D A CH I NL Vectrons 475 401 to 415. See "Swiss Railways" book for details.

CLASSES E.401 & E.402 A   Bo-Bo

Following the construction of five prototype locomotives in 1988, E.402.001 to 005 (now all withdrawn), 40 standard Class E.402 A locomotives were built with Siemens technology including separately-excited traction motors with microprocessor control. The locos were used to haul long-distance services across Italy, sharing this work with Classes E.402 B and E.444. In late 2013 it was announced that Trenitalia would rebuild these locomotives with a cab at one end only and replace traction equipment with similar equipment to that in Class E.403. The work was subcontracted to CAF but actually carried out in Trenitalia's Foligno works. Rebuilt locomotives are reclassified E.401 and are used on InterCity trains in push-pull mode with existing stock and new driving trailers.

Built: 1994–96.
Builder–Mechanical Parts: Firema 006–025; Sofer 026–045.
Traction Motors: 4 x MTA–F4–I asynchronous.   **Wheel Diameter:** 1250 mm.
Continuous Rating: 5200 kW.   **Weight:** 87 tonnes.
Maximum Tractive Effort: 250 kN.   **Length over Buffers:** 18.86 m, E.401; 18.44 m, E.402 A.
Maximum Speed: 200 km/h.
EVN: 91 83 240x 006-c and so on.

All Class E.401 are in the new red and grey IRS livery.

E.401.006	P	RL	E.401.019	P	MT	E.401.032	P	MT
E.401.007	P	MT	E.402.020	P	MT	E.402.033	P	MT
E.402.008	P	MT	E.401.021	P	MT	E.402.034	P	MT
E.401.009	P	MT	E.401.022	P	RL	E.401.035	P	MT
E.402.010	P	MT	E.401.023	P	MT	E.402.036	P	MT
E.402.011	P	MT	E.401.024	P	MT	E.401.037	P	MT
E.402.012	P	MT	E.401.025	P	RL	E.402.038	P	MT
E.401.013	P	RL	E.401.026	P	RL	E.401.039	P	MT
E.401.014	P	MT	E.401.027	P	MT	E.401.040	P	RL
E.401.015	P	RL	E.402.028	P	MT	E.401.042	P	MT
E.401.016	P	RL	E.402.029	P	MT	E.402.044	P	MT
E.402.017	P	MT	E.402.030	P	MT	E.402.045	P	MT
E.402.018	P	MT	E.401.031	P	MT			

▲ E.401.007, in the new IRS livery, is seen with an InterCity train at Bologna Centrale on 27 September 2018.   **Barry Tempest**

▼ E.402.124, in Frecciabianca livery, pushes an InterCity train towards Genova through Milano Lambrate on 6 April 2018.   **David Haydock**

CLASS E.402 B
Bo-Bo

Although derived from Class E.402 A, these locomotives have a completely different exterior and many different features. Passenger locos were passed for push-pull operation in late 2004 and have taken over InterCity services from Classes E.402 A and E.444. They operate across the country. Many locos have been finished in the red and white *Frecciabianca* livery and work in push-pull mode with *Frecciabianca* stock. The E.402.139 to 158 batch previously used on freight can no longer work into France. In late 2018 E.402.107 and 125 were equipped to operate in multiple for tests, with a view for the class to be used to haul freight on the Torino–Modane and Udine–Tarvisio routes.

Details as Class E.402 A except:

Built: 1997–2000.
Builder–Mechanical Parts: Ansaldo.
Builder–Electrical Parts: Sofer E.402.101–119, 131–158; Fiore E.402.120–130, 159–180.
Continuous Rating: 5600 kW. **Weight:** 89 tonnes.
Maximum Tractive Effort: 280 kN. **Length over Buffers:** 19.42 m.
Systems: 3000 V DC/25 kV AC 50 Hz overhead. **Maximum Speed:** 220 km/h.
EVN: 91 83 2402 101-c and so on.

* Based at Roma Tuscolana for *"Archimede"* test train.
m Equipped for operating in multiple.

E.402.101	*I*	*	RL	E.402.128	*P*	**FB**	MG	E.402.155	*P*		RL
E.402.102	*P*	**FB**	MG	E.402.129	*P*		RL	E.402.156	*P*		RL
E.402.103	*P*	**FB**	MG	E.402.130	*P*	*I*	MG	E.402.157	*P*		RL
E.402.104	*P*	*I*	MG	E.402.131	*P*		RL	E.402.158	*P*		RL
E.402.105	*P*	**FB**	MG	E.402.132	*P*		RL	E.402.159	*P*	**FB**	MG
E.402.106	*P*	**FB**	MG	E.402.133	*P*		RL	E.402.160	*P*	**FB**	MG
E.402.107	*P*	m	RL	E.402.134	*P*		RL	E.402.161	*P*		RL
E.402.108	*P*	**FB**	MG	E.402.135	*P*	*I*	RL	E.402.162	*P*	**FB**	MG
E.402.109	*P*	**FB**	MG	E.402.136	*P*	**FB**	MG	E.402.163	*P*		RL
E.402.110	*P*	**FB**	MG	E.402.137	*P*	**FB**	MG	E.402.164	*P*	**FB**	MG
E.402.111	*P*	**FB**	MG	E.402.138	*P*	**FB**	MG	E.402.165	*P*	**FB**	MG
E.402.112	*P*	**FB**	MG	E.402.139	*P*		RL	E.402.166	*P*	**FB**	MG
E.402.113	*P*		RL	E.402.140	*P*	*I*	MG	E.402.167	*P*		MG
E.402.114	*P*	**FB**	MG	E.402.141	*P*		RL	E.402.168	*P*	**FB**	MG
E.402.115	*P*		RL	E.402.142	*I*	*	RL	E.402.169	*P*		RL
E.402.116	*P*	**FB**	MG	E.402.143	*P*	*I*	RL	E.402.170	*P*	**FB**	MG
E.402.117	*P*		RL	E.402.144	*P*		RL	E.402.171	*P*	**FB**	MG
E.402.118	*P*	**FB**	MG	E.402.145	*P*	*I*	RL	E.402.172	*P*	*I*	RL
E.402.119	*P*		RL	E.402.146	*P*		RL	E.402.173	*P*		MG
E.402.120	*P*		RL	E.402.147	*P*	*I*	RL	E.402.174	*P*	**FB**	MG
E.402.121	*P*		RL	E.402.148	*P*		RL	E.402.175	*P*	**FB**	MG
E.402.122	*P*	*I*	MG	E.402.149	*I*	*	RL	E.402.176	*P*	**FB**	MG
E.402.123	*P*		RL	E.402.150	*P*		RL	E.402.177	*P*		RL
E.402.124	*P*	**FB**	MG	E.402.151	*P*		RL	E.402.178	*P*	**FB**	MG
E.402.125	*P*	m	RL	E.402.152	*P*		RL	E.402.179	*P*		RL
E.402.126	*P*	**FB**	MG	E.402.153	*P*		RL	E.402.180	*P*	**FB**	MG
E.402.127	*P*		RL	E.402.154	*P*		RL				

CLASS E.403   Bo-Bo

A class originally intended for freight services whose pre-series loco was delivered in mid-2006. The exterior is very similar to Class E.402 B – locos were originally to be classified E.402 C. After a very long running-in phase they were eventually allocated to IC passenger services and initially operated overnight services across the country. They are now being equipped to haul InterCity trains in push-pull mode with Type Z stock. E.403.010 was in an accident and will be scrapped.

Details as Class E.402 B except:

Built: 2006–14.
Builder–Mechanical Parts: AnsaldoBreda.
Builder–Electrical Parts: Bombardier.   **Weight:** 86 tonnes.
Systems: 3000 V DC/15 kV AC 16.7 Hz*/25 kV AC 50 Hz overhead*.
EVN: 91 83 2403 001-c and so on.

*   All 15/25 kV AC equipment was being removed in 2019.

E.403.001	P	RL	E.403.009	P	RL	E.403.017	P	RL
E.403.002	P	RL	E.403.010	P	RL(S)	E.403.018	P	RL
E.403.003	P	RL	E.403.011	P	RL	E.403.019	P	RL
E.403.004	P	RL	E.403.012	P	RL	E.403.020	P	RL
E.403.005	P	RL	E.403.013	P	RL	E.403.021	P	RL
E.403.006	P	RL	E.403.014	IC	RL	E.403.022	P	RL
E.403.007	P	RL	E.403.015	P	RL	E.403.023	P	RL
E.403.008	P	RL	E.403.016	P	RL	E.403.024	P	RL

CLASSES E.404   Bo-Bo

Following trials with five Class E.404.000 power cars (now withdrawn) plus trailers, FSI ordered 30 ETR.500 high-speed trains, each formed of two Class E.404.100 3000 V DC power cars and 11 trailers. These trains were initially used on *Eurostar Italia* Milano–Firenze–Roma–Napoli services running at 250 km/h over the *Direttissima* high-speed line between Firenze and Roma.

FSI then decided to electrify all future high-speed lines (starting with Roma–Napoli in 2005) at 25 kV AC 50 Hz and ordered 30 more ETR.500 sets with dual-voltage Class E.404.500 power cars. Trains with dual-voltage power cars were known as ETR.500 P (*Politensione*). Dual-voltage power cars can be identified by their central windscreen and rounder nose.

In 2002, FSI decided to replace Class E.404.100 with 60 dual-voltage E.404.600 power cars (with ERTMS cab signalling). E.404.600 power cars were delivered from 2005. At the same time, E.404.500 power cars were upgraded to the same standard, including being fitted with single-arm pantographs, upgraded transformers and ERTMS.

Class E.404.100 power cars have now been converted to operate with InterCity hauled coaches and have been renumbered as Class E.414 (see below).

Following the delivery of ETR.400 sets, it is probable that ETR.500 sets will be cascaded to work less prestigious trains, with considerable sections away from high speed lines.

In some earlier editions we listed ETR.500 trains by set number (01 to 59) and also showed trailer cars. However, power cars are constantly swapped between sets so we now only list those. Unfortunately, their numbers are in black so red and difficult to read. All ETR.500 sets are now in *Frecciarossa* (red arrow) livery except E.404.502 and 538 in blue and yellow for use with the DIA.MAN.TE diagnostics train Y2, and are mainly maintained at Napoli Centrale. E.404.649 and 652 power the Y1 test train. E.404.514 and 516 power the Mercitalia Fast test train.

Built: 1996–99, E.414; 1999–2001, E.404.500; 2004–06, E.404.600.
Builder: TREVI consortium (AnsaldoBreda, Firema, Alstom, Bombardier).
Continuous Rating: 4400 kW under 3000 V DC/25 kV AC, 2400 kW under 1500 V DC.
Maximum Tractive Effort: 290 kN.   **Wheel Diameter:** 1100 mm.
Weight: 68 tonnes.   **Maximum Speed:** E.404 300 km/h; E.414 200 km/h.
Length over Buffers: 20.25 m, E.414; 20.565 m, E.404.500/600.
Systems: 3000 V DC, E.414; 3000 V DC/25 kV AC 50 Hz overhead, E.404.500/600.

▲ E.403.022 heads a train of empty night stock through Milano Lambrate station on 6 April 2018.
David Haydock

▼ E.405.002 heads a mixed freight south through Branzolo station on 13 September 2018.
David Haydock

Class E.404.500. EVN: 91 83 2404 500-c and so on.

E.404.500	P	NC	E.404.520	P	NC	E.404.540	P	NC
E.404.501	P	NC	E.404.521	P	NC	E.404.541	P	NC
E.404.502	I	NC	E.404.522	P	NC	E.404.542	P	NC
E.404.503	P	NC	E.404.523	P	NC	E.404.543	P	NC
E.404.504	P	NC	E.404.524	P	NC	E.404.544	P	NC
E.404.505	P	NC	E.404.525	P	NC	E.404.545	P	NC
E.404.506	P	NC	E.404.526	P	NC	E.404.546	P	NC
E.404.507	P	NC	E.404.527	P	NC	E.404.547	P	NC
E.404.508	P	NC	E.404.528	P	NC	E.404.548	P	NC
E.404.509	P	NC	E.404.529	P	NC	E.404.549	P	NC
E.404.510	P	NC	E.404.530	P	NC	E.404.550	P	NC
E.404.511	P	NC	E.404.531	P	NC	E.404.551	P	NC
E.404.512	P	NC	E.404.532	P	NC	E.404.552	P	NC
E.404.513	P	NC	E.404.533	P	NC	E.404.553	P	NC
E.404.514	C	NC	E.404.534	P	NC	E.404.554	P	NC
E.404.515	P	NC	E.404.535	P	NC	E.404.555	P	NC
E.404.516	C	NC	E.404.536	P	NC	E.404.556	P	NC
E.404.517	P	NC	E.404.537	P	NC	E.404.557	P	NC
E.404.518	P	NC	E.404.538	I	NC	E.404.558	P	NC
E.404.519	P	NC	E.404.539	P	NC	E.404.559	P	NC

Class E.404.600. EVN: 91 83 2404 600-c and so on.

E.404.601	P	NC	E.404.621	P	NC	E.404.641	P	NC
E.404.602	P	NC	E.404.622	P	NC	E.404.642	P	NC
E.404.603	P	NC	E.404.623	P	NC	E.404.643	P	NC
E.404.604	P	NC	E.404.624	P	NC	E.404.644	P	NC
E.404.605	P	NC	E.404.625	P	NC	E.404.645	P	NC
E.404.606	P	NC	E.404.626	P	NC	E.404.646	P	NC
E.404.607	P	NC	E.404.627	P	NC	E.404.647	P	NC
E.404.608	P	NC	E.404.628	P	NC	E.404.648	P	NC
E.404.609	P	NC	E.404.629	P	NC	E.404.649	I	NC
E.404.610	P	NC	E.404.630	P	NC	E.404.650	P	NC
E.404.611	P	NC	E.404.631	P	NC	E.404.651	P	NC
E.404.612	P	NC	E.404.632	P	NC	E.404.652	I	NC
E.404.613	P	NC	E.404.633	P	NC	E.404.653	P	NC
E.404.614	P	NC	E.404.634	P	NC	E.404.654	P	NC
E.404.615	P	NC	E.404.635	P	NC	E.404.655	P	NC
E.404.616	P	NC	E.404.636	P	NC	E.404.656	P	NC
E.404.617	P	NC	E.404.637	P	NC	E.404.657	P	NC
E.404.618	P	NC	E.404.638	P	NC	E.404.658	P	NC
E.404.619	P	NC	E.404.639	P	NC	E.404.659	P	NC
E.404.620	P	NC	E.404.640	P	NC	E.404.660	P	NC

CLASS E.405   Bo-Bo

These locomotives were originally built for Polish Railways (PKP) as Class EU11 but PKP could not pay for them and Trenitalia Cargo came to the rescue. They mainly operate freight on the Verona–Brennero route, but also haul passenger trains. The design has much in common with Class E.412 but their body sides are smooth whilst E.412s are ribbed. E.405.032 was destroyed in an accident.

Built: 1999–2000. Introduced by Trenitalia 2003/04.
Builder–Mechanical Parts: Bombardier/Pafawag.
Builder–Electrical Parts: Bombardier.   **Wheel Diameter:** 1100 mm.
Continuous Rating: 5000 kW.   **Weight:** 82 tonnes.
Length over Buffers: 19.40 m.   **Maximum Speed:** 200 km/h.
EVN: 91 83 2405 001-c and so on.

E.405.001	C	VR	E.405.015	C	VR	E.405.029	C	VR		
E.405.002	C	VR	E.405.016	C	VR	E.405.030	C	VR		
E.405.003	C	VR	E.405.017	C	VR	E.405.031	C	VR		
E.405.004	C	VR	E.405.018	C	VR	E.405.033	C	VR		
E.405.005	C	VR	E.405.019	C	VR	E.405.034	C	VR		
E.405.006	C	VR	E.405.020	C	VR	E.405.035	C	VR		
E.405.007	C	VR	E.405.021	C	VR	E.405.036	C	VR		
E.405.008	C	VR	E.405.022	C	VR	E.405.037	C	VR		
E.405.009	C	VR	E.405.023	C	VR	E.405.038	C	VR		
E.405.010	C	VR	E.405.024	C	VR	E.405.039	C	VR		
E.405.011	C	VR	E.405.025	C	VR	E.405.040	C	VR		
E.405.012	C	VR	E.405.026	C	VR	E.405.041	C	VR		
E.405.013	C	VR	E.405.027	C	VR	E.405.042	C	VR		
E.405.014	C	VR	E.405.028	C	VR					

CLASSES EU 43 & E.412 — Bo-Bo

Class E.412 are three-voltage locomotives designed for international services, including passenger, into Austria and Germany (15 kV AC) but are only used on freight. Some of the locos' technology is based on the German Class 127. They mainly operate Verona–München via Brennero and sometimes reach München.

Class EU 43, owned by Rail Traction Company, are identical except that they cannot operate under 15 kV AC. Like Class E.405 they were originally built for Polish Railways (PKP). Also used, mainly in multiple, on the Verona–Brennero route.

Built: 1997–98, Class E.412; 1999, Class EU 43.
Builder–Mechanical Parts: Adtranz.
Builder–Electrical Parts: Adtranz.
Traction Motors: 4 x ABB 4FIA7065.
Continuous Rating: 6000 kW (3000 V DC); 5500 kW (15 kV AC) not Class EU 43; 2700 kW (1500 V DC).
Maximum Tractive Effort: 300 kN.
Wheel Diameter: 1100 mm.
Weight: 87 tonnes.
Length over Buffers: 19.40 m.
Maximum Speed: 200 km/h.

Class EU 43. EVN: 91 83 2043 001-c and so on.

EU 43 001	EU 43 003	EU 43 005	EU 43 007	EU 43 008
EU 43 002	EU 43 004	EU 43 006		

Class E.412. EVN: 91 83 0412 001-c and so on.

E.412.001	C	MS	E.412.008	C	MS	E.412.015	C	MS
E.412.002	C	MS	E.412.009	C	MS	E.412.016	C	MS
E.412.003	C	MS	E.412.010	C	MS	E.412.017	C	MS
E.412.004	C	MS	E.412.011	C	MS	E.412.018	C	MS
E.412.005	C	MS	E.412.012	C	MS	E.412.019	C	MS
E.412.006	C	MS	E.412.013	C	MS	E.412.020	C	MS
E.412.007	C	MS	E.412.014	C	MS			

CLASS E.414 — Bo-Bo

For details see Class E.404 above. These power cars are in *Frecciabianca* livery and top-and-tail sets of refurbished hauled stock. They are mostly used on the Milano–Bari route.

EVN: 91 83 2414 100-c and so on.

E.414.100	P	MT	E.414.113	P	MT	E.414.125	P	MT
E.414.101	P	MT	E.414.114	P	MT	E.414.126	P	MT
E.414.102	P	MT	E.414.115	P	MT	E.414.127	P	MT
E.414.103	P	MT	E.414.116	P	MT	E.414.128	P	MT
E.414.104	P	MT	E.414.117	P	MT	E.414.129	P	MT
E.414.105	P	MT	E.414.118	P	MT	E.414.130	P	MT
E.414.106	P	MT	E.414.119	P	MT	E.414.131	P	MT
E.414.107	P	MT	E.414.120	P	MT	E.414.132	P	MT
E.414.108	P	MT	E.414.121	P	MT	E.414.133	P	MT
E.414.109	P	MT	E.414.122	P	MT	E.414.134	P	MT
E.414.110	P	MT	E.414.123	P	MT	E.414.135	P	MT
E.414.111	P	MT	E.414.124	P	MT	E.414.136	P	MT

▲ E.412.005 passes through Castelfranco Veneto with a freight on 12 September 2018.

David Haydock

▼ E.414.128 heads a Lecce–Milano Frecciabianca service through Lodi on 6 April 2018.

David Haydock

E.414.137	P	MT	E.414.145	P	MT	E.414.153	P	MT
E.414.138	P	MT	E.414.146	P	MT	E.414.154	P	MT
E.414.139	P	MT	E.414.147	P	MT	E.414.155	P	MT
E.414.140	P	MT	E.414.148	P	MT	E.414.156	P	MT
E.414.141	P	MT	E.414.149	P	MT	E.414.157	P	MT
E.414.142	P	MT	E.414.150	P	MT	E.414.158	P	MT
E.414.143	P	MT	E.414.151	P	MT	E.414.159	P	MT
E.414.144	P	MT	E.414.152	P	MT			

CLASS E.436

These are the 30 SNCF Class BB 36300 tri-voltage locos which operate between France and Italy over the Modane–Torino route. Trenitalia owns two of them. See "French Railways" book for details.

CLASS E.444 R — Bo-Bo

Known as *"Tartaruga"* – tortoises – because of their original rounded shape, these were Italy's first high-speed locomotives, built to haul expresses over the *Direttissima* route between Firenze and Roma. E.444.001–004 were prototypes and had less bulbous front ends. E.444.001 is now in Pietrarsa museum. E.444.005 was actually built after the others, in 1976, as a prototype with "full chopper" equipment. It was transformed into a standard loco in 1989.

Now extinct Class E.447 were converted from Class E.444 in 1985–87 with a different gear ratio in order to operate at 200 km/h – originally Class E.444 were limited to 180 km/h. However, it was discovered that Class E.444 stood up very well to 200 km/h running without conversion. Now all locos are passed for 200 km/h. From 1989, locos were rebuilt with new cabs giving greater driver protection and known as E.444 R.

They can be found hauling InterCity passenger trains all over the country, running at up to 200 km/h on the *Direttissima*, but have lost the top jobs to Classes E.401, E.402 A, E.402 B and E.403. The last overhauls were carried out in early 2018 and the locos are gradually being withdrawn.

Built: 1967–76.
Builder–Mechanical Parts: Savigliano/TIBB/Casaralta/SOFER/Fiat/Reggiane/Breda.
Builder–Electrical Parts: Savigliano/TIBB/ALCE/OCREN/ASGEN/Marelli/CESA/Breda/Italtrafo.
Traction Motors: 4 x 42–200 FS.   **Wheel Diameter:** 1250 mm.
Continuous Rating: 4020 kW.   **Weight:** 83 tonnes.
Maximum Tractive Effort: 242 kN.   **Length over Buffers:** 17.12 m.
Maximum Speed: 200 km/h.
EVN: 91 83 2444 005-c and so on.

E.444.005	P	MC	E.444.048	P	MC	E.444.086	P	MC
E.444.006	P	MC	E.444.049	P	MC	E.444.087	P	MC
E.444.007	P	MC	E.444.051	P	MC	E.444.089	P	MC
E.444.009	P	MC	E.444.052	P	MC	E.444.090	P	MC
E.444.010	P	MC	E.444.053	P	MC	E.444.096	P	MC
E.444.016	P	MC	E.444.056	P	MC	E.444.098	P	MC
E.444.018	P	MC	E.444.057	P	MC	E.444.101	P	MC
E.444.019	P	MC	E.444.064	P	MC	E.444.103	P	MC
E.444.025	P	MC	E.444.066	P	MC	E.444.104	P	MC
E.444.034	P	MC	E.444.069	P	MC	E.444.106	P	MC
E.444.038	P	MC	E.444.070	P	MC	E.444.109	P	MC
E.444.040	P	MC	E.444.074	P	MC	E.444.112	P	MC
E.444.041	P	MC	E.444.079	P	MC	E.444.113	P	MC
E.444.043	P	MC	E.444.082	P	MC	E.444.115	P	MC
E.444.046	P	MC	E.444.085	P	MC			

CLASS E.464 Bo-Bo

A single driving-ended locomotive with a small baggage compartment, for powering regional push-pull services. An order for 50 locos in 1996 was followed by 90 more in 1999, and further orders took the total to 717 – one of the most numerous classes in Europe. They have replaced much older classes such as E.424, E.636 and E.646. E.464.029 was scrapped after an accident.

This design was also built for TPER & TFT, although the latter's only loco was transferred to Trenitalia in 2017. As TPER locos can be mainly found on RFI main lines with Vivalto stock they are now included here. TPER locos are based at Sermide but receive light maintenance at Trenitalia's Bologna Centrale depot.

From E.464.539, there are small differences, including a Type 52 pantograph, fault diagnostics, improved fire suppression and an improved cab.

Trenord locomotives carry Vehicle Keeper Marking I-TN instead of I-TI. All MF allocated locos are with Trenord.

Trenitalia is to use Class E.464, displaced by new EMUs, to haul InterCity trains in future, at first to replace Class E.656 in Sicily.

Built: 1999–2014, FSI locomotives; 2005, E.464.901–903; 2006, E.464.904–906; 2010, E.464.880, 890–893.
Builder–Mechanical Parts: Adtranz Italia; Bombardier from 2001.
Builder–Electrical Parts: Adtranz; Bombardier from 2001.

Continuous Rating: 3000 kW.	**Wheel Diameter:** 1100 mm.	
Maximum Tractive Effort: 200 kN.	**Weight:** 72 tonnes.	
Length over Buffers: 16.05 m.	**Maximum Speed:** 160 km/h.	

EVN: 91 83 2464 001-c and so on.

P   TPER livery of red, white and green.
*   Special red, white and green livery to celebrate E.464.464.
§   Ex TFT.
+   Equipped with ETCS.

No.			Dep	No.			Dep	No.			Dep
E.464.001	R		PA	E.464.037	R		NC	E.464.071	TR	N	MF
E.464.002	R	L	RS	E.464.038	R		BC	E.464.072	TR	N	MF
E.464.003	R	L	AN	E.464.039	R		BZ	E.464.073	TR	N	MF
E.464.004	R		AN	E.464.040	R		BZ	E.464.074	R		BC
E.464.005	R	L	PA	E.464.041	R		AL	E.464.075	TR		MF
E.464.006	TR	N	MF	E.464.042	R		RC	E.464.076	TR		MF
E.464.007	R		PA	E.464.043	R		NC	E.464.077	R		BC
E.464.008	R		PA	E.464.044	R		RC	E.464.078	TR		MF
E.464.009	TR		MF	E.464.045	TR	N	MF	E.464.079	TR	N	MF
E.464.010	TR		MF	E.464.046	R		PA	E.464.080	TR		MF
E.464.011	TR		MF	E.464.047	R		BC	E.464.081	R		GB
E.464.012	TR		MF	E.464.048	R		BC	E.464.082	R		BC
E.464.013	R		AL	E.464.049	R		BC	E.464.083	R		GB
E.464.014	R		AN	E.464.050	R		BC	E.464.084	R		PA
E.464.015	TR	N	MF	E.464.051	R		NC	E.464.085	R		PA
E.464.016	R		RC	E.464.052	R		BZ	E.464.086	R		PA
E.464.017	R		AN	E.464.053	R		AN	E.464.087	R		BC
E.464.018	TR		MF	E.464.054	R		NC	E.464.088	R		BC
E.464.019	R		AL	E.464.055	R		BZ	E.464.089	R		BC
E.464.020	TR	N	MF	E.464.056	TR	N	MF	E.464.090	R		BC
E.464.021	R		AL	E.464.057	R		BZ	E.464.091	R		BC
E.464.022	TR		MF	E.464.058	TR		MF	E.464.092	R		NC
E.464.023	TR		MF	E.464.059	TR	N	MF	E.464.093	R		AN
E.464.024	TR		MF	E.464.060	R		VR	E.464.094	R		RC
E.464.025	TR		MF	E.464.061	R		AL	E.464.095	R		NC
E.464.027	TR		MF	E.464.062	R		AL	E.464.096	R		AL
E.464.028	R		PA	E.464.063	TR		MF	E.464.097	R		NC
E.464.030	R		NC	E.464.064	R		FI	E.464.098	R		NC
E.464.031	R		BZ	E.464.065	R		AL	E.464.099	R		AN
E.464.032	R		BZ	E.464.066	R		AL	E.464.100	R		PA
E.464.033	R		BZ	E.464.067	R		PA	E.464.101	R		BC
E.464.034	R		NC	E.464.068	R		BZ	E.464.102	R		GB
E.464.035	R		BZ	E.464.069	TR		MF	E.464.103	R		GB
E.464.036	R		BZ	E.464.070	R		RS	E.464.104	R		FG

▲ E.444.041 heads an InterCIty service at Lecce on 25 May 2018. **David Haydock**

▼ A rare clean E.464.006 in Trenord livery, as is its train, is seen at Milano Lambrate on 6 April 2018. **David Haydock**

Code				Code				Code			
E.464.105	*R*		FG	E.464.169	*R*		RS	E.464.233	*R*		NC
E.464.106	*R*		PA	E.464.170	*R*		TC	E.464.234	*R*		NC
E.464.107	*R*		BC	E.464.171	*R*		TC	E.464.235	*TR*		MF
E.464.108	*R*		PA	E.464.172	*R*		RS	E.464.236	*TR*	**N**	MF
E.464.109	*R*		FG	E.464.173	*R*		RS	E.464.237	*TR*	**N**	MF
E.464.110	*R*		FG	E.464.174	*R*		RS	E.464.238	*TR*		MF
E.464.111	*R*		NC	E.464.175	*R*		RS	E.464.239	*TR*	**N**	MF
E.464.112	*R*		BC	E.464.176	*R*		TC	E.464.240	*TR*		MF
E.464.113	*R*		RC	E.464.177	*R*		BC	E.464.241	*TR*	**N**	MF
E.464.114	*R*		FG	E.464.178	*R*		VR	E.464.242	*TR*	**N**	MF
E.464.115	*R*		FG	E.464.179	*R*		TC	E.464.243	*TR*	**N**	MF
E.464.116	*R*		GB	E.464.180	*R*		RS	E.464.244	*R*		VR
E.464.117	*R*		FG	E.464.181	*R*		NC	E.464.245	*R*		VR
E.464.118	*R*		FG	E.464.182	*R*		PA	E.464.246	*R*		AL
E.464.119	*R*		FG	E.464.183	*R*		AL	E.464.247	*R*		VR
E.464.120	*R*		FG	E.464.184	*R*	**R**	RS	E.464.248	*R*		VR
E.464.121	*R*		FG	E.464.185	*R*		RS	E.464.249	*R*		VR
E.464.122	*R*		AL	E.464.186	*R*		NC	E.464.250	*R*		VR
E.464.123	*R*		FG	E.464.187	*R*		PA	E.464.251	*R*		VR
E.464.124	*R*	**R**	FI	E.464.188	*R*		RS	E.464.252	*R*		VR
E.464.125	*R*		AN	E.464.189	*TR*	**N**	MF	E.464.253	*R*		TS
E.464.126	*R*		RC	E.464.190	*TR*	**N**	MF	E.464.254	*R*		TS
E.464.127	*R*		FG	E.464.191	*TR*	**N**	MF	E.464.255	*TR*	**N**	MF
E.464.128	*R*		NC	E.464.192	*TR*	**N**	MF	E.464.256	*TR*	**N**	MF
E.464.129	*R*		NC	E.464.193	*TR*	**N**	MF	E.464.257	*TR*	**N**	MF
E.464.130	*R*		NC	E.464.194	*TR*	**N**	MF	E.464.258	*TR*	**N**	MF
E.464.131	*R*		AL	E.464.195	*TR*		MF	E.464.259	*R*		VR
E.464.132	*R*		BC	E.464.196	*TR*	**N**	MF	E.464.260	*TR*	**N**	MF
E.464.133	*R*		AN	E.464.197	*TR*	**N**	MF	E.464.261	*R*		SV
E.464.134	*R*		NC	E.464.198	*TR*	**N**	MF	E.464.262	*R*	**V**	RS
E.464.135	*R*		RC	E.464.199	*TR*	**N**	MF	E.464.263	*R*	**V**	RS
E.464.136	*R*		RC	E.464.200	*TR*	**N**	MF	E.464.264	*R*		TS
E.464.137	*R*		AL	E.464.201	*R*		TC	E.464.265	*R*		GB
E.464.138	*R*		RC	E.464.202	*R*		TC	E.464.266	*R*		BC
E.464.139	*R*		FG	E.464.203	*R*		TS	E.464.267	*R*	**R**	AN
E.464.140	*R*		RC	E.464.204	*R*		PA	E.464.268	*R*		NC
E.464.141	*R*		GB	E.464.205	*R*	**R**	FI	E.464.269	*TR*	**N**	MF
E.464.142	*R*		AN	E.464.206	*R*		NC	E.464.270	*TR*	**N**	MF
E.464.143	*R*		GB	E.464.207	*R*		FI	E.464.271	*TR*	**N**	MF
E.464.144	*R*		AN	E.464.208	*R*		RS	E.464.272	*TR*	**N**	MF
E.464.145	*R*		RS	E.464.209	*R*		RS	E.464.273	*R*		SV
E.464.146	*R*		GB	E.464.210	*R*		RS	E.464.274	*TR*	**N**	MF
E.464.147	*R*		GB	E.464.211	*R*	**R**	RS	E.464.275	*TR*	**N**	MF
E.464.148	*R*		AN	E.464.212	*R*		RS	E.464.276	*R*		GB
E.464.149	*R*		PA	E.464.213	*R*		RS	E.464.277	*R*		VR
E.464.150	*R*		PA	E.464.214	*R*	**R**	FG	E.464.278	*R*		VR
E.464.151	*R*		NC	E.464.215	*R*	+	FI	E.464.279	*TR*	**N**	MF
E.464.152	*R*		AN	E.464.216	*R*		RC	E.464.280	*R*		TS
E.464.153	*R*		NC	E.464.217	*R*		GB	E.464.281	*R*		VR
E.464.154	*R*		AN	E.464.218	*R*		RC	E.464.282	*TR*	**N**	MF
E.464.155	*R*		RS	E.464.219	*R*		NC	E.464.283	*TR*	**N**	MF
E.464.156	*R*		NC	E.464.220	*R*		NC	E.464.284	*TR*	**N**	MF
E.464.157	*R*		RS	E.464.221	*R*		NC	E.464.285	*TR*	**N**	MF
E.464.158	*R*		BC	E.464.222	*R*	**R**	RS	E.464.286	*TR*	**N**	MF
E.464.159	*R*		RS	E.464.223	*R*		NC	E.464.287	*R*		RS
E.464.160	*R*		RS	E.464.224	*R*		NC	E.464.288	*TR*	**N**	MF
E.464.161	*R*		RS	E.464.225	*R*		RS	E.464.289	*TR*		MF
E.464.162	*R*		RS	E.464.226	*R*		RS	E.464.290	*TR*	**N**	MF
E.464.163	*R*		RS	E.464.227	*R*		BC	E.464.291	*R*	**V**	RS
E.464.164	*R*		RS	E.464.228	*R*		RS	E.464.292	*R*	**R**	FG
E.464.165	*R*		AL	E.464.229	*R*	**V**	RS	E.464.293	*TR*	**N**	MF
E.464.166	*R*		NC	E.464.230	*R*		RS	E.464.294	*TR*	**N**	MF
E.464.167	*R*		BC	E.464.231	*R*		NC	E.464.295	*R*		TS
E.464.168	*R*		RS	E.464.232	*R*		AL	E.464.296	*R*		PA

ID				ID				ID			
E.464.297	R		BC	E.464.361	R		FG	E.464.425	R	R	GB
E.464.298	R		SV	E.464.362	R		FG	E.464.426	R		GB
E.464.299	R		RS	E.464.363	R	R	BC	E.464.427	R		AL
E.464.300	R		GB	E.464.364	R		FI	E.464.428	R	R	FI
E.464.301	R		NC	E.464.365	R	R	GB	E.464.429	R		FI
E.464.302	R	R	RS	E.464.366	R		NC	E.464.430	R		AL
E.464.303	R		PA	E.464.367	R	R	FI	E.464.431	R		AL
E.464.304	TR	N	MF	E.464.368	R		AN	E.464.432	TR		MF
E.464.305	R		TS	E.464.369	R		NC	E.464.433	R		FI
E.464.306	R		NC	E.464.370	R		VR	E.464.434	R	R	FI
E.464.307	R		VR	E.464.371	R		VR	E.464.435	R	R	FI
E.464.308	R		TS	E.464.372	R		AL	E.464.436	R		AL
E.464.309	R		VR	E.464.373	R		VR	E.464.437	R		TS
E.464.310	R		VR	E.464.374	R		NC	E.464.438	R		FG
E.464.311	R		RC	E.464.375	R	R	FI	E.464.439	R		FG
E.464.312	R		AN	E.464.376	R	R	FI	E.464.440	R		FG
E.464.313	R		AN	E.464.377	R	R	FI	E.464.441	R		AL
E.464.314	R	L	RS	E.464.378	R		FG	E.464.442	R		BC
E.464.315	R		GB	E.464.379	R		FI	E.464.443	R		NC
E.464.316	R		VR	E.464.380	R		GB	E.464.444	R		NC
E.464.317	R		TS	E.464.381	R		FI	E.464.445	TR		MF
E.464.318	R		AN	E.464.382	R		VR	E.464.446	TR		MF
E.464.319	R	R	RS	E.464.383	TR	N	MF	E.464.447	R		FI
E.464.320	R		VR	E.464.384	R	R	RS	E.464.448	R		AL
E.464.321	TR	N	MF	E.464.385	R		SV	E.464.449	R	R	FG
E.464.322	TR	N	MF	E.464.386	R		AL	E.464.450	R		BC
E.464.323	R		VR	E.464.387	TR	N	MF	E.464.451	R	R	VR
E.464.324	TR	N	MF	E.464.388	TR	N	MF	E.464.452	R		VR
E.464.325	R	R	RS	E.464.389	R		PA	E.464.453	R		BC
E.464.326	TR	N	MF	E.464.390	TR	N	MF	E.464.454	R		VR
E.464.327	TR	N	MF	E.464.391	TR		MF	E.464.455	R	R	FI
E.464.328	TR	N	MF	E.464.392	R		FI	E.464.456	R		FI
E.464.329	R		FG	E.464.393	R		FI	E.464.457	TR		MF
E.464.330	R		RS	E.464.394	R		FI	E.464.458	TR	N	MF
E.464.331	R		FG	E.464.395	TR	N	MF	E.464.459	TR	N	MF
E.464.332	R		RS	E.464.396	TR	N	MF	E.464.460	R		FI
E.464.333	TR	N	MF	E.464.397	R		BC	E.464.461	TR		MF
E.464.334	R		VR	E.464.398	R		GB	E.464.462	R		GB
E.464.335	TR		MF	E.464.399	R		FI	E.464.463	R		FI
E.464.336	R		FG	E.464.400	TR	N	MF	E.464.464	R	*	RS
E.464.337	R		FG	E.464.401	R		TS	E.464.465	TR	N	MF
E.464.338	R		VR	E.464.402	R		NC	E.464.466	R		FI
E.464.339	R		RS	E.464.403	TR		MF	E.464.467	R		AN
E.464.340	R		FI	E.464.404	TR	N	MF	E.464.468	R		AN
E.464.341	R		RS	E.464.405	TR	N	MF	E.464.469	R		NC
E.464.342	R		FG	E.464.406	R		TS	E.464.470	R		BC
E.464.343	R		BC	E.464.407	R		TS	E.464.471	R		AN
E.464.344	R		RC	E.464.408	TR	N	MF	E.464.472	R		FI
E.464.345	R		FI	E.464.409	TR	N	MF	E.464.473	R	R	BC
E.464.346	R	R	BC	E.464.410	TR	N	MF	E.464.474	R		FG
E.464.347	R		RS	E.464.411	R		FI	E.464.475	TR	N	MF
E.464.348	R		RS	E.464.412	TR	N	MF	E.464.476	R		FI
E.464.349	R		RS	E.464.413	TR	N	MF	E.464.477	R		FI
E.464.350	R		BC	E.464.414	R		FI	E.464.478	R	R	BC
E.464.351	R		FG	E.464.415	R	R	BC	E.464.479	TR		MF
E.464.352	R		FG	E.464.416	R		FI	E.464.480	R		AN
E.464.353	R		VR	E.464.417	R		FI	E.464.481	R		AN
E.464.354	R		AN	E.464.418	R		FI	E.464.482	R		AL
E.464.355	R		FI	E.464.419	R		FI	E.464.483	R		AN
E.464.356	R		BC	E.464.420	R		BC	E.464.484	TR		MF
E.464.357	R		FI	E.464.421	R		GB	E.464.485	R		GB
E.464.358	R		GB	E.464.422	R		RC	E.464.486	TR	N	MF
E.464.359	R		VR	E.464.423	R		BC	E.464.487	R		BC
E.464.360	R		FI	E.464.424	R		AL	E.464.488	R		VR

Code				Code				Code			
E.464.489	R	R	BC	E.464.553	TR	N	MF	E.464.617	R		PA
E.464.490	R		TC	E.464.554	R		AL	E.464.618	R		PA
E.464.491	R		VR	E.464.555	R		AL	E.464.619	R		PA
E.464.492	R		TC	E.464.556	R		AL	E.464.620	R		AL
E.464.493	R		VR	E.464.557	R		AL	E.464.621	R		AL
E.464.494	TR	N	MF	E.464.558	R	R	FI	E.464.622	R		PA
E.464.495	R		TC	E.464.559	R		SV	E.464.623	R		GB
E.464.496	R		GB	E.464.560	R	R	FI	E.464.624	R	R	GB
E.464.497	TR	N	MF	E.464.561	R		GB	E.464.625	R	R	SV
E.464.498	R		BC	E.464.562	R		VR	E.464.626	R	R	GB
E.464.499	R		VR	E.464.563	R	R	VR	E.464.627	R		GB
E.464.500	R		VR	E.464.564	R	R	RS	E.464.628	R	R	FI
E.464.501	R		GB	E.464.565	R	R	AL	E.464.629	R	R	GB
E.464.502	R		FI	E.464.566	R		RS	E.464.630	R		RS
E.464.503	R		NC	E.464.567	R		TS	E.464.631	R	R	FI
E.464.504	R		AN	E.464.568	R	R	BC	E.464.632	R		GB
E.464.505	R		FI	E.464.569	R		AN	E.464.633	R	R	GB
E.464.506	R		FI	E.464.570	R		GB	E.464.634	R		VR
E.464.507	R		AN	E.464.571	R	R	BC	E.464.635	R	R	FI
E.464.508	R		AL	E.464.572	R	R	BC	E.464.636	R	R	VR
E.464.509	R		GB	E.464.573	R	R	BC	E.464.637	R		VR
E.464.510	R		GB	E.464.574	R		BC	E.464.638	R		GB
E.464.511	R		AN	E.464.575	R	R	BC	E.464.639	R		FG
E.464.512	R		AN	E.464.576	R	R	BC	E.464.640	R	R	BC
E.464.513	R		AN	E.464.577	R		FI	E.464.641	R		RS
E.464.514	R		AN	E.464.578	R	R	BC	E.464.642	R	R	GB
E.464.515	R		GB	E.464.579	R	R	BC	E.464.643	R		VR
E.464.516	TR		MF	E.464.580	R		FG	E.464.644	R		VR
E.464.517	R		FI	E.464.581	R		GB	E.464.645	R		VR
E.464.518	R		FI	E.464.582	R		FG	E.464.646	R	R	VR
E.464.519	TR	N	MF	E.464.583	R	R	FI	E.464.647	R	R	FI
E.464.520	R		GB	E.464.584	R	R	FI	E.464.648	R		RS
E.464.521	R		GB	E.464.585	R	R	FI	E.464.649	R		AL
E.464.522	R		GB	E.464.586	R		AL	E.464.650	R	R	SV
E.464.523	R		GB	E.464.587	R		FG	E.464.651	R	R	FI
E.464.524	R	R	FI	E.464.588	R		RS	E.464.652	R		FI
E.464.525	R		GB	E.464.589	R	R	GB	E.464.653	R		FI
E.464.526	R		NC	E.464.590	R	R	FI	E.464.654	R		AL
E.464.527	R		FG	E.464.591	R		AL	E.464.655	R		FG
E.464.528	R		TC	E.464.592	R		GB	E.464.656	R	R	RS
E.464.529	R		TC	E.464.593	R	R	VR	E.464.657	R		MT
E.464.530	R		TC	E.464.594	R		AL	E.464.658	R		FI
E.464.531	R		AN	E.464.595	R		VR	E.464.659	R	R	FI
E.464.532	R		TC	E.464.596	R	R	BC	E.464.660	R		RS
E.464.533	R		TC	E.464.597	R	R	FI	E.464.661	R		RS
E.464.534	R		TC	E.464.598	R	R	BC	E.464.662	R		MT
E.464.535	R		TC	E.464.599	R	R	BC	E.464.663	R		RS
E.464.536	R		TC	E.464.600	R		AL	E.464.664	R	R	GB
E.464.537	R		TC	E.464.601	R		AL	E.464.665	R		RS
E.464.538	R		VR	E.464.602	R	R	FI	E.464.666	R		RS
E.464.539	R	R	AN	E.464.603	R	R	AL	E.464.667	R		AN
E.464.540	R	R	AL	E.464.604	R		VR	E.464.668	R		AN
E.464.541	R		AN	E.464.605	R	R	FI	E.464.669	R		AN
E.464.542	TR	N	MF	E.464.606	R	R	FI	E.464.670	R		AL
E.464.543	R	R	FI	E.464.607	R		AL	E.464.671	R		AN
E.464.544	R	R	FI	E.464.608	R		VR	E.464.672	R		AL
E.464.545	R		RS	E.464.609	R		FI	E.464.673	R		AL
E.464.546	TR	N	MF	E.464.610	R	R	FI	E.464.674	R		MT
E.464.547	TR	N	MF	E.464.611	R		RC	E.464.675	R		MT
E.464.548	TR	N	MF	E.464.612	R	R	PA	E.464.676	R		NC
E.464.549	R		AL	E.464.613	R		GB	E.464.677	R	R	FI
E.464.550	R		AL	E.464.614	R		SV	E.464.678	R		FI
E.464.551	TR	N	MF	E.464.615	R		AL	E.464.679	R	R	FI
E.464.552	R		FI	E.464.616	R	R	AL	E.464.680	R		FI

Number			Loc	Number			Loc	Number			Loc
E.464.681	*R*	**R**	FI	E.464.694	*R*	**R**	VR	E.464.706	*R*	**R**	SV
E.464.682	*R*	**R**	FI	E.464.695	*R*	**R**	SV	E.464.707	*R*	**R**	RS
E.464.683	*R*		FI	E.464.696	*R*	**R**	VR	E.464.708	*R*	**R**	RS
E.464.684	*R*		FI	E.464.697	*R*	**R**	RS	E.464.709	*R*	**R**	VR
E.464.685	*R*		RS	E.464.698	*R*	**R**	VR	E.464.710	*R*	**R**	VR
E.464.686	*R*		AN	E.464.699	*R*	**R**	RS	E.464.711	*R*	**R**	VR
E.464.687	*R*		AN	E.464.700	*R*	**R**	SV	E.464.712	*R*	**R**	SV
E.464.688	*R*		RS	E.464.701	*R*	**R**	RS	E.464.713	*R*	**R**	RS
E.464.689	*R*	**R**	SV	E.464.702	*R*	**R**	RS	E.464.714	*R*	**R**	RS
E.464.690	*R*	**R**	SV	E.464.703	*R*	**R**	VR	E.464.715	*R*	**R**	VR
E.464.691	*R*	**R**	RS	E.464.704	*R*	**R**	SV	E.464.716	*R*	**R**	SV
E.464.692	*R*	**R**	RS	E.464.705	*R*	**R**	SV	E.464.717	*R*	**R**	VR
E.464.693	*R*	**R**	RS								

E.464.880	*R*	**R§**	FI

E.464.890	*TPER*	**P**	SM	E.464.893	*TPER*	**P**	SM	E.464.894	*TPER*	**P**	SM
E.464.892	*TPER*	**P**	SM								

E.464.901	*TPER*	**P**	SM	E.464.903	*TPER*	**P**	SM	E.464.905	*TPER*	**P**	SM
E.464.902	*TPER*	**P**	SM	E.464.904	*TPER*	**P**	SM	E.464.906	*TPER*	**P**	SM

CLASS E.474   ES64F4   Bo-Bo

Siemens Type ES64F4 multi-voltage electric locomotives. These locos are the same as Class 189, version VF for Italy and Switzerland. Originally ordered by SBB Cargo, for contractual reasons SBB did not accept all the locomotives; the remaining locos were then taken over by Del Fungo Giera which then went bankrupt and sold them.

Details as Class 189.

Number	Owner	Built	Works no.	Notes
E.474.101	CFI	2004	20742	Built as SBB 474 001
E.474.102	CFI	2004	20762	Built as SBB 474 010
E.474.103	CFI	2005	21232	Built as SBB 474 007 (second version)
E.474.201	DB Cargo IT	2005	21233	Built as SBB 474 008 (second version)

CLASS E.483   TRAXX DC   Bo-Bo

Bombardier TRAXX version F140 DC locomotives for use off 3000 V DC supply only in Italy. E.483.101 to 108 are now approved to operate to Modane in France.

Details as Class 186

EVN: 91 83 2483 001-c and so on.

Number	Owner	Built	Works no.	Operator/Notes
E.483.001	AT	2006	34298	Oceanogate
E.483.002	AT	2007	7969	CTI
E.483.003	AT	2007	7970	CTI
E.483.004	AT	2007	7971	RTC
E.483.005	AT	2007	7972	RTC
E.483.006	AT	2007	7973	CTI
E.483.007	AT	2007	7974	Oceanogate
E.483.008	AT	2007	7975	DB Cargo IT
E.483.009	AT	2007	7976	DB Cargo IT
E.483.010	AT	2007	7977	DB Cargo IT
E.483.011	AT	2008	8230	Captrain
E.483.012	AT	2008	8231	Captrain
E.483.013	AT	2008	8232	Oceanogate

E.483.014	AT	2008	8233	Oceanogate
E.483.015	AT	2009	8234	Captrain
E.483.016	AT	2009	8235	Captrain
E.483.017	AT	2009	8236	Captrain
E.483.018	AT	2009	8237	Oceanogate
E.483.019	AT	2009	8238	Oceanogate
E.483.020	AT	2009	8239	Oceanogate
E.483.021	APS	2009	8248	MIR S&T
E.483.022	APS	2009	8249	MIR S&T
E.483.023	DP	2009	8250	
E.483.024	DP	2009	8251	
E.483.025	ST	2009	8252	
E.483.026	ST	2009	8253	
E.483.030	FAS	2012	8430	
E.483.031	FAS	2012	8431	Captrain
E.483.032	FAS	2015	8464	
E.483.040	FT	2013	8432	Oceanogate
E.483.041	FT	2013	8433	
E.483.042	FT	2016	8476	
E.483.043	FT	2017	8490	
E.483.051	GTS	2009	8254	"SASHA"
E.483.052	GTS	2009	8255	"FREEDOM"
E.483.053	GTS	2009	8256	"INDEPENDENCE"
E.483.054	GTS	2009	8378	"ELETTRA"
E.483.055	GTS	2009	8379	"ZOE"

▲ With a sprinkling of snow on the front end, Ferrotramviaria E.483.042 passes through Bari Centrale station on 4 January 2019 with a container train to Brindisi. **Philip Wormald**

E.483.056	GTS	2015	8463	"NICOLA"
E.485.057	GTS	2015	8465	"ALESSANDRIO"
E.483.058	GTS	2016	8487	"FELICIA"
E.483.059	GTS	2016	8488	"LEONIDA"
E.483.060	GTS	2017	8489	"APULIA"
E.483.101	DB Cargo IT	2009	8240	
E.483.102	DB Cargo IT	2009	8241	
E.483.103	DB Cargo IT	2009	8242	
E.483.104	DB Cargo IT	2009	8243	
E.483.105	DB Cargo IT	2009	8244	
E.483.106	DB Cargo IT	2009	8245	
E.483.107	DB Cargo IT	2009	8246	
E.483.108	DB Cargo IT	2009	8247	
E.483.301	Akiem		8466	Captrain IT
E.483.302	Akiem		8467	Captrain IT
E.483.303	Akiem		8468	Captrain IT
E.483.304	Akiem		8469	Captrain IT
E.483.305	Akiem		8470	Captrain IT
E.483.306	Akiem		8471	Captrain IT
E.483.307	Akiem		8472	Captrain IT
E.483.308	Akiem		8474	Captrain IT
E.483.309	Akiem		8475	Captrain IT
E.483.310	Akiem		8477	Captrain IT
E.483.311	Akiem		8478	Captrain IT
E.483.312	Akiem		8483	Captrain IT
E.483.313	Akiem		8484	DP
E.483.314	Akiem		8485	MIR
E.483.315	Akiem		8486	MIR
E.483.316	Akiem		8491	MIR
E.483.317	Akiem		8492	MIR
E.483.318	Akiem		8493	MIR
E.483.319	Akiem		8494	MIR
E.483.320	Akiem		8495	MIR

CLASS E.484   TRAXX   Bo-Bo

Bombardier TRAXX MS multi-voltage electric locomotives. SBB Cargo has locos 484 001–018. Full details in the Platform 5 Publishing book "Swiss Railways". 484 103 to 105 were originally built as 484 903 to 905. Capable of operating in Italy and Switzerland.

Details as Class 186.

Number	Owner	Built	Works no.	User/Notes
E.484.103	MRCE	2006	34293	Oceanogate
E.484.104	MRCE	2006	34294	Oceanogate
E.484.105	MRCE	2006	34295	Oceanogate
E.484.901	MRCE	2006	34290	ISC
E.484.902	MRCE	2006	34291	ISC

CLASS E.494   TRAXX DC3   Bo-Bo

Bombardier TRAXX version DC3. Mercitalia Rail has ordered 40 of these locos (E.494.001 to 040) plus an option for 20 more. Locoitalia has ordered four. Captrain Italia has ordered five with a last mile diesel engine through Deutsche Leasing. They will be numbered E.494.501 to 505. GTS Rail has ordered five.

Built: 2019–   **Maximum Tractive Effort:** 300 kN.
Builder: Bombardier, Kassel.   **Weight:** 84 tonnes.
Engine: Deutz 2013 BR-4V of 230 kW, (version with last mile engine).
Continuous Rating: 5600 kW.   **Wheel Diameter:** 1250 mm.
Length over Buffers: 18.90 m.   **Maximum Speed:** 160 km/h.
System: 3000 V DC.

MIR Locomotives

E.494.001	E.494.015	E.494.028
E.494.002	E.494.016	E.494.029
E.494.003	E.494.017	E.494.030
E.494.004	E.494.018	E.494.031
E.494.005	E.494.019	E.494.032
E.494.006	E.494.020	E.494.033
E.494.007	E.494.021	E.494.034
E.494.008	E.494.022	E.494.035
E.494.009	E.494.023	E.494.036
E.494.010	E.494.024	E.494.037
E.494.011	E.494.025	E.494.038
E.494.012	E.494.026	E.494.039
E.494.013	E.494.027	E.494.040
E.494.014		

Captrain Locomotives

E.494.501	E.494.503	E.494.505
E.494.502	E.494.504	

CLASS E.632 B-B-B

A passenger version of the E.633 design, this class known as *"Tigre"* (tiger), was mainly used on push-pull suburban workings in the north of Italy. These were the first B-B-Bs with a non-articulated body, thanks to monomotor bogies and the use of chopper electronics. Class E.633 locos allocated to *Regionale* started in 2005 to have gearing changes plus other minor modifications during overhaul to allow 160 km/h operation. They were therefore renumbered as Class E.632. Locos in the E.633.005–079 batch were to be numbered from E.632.067 and those in the E.633.080–111 batch, which have slightly different electrical equipment, from E.632.201. In mid-2006 the conversions stopped. There were only nine locos left in service in 2018, all used for train rescue and stock movements.

Built: 1982–87.
Builder–Mechanical Parts: Savigliano/TIBB.
Builder–Electrical Parts: Ansaldo/Marelli/TIBB.　**Wheel Diameter:** 1040 mm.
Traction Motors: 3 x T850 FS.　**Weight:** 103 tonnes.
Continuous Rating: 4320 kW.　**Length over Buffers:** 17.80 m.
Maximum Tractive Effort: 227 kN.　**Maximum Speed:** 160 km/h.
EVN: 91 83 2632 016-c and so on.

Rheostatic brakes. Equipped for push-pull operation.

E632.201 is ex E.633.105.

E.632.016	*R*	TC	E.632.030	*H*	MS	E.632.047	*R*	TC
E.632.022	*R*	VR	E.632.037	*R*	BC	E.632.048	*R*	BC
E.632.029	*R*	BZ	E.632.038	*R*	BC	E.632.201	*R*	TC

CLASS E.633 B-B-B

Class E.633 was the first of a new generation of electric locomotives for the 1980s, E.652 being the later, most powerful version. Whilst E.632 was the passenger version, E.633 was used on a variety of freight and passenger workings, mainly in the north of Italy. Class E.633.2 locos can work in multiple and have mainly operated freight on the Torino–Modane (France) route. Class E.633.0 have diamond pantographs whereas E.633.2 have single-arm models.

Built: 1981–88.
Builder–Mechanical Parts: Savigliano/TIBB/SOFER.
Builder–Electrical Parts: TIBB/Ansaldo/Marelli.　**Wheel Diameter:** 1040 mm.
Traction Motors: 3 x T 850 FS.　**Weight:** 104 tonnes.
Continuous Rating: 4320 kW.　**Length over Buffers:** 17.80 m.
Maximum Tractive Effort: 282 kN.　**Maximum Speed:** 130 km/h.

Rheostatic brakes. E.633.201–40 multiple working fitted; within class and with Class E.652. Some locos can be fitted with an uncoupling mechanism for banking through Mont Cenis tunnel (Modane–Bardonecchia).

*　In original livery.

Class E.633.0. EVN: 91 83 2633 083-c and so on.

E.633.083	TR	MF	E.633.108	TR	MF	E.633.111	C	MS
E.633.092	TR	MF	E.633.110	TR	MF			

Class E.633.2. EVN: 91 83 2633 201-c and so on.

E.633.201	C	MS	E.633.212	C	MS	E.633.233	C	MS
E.633.202	C	MS	E.633.214	C	MS	E.633.234	C	MS
E.633.203	C	MS	E.633.215	C	MS	E.633.237	C	MS
E.633.204	C	*	MS	E.633.224	C	MS	E.633.238	C	MS
E.633.205	C	MS	E.633.227	C	MS	E.633.240	C	MS
E.633.211	C	MS	E.633.228	C	MS			

CLASS E.652   B-B-B

The last and most powerful standard B-B-B type in the Trenitalia fleet, based on Class E.633. Originally also used on passenger workings, the class are now all allocated to freight duties and are now used on the Brennero, Tarvisio and Modane routes. E.652.039 was scrapped after a fire and E.652.100 after a crash. In 2014, gear ratios on E.652.048 were modified to reduce overheating. This reduces maximum speed from 160 to 120 km/h. This has now been applied to a few further members of the class. In 2018 the class started working in Sicily but none are allocated there.

Built: 1990–95.
Builder–Mechanical Parts: ABB/ITIN/SOFER/Casertane.
Builder–Electrical Parts: ABB/Ansaldo/Marelli.   **Wheel Diameter:** 1040 mm.
Traction Motors: 3 x T 910 FS.   **Weight:** 105 tonnes.
Continuous Rating: 4950 kW.   **Length over Buffers:** 17.80 m.
Maximum Tractive Effort: 273 kN.   **Maximum Speed:** 160 km/h. § 120 km/h.
EVN: 91 83 2652 001-c and so on.

Rheostatic brakes and multiple working within class and with Class E.633.2.

*   Repainted in original livery.

E.652.001	C		MA	E.652.033	C	§	CV	E.652.064	C		MS
E.652.002	C		MA	E.652.034	C		CV	E.652.065	C	M	MS
E.652.003	C	*	MA	E.652.035	C		MA	E.652.066	C		CV
E.652.004	C		MA	E.652.036	C	§	CV	E.652.067	C		MS
E.652.005	C	M	MA	E.652.037	C	§	CV	E.652.068	C		CV
E.652.006	C		MA	E.652.038	C		MS	E.652.069	C	M	CV
E.652.007	C	§	CV	E.652.040	C	§	CV	E.652.070	C	§	CV
E.652.009	C		MA	E.652.041	C	§	CV	E.652.071	C	§	VR
E.652.010	C		MS	E.652.042	C		MS	E.652.072	C		CV
E.652.011	C		CV	E.652.043	C		MS	E.652.073	C		MS
E.652.012	C		MS	E.652.044	C		MS	E.652.074	C	§	CV
E.652.013	C	§	CV	E.652.045	C		MS	E.652.075	C		VR
E.652.014	C		MS	E.652.046	C	§	CV	E.652.076	C	§	CV
E.652.015	C		MS	E.652.047	C		MS	E.652.077	C		MS
E.652.016	C	§	CV	E.652.048	C	§	CV	E.652.078	C		MS
E.652.017	C		CV	E.652.049	C		MS	E.652.079	C		MS
E.652.018	C		CV	E.652.050	C	§	CV	E.652.080	C		MS
E.652.019	C		CV	E.652.051	C		MS	E.652.081	C		MS
E.652.020	C	§	CV	E.652.052	C		MS	E.652.082	C		MS
E.652.021	C	§	CV	E.652.053	C	§	CV	E.652.083	C		MS
E.652.022	C		CV	E.652.054	C		MS	E.652.084	C		MS
E.652.023	C	M	MS	E.652.055	C	§	CV	E.652.085	C		MS
E.652.024	C		CV	E.652.056	C	§	CV	E.652.086	C		MS
E.652.026	C		CV	E.652.057	C		CV	E.652.087	C	M	MS
E.652.027	C	§	CV	E.652.058	C		MS	E.652.088	C		MS
E.652.028	C	§	CV	E.652.059	C		CV	E.652.089	C	§	CV
E.652.029	C	§	CV	E.652.060	C		CV	E.652.090	C		MS
E.652.030	C	§	CV	E.652.061	C		MS	E.652.091	C		MS
E.652.031	C		MA	E.652.062	C		MS	E.652.092	C		MS
E.652.032	C		CV	E.652.063	C	§	CV	E.652.093	C		MS

No.				No.				No.			
E.652.094	C		MS	E.652.123	C		CV	E.652.150	C	M	CV
E.652.095	C		CV	E.652.124	C		CV	E.652.151	C	M	CV
E.652.096	C		MS	E.652.125	C		CV	E.652.152	C		CV
E.652.097	C		CV	E.652.126	C	§	CV	E.652.153	C		CV
E.652.098	C		CV	E.652.127	C		CV	E.652.154	C		MS
E.652.099	C		CV	E.652.128	C	M	CV	E.652.155	C		MS
E.652.101	C		MS	E.652.129	C		CV	E.652.156	C		CV
E.652.102	C	§	CV	E.652.130	C	§	CV	E.652.157	C		CV
E.652.103	C		CV	E.652.131	C	M	MS	E.652.158	C		MS
E.652.104	C	§	CV	E.652.132	C		CV	E.652.159	C	M	MS
E.652.105	C		MS	E.652.133	C	§	CV	E.652.160	C	M	CV
E.652.106	C		CV	E.652.134	C		CV	E.652.161	C		MS
E.652.107	C		MS	E.652.135	C	M	CV	E.652.162	C		MS
E.652.108	C	M	MS	E.652.136	C		MS	E.652.163	C		MS
E.652.109	C	M	MS	E.652.137	C		CV	E.652.164	C		MS
E.652.110	C		CV	E.652.138	C		CV	E.652.165	C		MS
E.652.111	C		CV	E.652.139	C		CV	E.652.166	C	M	CV
E.652.112	C		MS (S)	E.652.140	C		MS	E.652.167	C	M§	CV
E.652.113	C		MS	E.652.141	C		MS	E.652.168	C	§	CV
E.652.114	C		MS	E.652.142	C	§	CV	E.652.169	C	M	CV
E.652.115	C		MS	E.652.143	C		MS	E.652.170	C		CV
E.652.116	C		MS	E.652.144	C	§	CV	E.652.171	C		CV
E.652.117	C		CV	E.652.145	C	M	CV	E.652.172	C		CV
E.652.118	C		MS	E.652.146	C	§	CV	E.652.173	C	M	CV
E.652.119	C		MS	E.652.147	C	§	CV	E.652.174	C	M	CV
E.652.120	C		MS	E.652.148	C	§	CV	E.652.175	C	§	CV
E.652.121	C		MS	E.652.149	C		MS	E.652.176	C		MS
E.652.122	C		MS								

▲ E.652.038 passes through Brescia with an eastbound freight on 5 April 2018.   **David Haydock**

CLASSES E.655 & E.656 — Bo-Bo-Bo

Class E.656, nicknamed "*Caimano*", or alligators, were the standard FS passenger locomotives of the 1980s. The class was built in successive batches, with some minor electrical differences. The class has now lost most of its long-distance passenger work and has been transferred to freight work. Freight locos were re-geared and renumbered as E.655, retaining the original serial numbers. Overhauls finished in 2013 and many locos are now stored. The final batch of locos finished work on Regionale passenger services in 2013. The final stronghold for the class on passenger work is Sicily. These locos will gradually be replaced by Class E.464 when freed by new EMUs. Others in passenger service are mainly used on empty stock movements.

Built: 1975–89.
Builder–Mechanical Parts: SOFER/Casaralta/Casertana/TIBB/Reggiane.
Builder–Electrical Parts: Italtrafo/ASGEN/TIBB/Marelli/Ansaldo/Retam/Lucana.
Traction Motors: 6 x 82–400 FS.   **Wheel Diameter:** 1250 mm.
Maximum Tractive Effort: 239 kN (300 kN Class E.655).
Continuous Rating: 4200 kW.   **Weight:** 120 tonnes.
Length over Buffers: 18.29 m.   **Maximum Speed:** 150 km/h. (120 km/h Class E.655).
EVN: 91 83 265x 009-c and so on.

p   Push-pull and multiple working fitted.
s   Equipped to operate into Slovenia, but no longer used there.

E.656.009	P		PA	E.655.413	R		TC	E.655.529	C		MA
E.656.018	P		PA	E.655.416	R		BZ	E.655.530	R		BE
E.656.024	P		PA	E.655.417	R		BC	E.655.531	C		MA
E.656.028	P		PA	E.656.424	P		PA	E.655.532	R		GB
E.656.030	P		MC	E.655.425	R		PE	E.655.533	R		RS
E.656.033	P		PA	E.655.426	R		GB	E.655.537	C		CV
E.656.039	P		MC	E.656.431	P		PA	E.655.541	C		MA
E.656.040	P		PA	E.656.435	P		PA	E.655.549	C		MA
E.656.046	P		RL	E.656.439	P		PA	E.656.551	I	p	GB
E.655.047	C	s	CV	E.656.443	P		PA	E.656.552	I	p	GB
E.656.052	P		PA	E.656.453	R		RS	E.656.557	I	p	GB
E.656.058	P		MC	E.656.462	P		PA	E.656.560	R	p	NS
E.656.059	C		MA	E.656.467	C		MS	E.656.564	C	p	PA
E.656.060	C		MA	E.656.468	R	p	RC	E.656.565	I	p	GB
E.656.063	P		RL	E.656.481	P		PA	E.656.568	R	p	AN
E.656.074	P		PA	E.656.489	P		PA	E.656.570	C	p	MS
E.655.085	R		AN	E.656.492	P		PA	E.656.573	R	p	GB
E.656.091	P		PA	E.656.497	P		PA	E.656.576	I	p	GB
E.656.093	P		PA	E.655.498	R		FG	E.656.577	C	p	MS
E.656.096	P		PA	E.655.502	R		AN	E.656.578	R	p	GB
E.656.099	P		PA	E.655.503	C		MA	E.656.579	R	p	GB
E.655.192	C		MS	E.655.509	C		MA	E.656.581	R	p	PE
E.655.248	R		VR	E.655.510	R		FI	E.656.586	C	p	MS
E.655.264	C		MA	E.655.513	R		FI	E.656.587	C	p	MS
E.655.267	C	s	CV	E.656.515	P		MC	E.656.588	R	p	FI
E.655.271	R		SU	E.655.521	C		MA	E.656.592	C	p	MS
E.656.289	P		RL	E.655.522	C		TO(S)	E.656.596	C	p	MS
E.656.294	P		PA	E.655.523	C		MA	E.656.601	R	p	TS
E.656.307	C		MA	E.655.524	R		CT	E.656.603	C	p	MS
E.655.410	R		RC	E.655.526	R		RC	E.656.607	C	p	MS
E.655.411	R		LV								

Robin Ralston

▲ E.656.431 is seen with an InterCity service at Cefalu in Sicily on 6 October 2017.

1.3. DIESEL AND BI-MODE MULTIPLE UNITS

Trenitalia has a large fleet of diesel railcars which operate the majority of trains on secondary lines as there are relatively few diesel-hauled passenger trains. The fleet mainly consists of single railcars and individual trailers which can be coupled in variable formations and were derived from the same Fiat design. Class numbers originally indicated the number of seats in the second and third digits, e.g. ALn 668 carry 68 passengers and ALn 663 carry 63 passengers. Most vehicles have been air conditioned in recent years. Trenitalia has recently started to prefix all DMUs ATR instead of ALn.

In mid 2018 Trenitalia signed a framework contract with Hitachi for 135 new DMUs (3-car or 4-car) for regional services. Their front ends will look similar to "Rock" EMUs. The first 30 will go to Toscana, Sicilia and Sardegna, and the order should allow most ALn 663 and 668 units to be withdrawn. All diesel railcar trailers (Class Ln 664.1400) have been withdrawn since the 2013 edition.

In this edition we have added to the section, most DMUs owned by other operators many of which are used on RFI main lines and in some cases operated by Trenitalia itself.

CLASSES ATR.100, 110, 115 & 116   2-SECTION ARTICULATED UNITS

These units are the third generation of Stadler GTW 2/6 DMUs which are formed of two driving trailers each on a single outer bogie, with a short power unit in the middle.

Initially the SAD units were numbered as Class 103 but in 2006 became Class ATR.100. The first order for eight SAD units was followed by four in late 2006. Their interior allows more space for bicycles in summer. 100.007 was severely damaged by a landslip and has been withdrawn. Parts are stored at Merano.

FUC units are used on the Udine–Cividale line. ST units operate on the Venezia–Adria line. Trenord (FNM) units operate on the Brescia–Edolo (Iseo units) and Milano–Lecco (Lecco units) lines.

Built: SAD ATR.100 2004/05 (ATR.100.009–012 2006); FUC/ST ATR.110 2006; FNM ATR.115 2009; ST ATR.116 2012/13.
Builder: Stadler.   **Weight:** 66 tonnes.
Engines: ATR.100/110: 2 x MAN D2876 LE621 of 390 kW each; ATR.115/116 2 x MAN D2876LE124 of 382 kW each.
Transmission: Electric.   **Length over Couplings:** 17.50 + 4.50 + 17.50 m.
Wheel Arrangement: 2-Bo-2.   **Driving Wheel Diameter:** 860 mm.
Maximum Speed: 140 km/h.   **Accommodation:** ATR.100: –/56 (3) + –/21 (16) 1TD.
ATR.110/115/116: –/56 (2) + –/46 (6) 1TD.
EVNs: ATR.100.001 is 95 83 8100 001-c + 1100 003-c + 8100 002-c and so on.
ATR.110.201 is 95 83 8110 201-c + 1110 203-c + 8110 202-c and so on.
ATR.115.001 is 95 83 8115 001-c + 1115 003-c + 8115 002-c.
ATR.116.001 is 95 83 8116 001-c + 1116 003-c + 8116 002-c.

SAD units.

ATR.100.001	ATR.100.005	ATR.100.010
ATR.100.002	ATR.100.006	ATR.100.011
ATR.100.003	ATR.100.008	ATR.100.012
ATR.100.004	ATR.100.009	

FUC units.

ATR.110.001	ATR.110.002

ST units.

ATR.110.201	ATR.110.202

ATR.116.001

Trenord units.

ATR.115.001	LC	ATR.115.004	IS	ATR.115.007	IS
ATR.115.002	LC	ATR.115.005	LC	ATR.115.008	LC
ATR.115.003	IS	ATR.115.006	LC		

CLASSES ATR.120, ATR.125 & ATR.126   4-SECTION ARTICULATED UNITS

Class ATR.120 are similar to Class ATR.110 and consist of two units back-to-back, each formed of a driving trailer, power unit and non-driving trailer. Half-sets of Class ATR.120/125/126 can, in theory operate in multiple with Class ATR.110/115/116. ATR.116 and ATR.126 have slight differences in the engines – this led to the Italian authorities adding a new classification. Class ATR.120 are numbered as half sets while ATR.125 and ATR.126 are numbered as full sets (see EVNs).

ST units mainly operate the Venezia–Adria line. Trenord units operate the Milano–Monza–Molteno–Lecco and Lecco–Como services and are allocated to Lecco depot. Later units work the Brescia–Edolo and Parma–Pavia lines and are based at Cremona or Iseo.

In late 2018 FNM ordered a further 30 new DMUs from Stadler plus 20 options. The units will be to an updated design and no more details are known yet.

Built: ST ATR.120 2006; Trenord ATR.125 2009-2017; ST ATR.126 2012/13.
Builder: Stadler/AnsaldoBreda.   **Weight:** 134.3 tonnes.
Engines: ATR.120: 4 x MAN DE2876LE621 of 390 kW each.
            ATR.125/126: 4 x MAN D2876LE124 of 382 kW each.
Wheel Arrangement: 2-Bo-2 + 2-Bo-2.   **Maximum Speed:** 140 km/h.
Transmission: Electric.
Accommodation: –/56 (3) + –/64 (3) + –/55 (3) 1TD + –/56 (3).
Length over Couplings: 17.65 + 4.50 + 16.22 + 16.22 + 4.50 + 17.65 m.
EVNs: ATR.120.401 is 95 83 8120 401-c + 1120 402 + 0120 403-c and so on.
        ATR.125.001 is 85 83 8125 001-c + 1125 003-c + 0125 002-c + 0125 005-c + 1125 006-c + 8125 004-c and so on.
        ATR.126.001 is 95 83 8126 001-c + 1126 003-c + 0126 002-c + 0126 005-c + 1126 006-c + 8126 004-c and so on.

ST units.

ATR.120.401	ATR.120.403	ATR.120.404
ATR.120.402		
ATR.126.001	ATR.126.002	ATR.126.003

▲ Trenord ATR.125.102 is seen at Edolo having arrived from Brescia on 5 April 2018. **David Haydock**

Trenord units.

ATR.125.001	LC	ATR.125.005	LC	ATR.125.009	LC
ATR.125.002	LC	ATR.125.006	LC	ATR.125.010	LC
ATR.125.003	LC	ATR.125.007	LC	ATR.125.011	LC
ATR.125.004	LC	ATR.125.008	LC		

ATR.125.101	CR	ATR.125.105	IS	ATR.125.108	CR
ATR.125.102	IS	ATR.125.106	CR	ATR.125.109	CR
ATR.125.103	CR	ATR.125.107	CR	ATR.125.110	CR
ATR.125.104	IS				

CLASS ATR.220   "SWING"   3-SECTION ARTICULATED UNITS

Following the purchase of ATR.220 articulated DMUs by local railways FSE, Trenord and TPER, Trenitalia ordered 40 of these units from PESA of Poland. There are also options for a further 20 units, of which 15 have been taken up and four delivered. At the time of going to press, there were ten more to come for Sardegna and one for Molise (AN). All are in the recent Regionale livery. The design is known by PESA as "*Atribo*" but by Trenitalia as "*Swing*".

Note that FSE, FNM and TPER numbers are virtually the same, and some duplicate each other – FSE has ATR.220.001 to 027, Trenord has ATR.220.024/025 and TPER has ATR.220.026 to 037!

Built: 2014/15.
Builder: PESA.
Engines: 2 x MAN R2876T3-390 of 390 kW each.
Transmission: Hydraulic. Voith T 211 re.4 + KB190 + HA.
Accommodation: –/152 (7) 1T 1TD.

Weight: 114 tonnes.
Maximum Speed: 130 km/h.

Length: 55.57 m.

EVN: Set 001 = 95 83 4220 101-c + 95 83 0220 301-c + 95 83 4220 201-c and so on.

ATR.220 Tr 001	PI	ATR.220 Tr 021	FG	ATR.220 Tr 041	TV
ATR.220 Tr 002	PI	ATR.220 Tr 022	FG	ATR.220 Tr 042	TV
ATR.220 Tr 003	PI	ATR.220 Tr 023	AN	ATR.220 Tr 043	AN
ATR.220 Tr 004	PI	ATR.220 Tr 024	FG	ATR.220 Tr 044	AN
ATR.220 Tr 005	PI	ATR.220 Tr 025	AN	ATR.220 Tr 045	
ATR.220 Tr 006	AN	ATR.220 Tr 026	CZ	ATR.220 Tr 046	
ATR.220 Tr 007	PI	ATR.220 Tr 027	SU	ATR.220 Tr 047	
ATR.220 Tr 008	PI	ATR.220 Tr 028	SU	ATR.220 Tr 048	
ATR.220 Tr 009	PI	ATR.220 Tr 029	AN	ATR.220 Tr 049	
ATR.220 Tr 010	PI	ATR.220 Tr 030	CZ	ATR.220 Tr 050	
ATR.220 Tr 011	PI	ATR.220 Tr 031	SU	ATR.220 Tr 051	
ATR.220 Tr 012	AN	ATR.220 Tr 032	AN	ATR.220 Tr 052	
ATR.220 Tr 013	PI	ATR.220 Tr 033	TV	ATR.220 Tr 053	
ATR.220 Tr 014	PI	ATR.220 Tr 034	TV	ATR.220 Tr 054	
ATR.220 Tr 015	PI	ATR.220 Tr 035	TV	ATR.220 Tr 055	
ATR.220 Tr 016	PI	ATR.220 Tr 036	SU	ATR.220 Tr 056	
ATR.220 Tr 017	PI	ATR.220 Tr 037	TV	ATR.220 Tr 057	
ATR.220 Tr 018	AN	ATR.220 Tr 038	TV	ATR.220 Tr 058	
ATR.220 Tr 019	AN	ATR.220 Tr 039	CZ	ATR.220 Tr 059	
ATR.220 Tr 020	FG	ATR.220 Tr 040	TV	ATR.220 Tr 060	

▲ ATR.220.043 stands at Bassano del Grappa on 8 April 2018. **David Haydock**

▼ ATR.365.002 is seen shortly after delivery to Cagliari depot on 7 September 2014.

Antonello Foddai

CLASS ATR.365 & ATR.465   3-CAR & 4-CAR TILTING UNITS

These were ordered from CAF of Spain by the Sardegna region in order to speed up the fastest, but still sluggish, trains from Cagliari to Sassari/Porto Torres and Olbia/Golfo Aranci, previously operated by Class ALn 501 *"Minuetto"* DMUs. They are derived from RENFE Class 598 and can tilt at a maximum of 6°. The units are by operated by Trenitalia. The first was delivered in 2013 and went through a series of tests on the mainland before the second train was delivered to Sardegna in July 2014. Most trains have entered service but they are not yet tilting and one or more were still on test at Velim (Czech Republic) in 2018.

Built: 2012/13.
Builder: CAF.   **Wheel Arrangement:** 1A-A1 + 1A-2 (+ 1A-2) + 1A-A1.
Length: 26.295 + 24.280 (+ 24.280) + 26.295 metres.
Engines: 6 x 6-cylinder MTU 6H 1800 of 390 kW each.
Weight: 56 + 48 (+ 48) + 56 tonnes.   **Maximum Speed:** 160 km/h.
Accommodation: –/68 1T + –/66 1TD 2W (+ –/76 1T) + –/68 1T.
Transmission: Hydro-mechanical.   **Wheel Diameter:** 850 mm (new).
EVN: 95 83 3365 001-c + 95 83 0365 201-c + 95 83 0365 301-c and so on.

Livery is white with red and black bands.

Class ATR.365.

ATR.365.001	ATR.365.003	ATR.365.005
ATR.365.002	ATR.365.004	ATR.365.006

Class ATR.465.

ATR.465.001	ATR.465.002

CLASS ALn 501   MINUETTO   3-SECTION ARTICULATED UNITS

A design produced in both diesel and electric (ALe 501) versions from 2004. The units are designed for low density routes. Over half the unit length and all entrances are low floor (600 mm). Units are known as MD 01 (Minuetto Diesel) or 001 upwards. The last four are officially owned by the Sardegna region but operated by Trenitalia.

Trento province also owns ten units in the ALn 501.600 series with set numbers Tn 01 to 10. These are allocated to Trento depot and jointly operated by Trenitalia and Trento Trasporti, mainly on the scenic Trento–Bassano del Grappa route. Trenitalia owns sets Tn 601, 608 and 610. These carry white/maroon or the more recent mainly lime green liveries.

Built: 2004–08.
Builder: Alstom Savigliano & Colleferro.
Engines: 2 x IVECO FVQE 2883X A201 8-cylinder of 560 kW each at 2100 rpm.
Transmission: Hydraulic. Voith T 212 bre.   **Weight:** 100 tonnes.
Wheel Arrangement: B-2-2-B.   **Maximum Speed:** 130 km/h.
Accommodation: 24/26 (4) + –/22 (16) 1TD + –/50 (4).
Length over Buffers: 19.125 + 13.650 + 19.125 m.
EVN: MD 01 = 95 83 4501 001-c + 95 83 0220 001-c + 95 83 4502 001-c and so on.

Trenitalia units.

MD 01	ALn 501.001	Ln 220.001	ALn 502.001	R	R	TC
MD 02	ALn 501.002	Ln 220.002	ALn 502.002	R	R	FI
MD 03	ALn 501.003	Ln 220.003	ALn 502.003	R	R	TC
MD 04	ALn 501.004	Ln 220.004	ALn 502.004	R	R	TC
MD 05	ALn 501.005	Ln 220.005	ALn 502.005	R	R	TV
MD 06	ALn 501.006	Ln 220.006	ALn 502.006	R	R	TC
MD 07	ALn 501.007	Ln 220.007	ALn 502.007	R	R	TV
MD 08	ALn 501.008	Ln 220.008	ALn 502.008	R	R	BE
MD 09	ALn 501.009	Ln 220.009	ALn 502.009	R	R	PA
MD 10	ALn 501.010	Ln 220.010	ALn 502.010	R	R	FI
MD 11	ALn 501.011	Ln 220.011	ALn 502.011	R	R	TC
MD 12	ALn 501.012	Ln 220.012	ALn 502.012	R	R	BE
MD 13	ALn 501.013	Ln 220.013	ALn 502.013	R	R	FI
MD 14	ALn 501.014	Ln 220.014	ALn 502.014	R	R	FI
MD 15	ALn 501.015	Ln 220.015	ALn 502.015	R	R	TC
MD 16	ALn 501.016	Ln 220.016	ALn 502.016	R	R	TC

MD 17	ALn 501.017	Ln 220.017	ALn 502.017	*R*	**R**	FI
MD 18	ALn 501.018	Ln 220.018	ALn 502.018	*R*	**R**	FI
MD 19	ALn 501.019	Ln 220.019	ALn 502.019	*R*	**R**	CG
MD 20	ALn 501.020	Ln 220.020	ALn 502.020	*R*	**R**	BE
MD 21	ALn 501.021	Ln 220.021	ALn 502.021	*R*	**R**	TC
MD 22	ALn 501.022	Ln 220.022	ALn 502.022	*R*	**R**	BE
MD 23	ALn 501.023	Ln 220.023	ALn 502.023	*R*	**R**	TV
MD 24	ALn 501.024	Ln 220.024	ALn 502.024	*R*	**R**	PA
MD 25	ALn 501.025	Ln 220.025	ALn 502.025	*R*	**R**	TR
MD 26	ALn 501.026	Ln 220.026	ALn 502.026	*R*	**R**	TC
MD 27	ALn 501.027	Ln 220.027	ALn 502.027	*R*	**R**	TC
MD 28	ALn 501.028	Ln 220.028	ALn 502.028	*R*	**R**	TR
MD 29	ALn 501.029	Ln 220.029	ALn 502.029	*R*	**R**	TR
MD 30	ALn 501.030	Ln 220.030	ALn 502.030	*R*	**R**	FI
MD 31	ALn 501.031	Ln 220.031	ALn 502.031	*R*	**R**	PA
MD 32	ALn 501.032	Ln 220.032	ALn 502.032	*R*	**R**	TR
MD 33	ALn 501.033	Ln 220.033	ALn 502.033	*R*	**R**	TC
MD 34	ALn 501.034	Ln 220.034	ALn 502.034	*R*	**R**	BE
MD 35	ALn 501.035	Ln 220.035	ALn 502.035	*R*	**R**	TV
MD 36	ALn 501.036	Ln 220.036	ALn 502.036	*R*	**R**	PA
MD 37	ALn 501.037	Ln 220.037	ALn 502.037	*R*	**R**	TC
MD 38	ALn 501.038	Ln 220.038	ALn 502.038	*R*	**R**	PA
MD 39	ALn 501.039	Ln 220.039	ALn 502.039	*R*	**R**	TV
MD 40	ALn 501.040	Ln 220.040	ALn 502.040	*R*	**R**	PA
MD 41	ALn 501.041	Ln 220.041	ALn 502.041	*R*	**R**	TV
MD 42	ALn 501.042	Ln 220.042	ALn 502.042	*R*	**R**	FI
MD 43	ALn 501.043	Ln 220.043	ALn 502.043	*R*	**R**	BE
MD 44	ALn 501.044	Ln 220.044	ALn 502.044	*R*	**R**	TV
MD 45	ALn 501.045	Ln 220.045	ALn 502.045	*R*	**R**	PA
MD 46	ALn 501.046	Ln 220.046	ALn 502.046	*R*	**R**	BE
MD 47	ALn 501.047	Ln 220.047	ALn 502.047	*R*	**R**	TC
MD 48	ALn 501.048	Ln 220.048	ALn 502.048	*R*	**R**	BE
MD 49	ALn 501.049	Ln 220.049	ALn 502.049	*R*	**R**	CG
MD 50	ALn 501.050	Ln 220.050	ALn 502.050	*R*	**R**	FI
MD 51	ALn 501.051	Ln 220.051	ALn 502.051	*R*	**R**	CG
MD 52	ALn 501.052	Ln 220.052	ALn 502.052	*R*	**R**	FI
MD 53	ALn 501.053	Ln 220.053	ALn 502.053	*R*	**R**	TC
MD 54	ALn 501.054	Ln 220.054	ALn 502.054	*R*	**R**	TC
MD 55	ALn 501.055	Ln 220.055	ALn 502.055	*R*	**R**	PA
MD 56	ALn 501.056	Ln 220.056	ALn 502.056	*R*	**R**	TC
MD 57	ALn 501.057	Ln 220.057	ALn 502.057	*R*	**R**	TC
MD 58	ALn 501.058	Ln 220.058	ALn 502.058	*R*	**R**	TC
MD 59	ALn 501.059	Ln 220.059	ALn 502.059	*R*	**R**	CG
MD 60	ALn 501.060	Ln 220.060	ALn 502.060	*R*	**R**	FI
MD 61	ALn 501.061	Ln 220.061	ALn 502.061	*R*	**R**	TC
MD 62	ALn 501.062	Ln 220.062	ALn 502.062	*R*	**R**	TC
MD 63	ALn 501.063	Ln 220.063	ALn 502.063	*R*	**R**	TC
MD 64	ALn 501.064	Ln 220.064	ALn 502.064	*R*	**R**	FI
MD 65	ALn 501.065	Ln 220.065	ALn 502.065	*R*	**R**	TC
MD 66	ALn 501.066	Ln 220.066	ALn 502.066	*R*	**R**	FI
MD 67	ALn 501.067	Ln 220.067	ALn 502.067	*R*	**R**	BE
MD 68	ALn 501.068	Ln 220.068	ALn 502.068	*R*	**R**	FI
MD 69	ALn 501.069	Ln 220.069	ALn 502.069	*R*	**R**	FI
MD 70	ALn 501.070	Ln 220.070	ALn 502.070	*R*	**R**	CG
MD 71	ALn 501.071	Ln 220.071	ALn 502.071	*R*	**R**	FI
MD 72	ALn 501.072	Ln 220.072	ALn 502.072	*R*	**R**	FI
MD 73	ALn 501.073	Ln 220.073	ALn 502.073	*R*	**R**	TV
MD 74	ALn 501.074	Ln 220.074	ALn 502.074	*R*	**R**	TV
MD 75	ALn 501.075	Ln 220.075	ALn 502.075	*R*	**R**	TR
MD 76	ALn 501.076	Ln 220.076	ALn 502.076	*R*	**R**	CG
MD 77	ALn 501.077	Ln 220.077	ALn 502.077	*R*	**R**	TV
MD 78	ALn 501.078	Ln 220.078	ALn 502.078	*R*	**R**	BE
MD 79	ALn 501.079	Ln 220.079	ALn 502.079	*R*	**R**	TC
MD 80	ALn 501.080	Ln 220.080	ALn 502.080	*R*	**R**	CG

MD 81	ALn 501.081	Ln 220.081	ALn 502.081	*R*	**R**	TC
MD 82	ALn 501.082	Ln 220.082	ALn 502.082	*R*	**R**	TC
MD 83	ALn 501.083	Ln 220.083	ALn 502.083	*R*	**R**	FI
MD 84	ALn 501.084	Ln 220.084	ALn 502.084	*R*	**R**	TV
MD 85	ALn 501.085	Ln 220.085	ALn 502.085	*R*	**R**	TV
MD 86	ALn 501.086	Ln 220.086	ALn 502.086	*R*	**R**	TV
MD 87	ALn 501.087	Ln 220.087	ALn 502.087	*R*	**R**	TV
MD 88	ALn 501.088	Ln 220.088	ALn 502.088	*R*	**R**	TC
MD 89	ALn 501.089	Ln 220.089	ALn 502.089	*R*	**R**	TV
MD 90	ALn 501.090	Ln 220.090	ALn 502.090	*R*	**R**	FI
MD 91	ALn 501.091	Ln 220.091	ALn 502.091	*R*	**R**	TC
MD 92	ALn 501.092	Ln 220.092	ALn 502.092	*R*	**R**	FI
MD 93	ALn 501.093	Ln 220.093	ALn 502.093	*R*	**R**	TC
MD 94	ALn 501.094	Ln 220.094	ALn 502.094	*R*	**R**	TV
MD 95	ALn 501.095	Ln 220.095	ALn 502.095	*R*	**R**	BE
MD 96	ALn 501.096	Ln 220.096	ALn 502.096	*R*	**R**	FI
MD 97	ALn 501.097	Ln 220.097	ALn 502.097	*R*	**R**	PA
MD 98	ALn 501.098	Ln 220.098	ALn 502.098	*R*	**R**	FI
MD 99	ALn 501.099	Ln 220.099	ALn 502.099	*R*	**R**	FI
MD 100	ALn 501.100	Ln 220.100	ALn 502.100	*R*	**R**	BE
MD 101	ALn 501.101	Ln 220.101	ALn 502.101	*R*	**R**	CG
MD 102	ALn 501.102	Ln 220.102	ALn 502.102	*R*	**R**	CG
MD 103	ALn 501.103	Ln 220.103	ALn 502.103	*R*	**R**	CG
MD 104	ALn 501.104	Ln 220.104	ALn 502.104	*R*	**R**	CG

Trentino Trasporti units.

Tn 601	Aln 501.601	Ln 220.601	Aln 502.601			TT
Tn 02	Aln 501.602	Ln 220.602	Aln 502.602			TT
Tn 03	Aln 501.603	Ln 220.603	Aln 502.603			TT
Tn 04	Aln 501.604	Ln 220.604	Aln 502.604			TT
Tn 05	Aln 501.605	Ln 220.605	Aln 502.605			TT
Tn 06	Aln 501.606	Ln 220.606	Aln 502.606			TT
Tn 07	Aln 501.607	Ln 220.607	Aln 502.607			TT
Tn 608	Aln 501.608	Ln 220.608	Aln 502.608			TT
Tn 09	Aln 501.609	Ln 220.609	Aln 502.609			TT
Tn 610	Aln 501.610	Ln 220.610	Aln 502.610			TT

▲ Trenitalia "Minuetto Diesel" set MD 28 plus TT unit Tn 601 are seen at Branzoli with a Bolzano–Bassano del Grappa service on 8 April 2018. **David Haydock**

CLASS ALn 663   SINGLE CARS

Class ALn 663 was developed from the last Class ALn 668.3100 and 668.3300, with which they can operate in multiple, and have very similar characteristics except that they have more seats in first class and lower capacity overall. They have flat rather than wrap-round cab windows as the latter were expensive and more vulnerable to breakage. Also operated by EAV/FA, FUC, ST and TPER.

Built: 1983–86.
Builder: Savigliano.
Engine: 2 x Fiat 8217.32 of 170 kW each.
Transmission: Mechanical.
Wheel Arrangement: 1A-A1.
Accommodation: 12/51 1T.

Wheel Diameter: 920 mm.
Weight: 40 tonnes.
Length over Buffers: 23.54 m.
Maximum Speed: 130 km/h (§ 120 km/h).

Class ALn 663.1000. EVN: 95 83 4663 001-c to 016-c. Note that 663 019 to 021 are with TPER.

ALn 663.1001	R	§	NO	ALn 663.1007	R	§	NO	ALn 663.1012	R	§	NO
ALn 663.1002	R	§	SI	ALn 663.1008	R	§	BE	ALn 663.1013	R	§	SI
ALn 663.1003	R	§	NO	ALn 663.1009	R	§	BE	ALn 663.1014	R	§	NO
ALn 663.1004	R	§	NO	ALn 663.1010	R	§	NO	ALn 663.1015	R	§	NO
ALn 663.1005	R	§	NO	ALn 663.1011	R	§	NO	ALn 663.1016	R	§	NO (S)
ALn 663.1006	R	§	RC								

Class ALn 663.1100. EVN: 95 83 4663 201-c to 304-c.

ALn 663.1101	R	BE	ALn 663.1136	R	SI	ALn 663.1170	R	RC
ALn 663.1102	R	SI	ALn 663.1137	R	SI	ALn 663.1172	R	RC
ALn 663.1103	R	RC	ALn 663.1138	R	SI	ALn 663.1173	R	CG
ALn 663.1104	R	BE	ALn 663.1139	R	CG	ALn 663.1174	R	SI
ALn 663.1105	R	SI	ALn 663.1140	R	CG	ALn 663.1175	R	BE
ALn 663.1106	R	SI	ALn 663.1141	R	PI	ALn 663.1176	R	BE
ALn 663.1107	R	SI	ALn 663.1142	R	BE	ALn 663.1177	R	RC
ALn 663.1108	R	CG	ALn 663.1143	R	BE	ALn 663.1178	R	RC
ALn 663.1109	R	BE	ALn 663.1144	R	SI	ALn 663.1179	R	CG
ALn 663.1110	R	SI	ALn 663.1145	R	CG	ALn 663.1180	R	RC
ALn 663.1111	R	SI	ALn 663.1146	R	CG	ALn 663.1181	R	BE
ALn 663.1113	R	RC	ALn 663.1147	R	SI	ALn 663.1182	R	RC
ALn 663.1114	R	RC	ALn 663.1148	R	CG	ALn 663.1183	R	BE
ALn 663.1115	R	SI	ALn 663.1149	R	CG	ALn 663.1184	R	BE
ALn 663.1116	R	BE	ALn 663.1150	R	BE	ALn 663.1185	R	BE
ALn 663.1117	R	BE	ALn 663.1151	R	RC	ALn 663.1186	R	BE
ALn 663.1118	R	BE	ALn 663.1152	R	BE	ALn 663.1187	R	BE
ALn 663.1119	R	BE	ALn 663.1153	R	BE	ALn 663.1188	R	BE
ALn 663.1120	R	BE	ALn 663.1154	R	SI	ALn 663.1190	R	RC
ALn 663.1121	R	BE	ALn 663.1155	R	SI	ALn 663.1191	R	RC
ALn 663.1122	R	BE	ALn 663.1156	R	CG	ALn 663.1192	R	RC
ALn 663.1123	R	SI	ALn 663.1157	R	RC	ALn 663.1193	R	RC
ALn 663.1124	R	SI	ALn 663.1158	R	SI	ALn 663.1194	R	RC
ALn 663.1125	R	CG	ALn 663.1160	R	RC	ALn 663.1195	R	RC
ALn 663.1126	R	BE	ALn 663.1161	R	BE	ALn 663.1196	R	BE
ALn 663.1127	R	BE	ALn 663.1162	R	RC	ALn 663.1197	R	BE
ALn 663.1128	R	CG	ALn 663.1163	R	BE	ALn 663.1198	R	BE
ALn 663.1129	R	BE	ALn 663.1164	R	BE	ALn 663.1199	R	RC
ALn 663.1130	R	BE	ALn 663.1165	R	BE	ALn 663.1200	R	RC
ALn 663.1131	R	BE	ALn 663.1166	R	RC	ALn 663.1201	R	RC
ALn 663.1132	R	BE	ALn 663.1167	R	BE	ALn 663.1202	R	RC
ALn 663.1133	R	BE	ALn 663.1168	R	RC	ALn 663.1203	R	BE
ALn 663.1135	R	BE	ALn 663.1169	R	BE	ALn 663.1204	R	BE

▲ ALn 663.1135 and two others of the class are seen at Isernia on 27 May 2012. **Antonin Bertagnin**

▼ ALn 668.3110 and two more of the class, on hire to FSE, wait to depart from Martina Franca with a train to Lecce on 24 May 2018. **David Haydock**

CLASS ALn 668   1A–A1

This highly successful series of Fiat railcars was developed in numerous versions over 30 years and derivatives have been exported to many other countries including the former Yugoslavia as well as being bought by almost all the non-electrified independent lines in Italy. The units are used all over Italy's secondary diesel lines in multiple with each other, and with ALn 663 for later groups. Railcars were built in a number of batches, starting with ALn 668.1400 in 1956 and continuing until 1983 with the most recent version, ALn 668.3300. Class ALn 663, a variant on the design, continued in production until 1986. All Type Ln trailer cars have now been withdrawn. Also operated by EAV/FA, GTT, ST, TPER and FNM/Trenord.

95 83 4668 013 to 018 are TPER 668.013 to 018.

95 83 4668 031 to 045 are FSE Ad 31 to Ad 45

Class ALn 668.1000. EVN: 95 83 4668 051-c to 170-c.

This group followed on from 668.1900. Details are identical as far as known, except:

Builder: Savigliano, 1001–1037, 1058–1120; OMECA 1038–1057.

ALn 668.1001	R		FG	ALn 668.1047	TR		CR	ALn 668.1086	R		FG
ALn 668.1004	R		PA	ALn 668.1048	R		CZ	ALn 668.1087	R		RC
ALn 668.1005	R		TV	ALn 668.1049	R		RC	ALn 668.1088	TR	N	CR
ALn 668.1006	R		PA	ALn 668.1050	R		CZ	ALn 668.1089	R		FG
ALn 668.1007	R		FG	ALn 668.1051	R		FG	ALn 668.1090	R		CZ
ALn 668.1010	R		CZ	ALn 668.1052	R		FG	ALn 668.1091	R		FG
ALn 668.1011	TR		CR	ALn 668.1053	TR		CR	ALn 668.1092	R		FG
ALn 668.1012	R		FG	ALn 668.1054	R		RC	ALn 668.1093	R		PA
ALn 668.1014	R		CZ	ALn 668.1055	R		RC	ALn 668.1094	R		FG
ALn 668.1015	R		RC	ALn 668.1057	R		CZ	ALn 668.1095	R		FG
ALn 668.1019	TR	N	CR	ALn 668.1058	TR	N	CR	ALn 668.1096	TR		CR
ALn 668.1021	TR	N	CR	ALn 668.1060	R		SI	ALn 668.1097	TR	N	CR
ALn 668.1023	R		RC	ALn 668.1061	R		PA	ALn 668.1099	TR		CR
ALn 668.1025	R		RC	ALn 668.1063	TR	N	CR	ALn 668.1100	R		RC
ALn 668.1027	R		RC	ALn 668.1064	TR	N	CR	ALn 668.1101	R		RC
ALn 668.1028	TR		CR	ALn 668.1066	TR		CR	ALn 668.1102	R		RC
ALn 668.1029	TR	N	CR	ALn 668.1067	R		RC	ALn 668.1103	R		RC
ALn 668.1030	TR		CR	ALn 668.1069	R		FG	ALn 668.1104	TR		CR
ALn 668.1031	R		PA	ALn 668.1070	R		FG	ALn 668.1106	TR	N	CR
ALn 668.1033	R		CZ	ALn 668.1071	R		FG	ALn 668.1107	TR	N	CR
ALn 668.1034	R		PA	ALn 668.1072	R		CZ	ALn 668.1108	R		RC
ALn 668.1035	R		CZ	ALn 668.1073	R		RC	ALn 668.1110	TR	N	CR
ALn 668.1036	TR	N	CR	ALn 668.1074	TR	N	CR	ALn 668.1111	TR		CR
ALn 668.1037	TR		CR	ALn 668.1075	R		CZ	ALn 668.1113	R		RC
ALn 668.1038	R		CZ	ALn 668.1076	TR	N	CR	ALn 668.1114	TR	N	CR
ALn 668.1040	R		FG	ALn 668.1077	R		RC	ALn 668.1115	TR		CR
ALn 668.1041	R		CZ	ALn 668.1079	TR	N	CR	ALn 668.1116	TR	N	CR
ALn 668.1042	R		CZ	ALn 668.1081	R		CZ	ALn 668.1118	TR		CR
ALn 668.1045	R		CZ	ALn 668.1083	TR	N	CR	ALn 668.1119	TR	N	CR
ALn 668.1046	R		CZ	ALn 668.1084	R		CZ	ALn 668.1120	TR		CR

Class ALn 668.1200. A slower, lower-powered version of ALn 668.1000 with single, central passenger door.

Built: 1979–80.
Builder: Savigliano 1201–40; OMECA 1241–60.
Engine: 2 x Fiat 8217.12 of 122 kW each. § 2 x Fiat 8217.32 of 122 kW each.
Transmission: Mechanical.   **Wheel Diameter:** 920 mm.
Accommodation: 8/60 1T.   **Weight:** 37 tonnes.
Length over Buffers: 23.54 m.   **Maximum Speed:** 110 km/h.
EVN: 95 83 4668 201-c and so on.

§   On hire to FSE in 2018.
s   On hire to Sistemi Territoriali in 2018.
t   On hire to Trenord in 2018.

ALn 668.1201	I		NO	ALn 668.1205	TR	t	CR	ALn 668.1212	R	s	TV
ALn 668.1204	TR		CR	ALn 668.1209	R	s	TV	ALn 668.1216	R	s	TV

ALn 668.1222	R	§	TV	ALn 668.1236	R	§	TV	ALn 668.1249	R	§	TV
ALn 668.1223	TR	t	LC	ALn 668.1237	R	§	TV	ALn 668.1251	R	s	TV
ALn 668.1225	TR	t	CR	ALn 668.1238	R	§	TV	ALn 668.1253	R	s	TV
ALn 668.1228	R	s	TV	ALn 668.1239	R	s	TV	ALn 668.1255	TR	t	CR
ALn 668.1231	TR	t	CR	ALn 668.1242	TR	t	CR	ALn 668.1256	R	s	TV

Class ALn 668.1900. These were the first of a new generation of Class ALn 668 with a longer, more modern body, in this case with two narrow passenger doors instead of one wider door and with more first class accommodation. The new generation also had significantly more powerful engines and a higher maximum speed. The original wrap-round cab windows were replaced with flat glass for security reasons. At the time of writing several units were loaned to Ferrovie del Sud-Est (FSE). ALn 668.1904, 1908 and 1936 have been preserved.

Built: 1975/76.
Builder: Savigliano, 1901–1920; OMECA, 1921–1940.
Engine: 2 x Fiat 8217.32 of 170 kW each.
Transmission: Mechanical.
Accommodation: 12/56 1T.
EVN: 95 83 4668 901-c and so on.

Wheel Diameter: 920 mm.
Weight: 37 tonnes.
Length over Buffers: 23.54 m.
Maximum Speed: 130 km/h.

F   On hire to FSE in 2018.

ALn 668.1901	R		NO	ALn 668.1915	R	F	FG	ALn 668.1928	R		FG
ALn 668.1903	R		FG	ALn 668.1918	R	F	FG	ALn 668.1929	R	F	FG
ALn 668.1905	R	F	FG	ALn 668.1919	R		NO	ALn 668.1930	R		FG
ALn 668.1906	R		FG	ALn 668.1920	R		NO	ALn 668.1931	TR		CR
ALn 668.1907	R		FG	ALn 668.1921	R	F	FG	ALn 668.1935	TR		CR
ALn 668.1909	R	F	FG	ALn 668.1922	R		FG	ALn 668.1938	TR		CR
ALn 668.1911	R		FG	ALn 668.1923	R		FG	ALn 668.1939	R	F	FG
ALn 668.1913	R		FG	ALn 668.1925	R		FG	ALn 668.1940	R	F	FG
ALn 668.1914	R		FG	ALn 668.1926	R		FG				

Class ALn 668.3000. Similar to ALn 668.1000 but with distinctive cowcatchers, less first class accommodation and a single, central door. All operate in Sicily.

Built: 1980/81.
Builder: Savigliano, 3001–3020; OMECA 3021–3040.
Engine: 2 x Fiat 8217.32 of 170 kW each.
Transmission: Mechanical.
Accommodation: 8/60 1T.
EVN: 95 83 4668 301-c and so on.

Wheel Diameter: 920 mm.
Weight: 38 tonnes.
Length over Buffers: 23.54 m.
Maximum Speed: 130 km/h.

ALn 668.3001	R	CT	ALn 668.3014	R	CT	ALn 668.3028	R	CT
ALn 668.3002	R	CT	ALn 668.3015	R	PA	ALn 668.3029	R	CT
ALn 668.3003	R	CT	ALn 668.3016	R	CT	ALn 668.3030	R	CT
ALn 668.3004	R	CT	ALn 668.3017	R	PA	ALn 668.3031	R	CT
ALn 668.3005	R	CT	ALn 668.3018	R	PA	ALn 668.3032	R	CT
ALn 668.3006	R	PA	ALn 668.3019	R	PA	ALn 668.3033	R	CT
ALn 668.3007	R	CT	ALn 668.3020	R	CT	ALn 668.3034	R	PA
ALn 668.3008	R	CT	ALn 668.3021	R	CT	ALn 668.3035	R	CT
ALn 668.3009	R	CT	ALn 668.3022	R	CT	ALn 668.3037	R	CT
ALn 668.3010	R	PA	ALn 668.3024	R	CT	ALn 668.3038	R	CT
ALn 668.3011	R	PA	ALn 668.3025	R	CT	ALn 668.3039	R	CT
ALn 668.3012	R	CT	ALn 668.3026	R	CT	ALn 668.3040	R	PA
ALn 668.3013	R	PA	ALn 668.3027	R	CT			

Class ALn 668.3100. Identical to ALn 668.3000 but fitted for working in multiple with up to two other railcars of the same class or ALn 668.3300 as well as Class ALn 663. Some were on loan to FSE at the time of writing. Details as ALn 668.3000 except:

Built: 1980–83.
Builder: Savigliano 3101–3120, 3181–3250; OMECA 3121–3180.
EVN: 95 83 4668 401-c to 550-c.

*   *Treno Galileo* – RFI test railcar, based at Roma Tuscolana. Front doors have been removed.
F   On loan to FSE in 2018.

ALn 668.3100	R	SI	ALn 668.3103	R	TV	ALn 668.3107	R	SI
ALn 668.3101	R	TV	ALn 668.3104	R	CT	ALn 668.3108	R	SS
ALn 668.3102	R	CT	ALn 668.3105	R	TV	ALn 668.3109	R	SS

Unit				Unit				Unit			
ALn 668.3110	R	F	FG	ALn 668.3158	R		TV	ALn 668.3206	TR		CR
ALn 668.3111	TR	N	CR	ALn 668.3160	R		FG	ALn 668.3207	R		SS
ALn 668.3112	R		CG	ALn 668.3162	R		TV	ALn 668.3208	R		SI
ALn 668.3113	R		BE	ALn 668.3163	R		FA	ALn 668.3209	R		SI
ALn 668.3114	R		CG	ALn 668.3164	R		TV	ALn 668.3210	R		FA
ALn 668.3115	R		TV	ALn 668.3165	TR	N	CR	ALn 668.3211	TR	N	CR
ALn 668.3116	R	F	FG	ALn 668.3166	R		TV	ALn 668.3212	R		SI
ALn 668.3118	R		CG	ALn 668.3167	R		TV	ALn 668.3213	R		SI
ALn 668.3119	R		CG	ALn 668.3168	R		SI	ALn 668.3214	TR	N	CR
ALn 668.3120	R		FA	ALn 668.3169	R		FG	ALn 668.3215	R		FG
ALn 668.3121	R		TV	ALn 668.3170	R		CT	ALn 668.3216	R		SI
ALn 668.3123	R		CG	ALn 668.3171	R		SI	ALn 668.3217	R		SI
ALn 668.3124	R		TV	ALn 668.3172	R		SI	ALn 668.3218	R		FA
ALn 668.3125	R		TV	ALn 668.3173	I		*	ALn 668.3219	R		SS
ALn 668.3126	R		TV	ALn 668.3174	R		FA	ALn 668.3220	R		PI
ALn 668.3127	R		TV	ALn 668.3175	R		CG	ALn 668.3221	TR		CR
ALn 668.3128	R		FG	ALn 668.3176	R		TV	ALn 668.3222	R		BE
ALn 668.3129	R		CT	ALn 668.3177	R		SI	ALn 668.3223	TR	N	CR
ALn 668.3130	R		TV	ALn 668.3178	R		SI	ALn 668.3224	TR		CR
ALn 668.3131	R		BE	ALn 668.3179	R		SI	ALn 668.3225	R		SI
ALn 668.3133	R		SI	ALn 668.3180	R		CG	ALn 668.3226	R		CG
ALn 668.3134	R		SI	ALn 668.3181	R		CT	ALn 668.3227	R		SS
ALn 668.3135	R		CT	ALn 668.3182	R		TV	ALn 668.3228	R		SS
ALn 668.3136	R		BE	ALn 668.3183	R		FA	ALn 668.3229	R		CT
ALn 668.3137	TR	N	CR	ALn 668.3184	R		SI	ALn 668.3230	R		CG
ALn 668.3138	R		TV	ALn 668.3185	TR		CR	ALn 668.3231	R		FG
ALn 668.3139	TR	N	CR	ALn 668.3186	R		FA	ALn 668.3232	R		SI
ALn 668.3141	R		BE	ALn 668.3187	R		SI	ALn 668.3233	R		CG
ALn 668.3142	R		FA	ALn 668.3188	R		FA	ALn 668.3234	R		CG
ALn 668.3143	R		FG	ALn 668.3189	R		FA	ALn 668.3235	R		FA
ALn 668.3144	R		FA	ALn 668.3191	R		SI	ALn 668.3236	R		SI
ALn 668.3145	R		FA	ALn 668.3192	R		TV	ALn 668.3237	R		PA
ALn 668.3146	R		FG	ALn 668.3193	R		SI	ALn 668.3238	TR	N	CR
ALn 668.3147	R		BE	ALn 668.3194	R		CG	ALn 668.3239	R		CT
ALn 668.3148	TR		CR	ALn 668.3195	R		SI	ALn 668.3240	R		SI
ALn 668.3149	R		SI	ALn 668.3196	R		SI	ALn 668.3241	R		CG
ALn 668.3150	R		SI	ALn 668.3197	R		SI	ALn 668.3242	R	F	FG
ALn 668.3151	R		CG	ALn 668.3198	R	F	FG	ALn 668.3243	R		FA
ALn 668.3152	R		TV	ALn 668.3199	R		FA	ALn 668.3244	R		SI
ALn 668.3153	R		CG	ALn 668.3200	R		SI	ALn 668.3245	R		SI
ALn 668.3154	R		CG	ALn 668.3202	R		CG	ALn 668.3246	R		FG
ALn 668.3155	R		SI	ALn 668.3203	R		SI	ALn 668.3248	TR	N	CR
ALn 668.3156	R		FG	ALn 668.3204	R	F	FG	ALn 668.3250	TR	N	SS
ALn 668.3157	R		SI	ALn 668.3205	R		SS(S)				

Class ALn 668.3300. The final version of ALn 668 before ALn 663 became the standard FS railcar. Originally similar to ALn 668.3100 but with a lower maximum speed of 120 km/h. This has now been raised to 130 km/h. Can operate in multiple with ALn 663. Details as ALn 668.3000 except:

Built: 1982/83.   **Builder:** Savigliano.
EVN: 95 83 4668 651-c to 690-c.

Unit				Unit			Unit			
ALn 668.3301	R		SU	ALn 668.3314	R	FG	ALn 668.3328	R		SU
ALn 668.3302	R		TV	ALn 668.3315	R	SU	ALn 668.3329	R		SU
ALn 668.3303	R	F	FG	ALn 668.3317	R	AN	ALn 668.3330	R		SU
ALn 668.3304	R		SU	ALn 668.3318	R	SU	ALn 668.3332	R		SU
ALn 668.3305	R		SU	ALn 668.3319	R	SU	ALn 668.3333	R		SU
ALn 668.3306	R		TV	ALn 668.3320	R	SU	ALn 668.3334	R		SU
ALn 668.3307	R		SU	ALn 668.3321	R	SU	ALn 668.3335	R		SU
ALn 668.3308	R		FG	ALn 668.3322	R	SU	ALn 668.3336	R		SU
ALn 668.3309	R		SU	ALn 668.3323	R	SU	ALn 668.3337	R		SU
ALn 668.3310	R		SU	ALn 668.3324	R	SU	ALn 668.3338	R		SU
ALn 668.3311	R		SU	ALn 668.3325	R	SU	ALn 668.3339	R		SU
ALn 668.3312	R		AN	ALn 668.3326	R	SU	ALn 668.3340	R		SU
ALn 668.3313	R		SU	ALn 668.3327	R	AN				

CLASS ALn 776 SINGLE CARS

Built for FCU, based on the Fiat ALn 663 design, there are two versions: M stands for mono-cabin – units have a single driving position and no corridor connection, which means that they have two large front windows; B means bi-cabin – these units are exactly like "regular" Class 663 with a door in the front end. The high top speed – FCU lines, despite excellent track, allow a 90 km/h maximum – is to allow main line running over RFI tracks. In recent years, FCU has taken over operation of certain local trains on RFI lines around Terni in the Umbria region. In 2005, FCU loaned a few units to Seatrain which operates "Roma Express" charters from cruise ships in Civitavecchia to Roma. They have been upgraded internally and are in a special livery. In general 776 B work Perugia–Sansepolcro and 776 M Perugia–Terni. Units 776 001, 002, 051, 053 and 054 have been sold to FAS.

Built: 1985–87 001–008, 051/052; 1990/91 009–024, 053–076.
Builder: Fiat.
Engines: 2 x Fiat of 170 kW each.
Transmission: Mechanical.
Wheel Arrangement: A1-1A.

Length over Buffers: 23.54 m.
Weight: 40 tonnes.
Maximum Speed: 150 km/h.
Accommodation: –/76.

*   Equipped to operate over RFI network to Roma and in special livery.
r   Refurbished for Seatrain service.

Type 776 M

ALn 776.001	FAS		ALn 776.013	FCU	
ALn 776.002	FAS		ALn 776.014	FCU	
ALn 776.003	FCU		ALn 776.015	FCU	
ALn 776.004	FCU		ALn 776.016	FCU	
ALn 776.005	FCU		ALn 776.017	FCU	
ALn 776.006	FCU		ALn 776.018	FCU	
ALn 776.007	FCU		ALn 776.019	r	FCU	"Piazza Navona"
ALn 776.008	FCU		ALn 776.020		FCU	
ALn 776.009	FCU		ALn 776.021		FCU	
ALn 776.010	FCU		ALn 776.022	r	FCU	"Via Veneto"
ALn 776.011	FCU		ALn 776.023	*	FCU	
ALn 776.012	FCU		ALn 776.024	*	FCU	

Type 776 B

ALn 776.051	FAS		ALn 776.064		FCU	
ALn 776.052	FCU		ALn 776.065		FCU	
ALn 776.053	FAS		ALn 776.066		FCU	
ALn 776.054	FAS		ALn 776.067		FCU	
ALn 776.055	FCU		ALn 776.068		FCU	
ALn 776.056	FCU		ALn 776.069		FCU	
ALn 776.057	FCU		ALn 776.070	*	FCU	
ALn 776.058	FCU		ALn 776.071		FCU	
ALn 776.059	r	FCU	ALn 776.072		FCU	
ALn 776.060	r	FCU	"Colosseo"	ALn 776.073	r	FCU	"Città deL Vaticano"
ALn 776.061	FCU		ALn 776.074		FCU	
ALn 776.062	FCU		ALn 776.075		FCU	
ALn 776.063	FCU		ALn 776.076		FCU	

BI-MODE MULTIPLE UNITS

At the time of going to press Italy had only one class of bi-mode multiple unit.

CLASS BTR.813   3-SECTION ARTICULATED UNITS

In May 2015 the Valle d'Aosta region in north-west Italy ordered five bi-mode units from Stadler, with an option for five more, to allow the restoration of through services from Torino to Aosta. Only the section from Torino to Ivrea is electrified and trains had been split there. Based on the FLIRT design, these trains consist of three long sections with passenger accommodation plus a short section with two diesel engines. The units should enter service in spring 2019. They are owned by the region but operated by Trenitalia. The Molise and Calabria regions also seem to be interested in the train. Trains are finished in a red livery.

Built: 2017/18.   **Systems:** 3000 V DC overhead and diesel.
Builder: Stadler.   **Wheel Diameter:** driving 920mm; trailing 760 mm.
Accommodation: –/56 (3) + –/42 (10) 1TD + –/56 (3).   **Weight:** 140 tonnes.
Length over Buffers: 21.20 + 17.60 + 6.90 + 21.20 m = 66.80 metres.
Maximum Power Rating: 2600 kW (electric); 700kW (diesel).
Engines: 2 x Deutz V8 of 450 kW each.   **Wheel Arrangement:** Bo-2-2-2-Bo.
Maximum Speed: 160 km/h (electric mode); 140 km/h (diesel mode).
EVN: 95 83 4813 001-c + 813 004-c + 813 003-c + 813 002-c .

BTR.813.001	TC	BTR.813.003		BTR.813.005	
BTR.813.002		BTR.813.004			

▲ BTR.813.001 is seen at Stadler's commissioning plant at Erlen, Switzerland.   **Courtesy Stadler**

1.4. ELECTRIC MULTIPLE UNITS

FS electric units were traditionally composed of independent power and trailer cars which could be formed in a variety of combinations. Numbering is confusing as power cars, prefixed ALe meaning *Automotrice Leggera elettrica* (light electric unit) and trailers, prefixed Le (originally meaning light trailer) sometimes have the same number. So, careful when taking notes! Class numbers are supposed to be based on passenger capacity – Le 108 indeed carry 108 passengers whilst ALe 644 carry 64 passengers, the last 4 indicating a 4-car set. However, there are so many exceptions to the rules that it is almost meaningless. Most power cars in this section have Bo-Bo wheel arrangement and all trailers are 2-2. All recent trains are fixed formation. In recent years the ALe prefix has been dropped and ETR is now used. This was previously only applied to high speed EMUs.

Since the 2013 edition, all of Classes Ale 801/940, 803 and 841 have been withdrawn

CLASS ETR.103 & 104   "POP"   3- OR 4-SECTION ARTICULATED UNITS

These are new EMUs being built by Alstom in Savigliano and known by the builder itself as Coradia Stream. Similar units will be built for Netherlands Railways. Class ETR.103 is 3-car and Class ETR.104 4-car. Alstom portrays the *Coradia Stream* as being a common platform for regional and intercity services with trains from three to ten cars, 160 or 200 km/h maximum speed. The Trenitalia version will operate from 3000 V DC, at a maximum of 160 km/h. By autumn 2018 31 3-car and 149 4-car had been ordered, a total of 180 sets. The first will go to Emilia-Romagna. The first unit will enter service in 2019.

Orders so far in early 2019 were: Abruzzo: Four 3-car; Emilia-Romagna: 27 3-car plus 20 4-car; Liguria: 15 4-car; Marche: Four 4-car; Piemonte : 15 4-car; Sicilia: 21 4-car; Puglia : 43 4-car; Veneto: 31 4-car.

Built: 2018–   **Wheel Diameter:** Power cars: 920 mm; trailer cars 850 mm.
Length: 23.60 + 18.50 (+18.50) + 23.60 m.   **Power Rating:** 2000 kW.
Accommodation: 3-car –/216 (21); 4-car –/292 (27).   **Maximum Speed:** 160 km/h.

ETR.104.001 is formed 104.001 + 104.251 + 104.501 + 104.701 and so on.

ETR.103 3-car sets

ETR.103.001	ETR.103.012	ETR.103.022
ETR.103.002	ETR.103.013	ETR.103.023
ETR.103.003	ETR.103.014	ETR.103.024
ETR.103.004	ETR.103.015	ETR.103.025
ETR.103.005	ETR.103.016	ETR.103.026
ETR.103.006	ETR.103.017	ETR.103.027
ETR.103.007	ETR.103.018	ETR.103.028
ETR.103.008	ETR.103.019	ETR.103.029
ETR.103.009	ETR.103.020	ETR.103.030
ETR.103.010	ETR.103.021	ETR.103.031
ETR.103.011		

ETR.104 4-car sets

ETR.104.001	BC	ETR.104.018	ETR.104.035
ETR.104.002	BC	ETR.104.019	ETR.104.036
ETR.104.003		ETR.104.020	ETR.104.037
ETR.104.004		ETR.104.021	ETR.104.038
ETR.104.005		ETR.104.022	ETR.104.039
ETR.104.006		ETR.104.023	ETR.104.040
ETR.104.007		ETR.104.024	ETR.104.041
ETR.104.008		ETR.104.025	ETR.104.042
ETR.104.009		ETR.104.026	ETR.104.043
ETR.104.010		ETR.104.027	ETR.104.044
ETR.104.011		ETR.104.028	ETR.104.045
ETR.104.012		ETR.104.029	ETR.104.046
ETR.104.013		ETR.104.030	ETR.104.047
ETR.104.014		ETR.104.031	ETR.104.048
ETR.104.015		ETR.104.032	ETR.104.049
ETR.104.016		ETR.104.033	ETR.104.050
ETR.104.017		ETR.104.034	ETR.104.051

▲ ETR.103.001 is seen on show at the Innotrans trade fair in Berlin on 17 September 2018 with a "Rock" unit to the left. **David Haydock**

▼ ETR.170.109, owned by the Trento province, is seen at Merano with a train to Brennero on 11 September 2018. **David Haydock**

ETR.104.052	ETR.104.085	ETR.104.118
ETR.104.053	ETR.104.086	ETR.104.119
ETR.104.054	ETR.104.087	ETR.104.120
ETR.104.055	ETR.104.088	ETR.104.121
ETR.104.056	ETR.104.089	ETR.104.122
ETR.104.057	ETR.104.090	ETR.104.123
ETR.104.058	ETR.104.091	ETR.104.124
ETR.104.059	ETR.104.092	ETR.104.125
ETR.104.060	ETR.104.093	ETR.104.126
ETR.104.061	ETR.104.094	ETR.104.127
ETR.104.062	ETR.104.095	ETR.104.128
ETR.104.063	ETR.104.096	ETR.104.129
ETR.104.064	ETR.104.097	ETR.104.130
ETR.104.065	ETR.104.098	ETR.104.131
ETR.104.066	ETR.104.099	ETR.104.132
ETR.104.067	ETR.104.100	ETR.104.133
ETR.104.068	ETR.104.101	ETR.104.134
ETR.104.069	ETR.104.102	ETR.104.135
ETR.104.070	ETR.104.103	ETR.104.136
ETR.104.071	ETR.104.104	ETR.104.137
ETR.104.072	ETR.104.105	ETR.104.138
ETR.104.073	ETR.104.106	ETR.104.139
ETR.104.074	ETR.104.107	ETR.104.140
ETR.104.075	ETR.104.108	ETR.104.141
ETR.104.076	ETR.104.109	ETR.104.142
ETR.104.077	ETR.104.110	ETR.104.143
ETR.104.078	ETR.104.111	ETR.104.144
ETR.104.079	ETR.104.112	ETR.104.145
ETR.104.080	ETR.104.113	ETR.104.146
ETR.104.081	ETR.104.114	ETR.104.147
ETR.104.082	ETR.104.115	ETR.104.148
ETR.104.083	ETR.104.116	ETR.104.149
ETR.104.084	ETR.104.117	

CLASS ETR.170   "FLIRT"   6-SECTION ARTICULATED UNITS

These are Stadler FLIRT EMUs built for operation in the Bolzano and Trento provinces of northern Italy. They are equipped for operation under 15 kV AC as well as 3000 V DC as they operate from Brennero to Innsbruck and from Innichen to Lienz in Austria. Some are owned by local operator SAD but most are owned and operated by Trenitalia, albeit carrying the local silver/multicolour livery. ETR.170.109 and 110 are owned by the Trento province and carry the latter's white/maroon livery although this is being replaced by a green livery on Trento's ALn 501 DMUs. The first four units were built as 4-car ETR.155.001 to 004 but were extended, becoming ETR.170.005 to 008, although out of order. ETR.170.211 to 217 were delivered with 25 kV AC capability because the Merano-Malles line is being electrified at 25 kV AC. The ETR.170.1 series are now being retrofitted for 25 kV AC by Stadler and renumbered – ETR.170.102 to 202 for example.

The ETR.170.0 subclass are mainly used on the Bolzano–Merano line and north of Bolzano. The others run the full length of the Brennero–Verona line. In late 2018 Bolzano province launched a tender for a further seven tri-voltage trains; it is almost certain that Stadler will win so we have added numbers 218 to 224.

Built: 2008 ETR.170.001–008 (ETR.170.005–008 as ETR.155.001–004); 2013 ETR.170.101–110; 2017 ETR.170.212–217.
Weight: ETR.170.001 to 008 170 tonnes; others 173 tonnes.
Length: 20.939 + 16.10 + 16.10 + 16.10 + 16.10 + 20.939 m = 106.278 m.
Systems: 3000 V DC/15 kV AC 16.7 Hz; ETR.170.2 also 25 kV AC 50 Hz.
Accommodation: –/48 + –/34 (8) 1TD + –/48 + –/48 + –/34 (8) 1TD + –/48.
Wheel Arrangement: Bo-2-2-2-2-2-Bo.
Numbering: ETR.170.001 is 170.001 + 170.006 + 170.005 + 170.004 + 170.003 + 170.002 and so on.

ETR.170.0

ETR.170.001	ETR.170.004	ETR.170.007
ETR.170.002	ETR.170.005	ETR.170.008
ETR.170.003	ETR.170.006	

ETR.170.1 and 170.2

ETR.170.101	ETR.170.109	ETR.170.217
ETR.170.202	ETR.170.110	ETR.170.218
ETR.170.103	ETR.170.211	ETR.170.219
ETR.170.104	ETR.170.212	ETR.170.220
ETR.170.105	ETR.170.213	ETR.170.221
ETR.170.106	ETR.170.214	ETR.170.222
ETR.170.107	ETR.170.215	ETR.170.223
ETR.170.108	ETR.170.216	ETR.170.224

CLASS ETR.234   4-SECTION ARTICULATED UNITS

These Alstom Coradia Meridian units, delivered to Torino operator GTT in 2013, are very similar to Class TTR (501.801 to 820) but with an extra centre section. Also very similar to Trenitalia ETR.425 "Jazz" units. They mainly operate in pairs on the Rivarolo–Torino–Chieri section, replacing sets of three Y0530 in multiple.

Details as Trenitalia Class ALe 501 except:

Built: 2013.   **Weight:**
Traction Motors: Four asynchronous of 512 kW each.
Wheel Arrangement: Bo-2-2-2-Bo.   **Length:** 19.125 + 13.65 + 13.65 + 19.125 m.
Accommodation: –/50 (4) + –/22 (16) + –/22 (16) + –/50 (4).

ETR.234.001	ETR.234.002	ETR.234.003

CLASS ETR.243   2-CAR UNITS

These units, known as ALFA2, were ordered by EAV in 2005 but only started to be delivered in 2014 after FIREMA suffered financial difficulties. The units are to be used on both the old FA line once electrified and the former FBN line.

Built: 2014–   **Builder:** Firema.
Power Rating: 1480 kW.   **Length:** 25.445 + 25.445 m.
Weight: 102 tonnes.   **Maximum Speed:** 160 km/h.
Wheel Arrangement: 2-Bo + Bo-2.
Accommodation: –/142 1TD.
EVN: 94 83 4 243 101-c + 94 83 4 243 102-c and so on.

ETR.243.101 + ETR.243.102	ETR.243.107 + ETR.243.108	ETR.243.113 + ETR.243.114
ETR.243.103 + ETR.243.104	ETR.243.109 + ETR.243.110	ETR.243.115 + ETR.243.116
ETR.243.105 + ETR.243.106	ETR.243.111 + ETR.243.112	ETR.242.117 + ETR.243.118

CLASS ETR.245   "CORADIA"   5-SECTION ARTICULATED UNITS

These sets only operate on FNM lines north of Milano so are shown in Section 2 under Trenord.

CLASS ETR.322   "IMPULS"   3-SECTION ARTICULATED UNITS

Five EMUs, with an option for ten more, were ordered by FSE from Newag in Poland. Newag has already produced this design for Poland where it is known as Type 36WEb. The first unit completed dynamic tests in Italy in spring 2018 and it was hoped that the first units could enter service in December. However, this depended on FSE finding the money to pay for them and complete electrification of the Bari–Putignano–Martina Franca line. The aim is to introduce an electric service all the way from Bari to Taranto with a half-hourly service on both lines between Bari and Putignano. Six more sets were ordered in late 2018 for delivery in 2020.

Built: 2017–
Builder: Newag.
Wheel Arrangement: Bo-2-2-Bo.   **Wheel Arrangement:** Bo-2-2-Bo.
Power Rating: 1600 kW.   **Length:** 58.50 m.
Accommodation: –/175 1TD.   **Maximum Speed:** 160 km/h.

ETR.322.001	ETR.322.005	ETR.322.009
ETR.322.002	ETR.322.006	ETR.322.010
ETR.322.003	ETR.322.007	ETR.322.011
ETR.322.004	ETR.322.008	

CLASSES ETR.324, 425 & 526 "JAZZ" 4, 5 & 6-SECTION ARTICULATED UNITS

Trenitalia and FNM (for Trenord) now have over 100 *"Coradia Meridian"* EMUs from Alstom – ETR.324 4-section, ETR.425 5-section and ETR.526 6-section units. There are options for 20 more.

The units are very similar to units delivered to GTT (ETR.234) and Trenord (ETR.245) and are based on the *Minuetto* units. They were nicknamed *"Jazz"* by Trenitalia after an internet poll.

There were no less than five versions of the unit in the Trenitalia order: five *Aeroportuale* for airport services, with more baggage space; 12 *Metropolitano* with more space for standees; 18 *Regionale* with the most seats, for Trenord. As we went to press we learned that Trenitalia had added 22 *Suburbano* and 13 *Regio Express* versions. The new trains will go to the Abruzzo (seven trains, Sulmona depot), Calabria (four, RC), Lombardia (18, MF), Marche (eight, AN), and Piemonte (14, TC) regions, allowing the withdrawal of Classes ALe 801/940, 803 and 840 EMUs ETR.425.041 to 045 are the *Aeroportuale* sets and operate the "Leonardo Express" service to Fiumicino airport. Seats are covered in cloth for Trenord units, fake leather for Trenitalia sets.

Trains carry numbers 001 upwards on the cabsides.

Units ETR.425.058 to 065 were lengthened and became ETR.526.005 to 012. E.425.102 belongs to TFT.

At the time of writing there were 12 Class E.425 for Campania still on order.

All units are in Regionale livery of silver-grey with dark blue front ends and lateral stripe, lime green doors and a yellow lateral strip, except those at MF which are in Trenord livery.

Built: 2013–　　　　　　　　　　　　　　　　**Builder:** Alstom, Savigliano.
Accommodation: 6-section *Regionale* version –/302 1TD (15); 5-section *Regionale* version –/248 1TD (15); 5-section *Aeroportuale* version –/251 1TD (15); 5-car *Metropolitano* version –/253 1TD (15); 4-car *Regio Express* version –/202 1TD (14); 5-car *Suburbano* version –/288 1TD (15).
Maximum Speed: 160 km/h (125 km/h under 1500 V DC).
Wheel Arrangement: Bo-2-2-2-Bo or Bo-2-2-2-2-Bo or Bo-2-2-2-2-2-Bo.
Power Rating: 2048 kW (four x 4 FXA 2842 asynchronous motors of 512 kW each).
Length: 19.20 + 14.65 + 14.65 (+ 14.65 + 14.65) + 19.20 m.
EVN: ETR.425.001 is 94 83 4425 001-c + 0425.002-c + 0425.003-c + 0425.004-c + 4425 .005-c and so on.

F　　Owned by FNM for Trenord services.
P　　As livery **L** but for Palermo airport.
§　　Used by TFT.

ETR.324 4-section units

ETR.324.001	*R*	PE	ETR.324.005	*R*	FI	ETR.324.009	*R*	PE
ETR.324.002	*R*	PE	ETR.324.006	*R*	FI	ETR.324.010	*R*	TA
ETR.324.003	*R*	PE	ETR.324.007	*R*	FI	ETR.324.011	*R*	TA
ETR.324.004	*R*	PE	ETR.324.008	*R*	FI	ETR.324.012	*R*	TA

ETR.425 5-section units

ETR.425.001	*R*		RS	ETR.425.022	*R*		TC	ETR.425.043	*R*	L	RS
ETR.425.002	*R*		AN	ETR.425.023	*TR*	F	MF	ETR.425.044	*R*	L	RS
ETR.425.003	*R*		AN	ETR.425.024	*TR*	F	MF	ETR.425.045	*R*	L	RS
ETR.425.004	*R*		AN	ETR.425.025	*TR*	F	MF	ETR.425.046	*R*		FI
ETR.425.005	*R*		AN	ETR.425.026	*TR*	F	MF	ETR.425.047	*R*		FI
ETR.425.006	*R*		AN	ETR.425.027	*TR*	F	MF	ETR.425.048	*R*		FI
ETR.425.007	*R*		AN	ETR.425.028	*TR*	F	MF	ETR.425.049	*R*		FI
ETR.425.008	*R*		AN	ETR.425.029	*TR*	F	MF	ETR.425.050	*R*		FI
ETR.425.009	*R*		TC	ETR.425.030	*TR*	F	MF	ETR.425.051	*R*		FI
ETR.425.010	*R*		TC	ETR.425.031	*TR*	F	MF	ETR.425.052	*R*		FI
ETR.425.011	*R*		TC	ETR.425.032	*TR*	F	MF	ETR.425.053	*R*		FI
ETR.425.012	*R*		TC	ETR.425.033	*TR*	F	MF	ETR.425.054	*R*		FI
ETR.425.013	*R*		TC	ETR.425.034	*TR*	F	MF	ETR.425.055	*R*		FI
ETR.425.014	*R*		TC	ETR.425.035	*TR*	F	MF	ETR.425.056		§	FI
ETR.425.015	*R*		TC	ETR.425.036	*TR*	F	MF	ETR.425.057	*R*		FI
ETR.425.016	*R*		TC	ETR.425.037	*TR*	F	MF	ETR.425.066	*R*	L	RS
ETR.425.017	*R*		TC	ETR.425.038	*TR*	F	MF	ETR.425.067	*R*	L	RS
ETR.425.018	*R*		TC	ETR.425.039	*TR*	F	MF	ETR.425.068	*R*	L	RS
ETR.425.019	*R*		TC	ETR.425.040	*TR*	F	MF	ETR.425.069	*R*		RS
ETR.425.020	*R*		TC	ETR.425.041	*R*	L	RS	ETR.425.070	*R*		RS
ETR.425.021	*R*		TC	ETR.425.042	*R*	L	RS	ETR.425.071	*R*		RS

ETR.425.072	R	RS	ETR.425.088	R	NF	ETR.425.104	R	SV
ETR.425.073	R	RS	ETR.425.089	R	NF	ETR.425.105	R	SV
ETR.425.074	R	RS	ETR.425.090	R	NF	ETR.425.106	R	SV
ETR.425.075	R	RS	ETR.425.091	R	NF	ETR.425.107	R	SV
ETR.425.076	R	RS	ETR.425.092	R	NF	ETR.425.108	R	SV
ETR.425.077	R	RS	ETR.425.093	R	PA	ETR.425.109	R	FI
ETR.425.078	R	RS	ETR.425.094	R	PA	ETR.425.110	R	FI
ETR.425.079	R	RS	ETR.425.095	R	PA	ETR.425.111	R	
ETR.425.080	R	RS	ETR.425.096	R	PA	ETR.425.112	R	
ETR.425.081	R	NF	ETR.425.097	R P	PA	ETR.425.113	R	
ETR.425.082	R	NF	ETR.425.098	R P	PA	ETR.425.114	R	
ETR.425.083	R	NF	ETR.425.099	R	NF	ETR.425.115	R	AN
ETR.425.084	R	NF	ETR.425.100	R	NF	ETR.425.116	R	
ETR.425.085	R	NF	ETR.425.101	R	AN	ETR.425.117	R	
ETR.425.086	R	NF	ETR.425.102	§		ETR.425.118	R	
ETR.425.087	R	NF	ETR.425.103	R	SV			

ETR.526 6-section units

ETR.526.001	TR	NV	ETR.526.007	TR	NV	ETR.526.013	TR
ETR.526.002	TR	NV	ETR.526.008	TR	NV	ETR.526.014	TR
ETR.526.003	TR	NV	ETR.526.009	TR	NV	ETR.526.015	TR
ETR.526.004	TR	NV	ETR.526.010	TR	NV	ETR.526.016	TR
ETR.526.005	TR	NV	ETR.526.011	TR	NV	ETR.526.017	TR
ETR.526.006	TR	NV	ETR.526.012	TR	NV	ETR.526.018	TR

CLASSES ETR.330, 340, 341, 342, 343, 350 & 360   "FLIRT"
3-, 4- 5- & 6-CAR ARTICULATED UNITS

These are very similar "FLIRT" EMUs built by Stadler alone or in cooperation with AnsaldoBreda for FG, FT, ST and TPER. They are also very similar to Class ET.170 6-car sets. Stadler is to build five 110 metre EMUs for the Messina–Palermo line for the Sicilia region but it is not yet known how they will be numbered.

Builder: Stadler.
Length: 20.939 + 16.10 (+ 16.10) (+ 16.10) (+ 16.10) + 20.939 m.
Weight: 102 tonnes 3-car; 120 tonnes 4-car ; 143 tonnes 5-car ; 170 tonnes 6-car.
Continuous Rating: 2000 kW.
Wheel Arrangement: Bo-2-2 (-2) (-2) (-2) -Bo.   **Maximum Speed:** 160 km/h.

Ferrovia del Gargano Class ETR.330
3-car sets used on Foggia–Lucera and Foggia–San Severo trains and maintained in Foggia. The first order was for three sets followed by a fourth. The second batch of three sets differ in having a modified front end with better crashworthiness. Built in 2008/9 and 2014.

Accommodation: –/56 (4) + –/24 (20) 1TD + –/56.
Numbering: ETR.330.001 is 94 83 4 330 001-c + 330 003-c + 330 002-c and so on.

ETR.330.001	ETR.330.003	ETR.330.004
ETR.330.002		
ETR.330.101	ETR.330.102	ETR.330.103

Ferrotramviaria Classes ETR.341 & ETR.342
4-car sets built 2009 in a luxury (ETR.341, built for a service which has been abandoned) and standard version (ETR.342), now operating on the Bari–Barletta service. ETR.341 TR 02 was severely damaged in a head-on crash in July 2016.

Accommodation: ETR.341: 56/– + 49/– 1TD + 56/– + 56/–. ETR.342: –/60(4) + –/31 (14) 1TD + –/48 (8) + –/60 (4).

ETR.341 TR 01

ETR.342 TR 01	ETR.342 TR 02

▲ ETR.425.052 is seen arriving at Pistoia on 9 February 2018.   **Robert Pritchard**

▼ An ETR.521 "Rock" EMU soon after delivery.   **Courtesy Trenitalia**

Sistemi Territoriali Classes ETR.340, ETR.343 & ETR.360
Classes ETR.340 and ETR.343 are two batches of 4-car sets built in 2008 and 2013/14; Class ETR.360 are 6-car sets built by Stadler and AnsaldoBreda in a joint order with TPER. They now work passenger trains on RFI lines in the Veneto region, driven and maintained (at Mestre depot) by Trenitalia staff.

Accommodation: 4-car –/52 8) + –/18 (15) 1TD + –/32 (16) + –/52 (8).
6-car –/60 (4) + –/56 (14) 1TD + –/56 (4) + –/56 (4) + –/56 (14) 1TD + –/60 (4).

ETR.340.001	ETR.340.002	

ETR.343.001	ETR.343.007	ETR.343.012
ETR.343.002	ETR.343.008	ETR.343.013
ETR.343.003	ETR.343.009	ETR.343.014
ETR.343.004	ETR.343.010	ETR.343.015
ETR.343.005	ETR.343.011	ETR.343.016
ETR.343.006		

ETR.360.001	ETR.360.003	ETR.360.004
ETR.360.002		

TPER Class ETR.350
5-car units. The first 12 units were built in cooperation by Stadler and Ansaldobreda in 2012/13. 14 more units with slight differences were built in 2017/18. They are used from Bologna to Portomaggiore, Rimini, Ferrara and Vignola plus once a day from Bologna to Milano Centrale. Others are operated by Trenitalia from Bologna to Prato.

Accommodation: –/52 (10) +–/20 (19) 1TD + –/32 (20) + –/28 (20) IT + –/52 (10).

ETR.350.001	ETR.350.005	ETR.350.009
ETR.350.002	ETR.350.006	ETR.350.010
ETR.350.003	ETR.350.007	ETR.350.011
ETR.350.004	ETR.350.008	ETR.350.012

ETR.350.101	ETR.350.106	ETR.350.111
ETR.350.102	ETR.350.107	ETR.350.112
ETR.350.103	ETR.350.108	ETR.350.113
ETR.350.104	ETR.350.109	ETR.350.114
ETR.350.105	ETR.350.110	

CLASSES ETR.421, ETR.521 & E.621 "ROCK" 4-, 5- & 6-CAR DOUBLE-DECK UNITS

This is a new double-deck EMU, the first new design to emerge from Hitachi Rail Italy, following its takeover of AnsaldoBreda.

The framework order is for a maximum of 300 units. Hitachi calls the units "Caravaggio" but Trenitalia has nicknamed them "Rock", following the recent musical theme. The first train, a 5-car unit, was moved to Velim for trials in spring 2018 but was promptly hit by a tree. The trains are due in service from spring 2019. Orders so far are as follows:

14 4-car and 25 5-car for Emilia-Romagna; 4 5-car for Toscana; 38 5-car and nine 6-car for Veneto
28 5-car for Liguria; 30 5-car for FNM; FNM has a framework order for up to 120 trains, including a minimum of 30 4-car and 20 5-car, to be delivered 2020 to 2025.

Length: 27.60 m + 27.20 m + 27.20 m (+ 27.20 m) (+ 27.20 m) + 27.60 m.
Wheel Diameter: 920 mm
Power Rating: ETR.421, ETR.521 3400 kW; ETR.621 4200 kW.
Maximum Speed: 160 km/h.
Wheel Arrangement: Bo-Bo + 2-2 + 2-2 (+ Bo-Bo) (+ 2-2) + Bo-Bo
Accommodation: 4-car 466; 5-car 598; 6-car 720. 4-car, 5-car 1T + 1TD; 6-car 2T + 1TD.
Numbering: ETR.521.001 = 521.001 + 521.201 + 521.401 + 521.601 + 521.801 and so on.

ETR.421 4-car

ETR.421.001	ETR.421.006	ETR.421.011
ETR.421.002	ETR.421.007	ETR.421.012
ETR.421.003	ETR.421.008	ETR.421.013
ETR.421.004	ETR.421.009	ETR.421.014
ETR.421.005	ETR.421.010	

ETR.521 5-car

ETR.521.001	ETR.521.043	ETR.521.085
ETR.521.002	ETR.521.044	ETR.521.086
ETR.521.003	ETR.521.045	ETR.521.087
ETR.521.004 BC	ETR.521.046	ETR.521.088
ETR.521.005	ETR.521.047	ETR.521.089
ETR.521.006	ETR.521.048	ETR.521.090
ETR.521.007	ETR.521.049	ETR.521.091
ETR.521.008	ETR.521.050	ETR.521.092
ETR.521.009	ETR.521.051	ETR.521.093
ETR.521.010	ETR.521.052	ETR.521.094
ETR.521.011	ETR.521.053	ETR.521.095
ETR.521.012	ETR.521.054	ETR.521.096
ETR.521.013	ETR.521.055	ETR.521.097
ETR.521.014	ETR.521.056	ETR.521.098
ETR.521.015	ETR.521.057	ETR.521.099
ETR.521.016	ETR.521.058	ETR.521.100
ETR.521.017	ETR.521.059	ETR.521.101
ETR.521.018	ETR.521.060	ETR.521.102
ETR.521.019	ETR.521.061	ETR.521.103
ETR.521.020	ETR.521.062	ETR.521.104
ETR.521.021	ETR.521.063	ETR.521.105
ETR.521.022	ETR.521.064	ETR.521.106
ETR.521.023	ETR.521.065	ETR.521.107
ETR.521.024	ETR.521.066	ETR.521.108
ETR.521.025	ETR.521.067	ETR.521.109
ETR.521.026	ETR.521.068	ETR.521.110
ETR.521.027	ETR.521.069	ETR.521.111
ETR.521.028	ETR.521.070	ETR.521.112
ETR.521.029	ETR.521.071	ETR.521.113
ETR.521.030	ETR.521.072	ETR.521.114
ETR.521.031	ETR.521.073	ETR.521.115
ETR.521.032	ETR.521.074	ETR.521.116
ETR.521.033	ETR.521.075	ETR.521.117
ETR.521.034	ETR.521.076	ETR.521.118
ETR.521.035	ETR.521.077	ETR.521.119
ETR.521.036	ETR.521.078	ETR.521.120
ETR.521.037	ETR.521.079	ETR.521.121
ETR.521.038	ETR.521.080	ETR.521.122
ETR.521.039	ETR.521.081	ETR.521.123
ETR.521.040	ETR.521.082	ETR.521.124
ETR.521.041	ETR.521.083	ETR.521.125
ETR.521.042	ETR.521.084	

E.621 6-car

E.621.001	E.621.004	E.621.007
E.621.002	E.621.005	E.621.008
E.621.003	E.621.006	E.621.009

CLASSES ALe 426/506   "TAF"   4-CAR DOUBLE-DECK UNITS

The first double-deck EMUs delivered to FS, this design is also in service with Trenord. The units are known as TAF – *Treni Alta Frequentazione* (high capacity trains). They were designed by Pininfarina and have egg-shaped front ends and ventilation grilles in the form of portholes. Builders were a consortium of Breda, Adtranz and Firema. Trains are formed ALe 426 + Le 736 + Le 736 + ALe 506 carrying a total of 475 seated passengers plus 398 standing. Class ALe 426 is identical to ALe 506 except for having spaces for disabled passengers. Seating is arranged 2+2, which is lower density than previous FS suburban stock. It seems that Trenitalia have not been happy with the units as no more have been delivered; instead double-deck Vivalto stock to be powered by Class E.464 locomotives has been ordered. Curiously, TAF sets cannot operate in multiple which seems to defeat the object of a multiple unit! Sets carry numbers "Treno 01" upwards on the cab sides. Units are used on a variety of suburban services including Roma Lines FR1 Fara Sabina–Fiumicino and FR3 Ostiense–Viterbo plus Milano's Varese–Pioltello service via the *Passante* cross-city tunnel. Set 04 was damaged in an accident.

Sets 07 to 15 were retro-fitted for operation in multiple in the Milano area and were renumbered 207 to 215 to show the difference. There have been several changes to centre cars in later units.

Built: 1999–2004.
Builder–Mech. Parts: Breda/Firema.   **Weight:** 63 + 44 + 44 + 62 tonnes.
Builder–Elec. Parts: Adtranz/Ansaldo.   **Maximum Speed:** 140 km/h.
Traction Motors: 4 x 910 kW.   **Floor Height:** 650 mm.
Accommodation: –/83 + –/146 + –/146 + –/100.
Length over Buffers: 25.895 + 26.090 + 26.090 + 25.895 m.
Wheel Arrangement: Bo-2 + 2-2 + 2-2 + 2-Bo.
EVN: 94 83 4426 001-c + 94 83 0736 002-c + 94 83 0736 001-c + 94 83 4506 001-c and so on.

Treno 01	ALe 426.001	Le 736.002	Le 736.001	ALe 506.001	R	RS
Treno 02	ALe 426.002	Le 736.004	Le 736.003	ALe 506.002	R	R	RS
Treno 03	ALe 426.003	Le 736.006	Le 736.005	ALe 506.003	R	RS
Treno 05	ALe 426.005	Le 736.010	Le 736.009	ALe 506.005	R	NF
Treno 06	ALe 426.006	Le 736.012	Le 736.011	ALe 506.006	R	NF
Treno 207	ALe 426.007	Le 736.014	Le 736.013	ALe 506.007	TR	NV
Treno 208	ALe 426.008	Le 736.016	Le 736.015	ALe 506.008	TR	NV
Treno 209	ALe 426.009	Le 736.018	Le 736.017	ALe 506.009	TR	NV
Treno 210	ALe 426.010	Le 736.020	Le 736.019	ALe 506.010	TR	NV
Treno 211	ALe 426.011	Le 736.022	Le 736.021	ALe 506.011	TR	NV
Treno 212	ALe 426.012	Le 736.024	Le 736.023	ALe 506.012	TR	NV
Treno 213	ALe 426.013	Le 736.026	Le 736.025	ALe 506.013	TR	NV
Treno 214	ALe 426.014	Le 736.028	Le 736.027	ALe 506.014	TR	NV
Treno 215	ALe 426.015	Le 736.030	Le 736.029	ALe 506.015	TR	NV
Treno 16	ALe 426.016	Le 736.032	Le 736.031	ALe 506.016	R	VR
Treno 17	ALe 426.017	Le 736.034	Le 736.033	ALe 506.017	R	TC
Treno 18	ALe 426.018	Le 736.036	Le 736.035	ALe 506.018	R	RS
Treno 19	ALe 426.019	Le 736.038	Le 736.037	ALe 506.019	R	TC
Treno 20	ALe 426.020	Le 736.040	Le 736.039	ALe 506.020	R	TC
Treno 21	ALe 426.021	Le 736.042	Le 736.041	ALe 506.021	R	RS
Treno 22	ALe 426.022	Le 736.044	Le 736.043	ALe 506.022	R	RS
Treno 23	ALe 426.023	Le 736.046	Le 736.045	ALe 506.023	R	RS
Treno 24	ALe 426.024	Le 736.048	Le 736.047	ALe 506.024	R	RS
Treno 25	ALe 426.025	Le 736.050	Le 736.049	ALe 506.025	R	VR
Treno 26	ALe 426.026	Le 736.052	Le 736.051	ALe 506.026	R	RS
Treno 27	ALe 426.027	Le 736.054	Le 736.053	ALe 506.027	R	RS
Treno 28	ALe 426.028	Le 736.056	Le 736.055	ALe 506.028	R	RS
Treno 29	ALe 426.029	Le 736.058	Le 736.057	ALe 506.029	R	RS
Treno 30	ALe 426.030	Le 736.060	Le 736.059	ALe 506.030	R	RS
Treno 31	ALe 426.031	Le 736.062	Le 736.061	ALe 506.031	R	RS
Treno 32	ALe 426.032	Le 736.064	Le 736.063	ALe 506.032	R	RS
Treno 33	ALe 426.033	Le 736.066	Le 736.065	ALe 506.033	R	RS
Treno 34	ALe 426.034	Le 736.068	Le 736.067	ALe 506.034	R	RS
Treno 35	ALe 426.035	Le 736.070	Le 736.069	ALe 506.035	R	RS
Treno 36	ALe 426.036	Le 736.072	Le 736.071	ALe 506.036	R	RS
Treno 37	ALe 426.037	Le 736.074	Le 736.073	ALe 506.037	R	TC
Treno 38	ALe 426.038	Le 736.076	Le 736.075	ALe 506.038	R	RS
Treno 39	ALe 426.039	Le 736.078	Le 736.077	ALe 506.039	R	RS

Treno 40	ALe 426.040	Le 736.080	Le 736.079	ALe 506.040	R	RS
Treno 41	ALe 426.041	Le 736.082	Le 736.081	ALe 506.041	R	RS
Treno 42	ALe 426.042	Le 736.084	Le 736.083	ALe 506.042	R	RS
Treno 43	ALe 426.043	Le 736.086	Le 736.085	ALe 506.043	R	NF
Treno 44	ALe 426.044	Le 736.088	Le 736.087	ALe 506.044	R	FI
Treno 45	ALe 426.045	Le 736.090	Le 736.089	ALe 506.045	R	VR
Treno 46	ALe 426.046	Le 736.092	Le 736.091	ALe 506.046	R	RS
Treno 47	ALe 426.047	Le 736.094	Le 736.093	ALe 506.047	R	VR
Treno 48	ALe 426.048	Le 736.096	Le 736.095	ALe 506.048	R	VR
Treno 49	ALe 426.049	Le 736.098	Le 736.097	ALe 506.049	R	RS
Treno 50	ALe 426.050	Le 736.100	Le 736.099	ALe 506.050	R	RS
Treno 51	ALe 426.051	Le 736.102	Le 736.101	ALe 506.051	R	RS
Treno 52	ALe 426.052	Le 736.104	Le 736.103	ALe 506.052	R	RS
Treno 53	ALe 426.053	Le 736.106	Le 736.105	ALe 506.053	R	RS
Treno 54	ALe 426.054	Le 736.007	Le 736.008	ALe 506.054	R	RS
Treno 55	ALe 426.055	Le 736.110	Le 736.109	ALe 506.055	R	RS
Treno 56	ALe 426.056	Le 736.112	Le 736.111	ALe 506.056	R	VR
Treno 57	ALe 426.057	Le 736.115	Le 736.114	ALe 506.057	R	NF
Treno 58	ALe 426.058	Le 736.118	Le 736.117	ALe 506.058	R	NF
Treno 59	ALe 426.059	Le 736.120	Le 736.119	ALe 506.059	R	FI
Treno 60	ALe 426.060	Le 736.122	Le 736.121	ALe 506.060	R	TC
Treno 61	ALe 426.061	Le 736.124	Le 736.123	ALe 506.061	R	VR
Treno 62	ALe 426.062	Le 736.126	Le 736.125	ALe 506.062	R	GB
Treno 63	ALe 426.066	Le 736.128	Le 736.127	ALe 506.061	R	GB
Treno 64	ALe 426.063	Le 736.132	Le 736.131	ALe 506.064	R	VR
Treno 65	ALe 426.065	Le 736.135	Le 736.113	ALe 506.065	R	NF
Treno 66	ALe 426.064	Le 736.131	Le 736.132	ALe 506.066	R	VR
Treno 67	ALe 426.067	Le 736.133	Le 736.134	ALe 506.067	R	FI
Treno 68	ALe 426.068	Le 736.113	Le 736.135	ALe 506.068	R	NF
Treno 69	ALe 426.069	Le 736.139	Le 736.140	ALe 506.069	R	RS
Treno 70	ALe 426.070	Le 736.140	Le 736.139	ALe 506.070	R	NF

▲ TAF set 87 is seen at Castelfranco Veneto on 9 September 2018.　　　**David Haydock**

Treno 71	ALe 426.071	Le 736.141	Le 736.142	ALe 506.071	R		TC
Treno 72	ALe 426.072	Le 736.143	Le 736.144	ALe 506.072	R		TC
Treno 73	ALe 426.073	Le 736.145	Le 736.146	ALe 506.073	R		TC
Treno 74	ALe 426.074	Le 736.149	Le 736.150	ALe 506.074	R		VR
Treno 75	ALe 426.075	Le 736.130	Le 736.129	ALe 506.075	R		VR
Treno 76	ALe 426.076	Le 736.151	Le 736.152	ALe 506.076	R		NF
Treno 77	ALe 426.077	Le 736.154	Le 736.153	ALe 506.077	R		VR
Treno 78	ALe 426.078	Le 736.156	Le 736.155	ALe 506.078	R		NF
Treno 79	ALe 426.079	Le 736.158	Le 736.157	ALe 506.079	R		TC
Treno 80	ALe 426.080	Le 736.160	Le 736.159	ALe 506.080	R		NF
Treno 81	ALe 426.081	Le 736.162	Le 736.161	ALe 506.081	R		TC
Treno 82	ALe 426.082	Le 736.164	Le 736.163	ALe 506.082	R		VR
Treno 83	ALe 426.083	Le 736.166	Le 736.165	ALe 506.083	R		NF
Treno 84	ALe 426.084	Le 736.168	Le 736.167	ALe 506.084	R		VR
Treno 85	ALe 426.085	Le 736.170	Le 736.169	ALe 506.085	R		VR
Treno 86	ALe 426.086	Le 736.172	Le 736.171	ALe 506.086	R		VR
Treno 87	ALe 426.087	Le 736.174	Le 736.173	ALe 506.087	R		VR
Treno 88	ALe 426.088	Le 736.176	Le 736.175	ALe 506.088	R		RS
Treno 89	ALe 426.089	Le 736.178	Le 736.177	ALe 506.089	R		VR
Treno 90	ALe 426.090	Le 736.180	Le 736.179	ALe 506.090	R		TC
Treno 91	ALe 426.091	Le 736.182	Le 736.181	ALe 506.091	R		VR
Treno 92	ALe 426.092	Le 736.184	Le 736.183	ALe 506.092	R		VR
Treno 93	ALe 426.093	Le 736.186	Le 736.185	ALe 506.093	R		RS
Treno 94	ALe 426.094	Le 736.188	Le 736.187	ALe 506.094	R		VR
Treno 95	ALe 426.095	Le 736.190	Le 736.189	ALe 506.095	R		VR
Treno 96	ALe 426.096	Le 736.192	Le 736.191	ALe 506.096	R		VR
Treno 97	ALe 426.097	Le 736.194	Le 736.193	ALe 506.097	R		VR
Treno 98	ALe 426.098	Le 736.196	Le 736.195	ALe 506.098	R		VR
Treno 99	ALe 426.099	Le 736.198	Le 736.197	ALe 506.099	R		RS

CLASS ALe 501   "MINUETTO"   3-SECTION ARTICULATED UNITS

An articulated EMU design produced in both electric and diesel (ALn 501) versions from 2004. The units are designed for low density routes. Over half the unit length and all entrances are low floor (600 mm). Units are known as ME (*Minuetto Electric*), numbered ME 1 upwards. Minuetto sets are also in service with private operators FAS, FCU, GTT and TFT. Alstom later produced a 5-car version of this design which is numbered ETR.245 and is in service with Trenord plus a 4-car version which GTT has as Class ETR.234. Units on the *Leonardo Express* service in Roma have been replaced by "*Jazz*" units.

Built: 2004–09.   **Wheel Diameter:** 850 mm.
Builder: Alstom (Savigliano).   **Weight:** 92 tonnes.
Traction Motors: Four asynchronous of 312 kW each.
Accommodation: 24/26 (4) + –/22 (16) 1T + –/50 (4).
Length over Buffers: 19.125 m + 13.650 m + 19.125 m.
Wheel Arrangement: Bo-2-2-Bo.   **Maximum Speed:** 160 km/h.
EVN: 94 83 4501 001-c + 94 83 0220 001-c + 94 83 4502 001-c and so on.

ME 1	ALe 501.001	Le 220.001	ALe 502.001	R		TV
ME 2	ALe 501.002	Le 220.002	ALe 502.002	R		PA
ME 3	ALe 501.003	Le 220.003	ALe 502.003	R		BC
ME 4	ALe 501.004	Le 220.004	ALe 502.004	R		PA
ME 5	ALe 501.005	Le 220.005	ALe 502.005	R	L	RS
ME 6	ALe 501.006	Le 220.006	ALe 502.006	R		PA
ME 7	ALe 501.007	Le 220.007	ALe 502.007	R		NF
ME 8	ALe 501.008	Le 220.008	ALe 502.008	R	L	RS
ME 9	ALe 501.009	Le 220.009	ALe 502.009	R		FI
ME 10	ALe 501.010	Le 220.010	ALe 502.010	R		PA
ME 11	ALe 501.011	Le 220.011	ALe 502.011	R		PA
ME 12	ALe 501.012	Le 220.012	ALe 502.012	R		FG
ME 13	ALe 501.013	Le 220.013	ALe 502.013	R		RC
ME 14	ALe 501.014	Le 220.014	ALe 502.014	R		FG
ME 15	ALe 501.015	Le 220.015	ALe 502.015	R		TS
ME 16	ALe 501.016	Le 220.016	ALe 502.016	R		PA

ME 17	ALe 501.017	Le 220.017	ALe 502.017	R		PA
ME 18	ALe 501.018	Le 220.018	ALe 502.018	R		SU
ME 19	ALe 501.019	Le 220.019	ALe 502.019	R		FG
ME 20	ALe 501.020	Le 220.020	ALe 502.020	R		PA
ME 21	ALe 501.021	Le 220.021	ALe 502.021	R		FG
ME 22	ALe 501.022	Le 220.022	ALe 502.022	R	L	RS
ME 23	ALe 501.023	Le 220.023	ALe 502.023	R	L	RS
ME 24	ALe 501.024	Le 220.024	ALe 502.024	R		PA
ME 25	ALe 501.025	Le 220.025	ALe 502.025	R		NF
ME 26	ALe 501.026	Le 220.026	ALe 502.026	R		RC
ME 27	ALe 501.027	Le 220.027	ALe 502.027	R		RC
ME 28	ALe 501.028	Le 220.028	ALe 502.028	R		PA
ME 29	ALe 501.029	Le 220.029	ALe 502.029	R		PA
ME 30	ALe 501.030	Le 220.030	ALe 502.030	R		TC
ME 31	ALe 501.031	Le 220.031	ALe 502.031	R		RC
ME 32	ALe 501.032	Le 220.032	ALe 502.032	R		BC
ME 33	ALe 501.033	Le 220.033	ALe 502.033	R		BC
ME 34	ALe 501.034	Le 220.034	ALe 502.034	R		PA
ME 35	ALe 501.035	Le 220.035	ALe 502.035	R		NF
ME 36	ALe 501.036	Le 220.036	ALe 502.036	R		PA
ME 37	ALe 501.037	Le 220.037	ALe 502.037	R		PA
ME 38	ALe 501.038	Le 220.038	ALe 502.038	R		FI
ME 39	ALe 501.039	Le 220.039	ALe 502.039	R		TC
ME 40	ALe 501.040	Le 220.040	ALe 502.040	R		PA
ME 41	ALe 501.041	Le 220.041	ALe 502.041	R		TS
ME 42	ALe 501.042	Le 220.042	ALe 502.042	R		SU
ME 43	ALe 501.043	Le 220.043	ALe 502.043	R		NF
ME 44	ALe 501.044	Le 220.044	ALe 502.044	R		PA
ME 45	ALe 501.045	Le 220.045	ALe 502.045	R	L	RS
ME 46	ALe 501.046	Le 220.046	ALe 502.046	R		NF
ME 47	ALe 501.047	Le 220.047	ALe 502.047	R		TC
ME 48	ALe 501.048	Le 220.048	ALe 502.048	R		TC
ME 49	ALe 501.049	Le 220.049	ALe 502.049	R		RS

▲ Both diesel and electric "Minuetti" – at Portogruaro on 11 September 2018, MD 44 with a train from Casarsa sits next to ME 061 which has arrived from Treviso. **David Haydock**

ME 50	ALe 501.050	Le 220.050	ALe 502.050	R		PA
ME 51	ALe 501.051	Le 220.051	ALe 502.051	R		CU
ME 52	ALe 501.052	Le 220.052	ALe 502.052	R		TV
ME 53	ALe 501.053	Le 220.053	ALe 502.053	R	L	RS
ME 54	ALe 501.054	Le 220.054	ALe 502.054	R		PA
ME 55	ALe 501.055	Le 220.055	ALe 502.055	R		FI
ME 56	ALe 501.056	Le 220.056	ALe 502.056	R		AN
ME 57	ALe 501.057	Le 220.057	ALe 502.057	R		NF
ME 58	ALe 501.058	Le 220.058	ALe 502.058	R		PA
ME 59	ALe 501.059	Le 220.059	ALe 502.059	R		TC
ME 60	ALe 501.060	Le 220.060	ALe 502.060	R		TS
ME 61	ALe 501.061	Le 220.061	ALe 502.061	R	L	RS
ME 62	ALe 501.062	Le 220.062	ALe 502.062	R		TC
ME 63	ALe 501.063	Le 220.063	ALe 502.063	R		TC
ME 64	ALe 501.064	Le 220.064	ALe 502.064	R		PA
ME 65	ALe 501.065	Le 220.065	ALe 502.065	R		PA
ME 66	ALe 501.066	Le 220.066	ALe 502.066	R		NF
ME 67	ALe 501.067	Le 220.067	ALe 502.067	R		CU
ME 68	ALe 501.068	Le 220.068	ALe 502.068	R		PA
ME 69	ALe 501.069	Le 220.069	ALe 502.069	R		PA
ME 70	ALe 501.070	Le 220.070	ALe 502.070	R	L	RS
ME 71	ALe 501.071	Le 220.071	ALe 502.071	R		TS
ME 72	ALe 501.072	Le 220.072	ALe 502.072	R		SU
ME 73	ALe 501.073	Le 220.073	ALe 502.073	R		PA
ME 74	ALe 501.074	Le 220.074	ALe 502.074	R		BC
ME 75	ALe 501.075	Le 220.075	ALe 502.075	R		NC
ME 76	ALe 501.076	Le 220.076	ALe 502.076	R	L	RS
ME 77	ALe 501.077	Le 220.077	ALe 502.077	R		TV
ME 78	ALe 501.078	Le 220.078	ALe 502.078	R		FI
ME 79	ALe 501.079	Le 220.079	ALe 502.079	R		TC
ME 80	ALe 501.080	Le 220.080	ALe 502.080	R		NF
ME 81	ALe 501.081	Le 220.081	ALe 502.081	R		FI
ME 82	ALe 501.082	Le 220.082	ALe 502.082	R		PA
ME 83	ALe 501.083	Le 220.083	ALe 502.083	R		PA
ME 84	ALe 501.084	Le 220.084	ALe 502.084	R		NF
ME 85	ALe 501.085	Le 220.085	ALe 502.085	R		RS
ME 86	ALe 501.086	Le 220.086	ALe 502.086	R		PA
ME 87	ALe 501.087	Le 220.087	ALe 502.087	R		AN
ME 88	ALe 501.088	Le 220.088	ALe 502.088	R		PA
ME 89	ALe 501.089	Le 220.089	ALe 502.089	R		SU
ME 90	ALe 501.090	Le 220.090	ALe 502.090	R		NC
ME 91	ALe 501.091	Le 220.091	ALe 502.091	R		TV
ME 92	ALe 501.092	Le 220.092	ALe 502.092	R		AN
ME 93	ALe 501.093	Le 220.093	ALe 502.093	R		AN
ME 94	ALe 501.094	Le 220.094	ALe 502.094	R		RS
ME 95	ALe 501.095	Le 220.095	ALe 502.095	R		PA
ME 96	ALe 501.096	Le 220.096	ALe 502.096	R		FI
ME 97	ALe 501.097	Le 220.097	ALe 502.097	R		PA
ME 98	ALe 501.098	Le 220.098	ALe 502.098	R		FI
ME 99	ALe 501.099	Le 220.099	ALe 502.099	R		PA
ME 100	ALe 501.100	Le 220.100	ALe 502.100	R		PA

TFT units. Ale 501.600; also known as ETT 21 to 24; nicknamed *"elfi"* (elves). Built 2005.

ETT 21	Ale 501.601	Le 220.601	ALe 502.601
ETT 22	Ale 501.602	Le 220.602	ALe 502.602
ETT 23	Ale 501.603	Le 220.603	ALe 502.603
ETT 24	Ale 501.604	Le 220.604	ALe 502.604

FAS units. Ale 501.700; also known as ETR/S03 01 to 04; nicknamed *"Lupetto"* (baby wolf) – the Abruzzo region is famous for its wolves. Built 2005.

01	Ale 501.701	Le 220.701	Ale 502.701
02	Ale 501.702	Le 220.702	Ale 502.702
03	Ale 501.703	Le 220.703	Ale 502.703
04	Ale 501.704	Le 220.704	Ale 502.704

GTT units. Ale 501.800; also known as Class TTR 001 to 020 (*Treno Trasporto Regionale*). Built 2009/10.

001	Ale 501.801	Le 220.801	Ale 502.801
002	Ale 501.802	Le 220.802	Ale 502.802
003	Ale 501.803	Le 220.803	Ale 502.803
004	Ale 501.804	Le 220.804	Ale 502.804
005	Ale 501.805	Le 220.805	Ale 502.805
006	Ale 501.806	Le 220.806	Ale 502.806
007	Ale 501.807	Le 220.807	Ale 502.807
008	Ale 501.808	Le 220.808	Ale 502.808
009	Ale 501.809	Le 220.809	Ale 502.809
010	Ale 501.810	Le 220.810	Ale 502.810
011	Ale 501.811	Le 220.811	Ale 502.811
012	Ale 501.812	Le 220.812	Ale 502.812
013	Ale 501.813	Le 220.813	Ale 502.813
014	Ale 501.814	Le 220.814	Ale 502.814
015	Ale 501.815	Le 220.815	Ale 502.815
016	Ale 501.816	Le 220.816	Ale 502.816
017	Ale 501.817	Le 220.817	Ale 502.817
018	Ale 501.818	Le 220.818	Ale 502.818
019	Ale 501.819	Le 220.819	Ale 502.819
020	Ale 501.820	Le 220.820	Ale 502.820

FCU units. Ale 501.900; nicknamed "*Pinturiccio*". Built 2007/8.

TRU 1	Ale 501.901	Le 220.901	Ale 502.901
TRU 2	Ale 501.902	Le 220.902	Ale 502.903
TRU 3	Ale 501.903	Le 220.903	Ale 502.903
TRY 4	Ale 501.904	Le 220.904	Ale 502.904

ETR.524   "FLIRT"   4- & 6-SECTION ARTICULATED UNITS

These are Stadler FLIRT EMUs which TILO services between the Swiss canton of Ticino and the Italian region of Lombardia, hence the branding. The units operate many services through to Como and via Mendrisio to Varese and Malpensa airport plus a few trains as far as Milano Centrale.

The units are all shown in our book "Swiss Railways" as 36 units (19 4-car 524.001 to 019 and 17 6-car 524 101 to 117) are owned by SBB and just four 4-car by FNM (ETR.524.201 to 204). In late 2018 FNM ordered a further nine 6-car units. These will be the new FLIRT 3 design so may have a different class number.

ETR.563 & 564   "CIVITY"   5-SECTION ARTICULATED UNITS

In 2010, the Friuli Venezia Giulia region of north-east Italy ordered eight *Civity* EMUs from CAF of Spain, the first in Italy to be ordered from this company. The region then ordered a further four sets which are also able to operate into Slovenia and Austria: there is an option for 22 more trains and 34 extra cars. The units are used from Trieste to Udine via Palmanova or Gorizia, Udine to Tarcento and Trieste to San Giorgio Nogaro, staffed by Trenitalia. ETR.563 sets started to operate into Slovenia in September 2018. They are maintained at Mestre depot.

Built: 2012/13; (ETR.564 2014).
Builder: CAF
Power Rating: 3210 kW.
Accommodation: 54/206.
Systems: Class 563 3000 V DC; Class 564 3000 V DC/15 kV AC 16.7 Hz.

Maximum Speed: 160 km/h.
Length: 21.50 + 16.20 + 16.20 + 16.20 + 21.50 m.
Wheel Arrangement: Bo-2-Bo-Bo-2-Bo.

Class ETR.563

ETR.563.001	TS	Città de Trieste	ETR.563.005	TS	Città de Cividale del
ETR.563.002	TS	Città de Gorizia			Friuli
ETR.563.003	TS	Città de Udine	ETR.563.006	TS	Città de Lignano
ETR.563.004	TS	Città de Acquileia			Sabbiadoro
			ETR.563.008	TS	Città de Grado

Class ETR.564

ETR.564.001	TS		ETR.564.003	TS		ETR.564.004	TS
ETR.564.002	TS						

▲ ETR.563.005 is seen at Udine on 12 September 2018.   **David Haydock**

▼ ALe 582.012 is seen near Faenza in July 2013, with a Rimini–Bologna local service.

Marco Cacozza

CLASS ALe 582   2, 3 & 4-CAR UNITS

Substantially similar to ALe 724 units, with the main exception of a redesigned front end, these are suburban units with chopper control, rheostatic and regenerative brakes. Around three-quarters of Class ALe 582 single-ended power cars are formed in 2- and 3-car units with Le 562 driving trailers. The others are formed into 4-car units comprising two ALe 582 power cars plus two Class Le 763 centre cars in the Milano area. These are now the majority and can be found mainly on orbital routes such as Lecco–Bergamo–Brescia. Can also be used with Class Le 884 trailers. The units are now sluggish and tired so are slowly being replaced and withdrawn

Class ALe 582. Motor Composite.

Built: 1987–89.
Builder–Mech. Parts: Breda Pt, 001–045; Fiore, 046–090.
Builder–Elec. Parts: Marelli/Ansaldo/Lucana.   **Wheel Diameter:** 860 mm.
Traction Motors: 4 x EXH 4046.   **Weight:** 57 tonnes.
Continuous Rating: 1218 kW.   **Length over Buffers:** 26.115 m.
Accommodation: 17/41 or –/58.   **Maximum Speed:** 140 km/h.
EVN: 94 83 4582 001-c and so on.

Multiple working within class and with Class ALe 724.

ALe 582.001	TR	N	LC	ALe 582.029	TR	N	LC	ALe 582.062	TR	N	CR
ALe 582.002	TR		LC	ALe 582.030	R		BC	ALe 582.063	TR		CR
ALe 582.003	TR	N	CR	ALe 582.031	R		PE	ALe 582.064	R		NF
ALe 582.005	TR	N	LC	ALe 582.034	TR	N	MF	ALe 582.067	R		FG
ALe 582.006	TR		CR	ALe 582.035	R		NF	ALe 582.068	TR		MF
ALe 582.009	TR	N	MF	ALe 582.038	TR		CR	ALe 582.069	TR	N	LC
ALe 582.010	TR	N	CR	ALe 582.039	TR	N	MF	ALe 582.071	R		BC
ALe 582.011	TR	N	LC	ALe 582.040	TR	N	MF	ALe 582.074	R		FG
ALe 582.012	R		FG	ALe 582.041	TR	N	MC	ALe 582.076	R		BC
ALe 582.013	TR		CR	ALe 582.042	R		BC	ALe 582.077	R		RC
ALe 582.014	TR		CR	ALe 582.043	R		PE	ALe 582.078	R		BC
ALe 582.015	TR	N	MF	ALe 582.044	TR	N	CR	ALe 582.079	R		FG
ALe 582.016	TR	N	CR	ALe 582.046	TR	N	CR	ALe 582.080	TR	N	CR
ALe 582.017	TR	N	CR	ALe 582.047	TR	N	CR	ALe 582.082	TR		MF
ALe 582.018	TR	N	LC	ALe 582.049	R		BC	ALe 582.083	TR		MF
ALe 582.019	TR	N	LC	ALe 582.051	TR		LC	ALe 582.084	TR		CR
ALe 582.020	TR	N	CR	ALe 582.053	TR	N	MF	ALe 582.085	R		NF
ALe 582.021	TR	N	LC	ALe 582.056	TR		CR	ALe 582.086	TR		CR
ALe 582.023	TR		CR	ALe 582.057	TR		CR	ALe 582.087	TR		CR
ALe 582.024	TR		CR	ALe 582.058	R		PE	ALe 582.088	TR	N	CR
ALe 582.026	TR		MF	ALe 582.059	TR	N	CR	ALe 582.089	TR		CR
ALe 582.027	R		RC	ALe 582.060	TR		LC	ALe 582.090	R		FG
ALe 582.028	TR		CR	ALe 582.061	TR		MF				

Name:

ALe 582.005   Maloja

Class Le 562. Driving Trailer Second.

Built: 1987–89.   **Wheel Diameter:** 860 mm.
Builder–Mech. Parts: Stanga, 001–045; Fiore, 046–068.
Builder–Elec. Parts: Ansaldo.   **Weight:** 37 tonnes.
Accommodation: –/56 2T.   **Maximum Speed:** 140 km/h.
Length over Buffers: 26.115 m.
EVN: 94 83 8562 001-c and so on.

Le 562.002	TR		CR	Le 562.014	TR	N	LC	Le 562.023	TR		MF
Le 562.003	R		FG	Le 562.015	R		MF	Le 562.024	TR	N	CR
Le 562.005	TR		CR	Le 562.016	TR	N	CR	Le 562.025	TR	N	MF
Le 562.006	TR		CR	Le 562.017	TR		CR	Le 562.028	TR	N	CR
Le 562.008	TR	N	CR	Le 562.018	TR		MF	Le 562.029	TR		LC
Le 562.010	TR		CR	Le 562.019	TR	N	LC	Le 562.031	TR	N	MF
Le 562.011	TR		CR	Le 562.020	TR	N	CR	Le 562.033	TR		CR
Le 562.012	TR		MF	Le 562.021	TR	N	CR	Le 562.035	TR		CR
Le 562.013	TR	N	LC	Le 562.022	TR	N	LC	Le 562.036	R		PE

Unit		N	Code	Unit		N	Code	Unit		N	Code
Le 562.037	TR		LC	Le 562.049	TR		LC	Le 562.059	R		FG
Le 562.038	TR		CR	Le 562.050	TR	N	LC	Le 562.060	TR	N	CR
Le 562.039	R		FG	Le 562.051	R		FG	Le 562.061	R		FG
Le 562.040	TR	N	LC	Le 562.052	TR	N	LC	Le 562.062	TR		CR
Le 562.041	TR	N	LC	Le 562.053	TR	N	CR	Le 562.063	R		FG
Le 562.042	TR	N	MF	Le 562.054	R		NF	Le 562.064	R		BC
Le 562.043	TR	N	LC	Le 562.055	R		FG	Le 562.065	R		BC
Le 562.044	TR	N	CR	Le 562.056	TR	N	CR	Le 562.066	TR	N	CR
Le 562.045	TR	N	MF	Le 562.057	R		BC	Le 562.067	TR		CR
Le 562.046	TR	N	LC	Le 562.058	R		BC	Le 562.068	TR	N	CR
Le 562.047	R		PE								

Class Le 763. Trailer Second.

Built: 1987–91.
Builder–Mech. Parts: Stanga, 101–155; Fiore, 156–163.
Accommodation: –/78.
Length over Buffers: 25.78 m.
EVN: 94 83 0763 101-c and so on.

Wheel Diameter: 860 mm.
Weight: 33 tonnes.
Maximum Speed: 140 km/h.

Unit		N	Code	Unit		N	Code	Unit		N	Code
Le 763.101	R		NF	Le 763.126	R		CR	Le 763.144	TR		CR
Le 763.102	TR		CR	Le 763.127	R		FG	Le 763.146	R		BC
Le 763.103	TR		MF	Le 763.128	TR	N	CR	Le 763.147	TR	N	MF
Le 763.104	R		PA	Le 763.129	TR	N	CR	Le 763.148	TR	N	CR
Le 763.105	TR	N	MF	Le 763.130	R		PE	Le 763.149	R		PE
Le 763.106	R		FG	Le 763.131	TR		LC	Le 763.150	TR	N	CR
Le 763.107	TR	N	MF	Le 763.132	TR	N	CR	Le 763.151	TR	N	CR
Le 763.108	TR		CR	Le 763.133	TR		CR	Le 763.152	TR	N	MF
Le 763.109	TR	N	CR	Le 763.134	TR	N	MF	Le 763.153	R		FG
Le 763.111	TR		CR	Le 763.135	R		FG	Le 763.154	R		BC
Le 763.115	TR		CR	Le 763.136	TR		CR	Le 763.156	TR	N	CR
Le 763.116	TR		LC	Le 763.137	R		BC	Le 763.157	TR		CR
Le 763.117	TR		MF	Le 763.138	TR	N	LC	Le 763.158	R		CR
Le 763.119	TR		LC	Le 763.139	TR	N	CR	Le 763.159	R		BC
Le 763.121	TR	N	LC	Le 763.140	R		PE	Le 763.160	R		CR
Le 763.122	R		NF	Le 763.141	R		BC	Le 763.161	R		BC
Le 763.123	TR		LC	Le 763.142	R		CR	Le 763.162	TR		CR
Le 763.124	TR	N	CR	Le 763.143	R		BC	Le 763.163	TR		CR
Le 763.125	TR	N	MF								

CLASS ALe 642   2, 3 & 4-CAR UNITS

Almost identical to ALe 582, Le 562 and Le 763, with only minor differences in electrical circuiting. 20 ALe 642 single end power cars operate as 2-car or 3-car units with Le 682 driving trailers. 20 4-car units are formed with two power cars plus two Le 764 centre cars. Occasional 5-car units have been spotted. Used on less-heavily-used suburban services.

Multiple working within class and with Class ALe 724.

Class Ale 642. Motor Second. EVN: 94 83 4642 001-c and so on.

Built: 1991–92.
Builder–Mech. Parts: Breda Pt, 001–030; Fiore, 031–060.
Builder–Elec. Parts: Ansaldo/Met. Lucana.
Traction Motors: 4 x EXH 4046.
Continuous Rating: 1218 kW.
Accommodation: –/64.

Wheel Diameter: 860 mm.
Weight: 57 tonnes.
Length over Buffers: 26.115 m.
Maximum Speed: 140 km/h.

Unit		Code	Unit		Code	Unit		Code
ALe 642.001	R	BC	ALe 642.009	R	BC	ALe 642.017	R	PI
ALe 642.002	R	BC	ALe 642.010	R	BC	ALe 642.018	R	BC
ALe 642.003	R	BC	ALe 642.011	R	BC	ALe 642.019	R	BC
ALe 642.004	R	BC	ALe 642.012	R	BC	ALe 642.020	R	PI
ALe 642.005	R	BC	ALe 642.013	R	BC	ALe 642.021	R	PI
ALe 642.006	R	BC	ALe 642.014	R	BC	ALe 642.022	R	BC
ALe 642.007	R	BC	ALe 642.015	R	BC	ALe 642.023	R	PI
ALe 642.008	R	BC	ALe 642.016	R	BC	ALe 642.024	R	BC

ALe 642.025	R	BC	ALe 642.037	R	PI	ALe 642.049	R	PI
ALe 642.026	R	BC	ALe 642.038	R	PI	ALe 642.050	R	PI
ALe 642.027	R	BC	ALe 642.039	R	PI	ALe 642.051	R	PI
ALe 642.028	R	BC	ALe 642.040	R	PI	ALe 642.052	R	PI
ALe 642.029	R	BC	ALe 642.041	R	PI	ALe 642.053	R	PI
ALe 642.030	R	BC	ALe 642.042	R	PI	ALe 642.054	R	PI
ALe 642.031	R	PI	ALe 642.043	R	PI	ALe 642.055	R	PI
ALe 642.032	R	BC	ALe 642.044	R	PI	ALe 642.056	R	PI
ALe 642.033	R	PI	ALe 642.045	R	PI	ALe 642.057	R	PI
ALe 642.034	R	PI	ALe 642.046	R	PI	ALe 642.058	R	PI
ALe 642.035	R	PI	ALe 642.047	R	PI	ALe 642.059	R	PI
ALe 642.036	R	PI	ALe 642.048	R	PI	ALe 642.060	R	PI

Class Le 682. Driving Trailer Second. EVN: 94 83 8682 001-c and so on.

Built: 1991–93, 001–020; 1994/95, 021–024.
Builder–Mech. Parts: Stanga.
Accommodation: –/68.
Wheel Diameter: 860 mm.
Weight: 37 tonnes.
Length over Buffers: 26.115 m.
Maximum Speed: 140 km/h.

Le 682.001	R	BC	Le 682.009	R	BC	Le 682.017	R	PI
Le 682.002	R	PI	Le 682.010	R	BC	Le 682.018	R	PI
Le 682.003	R	PI	Le 682.011	R	PI	Le 682.019	R	PI
Le 682.004	R	PI	Le 682.012	R	PI	Le 682.020	R	PI
Le 682.005	R	PI	Le 682.013	R	PI	Le 682.021	R	PI
Le 682.006	R	BC	Le 682.014	R	BC	Le 682.022	R	PI
Le 682.007	R	BC	Le 682.015	R	PI	Le 682.023	R	PI
Le 682.008	R	BC	Le 682.016	R	PI	Le 682.024	R	PI

Class Le 764. Trailer Second. EVN: 94 83 0764 101-c and so on.

Details as Class Le 763 except:

Built: 1991–93, 101–140; 1995, 141–148.
Builder–Mech. Parts: Fiore, 101–130, 141–148; Stanga, 131–140.

Le 764.101	R	BC	Le 764.117	R	PI	Le 764.133	R	BC
Le 764.102	R	PI	Le 764.118	R	BC	Le 764.134	R	BC
Le 764.103	R	PI	Le 764.119	R	PI	Le 764.135	R	BC
Le 764.104	R	BC	Le 764.120	R	PI	Le 764.136	R	BC
Le 764.105	R	BC	Le 764.121	R	PI	Le 764.137	R	PI
Le 764.106	R	BC	Le 764.122	R	PI	Le 764.138	R	PI
Le 764.107	R	BC	Le 764.123	R	PI	Le 764.139	R	BC
Le 764.108	R	BC	Le 764.124	R	PI	Le 764.140	R	PI
Le 764.109	R	BC	Le 764.125	R	PI	Le 764.141	R	BC
Le 764.110	R	BC	Le 764.126	R	PI	Le 764.142	R	BC
Le 764.111	R	BC	Le 764.127	R	PI	Le 764.143	R	PI
Le 764.112	R	BC	Le 764.128	R	PI	Le 764.144	R	PI
Le 764.113	R	BC	Le 764.129	R	BC	Le 764.145	R	PI
Le 764.114	R	PI	Le 764.130	R	BC	Le 764.146	R	PI
Le 764.115	R	PI	Le 764.131	R	BC	Le 764.147	R	PI
Le 764.116	R	PI	Le 764.132	R	BC	Le 764.148	R	PI

Class Le 764.2 Trailer Second. EVN: 94 83 0764 201-c and so on.

Built: 1978–81.
Builder–Mech. Parts: Breda Pt/AMT.
Accommodation: –/76.
Length over Buffers: 24.40 m.
Wheel Diameter: 860 mm.
Weight: 30 tonnes.
Maximum Speed: 140 km/h.

Le 764.201	R	BC	Le 764.208	R	BC	Le 764.212	R	BC
Le 764.203	R	BC	Le 764.210	R	BC			

▲ ALe 642.032 is pictured near Bologna in May 2016 with a Ferrara–Bologna train. **Marco Cacozza**

▼ TSR set R5-055 is seen at Lodi on 7 April 2018. On the right is TPER ETR.350.011 which is operating the daily TPER Bologna–Milano service. **David Haydock**

CLASS EB 711   "TSR"   3-, 5- & 6-CAR DOUBLE-DECK UNITS

These EMUs known as *Treno Servizi Regionali* (TSR), to a completely different design to TAF sets (see below), started to be delivered by a consortium led by AnsaldoBreda from August 2006. Following an initial order for 18 3-car and nine 5-car sets, many more were ordered and formed mainly into 3-car and 5-car sets – Milano Nord Cadorna can only fit 8-car trains in its platforms. All cars are powered with one motor bogie per car. Formations have changed frequently and may continue to do so. Set numbers are prefixed with the number of cars – R3 for 3-car, R5 for 5-car and R6 for 6-car sets. Most units work cross-Milano services via the *Passante* tunnel.

Built: 2006–12.
Builder: AnsaldoBreda.
Accommodation: –/91 + –/122 (+ –/122 + –/122 + –/122) + –/91.
Length over Buffers: 26.46 m + 26.025 m (+ 26.025 m + 26.025 m + 26.025 m) + 26.46 m.
Weight: 55 tonnes + 51 tonnes (+ 51 tonnes + 51 tonnes + 51 tonnes) + 55 tonnes.
Continuous Rating: 720 kW + 720 kW (+ 720 kW + 720 kW + 720 kW) + 720 kW.

Set no.

R3 001	711 053	710 027			711 054	MF
R3 002	711 060	710 045			711 067	MF
R3 003	711 055	710 028			711 056	NV
R3 004	711 057	710 029			711 058	NV
R3 005	711 007	710 050			711 064	NV
R3 006	711 059	710 030			711 061	NV
R3 007	711 009	710 046			711 014	NV
R3 008	711 062	710 035			711 063	MF
R3 009	711 012	710 010			711 013	MF
R5 010	711 065	710 036	710 037	710 038	711 066	MF
R3 011	711 016	710 009			711 017	MF
R3 012	711 006	710 032			711 008	NV
R3 013	711 015	710 012			711 018	NV
R5 014	711 021	710 033	710 040	710 042	711 023	MF
R3 015	711 020	710 015			711 022	MF
R5 016	711 033	710 047	710 048	710 049	711 034	MF
R3 017	711 001	710 001			711 003	MF
R5 018	711 030	710 003	710 004	710 051	711 032	MF
R3 019	711 019	710 034			711 068	NV
R3 020	711 089	710 054			711 118	MF
R5 021	711 069	710 007	710 008	710 011	711 071	MF
R3 022	711 010	710 031			711 011	NV
R3 023	711 024	710 044			711 085	MF
R5 024	711 039	710 013	710 014	710 017	711 073	MF
R5 025	711 037	710 020	710 021	710 061	711 041	MF
R5 026	711 040	710 063	710 065	710 067	711 042	MF
R5 027	711 044	710 129	710 070	710 166	711 045	NV
R3 028	711 086	710 002			711 087	MF
R3 029	711 005	710 043			711 025	NV
R3 030	711 028	710 041			711 088	MF
R3 031	711 026	710 039			711 029	NV
R3 032	711 027	710 052			711 031	NV
R6 033	711 043	710 023	710 110	710 022	710 074	711 046	NV
R5 034	711 075	710 068	710 071	710 073	711 077	NV
R5 035	711 078	710 026	710 062	710 064	711 079	NV
R3 036	711 036	710 019			711 136	NV
R3 037	711 072	710 016			711 074	MF
R5 038	711 051	710 075	710 069	710 025	711 052	MF
R3 039	711 081	710 024			711 082	MF
R6 040	711 083	710 131	710 132	710 170	710 135	711 084	NV
R6 041	711 131	710 134	710 133	710 180	710 178	711 133	NV
R5 042	711 135	710 130	710 179	710 005	711 035	MF
R3 043	711 038	710 018			711 070	MF
R5 044	711 137	710 167	710 168	710 136	711 139	MF
R5 045	711 090	710 060	710 059	710 057	711 091	MF
R5 046	711 092	710 082	710 053	710 006	711 093	MF

R5 047	711 004	710 055	710 083	710 077		711 095	MF
R5 048	711 094	710 058	710 081	710 084		711 096	MF
R5 049	711 097	710 056	710 085	710 079		711 098	MF
R5 050	711 099	710 086	710 088	710 087		711 100	NV
R5 051	711 101	710 078	710 089	710 090		711 102	MF
R3 052	711 048	710 125				711 049	MF
R5 053	711 103	710 080	710 081	710 092		711 104	MF
R3 054	711 047	710 106				711 050	MF
R5 055	711 105	710 094	710 095	710 096		711 107	NV
R5 056	711 145	710 172	710 173	710 174		711 146	MF
R5 057	711 106	710 097	710 098	710 099		711 108	NV
R6 058	711 143	710 169	710 161	710 175	710 162	711 144	NV
R5 059	711 109	710 101	710 093	710 100		711 110	NV
R6 060	711 138	710 148	710 141	710 138	710 137	711 140	MF
R5 061	711 111	710 103	710 102	710 104		711 112	MF
R6 062	711 113	710 105	710 107	710 066	710 109	711 114	NV
R5 063	711 116	710 111	710 120	710 112		711 117	NV
R5 064	711 121	710 115	710 117	710 118		711 122	MF
R5 065	711 132	710 126	710 165	710 177		711 134	NV
R5 066	711 141	710 163	710 164	710 171		711 142	NV
R6 067	711 147	710 143	710 139	710 142	710 144	711 148	MF
R6 068	711 163	710 190	710 201	710 200	710 194	711 166	NV
R5 069	711 164	710 186	710 187	710 188		711 165	MF
R5 070	711 162	710 183	710 184	710 185		711 161	MF
R5 071	711 123	710 108	710 116	710 121		711 124	MF
R5 072	711 127	710 119	710 124	710 128		711 128	MF
R5 073	711 129	710 122	710 127	710 123		711 130	MF
R3 074	711 115	710 114				711 125	NV
R3 075	711 119	710 113				711 120	NV
R3 076	711 002	710 176				711 126	NV
R6 077	711 159	710 189	710 191	710 198	710 182	711 160	NV
R3 078	711 076	710 076				711 080	NV
R6 079	711 157	710 204	710 193	710 202	710 203	711 158	NV
R5 080	711 167	710 192	710 195	710 197		711 168	MF
R4 081	711 169	710 199	710 196			711 172	NV
R4 082	711 170	710 210	710 209			711 173	NV
R4 083	711 149	710 146	710 145			711 151	NV
R4 084	711 150	710 147	710 149			711 152	NV
R4 085	711 154	710 150	710 140			711 155	NV
R6 086	711 156	710 151	710 152			711 153	NV
R6 087	711 180	710 155	710 157	710 158	710 159	711 177	NV
R6 088	711 178	710 212	710 205	710 206	710 207	711 179	NV
R6 089	711 181	710 160	710 219	710 222	710 223	711 182	NV
R6 090	711 174	710 208	710 215	710 216	710 217	711 171	NV
R6 091	711 188	710 224	710 226	710 225	710 229	711 183	NV
R6 092	711 175	710 176	710 211	710 213	710 220	711 176	NV
R6 093	711 185	710 225	710 227	710 231	710 234	711 186	NV
R6 094	711 184	710 233	710 235	710 230	710 232	711 187	NV
R4 095	711 189	710 214	710 218			711 190	NV
R4 096	711 197	710 241	710 242			711 198	NV
R4 097	711 191	710 221	710 236			711 192	NV
R4 098	711 199	710 243	710 244			711 200	NV
R4 099	711 193	710 237	710 238			711 194	NV
R4 100	711 201	710 245	710 246			711 202	NV
R4 101	711 195	710 239	710 240			711 196	NV
R4 102	711 203	710 247	710 248			711 204	NV
R4 103	711 205	710 249	710 250			711 206	NV
R4 104	711 207	710 251	710 252			711 208	NV

CLASS ALe 724   4-CAR UNITS

Suburban units developed from prototypes ALe 644 and ALe 804 but with many differences, the most obvious being completely different front ends. ALe 724.001–60 are formed with two ALe 724 plus two Le 884 centre cars whilst ALe 724.061–89 operate with an Le 724 driving trailer and two Le 884 centre cars. ALe 724.001–40 and Le 884.107–146 have fewer plastic seats for operating the Napoli–Villa Literno "metro" service. Other units with two power cars work mountainous lines in the Torino area. Units are now being withdrawn and none has been overhauled since 2014.

Class ALe 724. Motor Second. EVN: 94 83 4724 001-c and so on.

Built: 1983–85.
Builder–Mech. Parts: Breda Pt, 001–045; Fiore, 046–089.
Builder–Elec.Parts: Marelli/Ansaldo/Lucana.   **Wheel Diameter:** 860 mm.
Traction Motors: 4 x EXH 4046.   **Weight:** 55 tonnes (* 54 tonnes).
Continuous Rating: 1218 kW.   **Length over Buffers:** 24.78 m.
Accommodation: –/72 (* –/38).   **Maximum Speed:** 140 km/h.

Multiple working within class and with Class ALe 582.

ALe 724.001	R	*	NF	ALe 724.039	R	*	NF	ALe 724.063	R	NF
ALe 724.005	R	*	NF	ALe 724.040	R	*	NF	ALe 724.064	R	TC
ALe 724.006	R	*	NF	ALe 724.041	R		TC	ALe 724.065	R	TC
ALe 724.007	R	*	NF	ALe 724.042	R		TC	ALe 724.066	R	TC
ALe 724.011	R	*	NF	ALe 724.043	R		TC	ALe 724.067	R	NF
ALe 724.012	R	*	NF	ALe 724.045	R		TC	ALe 724.068	R	NF
ALe 724.014	R	*	NF	ALe 724.046	R		TC	ALe 724.071	R	NF
ALe 724.016	R	*	NF	ALe 724.047	R		NF	ALe 724.072	R	NF
ALe 724.017	R	*	NF	ALe 724.048	R		NF	ALe 724.073	R	TC
ALe 724.018	R	*	NF	ALe 724.049	R		NF	ALe 724.074	R	TC
ALe 724.020	R	*	NF	ALe 724.052	R		TC	ALe 724.077	R	TC
ALe 724.029	R	*	NF	ALe 724.053	R		TC	ALe 724.080	R	NF
ALe 724.031	R	*	NF	ALe 724.054	R		TC	ALe 724.082	R	NF
ALe 724.032	R	*	NF	ALe 724.055	R		TC	ALe 724.084	R	TC
ALe 724.033	R	*	NF	ALe 724.058	R		TC	ALe 724.086	R	TC
ALe 724.034	R	*	NF	ALe 724.060	R		NF	ALe 724.087	R	TC
ALe 724.036	R	*	NF	ALe 724.061	R		TC	ALe 724.089	R	NF
ALe 724.037	R	*	NF	ALe 724.062	R		NF			

Class Le 724.0. Driving Trailer Second. EVN: 94 83 8724 001-c and so on.

Built: 1982/83.
Builder–Mech. Parts: Stanga.   **Wheel Diameter:** 860 mm.
Accommodation: –/72 or –/80 (refurbished).   **Weight:** 31 tonnes.
Length over Buffers: 24.78 m.   **Maximum Speed:** 140 km/h.

Le 724.001	R	TC	Le 724.013	R	TC	Le 724.020	R	TC
Le 724.005	R	TC	Le 724.014	R	TC	Le 724.021	R	TC
Le 724.008	R	TC	Le 724.015	R	TC	Le 724.022	R	TC
Le 724.009	R	TC	Le 724.017	R	TC	Le 724.024	R	TC
Le 724.010	R	TC	Le 724.018	R	TC	Le 724.028	R	TC
Le 724.012	R	NF	Le 724.019	R	TC	Le 724.029	R	TC

Class Le 884. Trailer Second. EVN: 94 83 0884 108-c and so on.

Some used with Class ALe 582 in the Milano area.

Built: 1982–85.   **Wheel Diameter:** 860 mm.
Builder–Mech. Parts: Breda Pt, 108–165; Fiore, 168–226.
Accommodation: –/88 (* –/44) 1T.   **Weight:** 30 tonnes.
Length over Buffers: 24.40 m.   **Maximum Speed:** 140 km/h.

Le 884.108	R	*	NF	Le 884.119	R	*	NF	Le 884.128	R	*	NF
Le 884.110	R	*	NF	Le 884.120	R	*	NF	Le 884.129	R	*	NF
Le 884.112	R	*	NF	Le 884.121	R	*	NF	Le 884.130	R	*	NF
Le 884.113	R	*	NF	Le 884.122	R	*	NF	Le 884.132	R	*	NF
Le 884.114	R	*	NF	Le 884.125	R	*	NF	Le 884.134	R	*	NF
Le 884.117	R	*	NF	Le 884.126	R	*	NF	Le 884.135	R	*	NF
Le 884.118	R	*	NF	Le 884.127	R	*	NF	Le 884.138	R	*	NF

Le 884.140	R	*	NF	Le 884.170	TR	CR	Le 884.198	R	NF
Le 884.141	R	*	NF	Le 884.173	TR	LC	Le 884.199	R	TC
Le 884.143	R	*	NF	Le 884.175	TR	CR	Le 884.200	R	TC
Le 884.144	R	*	NF	Le 884.176	R	TC	Le 884.202	R	NF
Le 884.145	R	*	NF	Le 884.177	TR	LC	Le 884.203	R	NF
Le 884.149	TR		CR	Le 884.179	R	TC	Le 884.204	R	TC
Le 884.150	R		TC	Le 884.180	R	NF	Le 884.205	R	NF
Le 884.151	TR		CR	Le 884.181	R	TC	Le 884.208	R	TC
Le 884.153	TR		CR	Le 884.182	R	TC	Le 884.209	R	NF
Le 884.155	TR		CR	Le 884.183	R	TC	Le 884.210	TR	CR
Le 884.156	TR		CR	Le 884.184	R	NF	Le 884.211	R	NF
Le 884.157	TR		LC	Le 884.185	R	TC	Le 884.212	R	TC
Le 884.159	TR		CR	Le 884.186	TR	CR	Le 884.213	R	NF
Le 884.160	TR		LC	Le 884.187	R	TC	Le 884.215	R	TC
Le 884.161	TR		LC	Le 884.188	R	TC	Le 884.216	R	NF
Le 884.162	TR		MF	Le 884.189	R	TC	Le 884.218	R	TC
Le 884.163	TR		LC	Le 884.191	R	NF	Le 884.220	TR	CR
Le 884.164	TR		CR	Le 884.193	R	NF	Le 884.222	R	TC
Le 884.165	R		TC	Le 884.194	R	TC	Le 884.225	R	TC
Le 884.168	TR		CR	Le 884.195	R	NF	Le 884.226	R	NF
Le 884.169	TR		CR	Le 884.197	R	TC			

▲ ALe 724.007 is seen at Napoli Mergellina in May 2016 with a Napoli Margellina–Torre Annunziata regional service.
Antonio Bertagnin

1.5. HIGH SPEED ELECTRIC MULTIPLE UNITS

Italy has a long tradition of high-speed electric train operation. In the 1970s, Italy started to test the concept of tilting trains. Having stuck at it for almost 20 years, the pay off came with the start of services using Pendolino sets. Fiat (now Alstom), which developed the system, were able to export tilt technology although competitors have now developed their own systems. The last ETR.450 sets, the first Pendolinos built from 1987, were withdrawn in 2017. At the time of writing, major changes were expected to high speed train workings following the completion of ETR.400 deliveries and the purchase of the ETR.700s.

The ETR *"appellation"* is now being applied to non-high speed EMUs.

CLASS ETR.400   *"FRECCIAROSSA 1000"*   8-CAR UNITS

ETR.400 is Italy's most recent high speed train and entered service in 2015. The train, known by Bombardier as *"Zefiro"*, is designed for 360 km/h operation but Trenitalia's plans to run at more than 300 km/h were dropped as too expensive for the benefit offered in May 2018. In addition to replacing ETR.500 sets with much better acceleration, the new trains were aimed at countering NTV's modern Alstom trains and allowing Trenitalia to operate into or within other countries – even on Paris–Brussels. Unlike ETR.500 the new trains have distributed power, equipment being distributed through the train, and ETR.400s are more flexible – able to operate in multiple. Bogies have Bombardier's Active Lateral Suspension which improves comfort through curves. Accommodation is in four classes: Executive, Business, Premium and Standard.

The first 50 sets are, in principle, for Italy only. However, in 2018 sets 09 and 25 were equipped to operate in France as Trenitalia has plans to operate there. In early 2019 Trenitalia was considering buying ten more sets for domestic services, plus four for France and RFI was looking at acquiring one set for infrastructure testing.

There has been some confusion in class numbering for the train – announced as ETR.1000, the train has the branding *"Frecciarossa 1000"* but numbering is in the ETR.400 series. All trains are in *Frecciarossa* (red arrow) livery of red, with a black window band and pale grey lining.

The trains are based at Napoli but are also maintained at Milano Martesana.

Built: 2013–18.
Wheel Arrangement: Bo-Bo + 2-2 + Bo-Bo + 2-2 + 2-2 + Bo-Bo + 2-2 + Bo-Bo.
Length: 26.31 m + 24.90 m x 6 + 26.31 m = 202.02 m in total.
Maximum Rating: 9800 kW under 25 kV AC; 6700 kW under 300 V DC; 3050 kW under 1500 V DC.
Systems: 1500/3000 V DC, 25 kV AC 50 Hz.
Accommodation: 12/– 1T + –/50 2T + 19/– (2) Bar 1TD + 76/– 2T + –/92 2T + –/92 2T + –/68 1T.
Maximum Speed: 360 km/h.   **Total Weight:** 454 tonnes.
Signalling: ETCS Level 2, SCMT.
Coach Designation/Classes: DM1 Executive + TT2 Business + M3 Business/Bistro + T4 Premium + T5 Standard + M6 Standard + TT7 Standard + DM8 Standard.
EVN: 93 83 3400 101-c + 0400 201-c + 3400 301-c + 0400 401-c + 0400 501-c + 3400 601-c + 0400 701-c + 3400 801-c and so on.

E   Equipped with TVM cab signalling and KVB safety system to allow tests in France.

Set

01	ETR.400.101	to	ETR.400.801		NC	17	ETR.400.117	to	ETR.400.817	NC
02	ETR.400.102	to	ETR.400.802		NC	18	ETR.400.118	to	ETR.400.818	NC
03	ETR.400.103	to	ETR.400.803		NC	19	ETR.400.119	to	ETR.400.819	NC
04	ETR.400.104	to	ETR.400.804		NC	20	ETR.400.120	to	ETR.400.820	NC
05	ETR.400.105	to	ETR.400.805		NC	21	ETR.400.121	to	ETR.400.821	NC
06	ETR.400.106	to	ETR.400.806		NC	22	ETR.400.122	to	ETR.400.822	NC
07	ETR.400.107	to	ETR.400.807		NC	23	ETR.400.123	to	ETR.400.823	NC
08	ETR.400.108	to	ETR.400.808		NC	24	ETR.400.124	to	ETR.400.824	NC
09	ETR.400.109	to	ETR.400.809	E	NC	25	ETR.400.125	to	ETR.400.825	E NC
10	ETR.400.110	to	ETR.400.810		NC	26	ETR.400.126	to	ETR.400.826	NC
11	ETR.400.111	to	ETR.400.811		NC	27	ETR.400.127	to	ETR.400.827	NC
12	ETR.400.112	to	ETR.400.812		NC	28	ETR.400.128	to	ETR.400.828	NC
13	ETR.400.113	to	ETR.400.813		NC	29	ETR.400.129	to	ETR.400.829	NC
14	ETR.400.114	to	ETR.400.814		NC	30	ETR.400.130	to	ETR.400.830	NC
15	ETR.400.115	to	ETR.400.815		NC	31	ETR.400.131	to	ETR.400.831	NC
16	ETR.400.116	to	ETR.400.816		NC	32	ETR.400.132	to	ETR.400.832	NC

▲ ETR.400 set 49 whizzes through Milano Lambrate on 6 April 2018 with the 14.30 Milano Centrale–Roma Termini. **David Haydock**

▼ ETR.460 set 30 is seen stabled at Milano Squadra Riala on 6 April 2018. **David Haydock**

33	ETR.400.133	to	ETR.400.833	NC	42	ETR.400.142	to	ETR.400.842	NC
34	ETR.400.134	to	ETR.400.834	NC	43	ETR.400.143	to	ETR.400.843	NC
35	ETR.400.135	to	ETR.400.835	NC	44	ETR.400.144	to	ETR.400.844	NC
36	ETR.400.136	to	ETR.400.836	NC	45	ETR.400.145	to	ETR.400.845	NC
37	ETR.400.137	to	ETR.400.837	NC	46	ETR.400.146	to	ETR.400.846	NC
38	ETR.400.138	to	ETR.400.838	NC	47	ETR.400.147	to	ETR.400.847	NC
39	ETR.400.139	to	ETR.400.839	NC	48	ETR.400.148	to	ETR.400.848	NC
40	ETR.400.140	to	ETR.400.840	NC	49	ETR.400.149	to	ETR.400.849	NC
41	ETR.400.141	to	ETR.400.841	NC	50	ETR.400.150	to	ETR.400.850	NC

CLASSES ETR.460, ETR.463 & ETR.485   PENDOLINO   9-CAR TILTING UNITS

A development of Class ETR.450 (the first Pendolino trains, now all withdrawn) with redesigned front end and seating, asynchronous three-phase motors and extruded aluminium bodies. More importantly, the tilt system is completely underneath the chassis whereas the ETR.450 system included hydraulic rams within the body, taking up large quantities of space at each end of the coaches. Each set consists of six power cars grouped in pairs plus three trailers. Unlike ETR.450, the driving power cars have pantographs.

ETR.460 are 3000 V DC only whilst ETR.485 are almost identical but were additionally pre-equipped for 25 kV AC as Class ETR.480, then converted for 25 kV operation and re-classified as ETR.485.

ETR.460 sets 21, 27 and 28 were equipped to operate under 1500 V DC for services to Lyon in France but these ceased in 2003. These sets were modified with a lower gear ratio and 200 km/h maximum speed for better tractive effort on the route through the Alps. They have now been converted back to 250 km/h but remain capable of 1500 V DC operation and were renumbered ETR.463 in early 2006. Set 29 was severely damaged in an accident at Piacenza.

ETR.460/463 are now used on *Frecciabianca* services, mainly Roma–Genova–Torino/Milano and Roma–Ravenna. ETR.485 are mainly used on *Frecciargento* services from Roma to Foggia, Bari and Lecce plus Reggio di Calabria, Bergamo and Mantova and are finished in *Frecciargento* livery of silver, black and red. ETR.485 sets 32, 35, 36, 37 and 42 were malformed at the time of writing – formations have changed after fires and accidents. ETR.485 set 31 was tested in Greece during 2018 as a precursor to sending the ETR.470 sets there.

In December 2016 the tilt mechanism on ETR.460/463 was de-activated due to a lack of spares. They are likely to be withdrawn soon but ETR.485 sets will be modernised.

Built: 1995/96, ETR.460; 1997/98, ETR.485.
Builder–Mechanical Parts: Fiat.   **Builder–Electrical Parts:** Parizzi.
Wheel Arrangement: 1A-A1 + 1A-A1 + 2-2 + 2-2 + 1A-A1 + 1A-A1 + 2-2 + 1A-A1 + 1A-A1.
Continuous Rating: 5880 kW (3920 kW under 1500 V DC for ETR.463).
Traction Motors: 12 x 490 kW.   **Wheel Diameter:** 890 mm.
Weight: 452 tonnes, ETR.460 & 463; 454 tonnes, ETR.485.
Maximum Speed: 250 km/h.   **Overall Length:** 236.60 m.
Accommodation: 137/341 plus 2 disabled and 23 in restaurant car.

Class ETR.460.000 & ETR.485.000. Driving Motor First. Type BAC 1. With pantographs.

Length over Couplers: 27.20 m.   **Accommodation:** 49/– 1T (48/– 1T in ETR.463).

Class ETR.460.050 & ETR.485.050. Driving Motor Second. Type BAC 2. Details as ETR.460.000 except:

Accommodation: –/66 1T (–/63 in ETR.463).

Class ETR.460.100 & ETR.485.100. Motor Second with space for children. Type BA 2.

Length over Couplers: 25.90 m.   **Accommodation:** –/68 2T (–/69 in ETR.480).

Class ETR.460.200 & ETR.485.200. Motor First. Type BB 1. Details as ETR.460.100 except:

Accommodation: 52/– 1T.

Class ETR.460.250 & ETR.485.600. Motor Second. Type BB 2. Details as ETR.460.100 except:

Accommodation: –/69 2T

Class ETR.460.300 & ETR.485.300. Trailer Second. Type RA 2.

Length: 25.90 m.   **Accommodation:** –/69 2T.

Class ETR.460.400 & ETR.485.400. Trailer Restaurant/Bar. Type RB. Details as ETR.460.300 except:

Accommodation: 23 restaurant.

Class ETR.460.500 & ETR.485.500. Service Trailer. Type RH 1. Details as ETR.460.300 except:

Accommodation: 36/– 2W 1T.

Set formations

ETR.460 and ETR.463.

21 P	001	201	501	401	251	101	301	252	051	FB	RL
22	002	202	502	402	102	254	302	253	052	FB	RL
23	003	203	503	403	255	103	303	256	053	FB	RL
24	004	204	504	404	257	104	304	258	054	FB	RL
25	005	205	505	405	259	105	305	260	055	FB	RL
26	006	206	506	406	262	106	306	261	056	FB	RL
27 P	007	207	507	407	263	107	307	264	057	FB	RL
28 P	008	208	508	408	265	108	308	266	058	FB	RL
30	010	210	510	410	270	110	310	269	060	FB	RL

ETR.485.

31	001	201	501	401	616	101	301	601	051	FA	RL
32	012	212	512	402	617	102	302	602	052	FA	RL
33	003	203	503	403	618	103	303	603	053	FA	RL
34	016	216	516	416	631	104	304	604	054	FA	RL
35	005	205	505	405	620	105	307	607	057	FA	RL
36	006	207	507	406	621	106	306	606	056	FA	RL
37	002	202	502	407	622	107	305	605	055	FA	RL
38	008	208	508	408	623	108	308	608	058	FA	RL
39	009	209	509	409	624	109	309	609	059	FA	RL
40	010	210	510	410	625	110	310	610	060	FA	RL
41	011	211	511	411	626	111	311	611	061	FA	RL
42	007	206	506	412	627	112	312	612	062	FA	RL
43	013	213	513	413	628	113	313	613	063	FA	RL
44	014	214	514	414	629	114	314	614	064	FA	RL
45	015	215	515	415	630	115	315	615	065	FA	RL

CLASS ETR.470 CISALPINO 9-CAR TILTING UNITS

A version of ETR.460 with 15 kV AC capability for services from Italy to Switzerland and Germany. Trains have lower gearing for Swiss mountain lines and thus a lower maximum speed. Power cars and trailers are arranged into three traction units, each with two power cars and three trailers.

Originally operated by FS/SBB joint subsidiary company Cisalpino, then divided between Trenitalia and SBB, which scrapped all of its sets. Withdrawn from Milano–Zürich and Milano–Bern–Basel services in 2015 then used on some domestic services, Trenitalia now intends to convert all sets to 25 kV AC operation and export them to Greece, FS having taken over Greek Railways (OSE). They are all in *Frecciabianca* livery; three sets were working Roma–Reggio di Calabria services in late 2018.

Details as Class ETR.460 except:

Built: 1996/97.
Wheel Arrangement: 1A-A1 + 1A-A1 + 2-2 + 2-2 + 1A-A1 + 1A-A1 + 2-2 + 1A-A1 + 1A-A1.
Weight: 469 tonnes.
Maximum Speed: 200 km/h.
Accommodation: 151/322 plus 2 disabled and 29 in restaurant car.

Class ETR.470.000. Driving Motor First Type BAC 1. With 3000 V DC pantograph.

Length over Couplers: 27.20 m.   **Accommodation:** 50/– 1T

Class ETR.470.050. Driving Motor Second. Type BAC 2. With 3000 V DC pantograph. Details as ETR.470.000 except:

Accommodation: –/63 1T

Class ETR.470.100. Motor Second with disabled facilities. Type BAH 2.

Length over Couplers: 25.90 m.　　**Accommodation:** –/54 2W 2T.

Class ETR.470.200. Motor First. Type BB 1. Details as ETR.470.100 except:

Accommodation: 54/– 1T

Class ETR.470.250. Motor Second. Type BB 2. With 15 kV AC pantograph. Details as ETR.470.100 except:

Accommodation: –/69 2T

Class ETR.470.300. Trailer Second. Type RA 2.

Length over Couplers: 25.90 m.　　**Accommodation:** –/67 2T

Class ETR.470.400. Trailer Restaurant/Bar. Type RB. Details as ETR.470.300 except:

Accommodation: 29 restaurant

Class ETR.470.500. Service Trailer. Type RA 1. With 15 kV AC pantograph.

Length over Couplers: 25.90 m.　　**Accommodation:** 47/– 1T

Set formations

1	001	201	501	401	251	101	301	252	051	**FB**	RL
4	004	204	504	404	257	104	304	258	054	**FB**	RL
6	006	206	506	406	261	106	306	262	056	**FB**	RL
7	007	207	507	407	263	107	307	264	053	**FB**	RL
8	008	208	508	408	265	108	308	266	058	**FB**	RL

CLASS ETR.500　　　　　　　　　11-CAR NON-TILTING UNITS

These are high-speed trains without tilt, built for services over high-speed lines in Italy. Train sets are formed of two Class E.404 power cars plus 11 coaches – three ETR.199 open firsts, six ETR.299 open seconds, one ETR.889 bar/restaurant car and one ETR.899 service car. Trains were used entirely on the Torino–Milano–Roma–Napoli service until the arrival of Class ETR.400. They now have fewer duties and have taken over the Torino–Milano–Venezia route from Class E.414.

There are 59 sets, numbered 01 to 16 and 18 to 60; set 17 was damaged in an accident. Formations of trailer cars are relatively stable but power cars are swapped between sets very regularly. For this reason formations are not included in this book. RFI test trains Y1 and Y2 are formed with power cars 649/652 and 502/538.

Trains now have four classes, formations being:
Power car A + three Business + Business/Bistro + Premium + five Standard + power car B.

In November 2018 Mercitalia Rail started trials with a new high speed freight service running overnight between Bologna Interporto and Marcianise, near Napoli. The train, numbered M 01, has been created from spare power cars E.404.514 and 516 plus 12 of the 40 spare ETR.500 trailers, emptied of their interior furnishings. More trains will follow if the test is a success.

For details of Class E.404 Power Cars see Section 1.2.

Class ETR.199. Open First.

These coaches are similar in outline to those built for lorry drivers travelling by Le Shuttle through the Channel Tunnel.

Length over Couplers: 26.10 m.　　**Weight:** 42 tonnes.　　**Accommodation:** 52/– 2T.

Class ETR.299. Open Second.

Length over Couplers: 26.10 m.　　**Weight:** 42 tonnes.　　**Accommodation:** –/68 2T.

Class ETR.889. Bar/Restaurant Car.

Length over Couplers: 26.10 m.　　**Weight:** 42 tonnes.　　**Accommodation:** 30 seats.

Class ETR.899. Service Coach.

Length over Couplers: 26.10 m.　　**Weight:** 42 tonnes.　　**Accommodation:** 37/– 2W 1TD.

▲ ETR.500 set 34 stands at Bolzano Central having arrived from Roma Termini on 13 September 2018. **David Haydock**

▼ NTV .italo set 17 passes through Milano Lambrate on 6 April 2018 with 12.35 Milano Centrale–Roma Termini. **David Haydock**

CLASS ETR.575   ".italo"   11-CAR UNITS

These trains are operated by NTV, the first private company in Europe, if not the world, to operate high speed trains. NTV launched services in spring 2012 and is basically duplicating Trenitalia's high speed offer on the Torino/Milano–Bologna–Firenze–Roma–Napoli–Salerno corridor plus Venezia–Bologna–Roma. The company started with a fleet of 25 11-car articulated AGV sets, capable of 360 km/h, built by Alstom in France and Savigliano, Italy. These are marketed as .italo by NTV. The trains are maintained at a depot in Nola, east of Napoli. Alstom has the contract to maintain the trains and must turn out 21 plus one reserve of the 25 each day.

Coach 1 is Club class and has 11 seats arranged 2+1 in an open section, plus two business compartments with four seats each. Coaches 2 to 5 are classified Prima, with 2+1 seating. Coach 3 has a standing snack area with coffee machine and microwave. Coaches 6 to 11 are classified Smart with 2+2 seating. Coach 11 has video screens. Trains are designed for 360 km/h but are restricted to 300 km/h by RFI infrastructure.

As sets are articulated they will not normally be reformed. Coaches in set 01 are numbered 575 001, 002, 003 and so on to 575 011. Set 02 starts at 575 012 and so on. Class number 575 was apparently chosen to reflect the 574.8 km/h world record set by an Alstom TGV set, using bogies with the same permanent magnet traction motors now used in the AGV.

Built: 2008–12.   **Systems:** 3000 V DC/25 kV AC 50 Hz.
Builder: Alstom.   **Power Rating:** 7500 kW.
Accommodation: Club: 19, Prima 143, Smart 288. Total 450 seats.
Weight: 374 tonnes.   **Length:** 202 m.
Maximum Speed: 300 km/h.
EVN: 93 83 3575 xxx-c + 0575 xxx-c + 5575 xxx-c + 5575 xxx-c + 5575 xxx-c + 6575 xxx-c + 0575 xxx-c + 6575 xxx-c + 6575 xxx-c + 0575 xxx-c + 4575 xxx-c.

Set no.	Coach numbers										
01	575 001	002	003	004	005	006	007	008	009	010	011
02	575 012	013	014	015	016	017	018	019	020	021	022
03	575 023	024	025	026	027	028	029	030	031	032	033
04	575 034	035	036	037	038	039	040	041	042	043	044
05	575 045	046	047	048	049	050	051	052	053	054	055
06	575 056	057	058	059	060	061	062	063	064	065	066
07	575 067	068	069	070	071	072	073	074	075	076	077
08	575 078	079	080	081	082	083	084	085	086	087	088
09	575 089	090	091	092	093	094	095	096	097	098	099
10	575 100	101	102	103	104	105	106	107	108	109	110
11	575 111	112	113	114	115	116	117	118	119	120	121
12	575 122	123	124	125	126	127	128	129	130	131	132
13	575 133	134	135	136	137	138	139	140	141	142	143
14	575 144	145	146	147	148	149	150	151	152	153	154
15	575 155	156	157	158	159	160	161	162	163	164	165
16	575 166	167	168	169	170	171	172	173	174	175	176
17	575 177	178	179	180	181	182	183	184	185	186	187
18	575 188	189	190	191	192	193	194	195	196	197	198
19	575 199	200	201	202	203	204	205	206	207	208	209
20	575 210	211	212	213	214	215	216	217	218	219	220
21	575 221	222	223	224	225	226	227	228	229	230	231
22	575 232	233	234	235	236	237	238	239	240	241	242
23	575 243	244	245	246	247	248	249	250	251	252	253
24	575 254	255	256	257	258	259	260	261	262	263	264
25	575 265	266	267	268	269	270	271	272	273	274	275

CLASS ETR.600   PENDOLINO DUE   7-CAR TILTING UNITS

The latest generation of Pendolino set which features several innovations. The main differences compared with previous sets are a 7-car formation, the possibility of operating in multiple and more streamlined front ends. The units are dual-voltage with ERTMS Level 2 for use on all new high speed lines. They are all in *Frecciargento* red/silver livery and mainly work Venezia–Roma (–Napoli) services plus Roma–Mantova. Units are formed M + M + R + T + T + M + M where M is a power car, R a restaurant car and T a trailer. Coaches are numbered ETR.600.101, 201, 301, 401, 501, 601 and 701 in set 1, and so on.

Built: 2006–09.
Builder–Mechanical Parts: Alstom Ferroviaria.
Builder–Electrical Parts: Alstom Ferroviaria.
Traction Motors:
Continuous Rating: 5500 kW.
Wheel Arrangement: A1-1A + A1-1A + 2-2 + 2-2 + 2-2 + A1-1A + A1-1A.
Weight: 62 + 59 + 55 + 60 + 60 + 59 + 62 tonnes.
Overall Length: 28.20 m + 5 x 26.20 m + 28.20 m = total length 187.40 m
Accommodation: 100/332.

Wheel Diameter:
Weight: 387 tonnes.
Maximum Speed: 250 km/h.
Systems: 3000 V DC/25 kV AC 50 Hz.

Set						Set				
1	ETR.600.101	to	ETR.600.701	**FA**	RL	7	ETR.600.107	to	ETR.600.707	**FA**	RL
2	ETR.600.102	to	ETR.600.702	**FA**	RL	8	ETR.600.108	to	ETR.600.708	**FA**	RL
3	ETR.600.103	to	ETR.600.703	**FA**	RL	9	ETR.600.109	to	ETR.600.709	**FA**	RL
4	ETR.600.104	to	ETR.600.704	**FA**	RL	10	ETR.600.110	to	ETR.600.710	**FA**	RL
5	ETR.600.105	to	ETR.600.705	**FA**	RL	11	ETR.600.111	to	ETR.600.711	**FA**	RL
6	ETR.600.106	to	ETR.600.706	**FA**	RL	12	ETR.600.112	to	ETR.600.712	**FA**	RL

▲ ETR.600 set 1 speeds past Bronzolo station on 13 September 2018 with the 15.16 Frecchiargento service to Roma Termini.
David Haydock

CLASS ETR.610   PENDOLINO DUE   7-CAR TILTING UNITS

This is a version of Class ETR.600 for services between Italy and Switzerland. The main differences compared with the latter concern equipment for operating on 15 kV AC and signalling equipment for Switzerland. These include ERTMS Level 2 which is needed for the Lötschberg base tunnel, the Bern–Olten line and new high speed lines in Italy. Coaches are numbered ETR.610.101, 201, 301, 401, 501, 601 and 701 in set 1, and so on.

The sets were the victim of the Cisalpino split; seven sets (5, 6, 7, 9, 10, 13 and 14) are now used by SBB on services to Milano and the rest are with Trenitalia on the same services. SBB later ordered more and will renumber its sets as Class 503. Trenitalia says it hopes to use its sets on services extended from Zürich to Germany.

As Class ETR.600 except:

Built: 2007–10.
Systems: 3000 V DC/25 kV AC 50 Hz/15 kV AC 16.7 Hz.
Weight: 417 tonnes.
Accommodation: 44/– 1T + 54/– + –/28 1T + –/80 2T + –/80 2T + –/80 1T + –/64.

Set						Set					
1	ETR.610.101	to	ETR.610.701	FB	MM	8	ETR.610.108	to	ETR.610.708	FB	MM
2	ETR.610.102	to	ETR.610.702	FB	MM	11	ETR.610.111	to	ETR.610.711	FB	MM
3	ETR.610.103	to	ETR.610.703	FB	MM	12	ETR.610.112	to	ETR.610.712	FB	MM
4	ETR.610.104	to	ETR.610.704	FB	MM						

CLASS ETR.675   "EVO"   7-CAR UNITS

Private operator NTV decided to extend its fleet in 2016 and ordered 12 7-car dual-voltage (3000 V DC/25 kV AC) "Evo" trains from Alstom in Italy, followed by ten more in two orders for five. These are a significant update of the ETR.600 design with completely redesigned front ends and no tilt mechanism. Trains are based at NTV's Nola depot east of Napoli.

Built: 2017–19.   **Builder:** Alstom, Savigliano.
Systems: 3000 V DC, 25 kV AC 50 Hz.   **Power Rating:** 5500 kW.
Maximum Speed: 250 km/h.
Total Length: 28.15 m + 5 x 26.20 m + 28.15 m = total length: 187.30 m.
Wheel Arrangement: 1A-A1 + 1A-A1 + 2-2 + 2-2 + 2-2 + 1A-A1 + 1A-A1.
Total Weight: 407 tonnes.
Total Accommodation: 472 (Coach 1 Club/Prima, coaches 2/3 Prima, coaches 4 to 7 Smart).

Numbering of Set 1 is 675 001 to 007, Set 2 675 008 to 014 and so on.

Set					Set			
1	ETR.675.001	to	ETR.675.007		12	ETR.675.078	to	ETR.675.084
2	ETR.675.008	to	ETR.675.014		13	ETR.675.085	to	ETR.675.091
3	ETR.675.015	to	ETR.675.021		14	ETR.675.092	to	ETR.675.098
4	ETR.675.022	to	ETR.675.028		15	ETR.675.099	to	ETR.675.105
5	ETR.675.029	to	ETR.675.035		16	ETR.675.106	to	ETR.675.112
6	ETR.675.036	to	ETR.675.042		17	ETR.675.113	to	ETR.675.119
7	ETR.675.043	to	ETR.675.049		18	ETR.675.120	to	ETR.675.126
8	ETR.675.050	to	ETR.675.056		19	ETR.675.127	to	ETR.675.133
9	ETR.675.057	to	ETR.675.063		20	ETR.675.134	to	ETR.675.140
10	ETR.675.064	to	ETR.675.070		21	ETR.675.141	to	ETR.675.147
11	ETR.675.071	to	ETR.675.077		22	ETR.675.148	to	ETR.675.154

CLASS ETR.700   ex Fyra V250   8-CAR UNITS

These trains, nicknamed "Albatros", were built for use on the Amsterdam–Rotterdam–Breda and Amsterdam–Rotterdam–Brussels "Fyra" services. The first set was outshopped in 2009 – well after the trains were supposed to enter service in late 2007. Passengers were not carried in revenue service until autumn 2012 but by May 2013 operators NS and SNCB cancelled the contract with builder AnsaldoBreda due to chronic technical problems.

In 2017 Trenitalia agreed to buy 17 of the 19 trains and contracted Hitachi Rail Italy (formerly AnsaldoBreda) to make them ready for service. The sets originally had only five toilets as journeys are short in the Netherlands; Hitachi will add two more. Tests were carried out with sets 10, 13 and 16, renumbered from Fyra sets 4810, 4813 and 4816, during 2018. To be deployed on the Milano–Bologna–Bari route during 2019.

The original numbering of the sets was 4801 to 4819 (4817 to 4819 were originally 4881 to 4883, for Belgian Railways).

Built: 2008–13.   **Builder:** AnsaldoBreda.
Systems: 1500/3000 V DC, 25 kV AC 50 Hz.   **Power Rating:** 5660 kW under 3000 V DC;
      5800 kW under 25 kV AC.
Axle arrangement: Bo-Bo + 2-2 + Bo-Bo + 2-2 + 2-2 + Bo-Bo + 2-2 + Bo-Bo.
Accommodation: 47/– + 48/– 1TD + 30/23 + –/52 1T bistro + –/78 1T + –/78 1T + –/78 1T + –/66.
Total Weight: 423 tonnes.
Length over Couplers: 26.95 m + 6 x 24.50 m + 26.95 m = 200.90 metres.
Maximum Speed: 250 km/h.
Numbering: Set 1 is 93 83 3700 101 + 0700 201 + 0700 301 + 3700 401 + 0700 501 + 0700 601 + 0700 701 + 4700 801 and so on.

Set

1	ETR.700.101	to	ETR.700.801	MM	10	ETR.700.110	to	ETR.700.810	MM
2	ETR.700.102	to	ETR.700.802	MM	11	ETR.700.111	to	ETR.700.811	MM
3	ETR.700.103	to	ETR.700.803	MM	12	ETR.700.112	to	ETR.700.812	MM
4	ETR.700.104	to	ETR.700.804	MM	13	ETR.700.113	to	ETR.700.813	MM
5	ETR.700.105	to	ETR.700.805	MM	14	ETR.700.114	to	ETR.700.814	MM
6	ETR.700.106	to	ETR.700.806	MM	15	ETR.700.115	to	ETR.700.815	MM
7	ETR.700.107	to	ETR.700.807	MM	16	ETR.700.116	to	ETR.700.816	MM
8	ETR.700.108	to	ETR.700.808	MM	17	ETR.700.117	to	ETR.700.817	MM
9	ETR.700.109	to	ETR.700.809	MM					

▲ "EVO" ETR.675 set 03 passes Mezzocorona whilst working the 12.41 Bolzano–Salerno on 25 January 2019.   **Laurence Sly**

2. OTHER TRAIN OPERATORS

Italy has about 20 independent passenger railway companies, totalling over 3400 km, employing 12 000 staff and transporting 160 million passengers per year. These railways are much less well known and documented than those in Switzerland, perhaps because they keep changing names! Many are electrified, like the national RFI network, at 3000 V DC overhead and several have quite antediluvian rolling stock still in service. Travellers should note that passes such as InterRail are not accepted. In the recent past, control of most of these railways has passed from central to local government, mergers have taken place and some railways have started open access freight operations over the RFI network, and in some cases passenger services, either crewed by their own, or Trenitalia, staff. Most companies also run local buses.

We have also included all "open access" freight operators in this list and NTV which runs high speed passenger trains.

Not included in this book are urban tramways and metros, nor cable and funicular railways.

In this fourth edition, standard gauge DMU and EMU classes capable of operating over the RFI network have been transferred to Section 1 of the book.

INDEX FOR THIS SECTION

LINES CLOSED, RENAMED OR TAKEN OVER BY OTHER RAILWAYS

COTRAL	Consorzio Trasporti Lazio, later Met.Ro	now ATAC
FA	Ferrovia Alifana	now EAV
FABN	Ferrovia Alifana e Benevento-Napoli	now EAV
FAM	Ferrovia Adria-Mestre	now ST
FBN	Ferrovia Benevento–Napoli	now EAV
FBP	Ferrovia Bologna–Portomaggiore	now TPER
FBV	Suburbana Bologna–Vignola	now TPER
FCL	Ferrovie Calabro-Lucane	now FAL/FC
FCS	Ferrovie Complementari della Sardegna	now ARST
FCV	Ferrovia Casalecchio–Vignola	now TPER
FER	Ferrovia Emilia Romagno	now TPER
FETM	Ferrovia Elettrica Trento-Male	now TT
FP	Ferrovie Padane	now TPER
FPS	Ferrovia Parma–Suzzara	now TPER
FSAS	Ferrovia Sinalunga Arezzo Stia	now TFT
FSF	Ferrovia Suzzara–Ferrara	now TPER
FTC	Ferrovia Torino-Ceres	now GTT
FV	Ferrovie Venete	now ST
Met.Ro		now ATAC
SATTI	Società per Azioni Trasporti Torinesi Intercomunali	now GTT
SFM	Strade Ferrate del Mediterraneo.	now DB Cargo Italia
SFS	Strade Ferrate Sarde	now ARST
SFSM	Strade Ferrate Secondarie Meridionali	now Circumvesuviana
SNFT	Societa Nazionale di Ferrovie e Tranvie	now Trenord
SV	Societa Veneta Autoferovie	now ST

Notes

APTB	See TPER.
CTP	See EAV.
CCFR	See TPER.
FCB	See EAV.
FNP	See EAV.
SEFTA	See TPER.
SSIF	Societa Subalpina di Imprese Ferroviare. Details of this railway from Domodossola to Locarno in Switzerland are contained in the Platform 5 book "Swiss Railways Locomotives, Railcars and Trams".

2.1. ADRIAFER   ADFER

Adriafer is a company 100% owned by the Trieste port authority, which carries out shunting in the Trieste port area and currently operates five Henschel DHG 700 C, two Vossloh Class D.100, two Zephir road-rail shunters, one Class D.145 and one Class D.245 on hire from Trenitalia. The company also hires Class E.191 for Trieste–Villa Opicina freights.

The DHG 700 C are 31682 (1973), 31690 (1975), 31866 (1976), 31992 (1979), 31997 (1978).

2.2. AZIENDA REGIONALE SARDA TRASPORTI   ARST

This company, owned by the Sardegna region, runs all of the narrow gauge railway and tramway lines in Sardinia, as well as long distance bus services. Management of the narrow gauge network on the island was merged in 1989 as Ferrovie della Sardegna (FdS), from the Ferrovie Complementari della Sardegna (FCS) and Strade Ferrate Sarde (SFS). The network is divided into lines with a daily service and those with only tourist services in summer. In 2018 the 45 km Mandas–Dolianova section was closed for heavy maintenance.

In 2008 the section from Cagliari (Repubblica) to Monserrato (Gottardo) – 6.4 km with nine stations – was electrified and converted to light rail (*Metrocagliari*). Line 3 from Gottardo to Policlinico (1.8 km of new build) opened in December 2014 and the first line has been extended to Séttimo San Pietro over the Mandas line. This line will be extended at the city centre end from Repubblica to the main Trenitalia station (Piazza Mattetti) by 2020. In Sassari, a 1.4 km light rail line was built alongside the Sassari FS–Sorso line to Santa Maria di Pisa, then extended on street from Sassari FS to Emiciclo Garibaldi as *Metrosassari*. An extension is planned from Santa Maria di Pisa to Marginesu (1.9 km).

Trains are allocated to one of three divisions – Cagliari (C), Macomer (M) and Sassari (S).

Gauge: 950 mm.   **Electrification (tramways):** 750 V DC.
Routes (lines shown in bold have daily services whilst others have only tourist services):

ex SFS:

- Sassari FS–Nulvi–Palau Marina (150 km): only two train pairs Sassari–Nulvi during school terms.
- **Sassari FS–Sorso** (11 km).
- **Sassari FS–Alghero** (33 km).

ex FCS:

- Bosa–**Macomer–Nuoro** (89 km).
- **Cagliari San Gottardo–Mandas–Isili**–Sorgono (164 km).
- Mandas–Arbatax (159 km).

Depots (main depots in bold):

ex FCS: **Cagliari-Monserrato (C), Macomer (M)**, Mandas, Seui, Lanusei, Arbatax, Sorgono.
ex SFS: **Sassari (S)**, Tempio-Pausania.

DIESEL LOCOMOTIVES

CLASS LM   B

Small shunters formerly with Azienda Carboni Italiani coal mines in Carbonia. Five locos were built, with works numbers 25356 to 25360, becoming FCS or SFS locos LM 3, 2, 1, 5 and 4 in that order. LM 5 is used by the railway museum at Monserrato. LM 3 is rusting outside the museum.

Built: 1953.   **Length over Buffers:** 5.8 m.
Builder: O&K, Milano. Type MV4.   **Weight:** 8 tonnes.
Continuous Rating: 55 kW.   **Maximum Speed:** 30 km/h.
Transmission: Mechanical.

LM 3 (U)	LM 5

CLASS LDe 500 & 600   Bo-Bo

Centre-cab diesel locos. LDe 500–504 are ex SFS; LDe 600–614 are ex FCS. Haul schools, tourist and works trains. 601 is named "The Train of Love". 613 and 615 were scrapped.

Built: 1958–60.   **Length over Buffers:** 11.0 m.
Builders: Breda/TIBB.   **Weight:** 34 tonnes.
Continuous Rating: 514 kW.   **Maximum Speed:** 70 km/h.
Transmission: Electric.

500 S	503 S	601 M	604 C	606 C	608 C (U)	611 M	614 C (U)
501 S	504 S (U)	602 M (U)	605 M	607 C	609 M	612 C (U)	616 C
502 S		603 C					

DIESEL MULTIPLE UNITS

CLASS ADeS 01–07 2-CAR UNITS

New units similar to those on FAL built by Stadler. The first four units operate on the Sassari–Sorso/Alghero lines while 05–07 are on the Macomer–Nuoro line. Three more are on order.

Built: 2015 01–04; 2017 05–07. **Builder:** Stadler.
Details as FAL 2-car Stadler sets except:
Accommodation: –/100.

01 S "Maestral"	04 S "Sandalion"	07 M	09
02 S "Alguer"	05 M	08	10
03 S "Sardus Pater"	06 M		

CLASS ADe 01–20 & 301/302 SINGLE CARS

301–306 and accompanying trailers were ex Ferrovie Meridionali Sarde (FMS), on its closure in 1975. FMS included the Monteponi–San Giovanni Suergiu–Calasetta and San Giovanni Suergiu–Narcao lines. 01–20 operate with driving trailers RBe 101–110. 301/302 can run with trailers RP 351–354. 303 to 306 were withdrawn in 1994. However, all the trailers are stored. 07 is still stored at Tirso.

Built: 1957 except 301/302 1958–60. **Length over Buffers:** 16.75 m.
Builders: OMS/Fiat/TIBB. **Weight:** 28 tonnes.
Continuous Rating: 176 kW. **Maximum Speed:** 75 km/h.
Transmission: Electric. **Accommodation:** 15/40.
Wheel Arrangement: Bo-Bo.

Also numbered 15 0 31 2442 001-c upwards.

01 M	04 C	08 C	11 M	13 M	15 M	18 C	301 M
02 C	05 C	09 M	12 C	14 C	17 C	20 C	302 M
03 M	06 C	10 C					

CLASS ADm SINGLE CARS

Very similar to previous units but with mechanical transmission. Ex SFS. Operate with driving trailers RPm 151–158. All are based at Sassari. Following the delivery of Stadler units, they are now only used for tourist services.

Built: 1957. **Length over Couplers:** 16.95 m.
Builders: Fiat/OMS/TIBB. **Weight:** 24 tonnes.
Engines: 2 x 185 kW. **Maximum Speed:** 72 km/h.
Transmission: Mechanical. **Accommodation:** 15/40.
Wheel Arrangement: B-B.

51	53	55	57	58	59	60	61
52	54	56					

CLASS ADe 90 SINGLE CARS

Similar to single railcars on FAL. Used with driving trailers Rpe 901–905.

Built: 1995/96. **Length over Couplers:** 18.71 m.
Builder: Breda/ABB. **Weight:** 32 tonnes.
Engines: Two FIAT 8217.32.038S of 184 kW each.
Transmission: Electric. ABB Tecnomasio. **Accommodation:** –/54.
Wheel Arrangement: Bo-Bo. **Maximum Speed:** 100 km/h.

91 C	92 C	93 M	94 C	95 C	96 M (U)	97 S	98 S

▲ ARST ADe 92 runs onto Cagliari depot on 19 June 2013, with 2-6-2T 400 on the right.
David Haydock

▼ ARST tram SS 02 passes the depot entrance as it arrives at Sassari on 20 June 2013.
David Haydock

TRAMS

CLASS CA 01–09 5-SECTION TRAMS

Nine bidirectional trams for the section of the Cagliari line to Monserrato which was converted to a light rail line in 2007. CA 04 and 07 crashed in 2017.

Built: 2006/07.
Builder: Škoda Type 06T.
Continuous Rating: 460 kW.
Width: 2.46 m.
Wheel Diameter: 650 mm.
System: 750 V DC.

Length over Couplers: 29.50 m.
Weight: 36 tonnes.
Maximum Speed: 70 km/h.
Accommodation: –/42.
Wheel Arrangement: Bo-2-Bo.

| CA 01 | | CA 03 | | CA 04 (U) | CA 05 | | CA 06 | | CA 07 (U) | CA 08 | | CA 09 |
| CA 02 | | | | | | | | | | | | |

CLASS CA 10–12 URBOS 5-SECTION TRAMS

The Sardegna region has financed three bi-directional trams from CAF, with options for six more, for extensions in Cagliari.

Built: 2016/17.
Maximum Speed: 70 km/h.
Width: 2.40 m.

Builder: CAF.
Length: 32.966 m.
System: 750 V DC.

| CA 10 | | CA 11 | | CA 12 |

CLASS SS 5-SECTION TRAMS

Four bidirectional trams used on the tramway in Sassari.

Built: 2003/04.
Builder: AnsaldoBreda (Sirio).
Continuous Rating: 424 kW.
Width: 2.40 m.
Wheel Diameter: 660 mm.
System: 750 V DC.

Length over Couplers: 27.47 m.
Maximum Speed: 70 km/h.
Accommodation: –/34.
Wheel Arrangement: Bo-2-Bo.

| SS 01 | | SS 02 | | SS 03 | | SS 04 |

STEAM LOCOMOTIVES

No.	Type	Axles	Builder	Built	kW	km/h	Tonnes	Location	Notes
Ex FCS Locos									
1 (U)	v	2-6-0T	Breda	1914				Sorgono	
2 (U)	v	2-6-0T	Breda	1914				Mandas	
3 (U)	v	2-6-0T	Breda	1914				Mandas	
5 (U)	v	2-6-0T	Breda	1914				Macomer	1.
6 (U)	v	2-6-0T	Breda	1914				Mandas	
7	v	2-6-0T	Breda	1914				Monserrato	2.
43*	v	2-6-0T	SLM	1893				Monserrato museum.	3.
45	v	2-6-0T	SLM	1893				Plinthed at Via della Torre Clementina, Fiumicino	
201 (U)	v	0-4-4-0T	BMAG	1909				Monserrato	
202 (U)	v	0-4-4-0T	BMAG	1909				Monserrato	
300 (U)	v	2-8-0T	O&K	1914				Monserrato	
301 (U)	v	2-8-0T	O&K	1914				Mandas	
302 (U)	v	2-8-0T	O&K	1914				Monserrato	
303 (U)	v	2-8-0T	O&K	1914				Monserrato	

400	v	2-6-2T	Reggiane	1931	Monserrato. Active.	
402	v	2-6-2T	Reggiane	1931	Monserrato museum.	

Ex SFS Locos

3 (U)	v	2-6-0T	CEMSA	1931	Sassari	4.
5	v	2-6-0T	Breda	1930	Sassari. Active.	5.
6 (U)	v	2-6-0T	CEMSA	1931	Olmedo	
7 (U)	v	2-6-0T	Breda	1930	Tempio-Pausania	
11 (U)	v	2-6-0T	CEMSA	1931	Tempio-Pausania	

1. Named SULCIS.
2. Plinthed on roundabout, Via Cesare Cabras, Monserrato.
3. Named GOITO.
4. Named LAERRU / ELSA.
5. Named NULVI / WALLY.
* Some sources give this as 44.

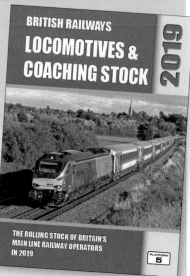

2.3. ATAC

Roma's urban and suburban transport system been reorganised many times, having been known as STEFER, COTRAL and Met.Ro in the past. All of Roma's public transport, including buses, trams, metro and three suburban rail lines, formerly operated by Met.Ro and Trambus were grouped as ATAC in 2010. The three ATAC suburban lines, sometimes known as Lines E, F and G, carry over 50 million passengers a year. The metro and Roma's tramway system are not included in this book. Some shunters are shared by the Lido line and the metro and are not mentioned here. Several pieces of former Roma stock are plinthed at Piramide station which is a gem in itself and other stock is preserved at Colonna Galleria, on the closed part of the Alatri line, 28 km from Roma near Galleria on the line to Frosinone. ATAC itself has never replied to our requests for data and no source in Italy has full details of Lido line stock, some of which is "permanent loan" from Line B. In February 2018 the Lazio region launched a tender for up to 20 6-car EMUs for the Lido line and up to 18 4-car EMUs for the Roma Nord line, of which 12 are for Roma–Montebello and six for Roma–Viterbo.

2.3.1. "LIDO DI OSTIA" – LINE "E"

This line interchanges with Metro Line B at three points, runs to Roma's nearest seaside resort and serves a station near the interesting ruins of Ostia Antica. The line shares a depot with Line B at Magliana and has the same operating voltage. In the past, rolling stock has been cascaded to the Lido line from Line B. All trains run in 6-car formations. At the time of writing the line is operated by two MA 100 trains ex metro Line A, eight MA 200 sets ex Line A, eight MA 300 sets (three ex Line B) and three MR 500 sets.

Gauge: 1435 mm.
Route: Roma Porta San Paolo (Piramide)–Ostia Cristoforo Colombo (28 km).
Electrical System: 1500 V DC overhead.
Depot: Magliana Ostiense.

ELECTRIC MULTIPLE UNITS

CLASS MA 200   6-CAR SETS

20 of these sets (40 half sets numbered MA 201 + RA 201 + MA 202 to MA 279 + RA 240 + MA 280) were built in 1976–79 for the extension of Metro Line A, but when Type MA 300 started to be delivered, some were refurbished and put into service on the Lido line with a special *Freccia del Mare* (Sea Arrow) branding. It is not known how many sets work on the Lido line, or their numbers; those below were observed in 2013. 24 half sets have been sold to MetroCampania NordEst and operate on the Piscinola–Aversa line.

Sets of Type MA 100 also appear on the Lido line. They are not listed in this book.

Built: 1997–99.   **Builders:** Breda, Fiat, Ansaldo, Firema.
Power Rating (set): 1760 kW.   **Maximum Speed:** 90 km/h.
Wheel Arrangement: Bo-Bo + 2-2 + Bo-Bo + Bo-Bo + 2-2 + Bo-Bo.
Accommodation: –/32 + –/40 + –/32 + –/32 + –/40 + –/32.
Length: 17.84 m x 6.

MA 201 + RA 203 + MA 206	MA 231 + RA 216 + MA 232
MA 211 + RA 206 + MA 212	MA 239 + RA 220 + MA 240

CLASS MA 300   6-CAR SETS

These units are part of a batch of 53 trains built by CAF for Line B and are dedicated to the Lido service. They are numbered in "half sets" and can "change partners" – 381/382 and 389/390 were together in 2013 but 379 was with 388. 322 to 327 are ex Line B. The Lido sets are in a special *Freccia del Mare* livery.

Built: 2007.   **Builder:** CAF
Power Rating: 2800 kW.   **Maximum Speed:** 90 km/h.
Wheel Arrangement: 2-2 + Bo-Bo + Bo-Bo + Bo-Bo + Bo-Bo + 2-2.
Accommodation: –/32 + –/38 + –/38 + –/38 + –/38 + –/32.
Weight: 29.5 + 30.5 + 30.5 + 30.5 + 30.5 + 29.5 tonnes.
Length: 18.20 + 17.92 + 17.92 + 17.92 + 17.92 + 18.20 m.

RA 322-0 + MA 322-1 + MA 322-2	MA 323-2 + MA 323-1 + RA 323-0
RA 324-0 + MA 324-1 + MA 324-2	MA 325-2 + MA 325-1 + RA 325-0
RA 326-0 + MA 326-1 + MA 326-2	MA 327-2 + MA 327-1 + RA 327-0
RA 379-0 + MA 379-1 + MA 379-2	MA 380-2 + MA 380-1 + RA 380-0
RA 381-0 + MA 381-1 + MA 381-2	MA 382-2 + MA 382-1 + RA 382-0
RA 383-0 + MA 383-1 + MA 383-2	MA 384-2 + MA 384-1 + RA 384-0
RA 385-0 + MA 385-1 + MA 385-2	MA 386-2 + MA 386-1 + RA 386-0
RA 387-0 + MA 387-1 + MA 387-2	MA 388-2 + MA 388-1 + RA 388-0
RA 389-0 + MA 389-1 + MA 389-2	MA 390-2 + MA 390-1 + RA 390-0

CLASS MR 500   5-CAR SETS

Operate with pairs of power cars either side of trailers in 551–562 series.

Built: 1987–99.
Builders: Fiat/Ansaldo/Marelli.
Continuous Rating:
Accommodation: –/40 + –/44.
Length over Couplers: 18.975 m.
Weight: 32 tonnes.
Maximum Speed:
Wheel Arrangement: Bo-Bo.

501 + 502	507 + 508	513 + 514	517 + 518	523 + 524
505 + 506	511 + 512	515 + 516	519 + 520	

"LIDO LINE" DIESEL SHUNTER

No.	Type	Axles	Builders	Built	kW	km/h	Tonnes	Seats	Notes
D 52	dh	0-6-0	Greco/Voith	1958	285	51	42	-	-

▲ On 19 June 2013, "Roma Nord" set 111 + 206 + 112 has just reversed at Prima Porta station.
David Haydock

2.3.2. "ROMA NORD" – LINE "F"

This line runs from a station near the Villa Borghese, close to Flaminio on Metro Line A. A suburban service runs approximately every 12 minutes on double track to Prima Porta. A patchy service runs over the single line from there to Civita Castellana (14 trains per day) and Viterbo (five trains per day). There is some stabling at Acqua Acetosa. Most of the stock, especially Type E84, is appallingly tagged.

Gauge: 1435 mm.
Route: Roma Piazzale Flaminio–Viterbo Nord (102 km).
Ex Società Romana per le Ferrovie del Nord (SRFN)
Electrical System: 3000 V DC overhead.
Depots: Civita Castellana Nord, Acqua Acetosa.

ELECTRIC LOCOMOTIVES

01 — Bo-Bo

01 to 03 were ancient motor luggage vans dating back to the initial order for EMUs. 01 is in working order at Civita Castellana. 02 is plinthed at Colonna Galleria.

Built: 1932.
Builders: Stanga/TIBB.
Continuous Rating: 4 x 122 kW.

Length over Buffers: 16.00 m.
Weight: 42 tonnes.
Maximum Speed: 60 km/h.

01

ELECTRIC RAILCARS & MULTIPLE UNITS

CLASS ECD — SINGLE CARS

Operate with intermediate and driving trailers. ECD 21 is now plinthed at Piramide station and 24 is at Colonna Galleria. 22 and 26 are preserved for heritage train *Trenino della Tuscia*.

Built: 1932.
Builders: OMS/TIBB.
Continuous Rating: 4 x 122 kW.
Accommodation: –/34.

Length over Buffers: 16.25 m.
Weight: 44 tonnes.
Maximum Speed: 72 km/h.
Wheel Arrangement: Bo-Bo.

22 | 26

TYPE E 84 — 3-CAR UNITS

Used on the *"Urbano"* service from Flaminio to Montebello. The second batch of units can be distinguished by the larger destination boards. Power cars are even numbered. The 151–154 batch have two doors per coach instead of three and are supposedly for outer suburban services. Power car 120 was scrapped.

Built: 101–113 1987 (centre cars 1990); others 1995.
Builders: FIREMA/Casaralta/OMS.
Length over Buffers: 21.56 + 21.61 + 21.56 m.
Continuous Rating: 1000 kW.
Accommodation: –/64 + –/72 + –/61 (2).

Weight: 41 + 32 + 41 tonnes.
Maximum Speed: 90 km/h.
Wheel Arrangement: 2-2 + 2-2 + Bo-Bo.

101 + 201 + 102	107 + 204 + 108	113 + 207 + 114	117 + 209 + 118
103 + 202 + 104	109 + 205 + 110	115 + 208 + 116	119 + 210 spare
105 + 203 + 106	111 + 206 + 112		
151 + 251 + 152	153 + 252 + 154		

TYPE MRP 236   3-CAR UNITS

Used on the *"Extraurbano"* service to Civita Castellana and Viterbo. Even numbered series 300 cars are powered.

Built: 2000.
Builders: Costaferroviaria/Alstom.
Continuous Rating:
Accommodation: –/75 + –/84 + –/71.

Length: 21.64 + 21.14 + 21.64 m.
Weight: 50 + 34 + 40 tonnes.
Maximum Speed: 90 km/h.
Wheel Arrangement: Bo-Bo + 2-2 + 2-2.

301 + 401 + 302	307 + 404 + 308	313 + 407 + 314	317 + 409 + 318
303 + 402 + 304	309 + 405 + 310 (S)	315 + 408 + 316	319 + 410 + 320
305 + 403 + 306	311 + 406 + 312		

2.3.3. "LAZIALI" – LINE "G"

This is what remains of the 94 km Roma–Alatri line. Fiuggi–Alatri closed in 1978 due to landslips. Further landslips and the worn-out overhead forced closure of all but the urban section at a time when new long distance stock was about to be delivered. In 1982, the urban branch from Centocelle to Piazza dei Mirti closed and in 1989 the remaining line was upgraded to light rail standards on reserved ways.

The line begins from a terminus close to platforms 23–26 of Roma Termini then runs on segregated track at the side or in the middle of the street. Vehicles are tramway type including some very old 4-wheelers. The outer Grotte Celoni–Pantano section reopened in early 2006 after doubling and rebuilding to allow conversion to standard gauge, but the line is now only operated to Giardinetti, the section from there to Pantano closing in July 2008. The Centocelle–Pantano section is to be taken over by new Metro Line C by 2020. The Roma–Centocelle section may be converted to standard gauge and operated with new light rail vehicles.

Gauge: 950 mm.
Route: Roma Laziali–Giardinetti (9 km).

Electrical System: 1650 V DC overhead.
Depot: Centocelle.

TRAMS

TYPES 0 & 100   2- OR 3-CAR TRAMS

One driving cab only. Operate with one driving trailer (DT) or between two DTs. Some DTs are in the 100 series. Sets carry the power car number (bold in the text); the other cars are not powered. Set 02 is in STEFER livery.

Built: 1958–62.
Builders: Stefer (01–03); MATER/Ranieri (101–110).
Weight: 24 tonnes except 01–03 22 tonnes.
Rating: 370 kW.
Accommodation: –/24 except 01–03: –/20. Trailers –/16.
Wheel Arrangement: Bo-Bo.

Length over Buffers: 14.21 m.

Maximum Speed: 40 km/h.

054 + **01** + 121 (U)	084 + **101** + 105	082 + **106** + 104
058 + **02** + 123	085 + **103** + 107	109 + **110**
03 + 122		

CLASS 420   3-CAR TRAMS

No driving cab. Operate sandwiched between driving trailers.

Built: 1926.
Rebuilt: 1958–62 by Stefer/MATER/Ranieri.
Weight: 24 tonnes.
Continuous Rating: 370 kW.
Accommodation: –/20; trailers –/16.

Builders: C&T/TIBB.
Length over Buffers: 12.24 m.

Maximum Speed: 40 km/h.
Wheel Arrangement: Bo-Bo.

062 + **420** + 064 (U) | 060 + **423** + 061 | 059 + **426** + 067 (U) | 052 + **428** + 065
056 + **421** + 063 | 068 + **424** + 071 | 070 + **427** + 073 (U) | 050 + **429** + 055 (S)
051 + **422** + 057 | 066 + **425** + 069

CLASS ET 820   3-SECTION ARTICULATED TRAMS

Similar in appearance to Manchester's original Metrolink vehicles.

Built: 1987–89.
Builders: Ansaldo/FIREMA/TIBB.
Continuous Rating: 720 kW.
Accommodation: –/66.

Length over Couplers:
Weight:
Maximum Speed: 80 km/h.
Wheel Arrangement: Bo-Bo-Bo-Bo.

820 | 821 (U) | 822 (U) | 823 | 824 (U) | 825

CLASS ET 830   2-SECTION ARTICULATED TRAMS

A shorter version of Class ET 820.

Built: 1999–2001.
Builders: Ansaldo/FIREMA.
Continuous Rating: 720 kW.
Accommodation: –/44 (2).

Length over Buffers:
Weight:
Maximum Speed: 80 km/h.
Wheel Arrangement: Bo-Bo-Bo.

831 | 832 | 833 (U) | 834 | 835 | 836 (U) | 837

OTHER MOTIVE POWER

No.	Type	Axles	Builder	Built	kW	km/h	Tonnes	Origin
Köf	D	B	Deutz (47268)	1943	95	45	16	ex DB 323 043

▲ On the "Laziali" line, set 425 (066 + 425 + 069), built in 1926, has just left Roma Laziali on 18 June 2013.
David Haydock

2.4. CAPTRAIN ITALIA   CTI

This is a subsidiary of French National Railways (SNCF), previously known as SNCF Fret Italia, which takes care of traffic in Italy. The company uses locomotives BB 36331 to 36360 (known as Class E.436 in Italy - see Platform 5 Publishing book "French Railways" for details) for main line traffic plus three Class Y 8000 shunters (see also "French Railways"), plus Class E.483 TRAXX electric locos leased from Akiem, two Class D.753 and five Vossloh G1000 diesels (Class D.100). BB 36339 to 350, of which 36339 and 36348 are owned by Trenitalia, are used only on the Torino Orbassano–Aiton (France) "rolling motorway" service. Most Captrain Italia trains are operated in the north of Italy.

Captrain Italia took over the former FS depot at Asti (previously run by Tiber.Co) in 2012.

2.5. COMPAGNIA FERROVIARIA ITALIANA   CFI

CFI started operations in August 2009 and has offices in Terni and Roma. Major shareholders include engineering company Demont and building company Di.Cos. The company works a variety of traffic, including two services moving steel coil from Terni. The company has also taken over operations in the port of Civitavecchia from Trenitalia. In February 2012 CFI took over staff and locomotives from Rail Italia. The company owns two Siemens ES64U4 (Class E.190) and two Vectron (Class E.191) locos and hires ES64F4 (Class 189) locomotives from MRCE.

In October 2015 CFI took over Rail One, which started out as Train One in 2007. Rail One owned three Class E.474 (Siemens ES64F4) electric locomotives and one Vossloh G2000 diesel, all originally operated by Del Fungo Ghiera.

CROSSRAIL ITALIA

Crossrail Italia ceased operations in April 2017, services being taken over by other operators.

2.6. DB CARGO ITALIA

The Italian subsidiary of DB Cargo was formerly known as Railion Italia and based in Alessandria. Railion created the company by taking over nascent open access operator Strade Ferrate del Mediterraneo (SFM) in 2004. DB Schenker took a majority share in DB Cargo Italia in 2010 and now operates freights in Italy using the latter's locomotives, having sold its Class D.752 locomotive and returned all of its hired G2000 diesels to Alpha Trains.

DB Cargo Italia has also absorbed the freight department of the FNM group, formerly known as Nordcargo (see also Trenord). This company brought with it Class DE.145 and DE.520 diesel locos (see under Trenord) plus one Class E.474 which it owns and several Class E.191 and E.483 which it hires.

2.7. DINAZZANO PO   DP

Dinazzano Po, 95.4% owned by TPER, was set up in 2012 to manage the intermodal terminals served by FER – at Dinazzano, which receives large quantities of clay from Germany and from Ravenna and dispatches ceramic tiles, and at S. Giacomo di Guastalla which handles steel. The company gained its own operating licence in 2012 then all of TPER's freight traction was transferred to DP in April 2014. Classes DE.145, 1900 and loco Dj 474 can only be used on FER lines. Classes 220 and 741.7 are shown in Section 1. The company also uses Class E.483 electrics.

In mid 2014 DP received a new Type MDD4 two-axle diesel shunter from Bulgarian builder Express Service. There is an option for a second loco. No number had been allocated as we went to press. Details are: Length: 9 metres. Weight: 41 tonnes. Engine: Caterpillar C15 CERT of 403 kW. Maximum speed: 60 km/h.

▲ DB Cargo Italia E.191.013 passes through Milano Lambrate with an eastbound freight on 6 April 2018.   **David Haydock**

▼ DP MDD 4 shunter, which carries no number, and TPER shunter 260 002 at Sermide depot on 7 April 2018.   **David Haydock**

DIESEL LOCOMOTIVES

CLASS DE.145   Bo-Bo

These centre-cab diesels are very similar to FS Class D.145.1000, with the same orange livery, but have higher power engines. Ex ACT Reggio Emilia.

Built: 1995.
Builder: Fiat.
Engines: Two Fiat Iveco Aifa 8297 of 551 kW each.
Maximum Speed: 100 km/h.

Transmission: Electric. Three-phase.
Wheel Diameter: 1040 mm.
Weight: 72 tonnes.
Length over Buffers: 15.20 m.

DE 145 012 | DE 145 013

CLASS 850   D

0-8-0 shunters which can be used for heavy trip freights. 850 003/4 are ex DB 279 001/2, formerly Söhrebahn V4/5 bought in 1971; 850 005 is ex Hersfelder Eisenbahn V 31, bought in 1977; 850.006 is ex Butzbach-Licher Eisenbahn V85, bought in 1980. Works numbers in brackets. Ex ACT Reggio Emilia.

Built: 1959–61.
Builder: Henschel (Type DH850).
Engine: MB of 625 kW.
Maximum Speed: 60 km/h.

Transmission: Hydraulic. Voith L217 ed.
Wheel Diameter: 1250 mm.
Weight: 60 tonnes.
Length over Buffers: 11.05 m.

850 003 (26530) | 850 004 (30308) | 850 005 (30339) | 850 006 (30310)

CLASS 1900   B-B

Ex DB locos 216 006/1 (V 160) with bulbous front ends which earned them the nickname "Lollos" after Gina Lollobrigida! The locos are only used on Guastalla–Reggio–Dinazzano freights. Ex ACT Reggio Emilia. 1900 008 is now in DB maroon livery and carries its original number V 160 001. It is thought that the locos are now stored.

Built: 1960. Purchased by ACT in 1981/82.
Builder: Krupp.
Engine: Maybach 870 B1 of 1400 kW*
        * slightly different power ratings in 007 and 008 due to different turbochargers.
Weight: 71 tonnes.
Maximum Speed: 120 km/h.

Transmission: Hydraulic. Voith.
Wheel Diameter: 1000 mm.

Length over Buffers: 16.40 m.

1900 007 | V 160 001 (1900 008)

CLASS V100   B-B

This is ex DB 211 138, B-B diesel-hydraulic, built by Deutz 1962, heavily rebuilt, named "RAILDOG". Ex FPS. Can only operate on FER lines.

Dj 474   (also known as 100 474)

OTHER LOCOMOTIVES

DP owns three Class E.483 TRAXX electric locos, 11 Vossloh G2000 diesels which are the main traction now on the Reggio–Dinazzano line, one Class D.184 Vossloh "Eurolight" diesel, three ex DB CLass 220 diesel-hydraulics, and four Class D.741.7 Czech diesels – see main section. The company also has Bulgarian MDD 4 shunter which carries no number and is hired to TPER for shunting at Sermide depot.

2.8. ENTE AUTONOMO VOLTURNO   EAV

All of the three "independent" operators in the Napoli area are now contained within this group, together with the Monte Faita cable car, although they retain their own identities.

2.8.1. CIRCUMVESUVIANA

Formerly known as SFSM, Circumvesuviana lines encircle the volcano *Monte Vesuvio* (Vesuvius) to the east of Napoli. The system carries around 40 million passengers per year. The double track Napoli–Torre Annunziata section has colour light signalling allowing a three-minute headway and units have repetition of signals in the cab and preset speed controls. The Torre Annunziata–Sorrento section replaced a rambling tramway in the 1940s. The network continues to be modernised and extended. Several sections are being doubled. The Volla line will be extended to the new Afragola high speed station, the Alfa Lancia branch has been extended to Acerra and an extension from Baiano to Avellino is under study. Fe220 stock is being refurbished. However,the network has been in a terrible state for several years, with no money to repair trains (or clean graffiti), leading to horrendously crowded conditions. In November 2018 tenders were invited for 40 new trains, of which 23 will be firm orders.

Gauge: 950 mm.
Routes: (total 142 km)

- Napoli Porta Nolana (PN)–Barra–Ottaviano–Poggiomarino–Sarno (38 km).
- Barra–San Giorgio a Cremano–Torre Annunziata–Poggiomarino (30 km).
- Torre Annunziata–Castellammare di Stabia (22 km).
- Napoli PN–Volla–Pomigliano d'Arco–Nola–Baiano (39 km).
- Pomigliano d'Arco–Acerra (6 km).
- San Giorgio a Cremano–Volla (7 km).

Electrical System: 1500 V DC overhead.
Depots: Ponticelli, San Giovanni a Teduccio, Napoli PN.

ELECTRIC MULTIPLE UNITS

TYPE Fe220   3-SECTION ARTICULATED UNITS

3-section units can be coupled up to three in multiple and with Type T21. 12 are currently being refurbished. 12 are to be refurbished, but many others are stored.

Built: 1971–78.
Builders: SOFER/ASGEN.
Continuous Rating: 2 x 350 kW.
Wheel Arrangement: 2-B-B-2.

Length over Buffers: 39.64 m.
Total Weight: 56 tonnes.
Maximum Speed: 90 km/h.
Accommodation: –/124

R   Refurbished.

001	010	019	028	037	046	054	062	070	078
002	011	020	029	038	047	055	063	071	079
003	012	021	030	039	048	056	064	072	080
004	013	022	031	040	049	057	065	073	081
005	014	023	032	041	050	058	066	074	082
006	015	024	033	042	051	059	067	075	083
007	016	025	034	043	052	060	068	076	084
008	017	026 R	035	044	053	061	069	077	085
009	018	027	036	045					

TYPE T21   3-SECTION ARTICULATED UNITS

Similar to Type Fe220 but with a flat front end, better acceleration and passenger information system. 25 are currently being refurbished, the first being 105. Others are stored.

Built: 1989–91.
Builders: SOFER/ASGEN.
Continuous Rating: 2 x 350 kW.
Wheel Arrangement: 2-B-B-2.

Length over Buffers: 39.64 m.
Weight: 56 tonnes.
Maximum Speed: 90 km/h.
Accommodation: –/124*

R   Refurbished.
*   Refurbished in 2005 for "Napoli Express" tourist service, operated for Seatrain, with 114 red leather seats and white, blue and yellow livery.

086	090	094	098	101	104	107	110	113	116
087 R	091	095	099	102	105 R	108	111	114	117 R
088	092	096	100	103	106	109	112	115	118
089 *	093	097							

ETR.200 3-SECTION ARTICULATED UNITS

EMUs designed by Pininfarina. Units have gangways between cars and air conditioning but very few seats. 210 was severely damaged and is stored at San Giovanni a Teduccio.

Built: 2009–15.
Builders: AnsaldoBreda/FIREMA.
Continuous Rating: 6 x 170 kW.
Wheel Arrangement: Bo-Bo-2-Bo.

Weight: 68 tonnes.
Length over Couplers: 40 m.
Maximum Speed: 120 km/h.
Accommodation: –/46.

x   Special livery for "Campania Express" tourist service.

201	204	207	210 (S)	213	216	219	221	223	225 x
202	205	208	211	214	217	220	222	224	226 x
203	206	209	212	215	218				

OTHER MOTIVE POWER

No.	Type	Axles	Builders	Built	kW	km/h	Tonnes	Seats	Notes
BD 0221	EMU	Bo-Bo	IMAM/TIBB	1948	880	-	43	56	1.
BD 0222	EMU	Bo-Bo	IMAM/TIBB	1948	880	-	43	56	1.
D 500	dh	0-4-0	Greco/Deutz	1967	74	30	15	-	
D 501	dh	0-6-0	Henschel/Voith	1966	260	50	33	-	
D 502	dh	0-6-0	Henschel/Voith	1966	260	50	33	-	

1.   Historic stock used for "Costiera Express" tourist service. 0223 and 0225 supply spares.

2.8.2. FERROVIA ALIFANA FA

Known in the past as Ferrovia Napoli-Piedimonte (FNP), and once part of the Consorzio Trasporti Pubblici di Napoli (CTP) group, this is a pleasant foothills route, which as the name Piedimonte suggests, terminates just at the foot of the 2050m Monte Miletto. Trains operate over RFI lines between Santa Maria CV and Napoli Centrale. The "Alifana" was briefly merged with the FBN (see below) as Metrocampania Nordest but the latter has been dropped within EAV.

The Santa Maria CV to Piedimonte Matese line is being electrified at present but the delay in delivery of electric trains meant that non-energised overhead wire was stolen and it is not known if work will ever restart! Seven 2-car "Alfa 2" EMUs were delivered from 2014, but went instead to the FBN line. The "Alifana" also owns historic railcar ALn 773.012, ex FS ALn 773.3542.

FA also has a historic route from Santa Maria CV to Napoli which was originally 950 mm gauge, electrified at 11 kV AC 25 Hz but closed in 1976. This is being rebuilt as standard gauge, and mostly put underground, at present and is initially being operated as a connection with the Napoli metro. The section from Piscinola to Aversa is currently open. Nine MA 100 2-car sets obtained from the Roma metro operate the line. Numbers are not known.

Gauge: 1435 mm.
Route: Santa Maria Capua Vetere FS–Piedimonte Matese (41 km).
Depot: Piedimonte Matese.

DIESEL MULTIPLE UNITS

CLASS ALn 663 1A-A1

Details as FS Class ALn 663 except:

Built: 1991.
Maximum Speed: 125 km/h.

Weight: 37 tonnes.
Accommodation: –/68 1T.

ALn 663.010 (ex 663.I.14) | ALn 663.011 (ex 663.I.15)

CLASS ALn 668.100 1A-A1

Converted from FS Class ALn 668.1400.

Built: 1956–60/63.
Builder: Fiat.
Engine: 2 x Fiat 203 of 110 kW each.
Transmission: Mechanical.
Weight: 32 tonnes.

Length: 22.11 m.
Wheel Diameter: 920 mm.
Maximum Speed: 110 km/h.
Accommodation: –/68.

ALn 668.103 (ex FS ALn 668.1442)
ALn 668.113 (ex FS ALn 668.1444)

ALn 668.116 (ex FS ALn 668.1470)
ALn 668.118 (ex FS ALn 668.1472)

CLASS ALn 668.300 1A-A1

Formerly 668.005 to 009. Details as FS Class ALn 668.3000 except:

Built: 1981/82.
Maximum Speed: 110 km/h.

Weight: 37 tonnes.
Accommodation: –/68 1T.

ALn 668.305 (ex 668.1.9)
ALn 668.306 (ex 668.1.10)
ALn 668.307 (ex 668.1.11)

ALn 668.308 (ex 668.1.12)
ALn 660 309 (ex 668.1.13)

2.8.3. FERROVIA BENEVENTO-NAPOLI FBN

Not to be confused with the FT, a.k.a. Ferrovia Bari Nord, or the SNFT, a.k.a. Ferrovie Brescia Nord, this line used to be the Ferrovia Cancello–Benevento (FCB)! The single line descends a pleasant valley from Benevento to Cancello where trains take the RFI line to Napoli Centrale. One train a day in each direction is formed by Trenitalia DMUs on a through service.

Gauge: 1435 mm.
Electrical System: 3000 V DC overhead.

Route: Cancello FS–Benevento FS (48 km).
Depot: Benevento Appia.

ELECTRIC MULTIPLE UNITS

CLASS ALe 125 SINGLE CARS

Similar to railcars used by FAS and FCU. Originally numbered E 501–504. Used with 1959 driving trailers Le 125 511–514 (ex 0432 013–015, ex Rp 512–514) as well as with 1991 stock. E 501 has been withdrawn but is still stored at Benevento Appia.

Built: 1959.
Builders: OMS/TIBB.
Continuous Rating: 4 x 180 kW.
Accommodation: 16/52.

Length over Buffers: 22.30 m.
Weight: 47 tonnes.
Maximum Speed: 120 km/h.
Wheel Arrangement: Bo-Bo

† Rebuilt with new cabs.

ALe 125 502 (ex 2442 002, ex E 502)
ALe 125 503 (ex 2442 003, ex E 503) †

ALe 125 504 (ex 2442 004, ex E 504) (S)

CLASS ALe 088 & 126 SINGLE CARS, 2- or 3-CAR UNITS

ALe 126 units have several different formations, being permuted together at will. Originally numbered E 507 to E 512, E 507 is a single car with two cabs whilst the others have one cab and a corridor connection. E 508/9 were formed into three-car sets with intermediate and driving trailers, E 510 was a two-car set with just a driving trailer whilst E 511 and 512 formed a three-car set with an intermediate trailer between them. Power cars were prefixed E, intermediate trailers R (*rimorchiata*) and driving trailers (*rimorchiata pilota*) Rp. Can be used in multiple with 1959 stock. ALe 088 units are very similar and were acquired from TPER (formerly ATCM) in 2012.

Built: 1991 (ALe 088 1984).
Length: ALe 088, E & Rp 23.02 m; R 23.2 m; E 507 24.0 m.
Weight: E 48 tonnes ; R 31 tonnes; Rp 32 tonnes; E 507 50 tonnes. ALe 088: 53 + 35 + 35 tonnes.
Continuous Rating: 720 kW.
Accommodation: E & Rp −/88 1T ; R −/96.

Builders: FIREMA/Casaralta.

Maximum Speed: 120 km/h.
Wheel Arrangement (power cars): Bo-Bo.

ALe 088.001+ Le 096.001 + Lep 088.101

ALe 126 507	(ex E 507)
ALe 126 508 (U) + Le 126 418 + Le 126 518	(ex E 508 + R 518 + Rp 518)
ALe 126 509 + Le 126 419	(ex E 509 + Rp 519)
ALe 126 510 + Le 126 420 + Le 126 520	(ex E 510 + R 520 + Rp 520)
ALe 126 511 + Ale 126 512	(ex E 511 + E 512)

OTHER MOTIVE POWER

No.	Type	Axles	Builders	Built	kW	km/h	Tonnes	Seats	Notes
Le 21 (E 125 021)	D e	Bo-Bo	OMS/TIBB	1959	4 x 180	90	?	-	
Le 22 (U)	D e	Bo-Bo	Breda/CEMSA	1936	4 x 180	100	58	-	
Köf	B dh	0-4-0	Deutz	?	95	45	16	-	1.

1.   Ex DB Class 323. Identity unknown.

2.8.4. SOCIETÀ PER L'ESERCIZIO DI PUBBLICI SERVIZI ANONIMA   SEPSA

This is a suburban railway, from an obscure Napoli terminus reached via a maze of sordid back streets from Montesanto FS "Metro" station, via the back sides of the western suburbs, to two seaside resorts. Services are frequent on both lines, which are known as the "*Cumana*" and "*Circumflegrea*". Both lines are being doubled and new branches are planned or under construction. Most stock is horribly tagged. Class EN 300 are now all withdrawn.

Gauge: 1435 mm.
Routes:

· Napoli Montesanto–Torregaveta (Cumana, 20 km).
· Napoli Montesanto–Marina di Licola (Circumflegrea, 21 km).
· Marina di Licola–Torregaveta (4 km).

Electrical System: 3000 V DC overhead.
Depots: Quarto Officina, Fuorigrotta.

ELECTRIC MULTIPLE UNITS

CLASS ET 100   2-CAR UNITS

Each unit is formed of two power cars numbered ET 101 + ET 101A, and so on. ET 104 was formerly numbered ET 111 and replaced a damaged unit. Most units are now out of use.

Built: 1958–60.
Builders: Aerfer/Ocren.
Rating: 4 x 185 kW.
Wheel Arrangement: 2-Bo + Bo-2

Length over Buffers: 26.40 + 26.40 m.
Weight: 39 + 39 tonnes.
Maximum Speed: 90 km/h.
Accommodation: −/84 + −/84

ET 101	ET 103	ET 105	ET 107	ET 109
ET 102	ET 104	ET 106	ET 108	ET 110

▲ Ferrovia Alifana ALn 668.118 (ex FS ALn 668.1472) and preserved ALn 773.012 (ex FS 773.3542) are seen at Caiazzo on 4 June 2016. **Antonio Bertagnin**

▼ Brand new SEPSA EMU ET 503 is seen at Quarto station with a Napoli Montesanto–Licola service on 13 March 2019. **Antonio Bertagnin**

CLASS ET 400 2-CAR UNITS

FIREMA Type E 82B EMUs. Formed ET 401a + ET 401b, etc. ET 414 was originally bought by FBN and was purchased by SEPSA in 2006. It has never run in service. Most units have now been modernised, with air conditioning and more seats.

Built: 1991/92 (ET 414 1998). | **Length over Buffers:** 24.70 + 24.70 m.
Builders: Firema/Stanga. | **Weight:** 42 + 45 tonnes.
Rating: | **Maximum Speed:** 120 km/h.
Wheel Arrangement: 2-Bo + Bo-2 | **Accommodation:** –/36 + –/36 (refurbished –/48 + –/48).

ET 401	ET 404	ET 407	ET 410	ET 413
ET 402	ET 405	ET 408	ET 411	ET 414 (S)
ET 403	ET 406	ET 409	ET 412	

CLASS ET 500 "ALFA 3" 2-CAR UNITS

These units were ordered in 2006 from FIREMA but the first one was not delivered until 11 years later due to the builder going bankrupt. They are similar to the ETR.243 units for Napoli–Benevento (see Section 1.4) but with three doors per side, higher entrance height and no toilet. ET 501 to 504 were in service by mid 2018. Individual cars are ET 501a + ET 501b and so on.

Built: 2017– | **Length over Buffers:** 25.445 + 25.445 m.
Builders: Titagarh Firema Adler. | **Weight:** 50 + 50 tonnes.
Rating: 1480 kW. | **Maximum Speed:** 100 km/h.
Wheel Arrangement: . | **Accommodation:** –/36 + –/36.

ET 501	ET 504	ET 507	ET 509	ET 511
ET 502	ET 505	ET 508	ET 510	ET 512
ET 503	ET 506			

OTHER MOTIVE POWER

No.	Type	Axles	Builders	Built	kW	km/h	Tonnes	Seats	Notes
DHL 2	dh	0-6-0	Henschel DH500C	1958	367	60	52	-	Rebuilt 1974.
ABL 4	dh	0-6-0	Badoni	1962	-	-	34	-	
ABL 5	dh	0-4-0	Badoni	-	-	-	-	-	

2.9. FERROVIE APPULO LUCANE FAL

This narrow gauge network was part of the Ferrovie Calabro Lucane (FCL) whose southern section split off to become the Ferrovie della Calabria (FC) in 1991. Rolling stock was divided between the two. Once out of Bari the network passes through a wild, hilly area and serves some interesting towns. The Bari–Modugno sections runs parallel to the RFI line most of the way and was being doubled over most of the line around Modugno in 2018. The section in central Matera was put underground in 1986. The steep Avigliano–Potenza line shares a mixed gauge section with RFI from Avigliano Lucania to a point just north of Potenza S. Maria (Superiore). The company has two operational divisions, in Bari (Puglia region) and Potenza (Basilicata region) which function quite separately, with separate fleets.

The new Stadler units saw off the last Class M2 railcars in Potenza by cascade. Unit 801 has also been scrapped. All trains are now equipped with air conditioning, free from graffiti and in a pleasant white, blue and green livery. A rake of old rolling stock is retained at Bari Scalo for tourist specials.

FAL is managing construction of an 11 km new line from Bari to Bitritto, but will probably not operate it as it is standard gauge.

Gauge: 950 mm.
Routes (total 183 km):

• Bari Centrale–Altamura–Matera (76 km).
• Altamura–Gravina in Puglia–Avigliano Lucania–Potenza Città (98 km).
• Avigliano Lucania–Avigliano Città (9 km).

Depots: Bari Scalo, Matera Villa Longo, Potenza.

DIESEL LOCOMOTIVES

CLASS LM₄ 600   B-2

Operate works trains and rescue breakdowns. Also numbered 12 2 31 1440 601–606.

Built: 1974.
Builders: Breda/Ferrosud.
Engines: Two BRIF of 370 kW each.
Transmission: Hydraulic.

Length over Buffers: 12.36 m.
Weight: 44 tonnes.
Maximum Speed: 70 km/h.

| 602 | 603 (S) | 604 (S) | 607 | 608 |

CLASS LM₂ 750   B

Depot shunters, usually at Bari Scalo. Also numbered 12 2 31 3420 751/752.

Built: 1983.
Builders: Greco (works numbers 3184/5).
Engine: ?? of 65 kW.
Transmission: Hydraulic.

Length over Buffers:
Weight:
Maximum Speed:

| 751 | 752 |

DIESEL MULTIPLE UNITS

CLASS M₄ 300   SINGLE CARS

Operate with trailers numbered 041–055 (–/64 1T, ex Class RA 4000). Allocated to Potenza and only used locally. Units 302, 304, 312 and 315 were sold to FC.

Built: 1987–89.
Builder: Ferrosud.
Engines: Two FIAT-Iveco 8217.32.000 of 206 kW each.
Transmission: Hydro-mechanical.
Maximum Speed: 100 km/h.

Length over Couplers: 18.17 m.
Weight: 35 tonnes.
Accommodation: –/52 1T.
Wheel Arrangement: B-B.

| 301 | 305 | 306 | 307 | 308 | 309 | 310 | 311 | 313 | 314 |
| 303 | | | | | | | | | |

CLASS 350   2-CAR UNITS

Individually numbered cars with corridor connections. 2+1 seating for more urban services. Used on outer suburban services from Bari to Toritto.

Built: 1988/89.
Builder: Fiat.
Engines:
Transmission:

Length over Buffers:
Weight: 27.8 tonnes.
Maximum Speed:
Accommodation: –/33.

| 351 + 352 | 355 + 362 | 356 + 357 | 358 + 359 | 360 + 361 |
| 353 + 354 | | | | |

CLASSES SB & ST   2- & 3-CAR UNITS

Eleven 2-car (Stadler Bi = SB) and six 3-car (Stadler Tri = ST) 50% low-floor, air-conditioned DMUs were originally ordered, then were supplemented by one 3-car and six centre cars (with toilets) in 2018. The extended sets are SBT6 and so on. Four more 3-car sets will be delivered in 2022, with an option for four more. The Stadler sets are used on the Bari to Matera/Gravina and Potenza services, replacing Class 300, most of which have moved to Potenza to replace the last Class M₂ 200 units. Unit SB1 has coaches lettered SB1A + SB1B, ST1 is ST1A + ST1C + ST1B, and so on.

Built: 2012/13, 2018.
Length over Couplers: 2-car 17.916 + 17.916 m; 3-car 17.916 + 16.700 + 17.916 m.
Wheel Arrangement: 2-car Bo-2 + 2-Bo; 3-car Bo-2 + 2-2 + 2-Bo.
Accommodation: **Weight:** 2-car 66 tonnes; 3-car 86 tonnes.
Engines: 2 x 6-cylinder Cummins of 395 kW.   **Maximum Speed:** 120 km/h.

SB1	SB3	SB4	SB5	SBT6	SBT7	SBT8	SBT9	SBT10	SBT11
SB2									

ST1	ST3	ST4	ST5	ST6	ST7	ST8	ST9	ST10	ST11
ST2									

OTHER MOTIVE POWER

No.	Type	Axles	Builders	Built	kW	km/h	Tonnes	Seats	Notes
402 *	v	2-6-0T	CEMSA	1930	440	45	41	-	Potenza (S)
421	v	2-6-0T	CEMSA	1932	440	45	41	-	Bari Scalo

*   also numbered 12 2 34 1420 402-7.

2.10. FERROVIA ADRIATICO SANGRITANA   FAS

Also known as Ferrovia Sangritana, after the river Sangro which it follows, and previously known as the Ferrovie Adriatico Appenino, this scenic line links the Adriatic coast with a hilly hinterland. However, Lanciano–Castel di Sangro is currently out of use but is to be rebuilt. Trains now operate through from Lanciano to Pescara over RFI metals from San Vito since a new line was built from Lanciano to S. Vito, replacing the former, tortuous line in 2008. The old depot at Lanciano is being decommissioned. The new depot is at Treglio, halfway between Lanciano and S. Vito. The Saletti depot is alongside the S 154 road. A line is under construction from Saletti to Archi (10.2 km). FAS also operates passenger trains on behalf of Trenitalia over the RFI network from S.Benedetto del Tronto, Pescara, Teramo and Termoli. The company has a vast reserve of stock at Lanciano, presumably waiting for reopenings and new contracts. FAS is increasingly active in freight transport, with diesels hauling vans from the SEVEL plant at Saletti to Fossacesia/Torino di Sangro and from there over RFI lines using Class E.483 electric locos – see Section 1.2. In June 2015 FAS became part of Transporto Unico Abruzzese which groups transport in the Abruzzo region.

▲ FAL DMUs SB3 and SB4 arrive empty at Bari Centrale to form the departure to Marera and Gravina respectively on 26 May 2018. On the left is an EMU in the FT terminal below. **David Haydock**

Since the 2013 edition we have removed most of the stored stock as it will never run again! The most modern EMUs can be found in Section 1.4 of this book.

Gauge: 1435 mm.
Routes:

- **San Vito-Lanciano FS – Lanciano (9.2 km).**
- Lanciano–Crocetta–Archi–Castel di Sangro (86 km out of use).
- Fossacesia–Saletti (10.8 km).
- Ortona–Villa Caldari (9.8 km).

Electrical System: 3000 V DC overhead, shown in bold. Fossacesia–Saletti under electrification.
Depots: Lanciano (old depot), Saletti, Treglio.

ELECTRIC LOCOMOTIVES

CLASS E.483   TRAXX   Bo-Bo

FAS has three of these locos which it uses on main line freights. See Section 1.2.

DIESEL LOCOMOTIVES

D 26/27   Bo-Bo

Centre-cab diesels for freight – very similar to Trenord Class DE.500. See Trenord for details.
Built: 1977.

D 26 | D 27

CLASS D.752   Bo-Bo

FAS has eight of these locos. See Section 1.1.

ELECTRIC MULTIPLE UNITS

CLASS 400 (ALe 056)   2-CAR UNITS

FAS bought several SNCB Type AM56 stainless steel-bodied EMUs, five of which were rebuilt for open access main line services but have never been approved. They are all stored at Lanciano. Units 142, 144 and 149 are rotting away at the modernising plant. Known as *"Orsetto"* – little bear.

401 + 402 (150) | 403 + 404 (140) | 405 + 406 (146) | 407 + 408 (136) | 409 + 410 (129)

OTHER MOTIVE POWER

No.	Type	Axles	Builders	Built	kW	km/h	Tonnes	Seats	Notes
6	v	0-6-0T	Henschel	1914	213	40	30	-	1.
(D30)	dh	B-B	MaK	1970	810	60	64	-	2.
(D31)	dh	B-B	MaK	1969	810	60	64	-	3.
(D33) (S)	dh	B	MaK	1986	246	22	32	-	4.
(D34)	dh	C	Henschel	1976	507	37	-	-	5.

1. Ex FAV. Henschel 13262. Purchased for an aborted tourist service. Named VALTELLINA.
2. Ex SEVEL. Ex Hüttewerke Itsede-Peine no. 42. MaK G1100BB works no. 800164.
3. Ex VLTJ (Denmark) ML24. MaK G1100BB works no. 800161.
4. Ex SIV. MaK G321 B works no. 220113. Carries number 275.
5. EX SAV. Henschel Type DHG 700 C, works no. 31991.

▲ FAS D 27 and E.483.031 stand outside Treglio depot on 9 April 2013. **David Haydock**

▼ A graffiti-free but smoky FC M₄ 406 leaves Cosenza on 21 May 2013. **David Haydock**

2.11. FERROVIE DELLA CALABRIA   FC

Formerly the southern half of the Ferrovie Calabro Lucane (FCL), this group of lines shared the FCL rolling stock with the FAL. Unfortunately this network seems to be in terminal decline due to a lack of public finance. At the time of writing the two lines from Gioia Tauro had been closed since 2011 and the depot locked shut, the Pedace–San Giovanni in Fiore line was closed and the Cosenza–Catanzaro Lido line was cut in the middle by a landslide. This was still shut in 2018 and the 26 km Gimigliano–Soveria Mannelli was closed for safety reasons in March 2017. In normal times the "main line" is worked in two sections: Cosenza–Catanzaro Città and Catanzaro Città to Catanzaro Lido, the latter needing rack-fitted stock. Apart from the new Stadler units most stock is hideously disfigured by graffiti. The only "new" stock since the 2013 edition are the four Class 300 railcars from FAL.

In February 2018 FC announced the future reopening of the S. Nicola Silvana Mansio–S. Giovanni in Fiore line for tourist trains. There is also a project to electrify from Cosenza to Rogliano (24 km) in connection with the construction of a 10.5 km tramway in Cosenza. Work started in August 2018.

Gauge: 950 mm.
Routes (total 231 km):

- Cosenza–Pedace–Camigliatello Silano–San Giovanni in Fiore (79 km).
- Pedace–Catanzaro Città–Catanzaro Lido (103 km).
- Catanzaro Pratica–Catanzaro Sala (2 km) is rack fitted (Strub system).
- Gioia Tauro–Cinquefrondi (32 km), Gioia Tauro–Palmi–Sinopoli (26 km).

Depots: Catanzaro Città, Cosenza, Gioia Tauro.

DIESEL MULTIPLE UNITS

CLASS M₂ 200   SINGLE CARS

These units were shared between FAL and FC when FCL split. Despite the arrival of newer trains and line closures, several are still running. 132 and 142 from an earlier, but similar class, are stored at Cosenza.

Built: 1966–68 201–210; 1973 211–233.   **Length over Buffers:** 18.25 m.
Builders: Breda 201–10; Ferrosud 211–233.   **Weight:** 32 tonnes.
Engine: 370 kW.   **Maximum Speed:** 70 km/h.
Transmission: Mechanical.   **Accommodation:** 6/46
Wheel Arrangement: B-2.

207 (S)	211 (S)	214 (S)	218 (S)	220 (S)	223 (S)	226 (S)	228 (S)	230	232 (S)
209	212 (S)	216 (S)	219	221 (S)	224 (S)	227 (S)	229	231 (S)	233 (S)

CLASS M₄ 300 & M₄ 350C   SINGLE CARS

See FAL for details. FAL sold four Class 300 units to FC in 2015.

Class 350C are a version of Class 300 equipped for the rack section (c = *cremagliera*). This is the reason for the higher weight of 38.5 tonnes. Maximum speed is 20 km/h on the rack section. All allocated to Catanzaro depot.

Built: 1987–89 (302–315); 1990 (351/2); 1996/97 (353–360).

302 (S)	304	312 (S)	315						
351 (S)	352	353	354	355	356 (S)	357	358 (S)	359	360

CLASS M₄ 400   SINGLE CARS

These are similar to FAL Class 300 (see FAL for details). Built in 1995–97. All allocated to Cosenza.

401	402	403	404	405	406	407	408

CLASS M₄ 500C   2-CAR UNITS

These part low-floor, rack-fitted, air-conditioned diesel-electric units were built by Stadler and are mainly used on the Catanzaro Lido–Catanzaro Città route. Numbers on front ends are DE M4C 501 A and 501 B. 501 is at Cosenza depot, the others at Catanzaro. Two more units were ordered in 2018, with an option for ten more. Their arrival will allow the withdrawal of all the old stock.

Built: 2009/10.
Wheel Arrangement: Bo-2 + 2-Bo.
Accommodation: –/47 (4) + –/43 (6).
Maximum Speed: 80 km/h.
Engines: 2 x Cummins 6-cylinder of 395 kW each.

Builder: Stadler.
Length: 17.916 + 17.916 m.
Weight: 71 tonnes.

| 501 | 502 | 503 | 504 | 505 | 506 | 507 |

DIESEL LOCOMOTIVES

CLASS LM₄ 600   B-2

Locos used on works trains. Other stored locos are shut away at Gioia Tauro.

For details see FAL.

| 601 (S) | 606 |

CLASS LM₂ 700   B

These locos were originally coupled to non-rack-fitted railcars in order to power them over the rack-fitted section. Rack equipment was removed in 2010. All stored at Cosenza.

Built: 1981–85.
Builder: SLM.
Continuous Rating:
Transmission:

Length over Buffers:
Weight:
Maximum Speed:

| 701 (S) | 702 (S) | 703 (S) |

CLASS LM₂ 750   B

See FAL for details. Stored at Cosenza. Built 1983.

753 (S)

STEAM LOCOMOTIVES

No.	Type	Axles	Builders	Built	kW	km/h	Tonnes	Seats	Notes
188	v	2-6-0T	Breda	1924				-	1
353	v	0-8-0T	Borsig	1926	590	45	46	-	2
358	v	0-8-0T	Borsig	1926	590	45	46	-	3
403 (S)	v	2-6-0T	CEMSA	1930	440	45	41	-	2
411	v	2-6-0T	CEMSA	1930	440	45	41	–	4
412	v	2-6-0T	CEMSA	1932	440	45	41	–	5
503	v rack	2-6-2T	CEMSA	1932	440	40/13	48	–	6
504	v rack	2-6-2T	CEMSA	1932	440	40/13	48	–	2
506	v rack	2-6-2T	CEMSA	1932	440	40/13	48	–	7

1. Monument. Gioia Tauro depot.
2. Cosenza depot.
3. Plinthed in Parco Selva di Paliano, south of Roma.
4. Plinthed at Città di Castello (Perugia).
5. Plinthed at Mileto.
6. Plinthed at Castrovillari.
7. Plinthed at Città del Ragazzi, Cosenza.

2.12. FERROVIA CIRCUMETNEA   FCE

This railway almost completely encircles Mount Etna, with some long stretches where old lava flows can be seen. The urban section in Catania is in the slow process of being put underground, converted to standard gauge and electrified – initially to Paternò, then Adrano (40 km). In June 1999, the 3.8 km underground section from Catania Porto–Catania Borgo opened. Work is under way to extend the line from Stesicoro to Palestro (2.2 km); Palestro to the airport (4.6 km) is expected by 2024. At the western end work is under way to extend the line from Nesima to Monte Po in 2019, then Monte Po to Misterbianco (2.1 km) by 2021.

FCE has ordered ten new 2-car diesel railcars from Newag of Poland for the narrow gauge line. Some older stock – ADe 01 to 03 plus AL 541 and 542 – is dumped at Riposto.

Gauge: 950 mm (110 km), 1435 mm (8.8 km).
Route: Porto/Stesicoro–Catania Borgo–Nesima (8.8 km), Catania Borgo–Riposto (110 km).
Depots: Catania Borgo, Bronte, Randazzo.
Electrification: (standard gauge "metro" section) 3000 V DC overhead.

ELECTRIC MULTIPLE UNITS

CLASS M 88   2-CAR UNITS

These units took over the "metro" section from Class E.100 electric railcars hired from FCU. The latter have all been scrapped except E.110 which returned to FCU. In order to work the extensions to the metro, FCE tendered for up to 54 2-car EMUs in 2018.

Built: 2001/02/08/10.
Builder: FIREMA (Type M 88).
Continuous Rating: 2400 kW.
Wheel Arrangement: Bo-Bo + Bo-Bo.

Length over Couplers: 19.765 + 19.765 m.
Weight: 89 tonnes.
Maximum Speed: 120 km/h.
Accommodation: –/36 + –/36.

M 88-01 Norma	M 88-03 Zaira	M 88-05 Rita	M 88-07 Brigante
M 88-02 Beatrice	M 88-04 Elvira	M 88-06	M 88-08 Donatello

DIESEL MULTIPLE UNITS

CLASS ADE 12–20   SINGLE CARS

These units were being refurbished. 18 was the first and 19 the second as their names suggest. Unit 11 was scrapped after a fire.

Built: 1970–73.
Builders: OMS/TIBB/Fiat.
Continuous Rating: 184 kW.
Transmission: Electric.
Wheel Arrangement: Bo-Bo.

Length over Buffers: 18.25 m.
Weight: 31 tonnes.
Maximum Speed: 75 km/h.
Accommodation: –/56.

R   Refurbished

12 (S)	14 (S)	16 R	18 R "La Prima"	20
13	15	17	19 R "La Seconda"	

CLASS ADE 21–25   SINGLE CARS

Similar to FAL Class M₄ 300.

Built: 1991/92.
Builders: IMPA.
Continuous Rating:
Transmission:

Length over Buffers:
Weight:
Maximum Speed: 100 km/h.
Accommodation: –/50 + –/50.

21 (U)	22	23	24	25

CLASS RALn 64   SINGLE CARS

These railcars were former FS Class RALn 60, purchased by FCE from the Castelvetrano–Ribera line which closed on 31 December 1985. Units RALn 60 02, 04, 05, 07, 14 and 18 became FCE 64.01 to 06.

Built: 1949–50.
Builders: Fiat.
Engine: Iveco 8217.32.032 of 170 kW.
Transmission: Mechanical.
Wheel Arrangement: B-B.

Length over Buffers: 19.12 m.
Weight:
Maximum Speed:
Accommodation: –/64 1T.

64.01 (S) | 64.02 (S) | 64.03 (S) | 64.04 (S) | 64.05 | 64.06

CLASS DMU   "VULCANO"   2-CAR UNITS

New DMUs built in Poland: Newag Type 226M. Four more were ordered in 2017. There is an option for two more.

Built: 2015/16.
Builders: Newag.
Engines:
Transmission: Electric.

Length over Buffers:
Weight:
Maximum Speed:
Accommodation: –/53 + –/53.

001 | 002 | 003 | 004 | 005 | 006 | 007 | 008

OTHER FCE MOTIVE POWER

No.	Type	Axles	Builders	Built	kW	km/h	Tonnes	Seats	Notes
10 "Mascali"	v	C	La Meuse	1909	-	-	-	-	Bronte
14	v	C	La Meuse	1909	-	-	-	-	1.
ALn 56.01	AB dm	1A-A1	Fiat	1937	2 x 55	100	19	12/44	
ALn 56.06	AB dm	1A-A1	Fiat	1937	2 x 55	100	19	12/44	

1. Plinthed at Catania Borgo.

2.13. FERROVIA CENTRALE UMBRA   FCU

The first part of this network to be built, in 1886, was the 950 mm gauge Umbertide–Sansepolcro line. The other, standard gauge, lines were built in 1915–20 being originally electrified at 11 kV AC 25 Hz. The Sansepolcro line was converted to standard gauge in 1956 and the whole network electrified at 3000 V DC in 1958. The overhead deteriorated and the company decided not to replace it and bought diesel railcars. The Terni–Perugia–Sansepolcro line (not the branch to Perugia Santa Anna yet) was then re-electrified in 2009 and FCU ordered four Alstom Minuetto EMUs for this line. However, the whole Sansepolcro–Perugia–Terni line was closed in 2018, with trains replaced by buses, due to poor track condition. The line reopened from Perugia PSG to Città di Castello (57 km) in October 2018. The rest was due to reopen in 2020.

In December 2010, FCU became the rail part of transport company Umbria Mobilità which administers most public transport in the Umbria region, then in 2014 Umbria Mobilità was taken over by Busitalia-Sita Nord, part of the FS group. FCU also operates a few trains over RFI lines to Orte and Terontola and operates the 104 km Terni–Rieti–L'Aquila line.

Gauge: 1435 mm.   **Depots:** Umbertide, Sansepolcro.
Routes:

• **Terni FS–Todi–Perugia Ponte San Giovanni FS–Sansepolcro (147 km).**
• Perugia PSG–Perugia Santa Anna (5 km).

Electrical System: 3000 V DC overhead (lines in bold).

ELECTRIC MULTIPLE UNITS

CLASS E.120   SINGLE CARS

Recently refurbished.

Built: 1980.
Power Rating: 588 kW.
Weight: 63 tonnes.
Accommodation: 10/76.

Builder: Stanga/TIBB.
Length: 23.02 m.
Maximum Speed: 90 km/h.
Wheel Arrangement: Bo-Bo.

E.121 | E.122

OTHER MOTIVE POWER

No.	Type	Axles	Builders	Built	kW	km/h	Tonnes	Seats
E.110	e	Bo-Bo	OMS/TIBB	1957	4 x 180	100	40	–/68.
E 152	e	Bo-Bo	Breda/Tosi/CGE	1918	4 x 180	100	40	-
E 153	e	Bo-Bo	Breda/Tosi/CGE	1918	4 x 180	100	40	-

E 152 & 153 are steeple-cab electric locos stored inside a shed at Sansepolcro, as is E.110.

▲ FG Le/ALe 200.003 and another EMU of the same type are seen at San Severo depot on 9 April 2013.   **David Haydock**

2.14. FERROVIE DEL GARGANO FG

This line links the RFI Adriatic coast line with the Gargano peninsula – the "spur" on the Italian "boot". The line is picturesque with some very beautiful hilly and lakeside stretches. Some services operate through from San Severo to Foggia. The company took over operation of the Foggia–Lucera line in 2009 and operates a half-hourly service with FLIRT EMUs there. A new 11.7 km cut-off near San Severo opened in 2015 but train services have been suspended between Cagnano Varano and Peschici Calanella due to problems with level crossings.

Gauge: 1435 mm.
Routes: San Severo FS–Peschici Calenella (79 km) and Foggia–Lucera (17 km).
Electrical System: 3000 V DC overhead.   **Depots:** San Severo, Foggia.

ELECTRIC MULTIPLE UNITS

CLASS ALe 080 SINGLE CARS

Identical in outline to Metrocampania NordEst Class ALe 126. Operate with trailers in the B200 and B300 series. Numbers were formerly ALe 80.01 upwards but now show 080.001 and so on.

Built: 1981–83.   **Length over Buffers:** 23.0 m.
Builders: OMS/Cittadella/Casaralta/TIBB.   **Weight:** 50 tonnes.
Continuous Rating: 720 kW.   **Maximum Speed:** 120 km/h.
Accommodation: 8/72.   **Wheel Arrangement:** Bo-Bo.
EVN: 94 83 4 080 001-c and so on.

| 080.001 | 080.003 (S) | 080.004 | 080.005 | 080.006 |
| 080.002 | | | | |

CLASS E.100 & ALe 200 SINGLE CARS & 2-CAR UNITS

Ten Class E.100 single railcars were built for FCU which still retains E.110 for heritage trains. E.101, 102, 104, 106, 107 and 108 were then acquired by FG whilst 105, 109 and 110 went to FCE. FG still has non-rebuilt, but modernised E.106–E.108 whilst the others have been converted by CORIFER into 2-car sets.

Built: 1957. Rebuilt by CORIFER.
Builders: OMS/TIBB.   **Weight:** E.100 47 tonnes; ALe 200 38 + 50 tonnes.
Length over Buffers: E.100 20.75 m; ALe 200 19.71 + 22.50 m.
Continuous Rating: 600 kW.   **Maximum Speed:** 95 km/h.
Accommodation: E.100 –/57. ALe 200 –/52 + –/52.
Wheel Arrangement: E.100 Bo-Bo; ALe 200 Bo-Bo + 2-2

| E.106 | E.107 (S) | E.108 |

| ALe 200.001 + Le 200.001 (ex E.101 + E.103) | ALe 200.003 + Le 200.003 (ex E.104 + R.212) |
| ALe 200.002 + Le 200.002 (ex E.102 + R.211) | |

DIESEL LOCOMOTIVES

ex DB CLASS 211 B-B

For details see HUPAC. Ex DB 211 270, and ex ÖBB. Used for track maintenance trains.

DD FMT BA 1318 B

CLASS DE 520 B-B

FG bought DE 520.006 and 007 from Nordcargo in 2015. Used for rescue and maintenance.
For details see Section 1.1.

ELECTRIC LOCOMOTIVE

CLASS L 80 Bo-Bo

A small locomotive, the last of four, formerly used with old coaching stock numbered 201–203 and 301–303.

Built: 1982.
Builder: OMS.
Continuous Rating: 544 kW.

Length over Buffers: 13.15 m.
Weight: 44 tonnes.
Maximum Speed: 100 km/h.

L 80.02 (S)

OTHER MOTIVE POWER

No.	Type	Axles	Builders	Built	kW	km/h	Tonnes	Seats	Notes
A 52(U)	ABD e	Bo-Bo	Savigliano/OFM	1934	4 x 147	83	51	14/46	

2.15. FERROVIA GENOVA–CASELLA FGC

A line climbing up into hills to the north of Genova from a terminus about one kilometre north of Genova Brignole station. Beware – this short distance is all uphill and unsigned – give yourself 30 minutes or take bus 49. The line has been rescued from a sure demise after management was taken over by AMT Genova, the city metro and bus operator. Units are now being turned out in a red livery with AMT Genova on the side. Railcars operate in the peaks with non-driving trailers in the B 50 and B 100 series. ET 007 has been transferred to TT.

Gauge: 1000 mm.
Route: Genova Piazza Manin–Casella (24.3 km).
Electrical System: 3000 V DC overhead (converted from 2800 V DC).
Depots: Genova Piazza Manin, Casella.

ROLLING STOCK

No.	Type	Axles	Builders	Built	kW	km/h	Tonnes	Seats	Notes
A 2	BD e	Bo-Bo	Ca&To/TIBB	1929	310	40	32	36	1.
A 5	BD e	Bo-Bo	Ca&To/TIBB	1926*	360	50	35	44	2.
A 6 (S)	BD e	Bo-Bo	Ca&To/TIBB	1926*	360	50	35	44	2.
A 8	BD e	Bo-Bo	Firema	1993	350	50	47	36	
A 9	BD e	Bo-Bo	Firema	1994	350	50	47	36	
A 10	BD e	Bo-Bo	Firema	1996	350	50	47	36	
A 11	BD e	Bo-Bo	Firema	1997	560	50	47	36	
A 12	BD e	Bo-Bo	Firema	1997	560	50	47	36	
29	B e	Bo-Bo	TIBB	1924	355	40	31	15	3.
D 1	de	B-B	Gmeinder/MaK	1964	375	40	33	-	4.

* Rebuilt 1957.

1. Ex Ferrovia Elettrica Val di Fiemme (Ora–Predazzo) in 1963.
2. Ex SSIF (Spoleto–Norcia, 950 mm gauge) in 1969.
3. Historic unit, sometimes used in normal service (see frontispiece of this book).
   Ex FAA, 950 mm gauge, in 1962.
4. Gmeinder 5326. Ex DB V52.902, ex SWEG, rebuilt with an IVECO engine in 2015.
   Sister V52 901 is with track company Ventura.

2.16. FERROVIE DEL SUD EST   FSE

With 473 km of line, this is the biggest private network in Italy, covering the heel of the "boot". In late 2016 the company was declared bankrupt and taken under FSI control. Subsequent investigations showed that managers had defrauded the company. It seems that FSI will not "integrate" FSE but this remains to be seen. In 2018, FSE was suffering from a 50 km/h speed limit due to a lack of modern signalling.

Trains are either DMUs or, from Bari in the peaks, loco-hauled trains formed with double-deck coaches. FSE 0-6-0 tank engine No. 6, built by St. Leonard, Liège, Belgium is plinthed on Bari Sud Est station. FSE is currently electrifying the Bari–Conversano–Putignano–Martina Franca and Bari–Casassima–Putignano lines and has ordered EMUs from Newag in Poland but these had not been delivered in 2018 due to lack of payment. The first section of "live" overhead was tested with a train in November 2015. When the EMUs arrive, some ATR.200 DMUs should move to Lecce. There is an enormous amount of old stock stored across the network. Since the last book, locos B 101–105, BB 151–163, Ad 51–80, Ad 121–132 and Class ATR.200 have all been withdrawn. The two D.753 diesels were for sale in 2018. On the other hand FSE was using Trenitalia Class ALn 668.1900, 3100 and 3300 units. These can be found in Section 1.3.

Gauge: 1435 mm.
Routes:

* Bari Centrale FS–Mungivacca–Conversano–Putignano–Martina Franca–Taranto FS (113 km).
* Mungivacca–Casamassima–Putignano (43 km).
* Martina Franca–Francavilla Fontana FS–Novoli–Lecce FS (103 km).
* Lecce FS–Zollino–Nardò Centrale–Gallipoli–Casarano (75 km).
* Zollino–Maglie–Gagliano Léuca (47 km), Novoli–Nardò Centrale–Casarano–Gagliano Léuca (75 km).
* Maglie–Otranto (18 km).

Depots: Bari Sud Est, Lecce.

ELECTRIC MULTIPLE UNITS

CLASS ETR.322   3-CAR UNITS

See Section 1.4 for details.

DIESEL MULTIPLE UNITS

Ad 31–44   SINGLE CARS

Derived from FS Class ALn 668.1900. Mainly used on services south from Lecce. Ad 37 is in the newer red/black livery.

Built: 1978.
Builders: OMECA/Fiat/Savigliano.
Engines: Two Fiat 8217.32 of 170 kW each.
Transmission: Mechanical.
Wheel Arrangement: 1A-A1.
EVN: 95 83 4668 031-c to 044-c.

Length over Buffers: 23.54 m.
Weight: 37 tonnes.
Maximum Speed: 130 km/h.
Accommodation: –/68 1T.

| 31 | 33 | 35 | 36 | 37 | 38 | 40 | 41 | 43 | 44 |
| 32 | 34 | | | | | | | | |

Ad 81–88   2-CAR UNITS

Air-conditioned DMUs of a similar design to TPER single railcars ALn 067–082. Used mainly on the Bari–Martina Franca service. 083/084 are in red/black livery.

Built: 2000.
Builder: Fiat.
Engines: Two Fiat 8217.31.0000A14 of 170 kW each per car.
Maximum Speed: 90 km/h.
Transmission: Hydraulic. Voith T211 rz.
EVNs: 95 83 4000 081-c and so on

Length: 23.84 m + 23.84 m.
Weight: 43 + 43 tonnes.
Accommodation: –/80 1T + –/80 1T.
Wheel Arrangement: 1A-A1 + 1A-A1.

| 081 + 082 | 083 + 084 | 085 + 086 | 087 + 088 |

CLASS ATR.220   3-SECTION ARTICULATED UNITS

These units are identical to Class ATR.220 units later delivered to TPER and Trenord. They now work most services on the FSE network north of Lecce.

Built: 2008–10.
Weight: 99 tonnes.
Engines: 2 x MAN D2876LUE623 of 382 kW each.
Maximum Speed: 120 km/h.
Wheel Arrangement: B-2-2-B.

Builder: PESA.
Length over Buffers: 55.57 m.

Transmission: Hydraulic. Voith.
Accommodation: –/151.

ATR.220.001 is 95 83 4220 801-c + 802-c + 803-c,
ATR.220.002 is 95 83 4220 805-c + 804-c +807-c and so on.

ATR.220.001	ATR.220.007	ATR.220.013	ATR.220.018	ATR.220.023
ATR.220.002	ATR.220.008	ATR.220.014	ATR.220.019	ATR.220.024
ATR.220.003	ATR.220.009	ATR.220.015	ATR.220.020	ATR.220.025
ATR.220.004	ATR.220.010	ATR.220.016	ATR.220.021	ATR.220.026
ATR.220.005	ATR.220.011	ATR.220.017	ATR.220.022	ATR.220.027
ATR.220.006	ATR.220.012			

DIESEL LOCOMOTIVES

CLASS DE.122   Bo-Bo

The locos power peak passenger trains Bari–Martina Franca with double-deck stock in push-pull mode.

Built: 1989–90.
Builder: DPA.
Engines: Two 610 kW Caterpillar engines.
Weight: 69 tonnes.
Continuous Rating: 1220 kW.
EVNs: 92 83 2122 410-c and so on.

Transmission: Electric.
Wheel Diameter: 1040 mm.
Maximum Speed: 100 km/h.
Length over Buffers: 15.84 m.
Train Heating: Electric.

| 410 (S) | 411 (S) | 412 | 413 | 414 | 415 |

OTHER MOTIVE POWER

No.	Type	Axles	Builders	Built	kW	km/h	Tonnes	Notes
14	v	0-8-0T		1914	-	-	-	MFP. Lucato Termica, Catelato Monferrato
315	v	0-6-0T		1913	-	-	-	Lecce museum
B 103	dh	0-4-0	Greco/Deutz	1959	184	55	25	Lecce museum
B 110	dh	0-4-0	Greco/Deutz	1962	22	13	10	Lecce museum
BB 159	de	Bo-Bo	Reggiane	1959	600	80	52	Lecce museum
Ad 05	dm	B-2	OMS/MAN	1939	250	90	40	Lecce museum
Ad 72	dm	B-2	Breda/Aerfer	1960	395	120	40	Lecce museum

▲ FSE DE.122.412 stands at Bari FSE station with empty stock for a Bari Centrale–Martina Franca train on 24 May 2018. **David Haydock**

▼ FT CAF EMU ETR.452 TR 07 passes through Fesca-San Girolamo station with a train to Bitonto on 26 May 2018. **David Haydock**

2.17. FERROTRAMVIARIA FT

Also known as Ferrovia Bari Nord, Ferrovia Bari–Barletta and most recently Ferrovie del Nord Barese which is painted on the side of units. Not to be confused with the Brescia Nord or Benevento-Napoli! Originally a narrow gauge tramway, converted to standard gauge and electrified at 3000 V DC in 1965. A new "metro" line from Bari Fesca S. Girolamo to Ospedale San Paolo opened in early 2008 and is being extended to Regioni. A 7.7 km underground loop off the Barletta line serving the airport opened in July 2013 (see map at front of book). The company also owns four Class E.483 locos, operating freights from Bari. All of the single car multiple units EL 01 to 15 are now scrapped or stored.

At the time of writing, the section of line from Ruvo to Barletta was still closed after an accident in July 2016 when ELT 210 and ETR.341 TR 02 collided head-on.

Gauge: 1435 mm.
Routes: Bari Centrale FS–Palese–Bitonto–Barletta FS (70 km), plus airport loop (7.7 km).
Bari Fesca S. Girolamo–Ospedale S. Paolo (5.1 km).
Electrical System: 3000 V DC overhead.
Depots: Bari Scalo, Barletta Scalo.

ELECTRIC MULTIPLE UNITS

ELT 200 3- & 4-CAR UNITS

Air conditioned units with high floors. 201–206 have more standing space and are used on the urban line to Ospedale San Paolo. 207–212 have more seats, were extended to four-car after delivery and work trains from Bari to Bitonto, Ruvo and Barletta.

Built: 2005 (201–206); 2008 (207–212).
Builder: Alstom.
Continuous Rating: 1280 kW.
Accommodation: ELT 201–206: –/43 + –/53 + –/43.
ELT 207–212: –/53 + –/66 + –/66 + –/53.
Wheel Arrangement: Bo-Bo + 2-2 (+ 2-2) + Bo-Bo.

Length over Buffers: 22.15 + 20.60 + 22.15 m.
Weight: 123 tonnes.
Maximum Speed: 110 km/h.

Unit ELT 201 is 94 83 4 200 101-c + 200 103-c + 200 102-c, and so on.
Unit ELT 207 is 94 83 4 200 119-c + 200 120-c + 200 121-c + 200 122-c and so on.

| 201 | 203 | 205 | 206 | 207 | 208 | 209 | 210 (U) | 211 | 212 |
| 202 | 204 | | | | | | | | |

ETR.452 "CIVITY" 4-SECTION ARTICULATED UNITS

In 2015 FT received a total of five 4-car Civity EMUs from CAF of Spain.

Built: 2014.
Length: 21.50 + 16.20 + 16.20 + 21.50 m.
Power Rating: 2080 kW.
Accommodation: –/51 (6) 1TD + –/64 + –/64 + –/58 (6).

Builder: CAF.
Maximum Speed: 160 km/h.
Wheel Arrangement: Bo-2-2-2-Bo.

ETR.452 TR 03 is 94 83 3 451 001-c + 452 201-c + 452 301-c + 452 401-c.

| ETR.452 TR 03 | ETR.452 TR 04 | ETR.452 TR 05 | ETR.452 TR 06 | ETR.452 TR 07 |

OTHER MOTIVE POWER

No.	Type	Axles	Builders	Built	kW	km/h	Tonnes	Seats	Notes
De 01 (S)	de	Bo-Bo	Ca&To/TIBB	1928	4 x 37	40	30	-	1.
De 02	de	0-4-0	OMS/TIBB	1963	2 x 44	30	16	-	
Le 101*	D e	Bo-Bo	OMS/TIBB	1963	4 x 180	90	47	-	
Le 102 (S)	D e	Bo-Bo	OMS/TIBB	1963	4 x 180	90	47	-	

1. Ex SAF (Bari San Spirito–Bitonto), rebuilt twice.
* Preserved.

2.18. FERROVIE UDINE–CIVIDALE   FUC

This short line was separated from Ferrovie Venete together with FAM to become Sistemi Territoriali in 2002, then in 2005 was split off as a separate company which is owned by the Friuli-Venezia-Giulia region. FUC also owns two Class E.190 electric locomotives which work freight and a Udine–Villach (Austria) passenger service with ÖBB stock. See Section 1.2.

Gauge: 1435 mm.
Route: Udine FS–Cividale del Friuli (15 km).
Depot: Udine.

DIESEL LOCOMOTIVES

CLASS Ld 400   C

Originally delivered to Società Veneta Autoferrovie Padova. Works no. 500076.

Built: 1976.
Builder: MaK (Type G700C).
Continuous Rating: 550 kW.
Transmission: Hydraulic.

Length over Buffers: 9.91 m.
Weight: 51 tonnes.
Maximum Speed: 50 km/h.

Ld 405

CLASS DE 424   Bo-Bo

Diesel luggage vans, ex SV, then FBP and FPS. 424.01/05–8 were with TPER, but are now withdrawn. DE 424.04 is preserved by SVF at Primolano.

Built: 1957/58.
Builders: TIBB/OM.
Engines: Two OM BXD-IL of 169 kW each.
Length over Buffers: 12.04 m.

Transmission: Electric.
Weight: 32 tonnes.
Maximum Speed: 75 km/h.

DE 424.02

CLASS DE 520 (D.753)   Bo-Bo

Acquired in 2012 for shunting and trip freights around Udine. See Section 1.1 for details.

DIESEL MULTIPLE UNITS

CLASS ADn 800   SINGLE CARS

The last of nine units – ADn 801 to 809, 803 is retained for heritage trains.

Built: 1958.
Builders: OMS/Fiat.
Engine: Fiat 700 of 147 kW.
Wheel Arrangement: B-2
Length: 20.10 m.

Transmission: Hydraulic.
Weight: 31 tonnes.
Maximum Speed: 90 km/h.
Accommodation: –/72

803

CLASS ALn 663.900 {SINGLE CARS}

Based on the FS Class ALn 663. 903 is now with TPER (ex FPS). 902, 905–909 are with ST. Operate with driving trailers Bp 664.372/3 (Fiat, 1985/91). See TPER ALn 663.900 for details.

Built: 1984–93

| ALn 663.901 | ALn 663.904 | ALn 663.910 |

CLASS ATR 110 {3-SECTION ARTICULATED UNITS}

See Section 1.3 for details.

2.19. FUORIMURO FMR

FuoriMuro Servizi Portuali e Ferroviari was set up by InRail in 2010 to take over "last mile" operations in the port of Genova. Originally InRail owned 15% of the company, the rest being in the hands of the port authority and port customers. In 2017 FNM took a 49% stake in the company with an option to increase this to 70%. Fuorimuro is now operating other services in the north of Italy, including the Italian section of a mixed freight train, launched in late 2012, from several points in Lombardia to the Marseille area of France.

The company has two Siemens Vectron electric locomotives E.191.002 and 003, two Vossloh G 2000 diesels, five LHB shunters (98 80 3 509–511, 526 and 537 ex VPS in Germany) and three Zephir road-rail tractors. The company hires up to ten diesel locomotives as required from Mercitalia (Class D.145) for use in the port of Genova and electric locos, for example Class E.483. The three MaK G764C shunters below were taken over by Mercitalia S&T from the port of Genova and are now hired to FuoriMuro.

1059   MaK 700064 / 1982 G 764 C ex port 3703-1059
1061   MaK 700066 / 1982 G 764 C ex port 3703-1061
1062   MaK 700067 / 1982 G 764 C ex port 3703-1062

▲ FUC units ALn 663.910 and ATR.110.001 are seen at Cividale del Friuli on 12 September 2018.
David Haydock

2.20. GTS RAIL GTSR

This is an intermodal freight train operator based in Bari. The company opened its own maintenance depot in Bari in December 2016. The company has ten TRAXX electric locos in a black and orange livery.

2.21. GRUPPO TORINESE TRASPORTI GTT

GTT was formed in 2003 as the merger of suburban passenger operator SATTI and ATM, Torino's urban transport operator. GTT operates two separate heavy rail lines as follows as well as trams and the Torino metro. In 2017 GTT teamed up with Arriva Italia in order to bid to operate the Torino SFM suburban network, in competition with Trenitalia.

The Ferrovia Centrale del Canavese, which became the Ferrovie Torino Nord in 1933, was taken over in 1959. Rivarolo–Torino trains today continue over RFI tracks to Lingotto then Chieri. DMUs are now banned from this route. The line from Rivarolo to Pont Canavese is not electrified but in March 2018 electrification was approved and financed.

The Ferrovia Torino-Ceres (FTC) became part of SATTI in 1980 along with local bus and tram routes. The Ponte Mosca–Ceres line was the first DC electrified line in Italy, electrified at 4000 V and later converted to standard Italian 3000 V. Ponte Mosca is now closed and the line runs into Dora station which is no longer connected to the rest of the rail network. Work is now programmed for the line to be reconnected. EMUs operate from Torino to Germagnano, then DMUs usually work from there to Ceres, despite the line being electrified.

Ponte Mosca (literally, bridge of flies and also known as Porta Milano or even Torino Cirié-Lanzo) is now used to store GTT locos and a variety of preserved stock.

Gauge: 1435 mm.
Routes:
- **Séttimo–Rivarolo (22 km) ex FCC.**
- Rivarolo–Pont Canavese (16.3 km) ex FCC.
- **Torino Dora–Ceres (41.2 km) ex FTC.**

Electrical System: 3000 V DC overhead. Electrified lines are shown in **bold** type.
Depots: Rivarolo (ex FCC) and Cirié (ex FTC).

ELECTRIC MULTIPLE UNITS

CLASS ALe 056 2-CAR UNITS

Ex SNCB Budd EMUs 133 and 148, purchased in 1999 and refurbished by Metalmeccanica Milanesio at Moretta in 1993/94. Units also carry set numbers 09 and 11. Only rarely used, on the Torino Dora–Germagnano route. Set 10 went to TPER in 2013. These units were believed to be stored in 2018.

Built: 1956.
Builder: BND (under licence from Budd, Pennsylvania).
Weight: 40 + 39 tonnes.
Continuous Rating: 4 x 155 kW.
Length over Couplers: 22.64 + 22.64 m.

Wheel Arrangement: A1-1A + A1-1A.

Maximum Speed: 130 km/h.
Accommodation: 28/56 1T + –/84 1T.

09 ALe 056.09 M1 + ALe 056.09 M2 (133) | 11 ALe 056.011 M1 + ALe 056.011 M2 (148)

CLASS Y0530   2-CAR UNITS

These modern EMUs have low-floor entrances and air conditioning. The numbering is the longest we know! ETR is unjustified as they are not fast. Y0530 is the Fiat type number. Between the Y0530 and the set number, each car also carries M1 and M2 meaning power cars 1 and 2! Units are only used on the Rivarolo line.

Built: 1996/97.
Builder: Fiat Ferroviaria/ABB Tecnomasio.
Continuous Rating: 1440 kW.
Length over Couplers: 49.72 m.
Wheel Diameter: 860 mm.

Wheel Arrangement: 2-Bo + Bo-2.
Weight: 93 tonnes.
Maximum Speed: 130 km/h.
Accommodation: –/136.

ETR Y0530 001	ETR Y0530 003	ETR Y0530 005	ETR Y0530 006	ETR Y0530 007
ETR Y0530 002	ETR Y0530 004			

CLASS ETR.234

See Section 1.3 for details.

DIESEL RAILCARS

CLASS ALn 668.900 (668.M)   SINGLE CARS

Ex FTC. Based on FS Class ALn 668.1800. Previously 668.M.001 to 007. Refurbished sets are equipped to operate on the RFI network and renumbered. M.002 and 004 are stored at Pont.

Built: 1972.
Builder: Fiat.
Engines: Two Iveco 8217.32 of 176 kW (non refurbished sets two Fiat 8217.12 of 114 kW each).
Length over Buffers: 22.11 m.
Accommodation: –/68 1T.

Transmission: Mechanical.
Weight: 35 tonnes.
Maximum Speed: 95 km/h.
Wheel Arrangement: 1A-A1.

668.901	668.903	668.905	668.906	668.907
668.M.002 (U)	668.M.04 (U)			

OTHER GTT MOTIVE POWER

No.	Type	Axles	Builders	Built	kW	km/h	Tonnes	Seats	Notes
FTC 13	D e	Bo-Bo	Ca&To/TIBB	1920	4 x 103	60	42	-	1.
FTC 15	D e	Bo-Bo	Ca&To/TIBB	1919	4 x 103	60	42	-	2.
-	dh	0-8-0	Deutz	1962	230	-	-	-	3.
-	dh	0-8-0	Deutz	1964	230	-	-	-	3.
DE 101 (U)	de	B-B	Fiat/OM/CGE	1965	420	85	48	-	
DL 200 (U)	dh	0-6-0	Badoni/OM	1968	397	65	43	-	4.
245.01	dh	0-6-0	Badoni/OM	1967	400	70	41	-	5.
E.626.187	e	Bo-Bo-Bo						-	6.

Also SATTI III, TTR IV and TTR VI are still stored at Germagnano.

1. Preserved by MFP at Torino Ponte Mosca.
2. Preserved at Cirié.
3. Deutz Type KG230D, works nos. 57219 and 57810. Rivarolo depot pilots.
4. Officially still a GTT loco but stored at Torino Ponte Mosca "museum".
5. Ex FTC. Based on FS Class 245.0000. Cirié depot pilot.
6. Ex FS. Stored at Cirié.

▲ ETR Y0530 001 is seen at Rivarolo depot on 29 November 2011.   **David Haydock**

▼ RTC Vectron 193 775 runs light engine through Portogruaro on 11 September 2018 to pick up a tank train for Vlissingen in the Netherlands.   **David Haydock**

2.22. HUPAC   HUPAC

HUPAC is a Swiss company specialising in intermodal transport and operating RoLa piggyback trains through Switzerland into Italy. The company started operating its own trains from the Milano area to the Swiss border stations in 2002, although delegating traction to other operators. The company also has Vossloh G1000 locos on hire – see Section 1.1.

CLASS 211   B-B

Former DB Class 211, used for shunting at the Busto Arsizio terminals. 211 002 was formerly with Ferrovia Alifana (see EAV), 211 121 with ÖBB as 2048 032 and 211 150 with track contractors. There are still several other locos of this class with track contractors, one with FG and another with Oceanogate, which also has one Class 212. Class 212 – which can also be found in Italy – are very similar but are 12.30 metres long and have a 1005 kW engine.

Built: 1958–63.
Builder: MaK/Henschel.
Engine: MTU MD 12V538 TA of 820 kW.
Transmission: Hydraulic. Voith L216 rs.

Length over Buffers: 12.10 m.
Weight: 62 tonnes.
Maximum Speed: 100 km/h.

L 05 (211 002) | L 06 (211 150) | L 11 (211 121)

2.23. InRail   INR

InRail is a private company, 35% of shares being owned by the Friuli Venezia Giulia region, with offices in Genova and Udine and operating freight since 2009 in the north of Italy. Most traffic is in the Udine area, where InRail works with FUC. In January 2018 InRail took over the former FS depot at Udine. InRail already owns the MeReSEr depot in Genova and the ODA depot at Arquata Scrivia. The company owns a 15% share in FuoriMuro.

The company owns four Class E.190 and four Class E.191 locomotives, and hires several Class E.189 and E.193 electric locos plus three D.100 diesels. See Sections 1.1 and 1.2.

2.24. INTERPORTO SERVIZI CARGO   ISC

ISC is a subsidiary set up in 2009 by Interporto Campano which manages the Interporto freight terminal in Nola, 30 km east of Napoli. The company operates intermodal services from Nola to Gioia Tauro, Bologna, Padova, Verona and Milano plus Bologna to Bari and Milano to Pomezia.

In 2017 ISC started preparations to operate freight services running over high speed lines at night from 2019. Trains will run between Novara, Melzo and Verona in the north and Pomezia and Nola in the south carrying semi-trailers. The company will have to acquire locomotives to operate from both 3000 V DC and 25 kV AC.

ISC leases several Siemens ES64F4 (Class E.189) and Bombardier TRAXX (Class E.484) electric locomotives. See Section 1.2.

2.25. MERCITALIA SHUNTING & TERMINAL   MIST

The FSI subsidiary formerly known as Servizi Ferroviari (Ser.Fer), charged with operating industrial branches, was renamed MIST in 2017. The subsidiary operates some short-distance freights, supplies drivers for other companies' locomotives, and has gradually taken over shunting on behalf of Trenitalia with its own locomotives. MIST now has a fleet of around 200 former Trenitalia locomotives but also has a motley fleet of other locos listed here.

The depot north of Udine, formerly run by Bulfone, maintains the company's own locos but also does work for other companies including Trenitalia. Loco numbers are usually prefixed with "K". UD indicates Udine MIST depot. Udine depot is modernising a small number of locos for use on main lines and is adding a "1" prefix to their numbers – former DB 211 003 was renumbered from 077 to 1 077. The others can only work in factories or are restricted to yards. The oldest of these locos are likely to be withdrawn soon.

Loco	Builder	Type	Works no.	Axles	h.p.	Built	Location/Notes
013	Henschel	DH 850 D	30309	D	1000	1961	Rosignano.
018	FIAT	-	7142	B-B	650	1962	Brindisi
023	Henschel	DHG 700 C	31560	C	700	1972	Rosignano
026	MaK	600 C	600342	C	600	1960	Ferrara
029	Greco	TP 300 B	3147	B	285	1962	Giammoro Milazzo.
031	Henschel	V100.1	30525	B-B	1350	1962	Rosignano. Ex DB 211 176
032	Jung	R 60 D	13932	D	700	1966	Rosignano.
043	MaK	V60	600219	C	650	1958	Giammoro Milazzo. Ex DB 261 630.
046	Henschel	V100.1	30566	B-B	1100	1962	Castelguelfo (Interporto). Ex DB 211 217
051	Jung	RK 20 B	12141	B	210	1954	Ravenna (S).
056	MaK	450 C	400043	C	440	1962	Cervignano.
059	Krauss-Maffei	ML 440 C	-	C	440	1960	Porcia.
067	Krupp	V60	3976	C	650	1960	San Zeno sul Naviglio. Ex DB 260 553
073	Zephir	1000	00-848	B	155	1989	UD
075	Krauss-Maffei	ML 500 C	-	C	500	-	Livorno.
1 077	MaK	V100.1	1000071	B-B	1100	1965	Osoppo. Ex DB 211 053
087	Greco	TC 285 B	2971	B	285	1975	Mantova
089	Krauss-Maffei	ML 550 D	18341	D	550	1956	Brindisi
1 090	Krauss-Maffei	V100.1	18899	B-B	1100	1962	Osoppo. Ex DB 211 303
091	Deutz	KS 230 B	57066	B	220	1959	San Vincenzo (Solvay).
092	Krauss-Maffei	ML 500 C	18218	C	440	1963	Udine.
097	Deutz	KG 230 B	57502	B	230	1963	Mantova.
100	Deutz	DG1000BB	58233	B-B	1000	1968	Livorno.
102	Gmeinder	Köf II	4860	B	128	1955	UD. Ex DB 323 538
104	Krauss-Maffei	ML 550 D	18340	D	550	1956	Rosignano
110	Krauss-Maffei	ML 225 B	-	B	300	1961	Ravenna
113	Deutz	KS 230 B	56452	B	220	1959	Sannazzaro de' Burgondi.
114	O&K	MV 10	26244	B	250	1963	Giammoro Milazzo.
115	Henschel	DH 200 B	25089	B	200	1952	Susegna (Electrolux)
120	ABR	250.1	-	C	550	1960	Trieste Campo Marte. Ex SNCB 8438
122	ABR	250.1	-	C	550	1962	Osoppo. Ex SNCB 8436.
123	Jung	RK 20 B	13264	B	240	1960	Giammoro Milazzo.
1 132	Esslingen	V100.1	5299	B-B	1100	1962	UD. Ex DB 211 363
136	Deutz	DG1000BB	58232	B-B	1000	1968	UD (S).
148	Deutz	DG1200BB	57689	B-B	1000	1964	UD (S). Ex AKN 2.012
149	Deutz	DG1000BB	58234	B-B	1000	1968	Dalmine.
153	GE	85 T	38998	B-B	570	1974	Brindisi.
154	GE	85 T	39033	B-B	579	1975	Dalmine.
155	Krauss-Maffei	ML 225 B	18864	B	250	1962	Giamorro Milazzo.
157	MaK	G 764 C	700063	C	700	1982	Mortara.
1 158	MaK	G 764 C	700064	C	700	1982	UD.
159	MaK	G 764 C	700065	C	700	1982	UD.
160	MaK	G 764 C	700066	C	700	1982	Mortara.
161	MaK	G 764 C	700067	C	700	1982	UD.
162	MaK	G 764 C	700068	C	700	1982	UD.
163	MaK	600 C	600338	C	600	1958	Sannazzaro de' Burgondi.
165	Zephir	800 TT SR	00-274	B	135	1981	UD.
168	Zephir	800 TT	00-515	B	135	1985	UD.
169	Zephir	800 TT SR	00-640	B	135	1986	UD.
172	GE	85 T	39029	B-B	570	1975	Dalmine.
173	GE	85 T	41126	B-B	570	1982	Dalmine.
177	GE	85 T	-	B-B	570	-	Dalmine.
183	Badoni	V A	-	B	-	-	UD.
187	Eurotract	E2000	A97	B	250	2000	UD.
190	Zephir	800 TT	00-639	B	135	-	Livorno.
192	Translok	DH140	142	B	232	-	UD.
205	Zephir	E3500	A104	-	300	-	Giamorro Milazzo.
206	Zephir	E3500	A105	-	300	-	Pallanzeno.

207	Zephir	E3500	A108	-	300	-	Cremona Aquanegra.
208	Zephir	E3500	A109	-	300	-	UD.
209	Zephir	E3500	A111	-	300	-	Mantova.
1 211	MaK	V100.1	1000127	B-B	1000	1963	Castelguelfo (Interporto). Ex DB 211 109.
212	Henschel	DHG 300 B	31874	B	-	1974	Port of Savona "3"
213	Henschel	DHG 300 B	32837	B	-	1986	Port of Savona
214	Henschel	DHG 300 B	31873	B	-	1974	Port of Savona "2"
215	Henschel	DHG 300 B	31986	B	-	1978	Port of Savona "8"
216	Henschel	DHG 700 C	32480	C	-	1981	Port of Savona "9"
217	Henschel	DHG 700 C	31692	C	-	1974	Port of Savona "1"
218	Zephir	E3500	A122	B	300	2002	Verzuolo.
219	Zephir	E3500	A125	B	300	-	Cremona Aquanegra.
220	MaK	G 1100 BB	800169	B-B	810	1971	UD. Ex AKN.
222	Henschel	DH 500 C	30514	C	500	1963	Mortara.
225	Henschel	V60	29300	C	650	1957	San Zeno sul Naviglio. Ex DB 360 220.
226	MaK	V60	600111	C	650	1958	Castelguelfo (Interporto). Ex DB 360 013
232	Zephir	14.240	1426	B	235	1997	Novara Radici.
233	Zephir	16.300	1604	B	290	-	Savona.
237	Gmeinder	Köf III	26475	B	270	1974	UD. Ex DB 335 166
239	Zephir	16.300	1943	B	290	2005	S. Polo Torille.
242	MaK	V60	600419	C	650	1963	Osoppo. Ex DB 361 104
243	MaK	V100	1000024	B-B	1350	1959	UD. Ex DB 211 005.
244	Zephir	16.300	2104	B	300	2008	Savona.
245	Zephir	16.300	2105	B	300	2008	Savona.
246	Jenbacher	DH600C	-	-	600	1969	UD.
247	Đuro Đakovic	731	-	-	600	1958	Sannazzaro de' Burgondi.
250	ČKD	T334	-	B	-	-	Trecate
251	ČKD	T334	32001	B	-	-	Ex ŽSR 334-1621. Trecate. Cargo Chemical 314.1621
252	Gmeinder	D35B	5249	D	-	1961	Trecate.
253	Badoni	VII B	-	-	-	-	Novara Radici.
254	Ironmit	DH 300 I	-	-	-	-	Novara Radici.

MIST also has two Class D.200 (G2000) and five Class D.744 locos. See Section 1.1.

2.26. NUOVO TRASPORTO VIAGGIATORI   NTV

This was the first private company in Europe to operate high speed trains. NTV was set up in 2006 by a group of businessmen, including the head of Ferrari! French Railways (SNCF) acquired a 20% share in NTV in 2008, but later pulled out. NTV launched services in spring 2012, basically duplicating Trenitalia's high speed offer on the Torino/Milano–Bologna–Firenze–Roma–Napoli–Salerno corridor plus Venezia–Bologna–Roma. The company has since expended to operate Torino–Milano–Venezia.

The company initially used a fleet of 25 11-section Class ETR.575 articulated AGV sets, capable of 360 km/h, built by Alstom in France and Savigliano, Italy. These are marketed as Italo by NTV. The trains are mostly maintained at a depot in Nola, east of Napoli, but also at NTV facilities at Mestre (Venezia) and Milano (San Rocco). Alstom has the contract to maintain the trains.

The company has now ordered 22 ETR.675 EMUs from Alstom. Delivery will be completed in 2019.

NTV hires Vossloh G2000 diesels from FER to shunt at Nola.

2.27. OCEANOGATE   OCG

This company was created in 2010 by Sogemar, a subsidiary of shipping company Contship Italia, and TPER, then took over the long distance freight services previously run by FER, from January 2012.

Oceanogate leases E.483 and E.484 electric locos to operate trains from the ports of Genova, La Spezia, Livorno and Ravenna, to terminals at Rho, Melzo, Rivalta Scrivia, Bologna, Dinazzano and Padova. Loco maintenance is carried out at Asti and Nola. See Section 1.2.

Oceanogate also owns former DB diesel locos 211 271 (numbered 1001 271) and 212 082 for shunting at Melzo. See HUPAC for technical details.

2.28. RAIL CARGO CARRIER ITALY   RCCIT

RCCIT is a freight operator founded, as Linea, by Tiber.Co and TI Ferest of Bratislava, Slovakia. In 2008 Austrian Federal Railways' (ÖBB) subsidiary Rail Cargo Austria (RCA) acquired a 55% shareholding, then in September 2011 the remaining shares. The company, renamed Rail Cargo Italia, then Rail Cargo Carrier Italy, is now working the Italian part of RCA cross-border services.

RCCIT has a fleet of Class E.190 electric locos from the ÖBB fleet plus leased Class 186 and 189, electric locos. See Section 1.2.

RAIL ONE

Taken over by CFI in October 2015.

2.29. RAIL TRACTION COMPANY   RTC

The first Italian open access company, with its HQ in Bolzano, started operations in October 2001. RTC operates mainly on the Verona–Brennero route, with German company Lokomotion taking the trains from Brennero to München. The two companies now work 30% of freight over the Brennero route.

RTC owns eight Class EU 43 plus some Class 189 electric locos and hires others, plus Classes 186, 193 and E.483 – see Section 1.2.

In 2015 RTC bought two ex DB Class 220 diesels from DP and uses them for heavy shunting; it also has two Class D.753 diesels.

RTC also uses locomotives hired from Lokomotion in Italy and applies the same livery as Lokomotion – tiger stripes along the loco sides.

Depot: Verona.   **Outstation:** Nola.

2.30. SAD TRASPORTO LOCALE   SAD

This company operates bus and train services in the Alto Adige (Südtirol) region of northern Italy which for historic reasons is mainly German speaking. Infrastructure is owned and managed by Strutture Trasporto Alto Adige (STA), previously owned by Bolzano province but now private. In May 2005, STA reopened the Merano (Meran)–Mallès Venosta (Mals) line using Class ATR.100 DMUs (see Section 1.4). SAD then took over operation of Merano–Bolzano from Trenitalia using Class ETR.170 EMUs (see Section 1.3) and is now operating some trains on the Bolzano–Brennero RFI line. In August 2018 SAD was granted a contract to operate trains on the Fortezza–San Candido, Brennero–Bolzano–Trento and Bolzano–Merano–Malles Venosta routes on top of the contract signed with Trenitalia. A further seven FLIRT EMUs will be needed.

Gauge: 1435 mm.
Route: Merano–Mallès Venosta (60 km). To be electrified at 25 kV AC.
Depot: Mallès Venosta (diesel), Merano (electric).

2.30.1. RITTNERBAHN (operated by SAD)

This line is in the scenic Südtirol tourist region high up above Bozen/Bolzano. Also known as the Ferrovia del Renon. Oberbozen can be reached by taking the cable car (*Seilbahn* or *Funivia*), 500 m from Bozen FS station. Operation is in two sections with a mainly half-hourly service from Oberbozen to Klobenstein but only four services per day from Oberbozen to Maria Himmelfahrt. Wooden-bodied stock dating almost from the line's opening in August 1907 is still occasionally used for normal services. Düwag tram 12 no longer operates in normal circumstances.

Route: Maria Himmelfahrt (L'Assunta)–Oberbozen (Soprabolzano)–Klobenstein (Collalbo) (6.6 km).
Gauge: 1000 mm.
Electrical System: 1500 V DC overhead.
Depots: Oberbozen (Soprabolzano), Klobenstein.

ELECTRIC MULTIPLE UNITS

TYPE BDe 4/8   2-CAR UNITS

These EMUs were purchased between 2008 and 2017 from the Trogenerbahn (TB) in Switzerland and operate the main service, the vintage stock only appearing on special occasions. The units were converted from 1000 to 1500 V DC. They retain their original numbers.

Built: 1975.
Builders: FFA/BBC/SWP.
Accommodation: –/40 + –/34.
Power Rating: 405 kW.

Length: 30.20 m.
Maximum Speed: 65 km/h.
Weight: 39 tonnes.
Wheel Arrangement: Bo-Bo + 2-2.

| 21 | 22 | 23 | 24 |

▲ SAD ex Trogenerbahn units 21 and 24 cross at Lictenstern/Stella on 13 September 2018.
David Haydock

OTHER MOTIVE POWER

No.	Type	Axles	Builders	Built	kW	km/h	Tonnes	Seats	Notes
L.2	e	Bo	SLM		280	7		0	1.
2	BD e	A1-1A	AEG/Graz	1908	2 x 29	25	21	60	
11	B e	Bo	AEG/Graz	1908	2 x 29	25	12	36	
12	B e	Bo	AEG/Graz	1908	2 x 29	25	12	36	
12	B e	Bo-Bo	Düwag	1958	?	?	?	48	2.
105	BD e	A1-1A	Alioth/Ness	1910	2 x 55	25	12	40	3.

1. L.4 is preserved by Tiroler Museumseisenbahn in Innsbruck, Austria.
2. Ex Esslingen in 1992.
3. Ex Dermulo-Mendola in 1936.

2.31. SOCIETÀ FERROVIARIA APUO VENETA   SAV

This company was founded in 2001 and works trains from the port at Marina di Carrara to the main line station at Massa Zona Industriale. The company formerly used an ex FS Class 225.6000 shunter and no. 14, ex DB B-B diesel 202 207 (LEW 12489, 1970). The company now only uses D.146.0001, built by Firema in 2002 (see Class D.146 in section 1.1 for details).

D.146.0001

2.32. SEATRAIN

This company organises trains to carry cruise ship passengers to city centres, but does not directly operate the trains itself. The *Rome Express* runs from the port of Civitavecchia to Roma with trains and staff provided by FCU.

2.33. SISTEMI TERRITORIALI   SI or ST

ST was renamed from Ferrovie Venete on 1 April 2002 and is now owned by the Veneto region. ST also covers inland shipping, ports and buses. Initially covering the former FAM and FUC lines, FUC was separated in 2005. These two lines once made up the Società Veneta Autoferrovie (SV) together with the FBP and FPS, now both part of FER/TPER.

The line from Mestre to Mira Buse (11 km) was electrified in 2010 but traffic has been so disappointing that FLIRT EMUs have been replaced with single diesel railcars! ST now operates both passenger and freight services across the region, over the RFI network. ST also owns two Class E.483 electric locomotives which haul cereals from Slovenia to Rovigo. See Section 1.2. At the time of writing ST had a number of ALn 668.1200 railcars on hire from Trenitalia.

Gauge: 1435 mm.   **Routes:** Mestre FS–Adria FS (57 km).
Depot: Piove di Sacco.

DIESEL RAILCARS

CLASSES ATR.110, 116, 120 & 126

See Section 1.3.

ALn 668.600   SINGLE CARS

Based on FS Class ALn 668.1000. ALn 668.607/08 are with TPER. Details as Trenitalia Class ALn 668.1000 except:

Built: 1979/80.   **Builder:** OMECA.
Maximum Speed: 88 km/h.   **Accommodation:** –/78.

| ALn 668.605 | ALn 668.606 | ALn 668.609 | ALn 668.610 |

CLASS ALn 663.900
SINGLE CARS

Based on the FS Class ALn 663 design. Used with trailers Bp 663.372–376. 902 and 903 are now with TPER (ex FPS). 901, 904 and 910 are with FUC. 906 was tested with agri-diesel in 2006. Details as Trenitalia Class ALn 663 except:

Built: 1991–93.
Maximum Speed: 90 km/h.
Accommodation: –/68.

Weight: 34 tonnes.
Transmission: Hydraulic.

EVN: 95 83 4663 905-c and so on.

| ALn 663.905 | ALn 663.906 | ALn 663.907 | ALn 663.908 | ALn 663.909 |

DIESEL LOCOMOTIVES

CLASS D.753
Bo-Bo

Former Czech Railways (ČD) Class D.753 are used on local freight. Of D.753.001 to 007, 002/007 are stored while 005/006 were sold to Captrain. See Section 1.1.

TYPE F364A
B

This diesel-hydraulic loco was acquired in 2006. It was originally delivered to Ormec of Gozzano.

Badoni works no. 5179. Built 1964.

2.34. TERMINALI ITALIA

A company which shunts intermodal terminals and yards. Owned 89% by infrastructure manager RFI and 11% Mercitalia Intermodal (formerly CEMAT). Owns Class D.741 diesel locos.

▲ ST DMU ALn 663.905 is seen at Piove di Sacco on 8 September 2018.   **David Haydock**

2.35. TRASPORTO FERROVIARIO TOSCANO TFT

After some years as FSAS (Ferrovia Sinalunga Arezzo Stia), this network was renamed La Ferroviaria Italiana (LFI) in 1991, then LFI became a holding in 2006 consisting of operator TFT and infrastructure manager Rete Ferroviaria Toscana (RFT). This was the beginning of operations on the RFI network with the TFT branding replacing LFI on trains.

The Arezzo–Stia line was originally intended as narrow gauge to connect with another railway from Arezzo to Sansepolcro but was eventually built as standard gauge. In 1950, LFI took it over from SV and started electrification of a previously steam-hauled line, completing work in 1954.

Passenger services were operated by a veritable traction museum in the past. Of great interest is the ex LMS jackshaft drive shunter which has a very familiar profile! Most electric locos and units are fitted for push-pull operation. A blue, turquoise and white livery is now replacing black and red for locos and white and brown for EMUs. Graffiti is rampant on the older stock.

Four ex FS steam locos are based at Arezzo but are privately-owned, by Nettunia Sud. See list in Section 6. Several items of stock are stored around the network.

TFT exchanged its single Class E.464 electric loco plus double-deck stock for Trenitalia EMUs ETR.425.056 (from Trenitalia) and 102 (direct from the builder) in 2017. The company now operates a train from Stia to Firenze via Arezzo each day with these units. In 2017/18 the company took over three former Trenitalia Class ALe 801/940 EMUs. It now looks like the oldest trains are sadly on the way out.

Gauge: 1435 mm. **Electrical System:** 3000 V DC overhead.
Route: Sinalunga FS–Arezzo FS–Pratovecchio Stia (84 km).
Depot: Arezzo Pescaiola.

DIESEL LOCOMOTIVES

CLASS D.341.1000 Bo-Bo

Built: 1960–63.
Builder: OM.
Engine: Fiat 2312 SF of 1030 kW.
Transmission: Electric (CGE Amplistat).
Continuous Rating: 805 kW.

Wheel Diameter: 1040 mm.
Weight: 66 tonnes.
Length over Buffers: 14.54 m.
Maximum Speed: 110 km/h.

D.341.1041 | D.341.1063

ELECTRIC LOCOMOTIVES

EDz 12–14 "CALIMERO" Bo-Bo

Ex SAIF Sédico-Bribano–Agordo line, closed in 1955. Similar motor luggage vans used to push-pull passenger trains. All have been rebuilt two or three times, 12 and 13 with a single cab, for use at either end of a schools train, 14 for freight in 2013. 11 is plinthed at the Centro Minerario di Valle Imperina near Agordo.

Built: 1924. Rebuilt several times.
Builder–Mechanical Parts: Ca&To.
Builder–Electrical Parts: CGE.
Continuous Rating: 4 x 136 kW.

Length over Buffers: 11.03 m.
Maximum Speed: 100 km/h.
Weight: 37–45 tonnes.

EDz 12 | EDz 13 | EDz 14

EDz 17, 18 — Bo-Bo

Rebuilt in 1979 and 1980 by LFI from SACFEM electric railcars EDz 1 and 2. Used at either end of a schools train.

Built: 1930.
Builder–Mechanical Parts: LFI.
Builder–Electrical Parts: TIBB.
Continuous Rating: 4 x 125 kW.

Length over Buffers:
Maximum Speed: 120 km/h.
Weight: 56 tonnes.

EDz 17 | EDz 18

CLASS E.626 — Bo-Bo-Bo

Ex FS locos. E.626.006 was refurbished with modified front ends. E.626.012 was scrapped. All stored in 2018.

Built: 1928–37.
Builder–Mechanical Parts: OM/Breda/TIBB.
Builder–Electrical Parts: CGE/Breda/TIBB.
Continuous Rating: 1890 kW.
Maximum Tractive Effort: 262 or 224 kN.

Traction Motors: 6 x 32.200 FS.
Wheel Diameter: 1250 mm.
Weight: 93 tonnes.
Maximum Speed: 95 km/h.
Length over Buffers: 14.95 m.

E.626.006 (S) | E.626.223 (S) | E.626.311 (S)

ELECTRIC MULTIPLE UNITS

CLASS E.624 — "VARESINA" — SINGLE CARS

Ex FS electric railcars, still in regular service. E.624.001 and 002 were scrapped. These will probably be replaced on schools trains by the Class ALe 801/940 units.

Built: 1932/35.
Builder–Mechanical Parts: Meridionali, Breda.
Builder–Electrical Parts: CGE.
Continuous Rating: 4 x 150 kW.
Wheel Arrangement: Bo-Bo.

Length over Buffers: 21.00 m.
Maximum Speed: 120 km/h.
Weight: 65 tonnes.
Accommodation: –/47 or –/34.

EBz 624.009 | EBz 624.012

CLASS ALe 054 — "LEPRINA" — 2-CAR UNITS

Units 02, 03 and 07 were Type AM54 EMUs purchased from Belgian Railways (SNCB set numbers in brackets) by SATTI (now GTT) and acquired by TFT in 2011. For details, see GTT. It is not known if they will operate in service. Sets in the 96x series were converted into postal vans by SNCB then converted back by OMS of Porrena for TFT! 965 has not been converted.

02 ALe 054.02 M1 + ALe 054.02 M2 (061) (U)
03 ALe 054.03 M1 + ALe 054.03 M2 (099) (U)

07 ALe 054.07 M1 + ALe 054.07 M2 (083) (U)

ALe 054.961 + Le 054.961 (080)
ALe 054.965 + Le 054.965 (117)

ALe 054.969 + Le 054.969 (091)

CLASS ALe 801 & ALe 940   4- OR 5-CAR UNITS

Former Trenitalia suburban EMUs. These units have the same outline and motors as express Class ALe 601. The second series of units, formed of ALe 801/940.026–065 and 108.051–130, have Scharfenberg automatic couplers and are therefore 120 mm longer overall.

Classes ALe 801/940

Built: 1975–79.
Builder–Mech. Parts: ALe 801 Stanga. ALe 940 Fiore/Stanga.
Wheel Diameter: 1040 mm.   **Weight:** 72 (* 70) tonnes.
Builder–Elec.Parts: ALe 801 Marelli/Italtrafo. ALe 940 Lucana/Italtrafo.
Traction Motors: 4 x FS T.165 of 262 kW.
Length over Couplers: 27.305 m (* 27.365 m).
Continuous Rating: 872 kW.   **Maximum Speed:** 140 km/h.

Class Le 108.

Built: 1975–79.   **Wheel Diameter:** 940 mm.
Builder–Mech. Parts: Breda Pt, 001–035, 075–130; Cittadella, 036–074.
Builder–Elec. Parts: ASGEN/Italtralfo/Lucana/Ansaldo.
Weight: 39 tonnes.
Length over Buffers: 26.41 m.   **Maximum Speed:** 140 km/h.

Accommodation 5UNITS°: –/80 + –/108 + –/108 (+ –/108) + –/94.

ALe 801.016 + Le 108.040 + Le 108.078 + Le 108.091 + ALe 940.049*   Stia line
ALe 801.032* + Le 108.085 + Le 108.065 + ALe 940.050*   Sinalunga line
ALe 801.049 + Le 108.051 + Le 108.124 + ALe 940.030   Sinalunga line

OTHER MOTIVE POWER

No.	Type	Axles	Builders	Built	kW	km/h	Tonnes	Seats	Notes
213.930	d	B	O&K	1933	37	18	23	-	1.
225.7051	dh	B	Greco	1959	125	30/50	28	-	2.
225.7069	dh	B	Greco	1963	125	30/50	28	-	2.
700.003 (S)	de	C	LMS Derby	1941	-	30	56	-	3.
D.l.183 (U)	de	C	Werkspoor	1957	370	60	48	-	4.
DE 51	d	B	Borsig	1934	45	18	15	-	5.
E 6	B e	Bo	SACFEM/LFI	1950	2 x 125	60	23	-	
EAz.623.100	AD e	Bo-Bo	Breda/CGE	1931	840	-	66	54/–	6.

1. Ex DB 322 655, ex DRG Kö 4170, ex Italian track contractor, O&K 20264.
2. Ex FS.
3. Ex LMS shunter 7106, ex War Department 55, ex FS Ne 700.003.
4. Ex Dutch mining railway.
5. Ex DRG KöE 4080, ex FTV 51, Borsig 14457.
6. Historic unit. Ex FS.

2.36. FERROVIE EMILIA-ROMAGNA   FER
TRASPORTO PASSEGGERI EMILIA ROMAGNA   TPER

FER, with its headquarters in Bologna, was formed in 2001 to operate in the Emilia-Romagna region, a merger of the Ferrovia Bologna-Portomaggiore (FBP), Ferrovie Padane (FP), Ferrovia Suzzara-Ferrara (FSF) and Ferrovia Parma-Suzzara (FPS), the last formerly part of Ferrovie Venete (FV). The FBP was originally part of the Società Veneta and shared out motive power with the FV. In 2008, FER absorbed ATCM, the last line of the once extensive Società Emiliana di Ferrovie, Tranvie ed Automobili (SEFTA) network. In 2009, FER absorbed ACT Reggio Emilia, once known as Consorzio Cooperativo Ferrovie Reggiane (CCFR), and Azienda Trasporti Consorziali Bologna (ATC), formerly Azienda Provincializzata Trasporti Bologna then Ferrovia Casalecchio-Vignola.

In 2012, the passenger arm of FER merged with Bologna's bus operator to become TPER. In 2014 the freight operator became Dinazzano Po (DP), but Oceanogate has taken over some long distance freights.

In general, the company has gradually integrated its previously separate fleets, but the former ATCM Modena–Sassuolo line is now a separate operation, using only former SNCB EMUs while ACT is still more-or-less as before, retaining its ALn 067–082 railcars. ACT lived mainly from heavy freight – almost 2 million tonnes a year of clay in, tiles out – serving the ceramics industry at Dinazzano on the Reggio Emilia–Sassuolo line. This is now managed by DP.

In 2005, FER formed a joint venture known as Società Ferroviaria Passeggeri (SFP) with ACT and ATCM in order to bid for passenger service contracts in the Emilia-Romagna region. SFP won a contract to operate local services which means that TPER now runs trains over the RFI lines from Bologna to Poggio Rusco, Rimini, Ravenna, Ferrara, Milano and Parma plus Modena–Mantova.

Infrastructure projects in progress include electrification from Reggio Emilia to Bagnolo in Piano. Electrification is planned for Reggio Emilia to Sassuolo and Guastalla, plus Poggio Rusco–Suzzara.

The TPER fleet is very varied, the heritage of six different lines, but a start has been made on a standard fleet with ATR.220 DMUs and ETR.350 EMUs. The introduction of the EMUs on the Bologna to Vignola and Portomaggiore lines in cascaded DMUs and should allow withdrawal of the oldest units. TPER's Class E.464 electric locos are shown in Section 1.2.

Roveri maintains some DMUs including the PESA ATR.220s plus ETR.350 EMUs. Suzzara is only used to store preserved stock. Sermide is the main workshops.

We have removed the ex SŽ Class E.640 and LD 61/62 as they are still stored at Sermide.

TPER also has the following preserved railcars: ALn 1201 (former ACT), ALn 1204 (former ACT "Schienenbus" built by Macchifer in 1957, active from Trenord's depot at Iseo, plus trailer RP 2002), ALn 1208 (former ACT, preserved by FBS), ALn 2451 (former ACT, preserved by GRAF at Civita Castellana ATAC depot), ALn 2455 (former ACT), ALn 556.1236 and 1277 (both former FS, ex FSF, Suzzara) and ALn 772.1004 (former FP, Suzzara).

Gauge: 1435 mm.
Routes:

- **Bologna Centrale FS–Budrio–Portomaggiore FS** (former FBP, 48 km).
- Ferrara FS–Codigoro (former FP, 53 km).
- **Ferrara FS–Sermide–Poggio Rusco FS**–Suzzara FS (former FSF, 82 km).
- Reggio S.Lazzaro–Reggio Emilia FS–Guastalla (31 km).
- Parma FS–Guastalla–Suzzara FS (former FPS, 44 km).
- Reggio Emilia FS–Guastalla (former ACT, 28 km).
- Reggio Emilia FS–Sassuolo (former ACT, 22 km).
- Reggio Emilia FS–Ciano d'Enza (former ACT, 26 km).
- **Casalecchio di Reno–Vignola** (former ATC, 24 km).
- **Modena FS–Sassuolo** (former ATCM, 18 km).

Electrical System: 3000 V DC overhead. Electrified routes shown in bold.
Depots: **RO** Roveri (FBP), Suzzara (FPS), **RE** Reggio Emilia Santa Croce (ACT), Guastalla (ACT), Modena Piazza Manzoni (ATCM), **SE** Sermide (FSF) works and depot.

DIESEL LOCOMOTIVES

CLASS DE 122 Bo-Bo

These were used on push-pull suburban trains on the Sassuolo line with rakes of ex SBB stock until 2012. FSE has the same type. Ex ACT Reggio Emilia.

Built: 1989–90.
Builder: IMPA.
Engines: Two Isotta Fraschini ID 36 SS 8V of 610 kW each.
Weight: 69 tonnes.
Maximum Speed: 100 km/h.
Continuous Rating: 1220 kW.

Transmission: Electric.
Wheel Diameter: 1040 mm.

Length over Buffers: 15.84 m.
Train Heating: Electric.

DE 122 009 | DE 122 010

CLASS 260 B

Very similar to FS Class 225.7000. Ex ACT Reggio Emilia. Depot shunters.

Built: 1957.
Builder: Greco (Type T4M 625). Deutz licence.
Engine: Deutz VM of 190 kW.
Maximum Speed: 30/55 km/h.

Transmission: Hydraulic. Voith L24U.
Wheel Diameter: 900 mm.
Weight: 26 tonnes.
Length over Buffers: 7.40 m.

260 001 | 260 002

ELECTRIC MULTIPLE UNITS

CLASS ALe 054 2-CAR UNITS

Former Belgian Railways Type AM 54 EMUs, with rebuilt front ends and air conditioning, ex ATC Bologna. Based in Modena for former ATCM.

Built: 1954.
Builders: BN/ACEC.
Continuous Rating: 4 x 155 kW.
Wheel Arrangement: A1-1A + A1-1A.
Accommodation: 28/58 + –/85.

Length over Buffers: 22.64 m + 22.64 m
Weight: 43 + 42 tonnes.
Maximum Speed: 130 km/h.

ALe 054.201 + ALe 054.202 (077) | ALe 054.203 + ALe 054.204 (107)

CLASS ALe 056 2-CAR UNIT

Ex SNCB Budd EMU 145, ex GTT. See GTT for details. Based at Modena for former ATCM.

10 ALe 056.010 M1 + ALe 056.010 M2

CLASS ALe 088 2-CAR UNIT

Details as EAV (FBN) Class ALe 88. Operates from Modena.

ALe 088.002 + Le 088.102

CLASS ALe 122　　　　　　　　　　　　　　　　　　　　　2-CAR UNITS

Delivered in 2005 to ATC Bologna (now TPER) and finished in silver livery with red and blue flashes. Sold to SEPSA in 2010 but never reached Napoli. Being overhauled in 2017.

Built: 1999.
Builder: Firema/Ansaldo (Type E122).
Continuous Rating: 1100 kW.
Accommodation: –/120.

Length over Couplers: 50.60 m.
Weight: 91 tonnes.
Maximum Speed: 100 km/h.
Wheel Arrangement: 2-Bo + Bo-2.

| ALe 122.01 + ALe 122.02 | ALe 122.03 + ALe 122.04 |

DIESEL MULTIPLE UNITS

CLASS ATR.220　　　　　　　　　　　　　　3-SECTION ARTICULATED UNITS

These units were built as a follow-on order for those built for FSE (220.001 to 023) and FNM (220 024 and 025). This is the reason for them being numbered from 026. Individual cars for ATR.220.026 are 94 83 4 220 004 + 94 83 0 220 006 + 94 83 220 005 and so on. Details as FSE units except built in 2009/10.

ATR.220.026	ATR.220.029	ATR.220.032	ATR.220.034	ATR.220.036
ATR.220.027	ATR.220.030	ATR.220.033	ATR.220.035	ATR.220.037
ATR.220.028	ATR.220.031			

CLASS ALn 663.000, 100 & 1000　　　　　　　　　　　　　SINGLE CARS

Based on FS Class ALn 663. ALn 663.019 to 021 are ex FSF; ALn 663.101–105 are ex FBP; ALn 663.1016–1021 are ex FP. Details as Trenitalia Class ALn 663 except:

Built: 1989 ALn 663.019–21, 101; 1991 ALn 663.103–105. 1993 ALn 663.1016–1021.
Weight: 46 tonnes.
Accommodation: –/63 (* 8/60).

Maximum Speed: 110 km/h (* 118 km/h).
Wheel Arrangement: 1A-A1.

ALn 663.019	SE	ALn 663.101	RO	ALn 663.104	RO	ALn 663.1016*	SE	ALn 663.1019*	SE
ALn 663.020	SE	ALn 663.103	RO	ALn 663.105	RO	ALn 663.1017*	SE	ALn 663.1020*	SE
ALn 663.021	SE					ALn 663.1018*	SE	ALn 663.1021*	SE

ALn 663.067–082　　　　　　　　　　　　　　　　　　　SINGLE CARS

Used on most passenger trains on branches from Reggio Emilia. Do not carry the 663 class number on front end. Ex ACT Reggio Emilia.

Built: 1996.
Builder: Fiat.
Engines: Two Fiat 8217.31.00.00 A14 of 170 kW each.
Maximum Speed: 90 km/h.
Accommodation: –/80.

Weight: 43 tonnes.
Length over Buffers: 23.84 m.

Transmission: Hydraulic. Voith T211 rz.
Wheel Arrangement: 1A-A1.

| ALn 067 | ALn 069 | ALn 071 | ALn 073 | ALn 075 | ALn 077 | ALn 079 | ALn 081 |
| ALn 068 | ALn 070 | ALn 072 | ALn 074 | ALn 076 | ALn 078 | ALn 080 | ALn 082 |

CLASS ALn 663.900　　　　　　　　　　　　　　　　　　SINGLE CARS

Based on the FS Class ALn 663. 902 has been withdrawn. Other units are with FUC and ST. Ex FPS Class AD 900. Details as Trenitalia Class ALn 663 except:

Built: 1991.
Weight: 34 tonnes.
Accommodation: –/68.

Transmission: Hydraulic.
Maximum Speed: 90 km/h.
Wheel Arrangement: 1A-A1.

ALn 663.903　　RO

ALn 668.013–018   SINGLE CARS

Based on FS Class ALn 668.1000/1900. Ex FSF. Details as Trenitalia Class ALn 668.1900 except:

Built: 1978/79.
Maximum Speed: 135 km/h.

Builder: Savigliano.
Wheel Arrangement: 1A-A1.

| ALn 668.013 | SE | ALn 668.015 | SE | ALn 668.016 | SE | ALn 668.017 | SE | ALn 668.018 | SE |
| ALn 668.014 | SE | | | | | | | | |

ALn 668.611–613   SINGLE CARS

Based on FS Class ALn 668.3000. Ex FPS Class ADn 600. Details as Trenitalia ALn 668.300 except:

Built: 1981.
Weight: 37 tonnes.
Accommodation: –/78.

Builder: Savigliano.
Maximum Speed: 89 km/h.
Wheel Arrangement: 1A-A1.

| ALn 668.611 | SE | ALn 668.612 | RO | ALn 668.613 | RO |

ALn 668.1012/1013   SINGLE CARS

Based on FS ALn 668.1000. Operate with Class Ln 880.300 trailers built in the same period by Savigliano. Ex FP. Details as Trenitalia ALn 668.1000 except:

Built: 1976/77.
Wheel Arrangement: 1A-A1.

Builders: Savigliano.

| ALn 668.1012 | RO | ALn 668.1013 | RO |

ALn 668.1014/5   SINGLE CARS

Based on FS ALn 668.3000. Ex FP. Details as Trenitalia ALn 668.3000 except:

Built: 1983.
Weight: 37 tonnes.
Wheel Arrangement: 1A-A1.

Builder: Savigliano.
Maximum Speed: 110 km/h.

| ALn 668.1014 | SE | ALn 668.1015 | SE |

▲ TPER ALn 668.612 stands at Suzzara on 7 April 2018.   **David Haydock**

ALn 668.2463–2466   SINGLE CARS

Based on FS Class ALn 668.1900. Mainly used on the Reggio Emilia–Guastalla line. Ex ACT Reggio. The first unit has been restored to its original orange livery and carries number ALn 2463. Details as Trenitalia Class ALn 668.1900 except:

Built: 1980.   **Builder:** Savigliano.
Engine: Two Fiat 8217.32.03 of 170 kW each.   **Maximum Speed:** 90 km/h.
Accommodation: –/80.   **Wheel Arrangement:** 1A-A1.

ALn 668.2463 RE | ALn 668.2464 RE | ALn 668.2465 RE | ALn 668.2466 RE

All TPER ALn 663 and 668 railcars can operate with trailers Ln 778 401–404 and 880 031–038, 306–313 and 371.

OTHER MOTIVE POWER

No.	Type	Axles	Builders	Built	kW	km/h	Tonnes	Notes
A 7	e	Bo-Bo	Breda	1932	472	80	42	Plinthed. Mezzano di Ravenna.
A 8	e	Bo-Bo	Breda	1932	472	80	42	Preserved. Modena.
ALn 1204	dm	A-1	Macchi	1956	110	100	–	Preserved. Iseo.
ALn 668.05	d	1A-A1	Fiat/OM	1959	220	90	32	Preserved. Sermide
CCFR 7	v	0-6-0T	Henschel (8138)	1907	?	50	38	Active. Ex ACT.
SAFRE 21	v	0-4-0T	Reggiane	1927	?	?	?	Plinthed
L 51	e	Bo-Bo	Breda	1932	472	50	39	Preserved. Modena
L 52	e	Bo-Bo	Breda	1932	472	50	39	Preserved. Modena
L 915	d	B	Greco/Deutz	1957	95	?	?	Ex ATC. Ex SAF
L 916	d	B	Krauss-Maffei	1961	210	50	18	Type ML225. Ex ATC.
Ld 404 (S)	dh	0-8-0	MaK	1960	590	60	58	1.

1.   Ex Bentheimer Eisenbahn in 1974. Ex FPS.

2.37. TRENORD / FNM

Trenord is a joint venture formed in 2011 by the merger of Trenitalia's regional passenger activities in the Lombardia region and LeNord, the passenger activity of Ferrovie Nord Milano (FNM), part-owned by the Lombardia region and the historic operator of a 228 km network of four major suburban routes in the north of Milano, as well as the 103 km Brescia–Edolo non-electrified line. Plans to create a merged company mainly stemmed from the construction of the *Passante* cross-city underground line which links suburban routes on each side of the city, and the FNM and RFI networks.

The FNM group still exists. Passenger operator LeNord has been subsumed into Trenord while freight subsidiary DB Cargo Italia is now DB Cargo's subsidiary in Italy. FNM supplies staff within Italy for the Verona–Innsbruck–München EuroCity service, working with DB and ÖBB.

The FNM depot at Novate Milanese still looks after "former FNM" stock, including the more recent 'TSR' double-deck EMUs and ETR.245 EMUs for the *Malpensa Express* service, whilst the FNM depot at Iseo deals with stock used on the Brescia–Edolo line. However, TSR units are also maintained by Milano Fiorenza depot and Iseo depot now overhauls "former FNM" diesel railcars. FNM itself is also used for rolling stock acquisition. This started with the ATR.115 and ATR.125 DMUs and has continued since. The former were for the "former FNM" Brescia–Iseo line but the latter for the Milano–Molteno–Lecco service and are maintained at Lecco depot.

FNM still continues to maintain its 321 km historic network and upgraded the Saronno–Seregno line for passenger traffic in 2012. This is only a small part of the 1900 km Trenord network but carries about one-third of all passenger-km in the region. FNM is still doubling the Saronno–Novara line and has built an extension to the Malpensa airport branch which will eventually loop round to Gallarate.

The passenger fleet shown below is ex FNM or purchased recently by FNM. The "former Trenitalia" part of the Trenord fleet is shown in the Trenitalia section of this book and mainly consists of (excluding odd locos from other classes): Class E.464 electric locomotives, based at Milano Fiorenza depot, plus a large amount of single- and double-deck stock, Class D.445 diesel locomotives, based at Cremona depot, Class ALe 582 EMUs at Milano Greco, Lecco and Cremona depots, diesel railcars at Lecco and Cremona.

Trenord also owns EMUs ETR.524.201 to 204 which are included in the SBB fleet. See 'Swiss Railways' book.

We have removed Classes E.610, E.640, E.660 and E.661 locomotives which are all now withdrawn.

In 2018 FNM subsidiary Ferrovienord ordered 50 FLIRT 3 DMUs of which 30 were to be delivered in 2021. They will be 66.8 metres long with 168 seats. They will have batteries which will be charged by braking energy. FNM has ordered nine 6-car FLIRT 3 EMUs for TILO services to be delivered in 2020/21. In late 2018 FNM tendered for two 800 kW shunting locos.

In 2017 FNM bought a 51% share in the emerging leasing company Locoitalia, the other shareholder being Tenor, an investment company in Genova which part-owns FuoriMuro.

Gauge: 1435 mm.

FNM routes:

- **Milano Nord Cadorna–Bovisa–Seveso–Canzo-Asso (52 km).**
- **Seveso–Camnago-Lentate (2 km).**
- **Bovisa–Saronno–Varese Nord–Laveno Mombello Nord (68 km).**
- **Saronno–Como Nord Lago (24 km).**
- **Saronno–Bivio Sacconago–Novara Nord (40 km).**
- **Bivio Sacconago–Aeroporto della Malpensa (9 km).**
- **Saronno–Seregno (15 km).**

Former Società Nazionale di Ferrovie e Tranvie (SNFT) lines

- Brescia FS–Bornato-Calino–Edolo (103 km).
- Bornato-Calino–Rovato FS (5.8 km, now open to passengers).

Electrical System: 3000 V DC overhead. Electrified lines are shown in **bold** type.
Depots: Camnago-Lentate, Novate Milanese, Iseo.

DIESEL LOCOMOTIVES

CLASS DE.145   Bo-Bo

These are similar to FS Class D.145.1000 but have a higher rating of 950 kW. Stored at Iseo but may be refurbished by Bombardier and/or sold. These locos are actually owned by DB, not Trenord.

Built: 1995.
Builder: Fiat.
Engines: Two Fiat of 475 kW each.
Maximum Tractive Effort: kN

Transmission: Three-phase electric
Weight: 72 tonnes.
Maximum Speed: 100 km/h.
Length over Buffers: 15.20 m.

DE.145.01 (S) | DE.145.02 (S) | DE.145.03 (S)

CLASS DE.500   Bo-Bo

Centre-cab diesel shunters, mainly used for depot shunting and track work. 500.02 has been preserved by Club del San Gottardo. FAS has two of this type (D 26 and 27) in its fleet.

Built: 500.1–3 1971; 500.4/5 1975.
Builder: TIBB.
Engine: Two Fiat of 296 kW.
Transmission: Electric.

Weight: 46 tonnes.
Maximum Speed: 75 km/h.
Length over Buffers: 10.44 m.
Maximum Tractive Effort:

DE.500.1 (S) | DE.500.3 | DE.500.4 (S) | DE.500.5 (S)

CLASS Cne 510   0-6-0

Based at Iseo. Cne means *Carro a nafta elettrico*. 517, based at Iseo, is used to haul the tourist service *"Il Treno dei Sapori"* – the "train of tastes" on the Edolo line. 510 to 516 and 518, 519 were withdrawn.

Built: 1979.
Builders: Reggiane/BRIF.
Engine: Breda D26 rated at 400 kW.
Maximum Tractive Effort: 94 kN.

Transmission: Electric.
Weight: 42 tonnes.
Maximum Speed: 80 km/h.
Length over Buffers: 9.80 m.

517

CLASS DE 520   Bo-Bo

Former Czech Railways (CD) Class D.753. Used for freight traffic well out of the traditional operating area of the company. Maintained at Iseo. See Section 1.1.

ELECTRIC LOCOMOTIVES

CLASS E.600   Bo-Bo

The last of these ancient electrics, formerly E.600.1 to 6. The loco is preserved, in black livery, and occasionally used for odd stock movements from Novate. E.600.2 is plinthed at Malnate and E.600.6 at Saronno museum. Others are still stored at Novate.

Built: 1928.
Builder–Mechanical Parts: OM.
Builder–Electrical Parts: CGE.
Power Rating: 1125 kW.

Weight: 63 tonnes.
Maximum Speed: 75 km/h.
Length over Buffers: 11.92 m.

E.600.3

ELECTRIC MULTIPLE UNITS

CLASS ETR.245   "CORADIA"   5-CAR SINGLE DECK UNITS

It was rapidly found that 'TAF' double-deck EMUs were not suited to the *Malpensa Express* airport service so FNM ordered these wholly first class units from Alstom in Savigliano. They are basically an extended version of the *Minuetto* built for Trenitalia and others. The first six units were allocated to the new Milano Centrale–Malpensa service then a second batch of eight was ordered for Milano Cadorna–Malpensa. These freed 'TAF' units which now operate normal suburban services. These units also carry the following class numbers in the FNM system – EA 720, EA 906, EA 905, EA 907 and EA 721. Units are all allocated to Novate. ETR.245.01 to 06 are owned by FNM and 07 to 14 by Trenord.

Trenord is also receiving very similar ETR.425 EMUs as part of the order for "Jazz" units being built for Trenitalia. See Section 1.4 for numbers and technical details.

EVN: Driving power cars are 94 83 3245 001-c and so on; trailers are 94 83 0245 002-c and so on.

ETR.245.01	245 001	245.002	245.003	245.004	245.005
ETR.245.02	245 006	245.007	245.008	245.009	245.010
ETR.245.03	245 011	245.012	245.013	245.014	245.015
ETR.245.04	245 016	245.017	245.018	245.019	245.020
ETR.245.05	245 021	245.022	245.023	245.024	245.025
ETR.245.06	245 026	245.027	245.028	245.029	245.030
ETR.245.07	245 031	245.032	245.033	245.034	245.035
ETR.245.08	245 036	245.037	245.038	245.039	245.040
ETR.245.09	245 041	245.042	245.043	245.044	245.045
ETR.245.10	245 046	245.047	245.048	245.049	245.050
ETR.245.11	245 051	245.052	245.053	245.054	245.055
ETR.245.12	245 056	245.057	245.058	245.059	245.060
ETR.245.13	245 061	245.062	245.063	245.064	245.065
ETR.245.14	245 066	245.067	245.068	245.069	245.070

CLASS EA 750   POWER CARS

750.01 to 18 are very similar to FS Class ALe 724 power cars but used to power single- or double-deck trailers. Most units are now mostly or all double-deck – EAB 850 driving trailers were built by Fiat under licence from France, 42 tonnes, 140 km/h, 68/72 seats, EB 950 intermediate trailers are Fiat, 41 tonnes, 140 km/h, –/150 seats. EB 750.19–24 are based on FS Class ALe 582. Remaining units up to 750.12 are 3-car, the rest 4-car. Trenord was trying to decide whether to refurbish these units in 2018 but they are more likely to be withdrawn.

Built: 1982; 1994/95†.   **Weight:** 53 tonnes.
Builder–Mechanical Parts: Breda/FIAT.   **Maximum Speed:** 130 km/h.
Builder–Electrical Parts: Ansaldo/TIBB.   **Length over Buffers:** 24.76 m.
Accommodation: 58/–.   **Traction Motors:** 4 x 280 kW.
Wheel Arrangement: Bo-Bo.

750.01 (S)	750.12 (S)	750.16 (S)	750.19† (U)	750.22† (S)
750.02 (S)	750.14 (S)	750.17 (S)	750.20† (U)	750.23† (U)
750.05 (S)	750.15 (S)	750.18 (S)	750.21† (S)	750.24† (S)

CLASS EB 760 & EA 761   "TAF"   4-CAR DOUBLE-DECK UNITS

Double-deck EMUs, identical to FS Classes ALe 426, ALe 506 and Le 736, mainly for the *"Passante"* route under the centre of Milano. This involves through running onto RFI metals and FS stock operating onto the FNM network. Of the six units built to operate the *Malpensa Express* service 07 was scrapped after an accident and the others now work normal services after ETR.245 took over. They are classified as first class but have the same seats as other units, a few being removed to make luggage space. Units 08 to 15 have been "sold" to Trenitalia and are now numbered 108 to 115.

Details as FS Class ALe 426 (EB 760), ALe 506 (EA 761) and Le 736 (EB 990).

Set no.

01	EB 760.001	EB 990.001	EB 990.002	EA 761.001
02	EB 760.002	EB 990.003	EB 990.004	EA 761.002
03	EB 760.003	EB 990.005	EB 990.006	EA 761.003
04	EB 760.004	EB 990.007	EB 990.008	EA 761.004
05	EB 760.005	EB 990.009	EB 990.010	EA 761.005
06	EB 760.006	EB 990.011	EB 990.012	EA 761.006
108	EB 760.008	EB 990.015	EB 990.016	EA 761.008
109	EB 760.009	EB 990.017	EB 990.018	EA 761.009
110	EB 760.010	EB 990.019	EB 990.020	EA 761.010
111	EB 760.011	EB 990.021	EB 990.022	EA 761.011
112	EB 760.012	EB 990.023	EB 990.024	EA 761.012
113	EB 760.013	EB 990.025	EB 990.026	EA 761.013
114	EB 760.014	EB 990.027	EB 990.028	EA 761.014
115	EB 760.015	EB 990.029	EB 990.030	EA 761.015
16	EB 760.016	EB 990.031	EB 990.032	EA 761.016
17	EB 760.017	EB 990.033	EB 990.034	EA 761.017
18	EB 760.018	EB 990.035	EB 990.036	EA 761.018
19	EB 760.019	EB 990.037	EB 990.038	EA 761.019
20	EB 760.020	EB 990.039	EB 990.040	EA 761.020
21	EB 760.021	EB 990.041	EB 990.042	EA 761.021
22	EB 760.022	EB 990.043	EB 990.044	EA 761.022
23	EB 760.023	EB 990.045	EB 990.046	EA 761.023 (S)
24	EB 760.024	EB 990.047	EB 990.048	EA 761.024
25	EB 760.025	EB 990.049	EB 990.050	EA 761.025
26	EB 760.026	EB 990.051	EB 990.052	EA 761.026
27	EB 760.027	EB 990.053	EB 990.054	EA 761.027

DIESEL MULTIPLE UNITS

All except Class ATR.115 and ATR.125 (see Section 1.3) are used on the Brescia–Edolo line.

CLASS ATR.220   3-SECTION ARTICULATED UNITS

These units were built by PESA in 2009 and are identical to those operated by FSE and TPER. The numbers duplicate those of FSE sets. They were stored in 2018 and could be sold. See FSE for details.

Set no.

| ATR.220.024 | 221.024 | 222.024 | 223.024 | ATR.220.025 | 221.025 | 222.025 | 223.025 |

CLASS ALn 668.120   SINGLE CARS

Based on FS Class ALn 668.1000 (121/2) or 668.3100 (123-126). 668.123 was destroyed in an accident. 668.121 is in historic livery.

Built: 668.121/2 1979; 123–26 1983.
Builders: 121/2 OMECA/Fiat; 123–26 Savigliano.
Engines: Two Fiat 8217.32 of 175 kW each.
Wheel Arrangement: 1A-A1.

Transmission: Mechanical.
Weight: 37 tonnes.
Maximum Speed: 95 km/h.
Accommodation: 8/56 1T.

| (668.)121 | 668.122 | 668.124 (S) | 668.125 (S) | 668.126 |

CLASS ALn 668.130   SINGLE CARS

Based on FS Class ALn 663.

Built: 668.131/2 1987; 133 1991.
Builder: Savigliano.
Engines: Two Fiat 8217.32 of 170 kW each.
Wheel Arrangement: 1A-A1.

Transmission: Mechanical.
Weight: 40 tonnes.
Maximum Speed: 95 km/h.
Accommodation: –/68 1T.

| 668.131 | 668.132 | 668.133 |

▲ Trenord Cn 531 is seen at Iseo depot on 6 April 2018. On the right is former Czech Railways DE 520.016. **David Haydock**

CLASS ALn 668.140 SINGLE CARS

Based on FS Class ALn 663. 668.147 was destroyed in an accident.

Built: 1993/94.
Builder: Savigliano.
Engine: Two Fiat 8217.32 of 175 kW each.
Wheel Arrangement: 1A-A1.

Transmission: Mechanical.
Weight: 39 tonnes.
Maximum Speed: 118 km/h.
Accommodation: –/68 1T.

668.141	668.143	668.144	668.145	668.146	668.148
668.142					

OTHER MOTIVE POWER

No.	Type	Axles	Builders	Built	kW	km/h	Tonnes	Seats	Notes
200.05	v	0-4-0T	MaCo	1883	330	60	22	–	Active
240.05	v	0-8-0T	La Meuse	1909	780	60	61	–	Active
270.04	v	0-6-0T	Esslingen	1897	575	60	34	–	Plinthed
DE 510.2	de	0-4-0	TIBB/Fiat	1967	2 x 32	30	18	–	
Cn 531	dh	0-4-0	Badoni/Fiat	1966	96	20	41	–	
E.600.3	e	Bo-Bo	OM/CGE	1928	1125	75	63	–	Novate
E.610.03	e	Bo-Bo	Breda/CGE	1949	1125	80	61	–	1
E.700.02	e	Bo-Bo	OM/TIBB	1928	544	80	55	82	2
E.700.09	e	Bo-Bo	OM/TIBB	1930	544	80	55	82	1
E.700.18	e	Bo-Bo	OM/TIBB	1948	544	80	55	57	Active
EB 740.01	e	Bo-Bo	OM/CGE	1928	736	80	57	78	Active
EB 740.02	e	Bo-Bo	OM/CGE	1928	736	80	57	78	3

1. Preserved at Saronno museum.
2. Preserved by MFP, Savigliano.
3. Plinthed at Museo delle Industrie e del Lavoro del Saronnese.

2.38. TRENTINO TRASPORTI TT

TT is the transport department of Trento province. In 2002 TT took control of metre gauge Ferrovia Elettrica Trento-Malè (FETM) and now has standard gauge Class ALn 501 DMUs for which a depot has been built at Spini di Gàrdolo just north of Trento. The DMUs work Trento–Bassano–Venezia over RFI tracks, now using TT staff. TT now also operates two FLIRT EMUs and six ETR.526 EMUs on the line to Bolzano. These are shown in Section 1.4.

The metre gauge line at first runs on the flat, hugging the main road northwards, then near the Trento–Bolzano RFI line. From Mezzolombardo, the line climbs rapidly, most of the upper section, in the *Gruppo di Brenta* mountains, being highly scenic. The line was extended 10 km from Malè to Marilleva in March 2003 and then to Mezzana (810 metres) in 2016. Extension to Fucine (6.5 km) is at the planning stage. The service is approximately hourly with some short workings to Mezzolombardo. TT also operates many connecting bus services. The section in the suburbs of Trento is gradually being put underground.

Gauge: 1000 mm.
Electrical System: 3000 V DC overhead.

Route: Trento Piazza Centa–Marilleva (66 km).
Depots: Trento, Mezzolombardo, Malè.

METRE GAUGE ELECTRIC MULTIPLE UNITS

EL 01/03 Bo-Bo

Single vehicles, similar in looks to FT's EL 01–12. EL 03 and 05 are retained as heritage units.

Built: 1963/64.
Builders: Stanga/TIBB.
Rating: 4 x 96 kW.
Accommodation: –/42.

Length over Buffers: 19.60 m.
Weight: 35 tonnes.
Maximum Speed: 90 km/h.

EL 01 (S)	EL 02 (S)	EL 03	EL 04 (S)	EL 05

ET 15–18   3-SECTION ARTICULATED UNITS

FIREMA Type E86 3-section units featuring GTO thyristor current supply and a lift for disabled passengers. Usually operate Trento suburban and the Malè–Marilleva shuttle.

Built: 1994/95.
Builder: FIREMA.
Continuous Rating: 720 kW.
Accommodation: –/95.

Length over Buffers: 35.78 m.
Weight: 69 tonnes.
Maximum Speed: 90 km/h.
Wheel Arrangement: Bo-Bo-Bo-Bo.

ET 15 Cles	ET 17 Mezzolombardo	ET 18
ET 16		

CLASS ETi 400   2-CAR UNITS

Also known as Type ETi 8/8 (numbered 401A + 401B, etc.), built by Alstom with a similar outline to standard gauge units for FT. Introduced with the opening of the extension to Marilleva.

Built: 2005–06.
Builder: Alstom.
Continuous Rating: 1360 kW.
Accommodation: –/100.

Length over Couplings: 40.20 m.
Weight: 73 tonnes.
Maximum Speed: 120 km/h.

401	403	405	407	409	411	413	414
402	404	406	408	410	412		

OTHER METRE GAUGE MOTIVE POWER

No.	Type	Axles	Builders	Built	kW	km/h	Tonnes	Seats	Notes
13	ABe	Bo-Bo	CET/BBC	1923	310	45	33	6/30	Ex SSIF
LC 21	D e	Bo-Bo	OMS/TIBB	1965	4 x 220	65	48	-	-
B.51	e	Bo-Bo	C&T/TIBB	1929	4 x 7540	32-36	-	-	*

*   originally FEVF, then FAS, then FGC. For historic trains.

▲ TT ETi 400 set 405 is seen at Mezzocorona on 11 September 2018.   **David Haydock**

3. OTHER RAILWAYS OPERATING IN ITALY

BLS Cargo Italia   BLSC

This Swiss company has a subsidiary in Italy and operates freights into the north of the country using its own Class 475 and 486 electric locos or hired Class 186 electrics (see Section 1.2).

Lokomotion Gesellschaft für Schienentraktion   LM

A German company which operates from München over the Brennero and Tarvisio routes to northern Italy in concert with RTC. The company's Class 193 locos (see Section 1) operate south of border stations.

Austrian Federal Railways   ÖBB

ÖBB's passenger division supplies the traction for the Verona–Brennero–Innsbruck–München EuroCity service, whose stock is supplied by DB and staff in Italy by FNM. ÖBB locos also work Wien–Venezia. Locos used are Class 1216, known as Class E.190 in Italy – see Section 1.2. See RCCIT for details of ÖBB's freight activities in Italy and Section 1.2 for locos used.

French National Railways   SNCF

SNCF operates the TGV service from Paris to Milano Porta Garibaldi using TGV Réseau sets 4501–4506 (see Platform 5 Publishing book "French Railways" for full details). See Captrain Italia for details of SNCF's freight activities in Italy.

Slovenian Railways   SŽ

SŽ operates freight as far as Villa Opicina with its Class 541 electric locos. Trenitalia locos no longer work into Slovenia.

Swiss Federal Railways   SBB

SBB Cargo Italia operates into Italy using 12 Siemens Class Re 474 on the Chiasso route and 18 Bombardier Class Re 484 electric locos (E.484.001–018) on the Luino route. SBB Cargo Italia also uses three Class D.100 diesel locos – see Section 1.1. Swiss Railways operates passenger trains into Milano Centrale using its Class 503 Pendolino Due tilting EMUs – the same design as Trenitalia's ETR.610.

THELLO

Thello is a Trenitalia subsidiary whose aim is to preserve and develop services between Italy and France. Thello first took over the Paris–Venezia overnight service, then the Paris–Roma overnight, later withdrawing the latter. The next service to be reintroduced was Milano–Nice–Marseille daytime trains. So far services have been operated by French BB 36000 locos in France (as far as Ventimiglia in Italy for the Milano service), and Trenitalia locos in Italy.

TILO

TILO is a joint venture between Trenitalia and Swiss Federal Railways, formed to improve cross-border local passenger services between the Swiss canton of TIcino and the Italian region of Lombardia – thus the name. TILO livery combining white with Italian green and Swiss red has been applied to Class E.464 locos and stock used on the Milano–Chiasso service. TILO owns 19 4-car (524 001–019) and 11 6-car (524.101–111) Class 524 FLIRT EMUs (see Platform 5 Publishing "Swiss Railways" book for full details). These are known internally as Class ETR.150 by Trenord and now work through to Milano Centrale and Malpensa airport via the new Mendrisio–Varese line.

TX Logistik   TXL

A German company, majority owned subsidiary of Trenitalia, working on the corridors to Germany via both Switzerland and Austria. Trenitalia Class E.412 electric locos are driven from Brennero to München by TXL staff. TXL also uses other electric locos in Italy – see Section 1.

4. LOCOMOTIVES IN INDUSTRIAL SERVICE

There are very large numbers of locomotives in industrial service in Italy, particularly with private track maintenance contractors. Because of limitations on space, we only list here those engines which used to operate for one of the national railway companies. Large numbers of "Köf" shunters exist but many cannot be identified or never operated for DB or DR. Track maintenance company locos can range far and wide, while in the case of those with loco refurbishment firms, the loco has probably been sold on since this book was published. Numbering is confusing and has changed several times. The first system consisted of a number prefixed with "T" – some locos still carry these. Then, until 2013, a long code starting with letters DD FMT and finishing with two letters, four numbers and another letter was applied. The two letters before the number give the local division – NA is Napoli, VR Verona and so on. As the numbers are almost never duplicated, we show them here. During 2013, Italy started to apply 12-figure European Vehicle Numbers to main line locos although few had been applied at the time of writing. For example, 211 145 and 017 with GCF had become 99 83 9 484 005-7 and 006-5 IT-GCF. Where we have these numbers we show them in the shortened version: for the above, 484 005 and 006 for example. Unfortunately, locos also carry numbers given by infrastructure manager RFI. For example, the above two locos are IT-RFI 270 015-7 and 270 069-4.

CZ	Ex Czech industrial locomotive		§	Converted to 950 mm gauge	
SK	Ex Slovak industrial locomotive				

No.	Former No.	Owner/Location	No.	Former No.	Owner/Location
NA 0001	NSB Di.3 622	Globalfer (red)	VE 0189	ÖBB 2043 054	SOGRAF, Cava Tigozzi
NA 0002	NSB Di.3 626	Globalfer (red)			
NA 0004	NSB Di.3 631	Globalfer (red)	NA 0190	DB 323 959	COMES, Villaricca (ex T 6265)
VR 0005	DB 323 452	Mazzi, Castel d'Azzano	RC 0203	SNCB 5122	Ventura
RC 0021	DB 211 148	Ventura (ex T 7234)	RC 0204	SNCB 5135	Ventura
RC 0022	DB 323 571	Ventura	BO 0216	DB 211 080	CLF No. 15, ex T 1868.
RC 0025	DB 323 647	Ventura (ex T 7212)	RC 0227	SNCB 5104	Ventura
GE 0026	DB 211 241	Valditerra (Tk 1542)	RC 0228	SNCB 5127	Ventura
	EVN: 484 011	RFI: 270 057	RC 0229	SNCB 5133	Ventura
RC 0026	SNCB 6070	Ventura (ex T 7222)	PA 0248	DB 332 111	ICA, Palermo
RC 0027	SNCB 6067	Ventura (ex T 7221)	GE 0242	DB 201 883	Valsecchi
RC 0030	SNCB 6047	Ventura (ex T 7204)	GE 0248	DB 280 008	Ser.Fer., Udine (ex T 3569)
PA 0034	DB 323 544	??, Palermo			
GE 0045	FS 225.6010	Valditerra (ex T 3305)	BO 0252	DB 323 815	CLF No. 18 (ex T 3693)
RC 0087	DB 260 144	Ventura (ex T 7104)	VR 0259	SNCB 8006	Logyca
AN 0091	SJ V4 147	Tuzi, Balsorano	RC 0266	DB 322 049	ex T 7555 Multitel, Crotone
AN 0092	SJ V4 149	Tuzi, Balsorano			
GE 0093	CFR 60-1296	Valditerra (ex TK 1775)	VR 0271	DB 333 002	Gemmo, Vicenza
RC 0096	DB 323 111	Ventura (ex T 7100)	RC 0279	SNCB 5105	Ventura
RC 0102	PKP ST43-62	Ventura Ex 060-DA 375	NA 0314	DB 323 831	ex T 6000 FADEP, Napoli
NA 0114	SNCB 6039	Globalfer (ex T 6577)	GE 0318	FS 225.7057	??
NA 0115	SNCB 6089	Globalfer (ex T 291, ex T 6578)	TO 0320	DB 211 224	Ar.Fer (ex T 1756)
RC 0115	DB 323 573	Ventura (ex T 7182)	RC 0323	SNCB 5167	Ventura
RC 0116	DB 323 865	Ventura (ex T 7170)	GE 0328	DB 211 134	GCF 481 010 RFI: 270 194
AN 0118	DB 323 630	Impresa IRT	RC 0332	SNCB 5185	Ventura
TS 0119	DB 323 962	Gleisfrei (T 6232)	VR 0336	ÖBB 2062 047	Quadro Gaetano
RC 0120	DB 211 153	Ventura (T 16245)	VR 0357	ÖBB 2062 021	Notari RFI: 270 153
RC 0121	ÖBB 2060 054	Ventura (ex Tk 7007)	NA 0367	SNCB 6019	Globalfer
RC 0122	ÖBB 2060 059	Ventura (ex Tk 7008)	TO 0371	DB 211 126	Ar.Fer (ex T 1758)
RM 0161	DB 333 226	Geo Costruzioni, Patti	BO 0394	DB 260 552	Bonciani "316" 270 256 (ex T 16524)
RM 0174	DB 211 010	GCF (ex T 1544) RFI: 270 450	BO 0395	DB 260 120	Bonciani, Ravenna "315" (ex Tk 1734)
RM 0175	DB 211 259	Ge.Fer RFI: 270 056	NA 0400	FS D.341.1060	Globalfer (ex T 7227)
			NA 0401	FS D.341.1027	Globalfer (ex T 7228)
RM 0176	DB 211 130	Ge.fer (ex Tk 3631) RFI: 270 353	BO 0411	DB 323 018	CLF no. 21
			BO 0412	DB 323 813	CLF (T 3704, no. 20)

TO 0413	DB 335 237	Sifel, Spigno Monferrato	VE 2035	DB 211 223	SeGeCo, Mestre (ex T 819)
NA 0488	FS D.341.1048	Globalfer	VE 2036	DB 323 769	SeGeCo, Mestre
NA 0489	FS D.341.1054	Globalfer	MI 2054	FS D.341.2004	Salcef (ex T 3794, for Romania)
TO 0490	DB 323 514	Hi-Tec Italia (T 14045)	MI 2053?	FS D.341.2025	Salcef (ex T 3795, for Romania)
TO 0491	DB 323 240	Hi-Tec Italia (T 14032)	RM 2056	DB 212 090	Salcef (ex T 1803)
NA 0499	DB 322 034	Gleisfrei (270 416)	RM 2058	DB 211057	Salcef
NA 0502	SNCB 5182	Globalfer	RM 2060	DB 212 106	Salcef
RC 0511	DB 323 989	Esperia, Paola (ex T 22036)	RM 2061	SNCB 8042	Salcef (ex T 882)
NA 0554	SNCB 5132	Globalfer (dk green)	RM 2066	DB 212 301	Salcef EVN: 484 037 RFI: 270 017
NA 0565	SNCB 5107	Globalfer	RM 2069	DB 211 358	Salcef RFI: 270 089
NA 0599	FS 234.2009	OMTE	RM 2072	DB 212 044	Salcef
NA 0601	DB 323 589	??	RM 2073	DB 212 045	Salcef RFI: 270 019
BO 0621	T448 0836	CLF (CZ)	VE 2109	DB 211 ???	Cenedese RFI 270 023
BO 0621"	T448 0936	CLF (CZ)			
BO 0626	T448 0779	CLF (SK)	VE 2172	DB 323 454	Petrangeli, Orvieto RFI: 270 101
BO 0626"	T448 0954	CLF (CZ)			
BO 0680	SNCB 7506	CLF No. 28	VE 2301	DB 211 343	Co.Rac.Fer (ex T 2208, ex Tk 1749)
BO 0681	SNCB 7504	CLF No. 26			
BO 0682	SNCB 7505	CLF No. 27			
BO 0693	HŽ 2141 001	CLF (ex JŽ 743-001)	RM 2350	SNCB 6042	Salcef (ex T 5958)
TO 0706	SNCB 8052	Gleisfrei	RM 2351	SNCB 6034	Salcef (ex T 6411)
BO 0712	SNCB 7101	CLF No. 24	RM 2359	DB 323 354	Salcef (in UAE)
BO 0713	SNCB 7103	CLF No. 25	RM 2501	FS 225.6008	Micos (ex Tk 5820) RFI: 270 337
NA 0722	SBB Tm 9570	Mercuri, Napoli			
NA 0724	DB 211 211	CLF "14"	RM 2516	FS 225.6016	Mi.Cos (ex Tk 5821) RFI: 270 185
NA 0841	DB 211 020	GCF (ex T 3596, ex Tk 1900) RFI: 270 337			
NA 0866	DB 323 168	Armafer	RM 2782	DB 324 001	Ceprini (ex T 4031) RFI: 270 004
BA 1023	DB 212 128	Fersalento			
BA 1037	DB 212 131	Fersalento	RM 2806	FS 225.6xxx	MF SRL (ex T 5763)
BA 1038	DB 211 108	SILF, Bari	BA 4062	DB 260 024	Armafer, Lecce
BA 1048	DB 211 229	Fersalento RFI: 270 196	BA 4068	DB 211 004	Armafer (ex T 6158)
			BA 4069	FS D.341.2005	Armafer (ex T 6159)
RM 1052	FS 225.6011	SEGI (ex Tk 5950)	BA 4110	DB 280 010	Armafer (ex T 6215)
RM 1053	FS 225.6020	SEGI (ex Tk 5831)	BA 4118	DB 323 275	Armafer
RM 1054	FS 235.6007	SEGI (ex T 5752)	BA 4140	FS D.341.2029	Armafer (ex T 6459)
VE 1086	DB 323 230	Gleisfrei	BA 4145	DB 211 001	Armafer (ex T 7546)
NA 1097	SNCB 6045	Globalfer (ex Tk 1632)	BA 4167	SNCB 5175	Globalfer
FI 1125	DB 323 949	CEMES	BA 4227	DB 323 410	GCF (ex T 14094)
FI 1154	DB 211 xxx	Scala (ex T 1817, ex FI 1155)	BA 4228	DB 332 044	GCF
FI 1155	DB 211 334	Scala (ex FI 1154)	BA 4266	DB 323 914	Ceprini (ex RM 1753)
FI 1276	DB 212 xxx	Scala (ex Tk 1948)	BE 4270 484 004	DB 211 ???	GCF RFI: 270 088
BA 1318	DB 211 270	See FG	BA 4321	DB 323 236	GCF
FI 1363	DB 333 247	CERES, Pisa	BA 4366	DB 211 145	GCF (ex T 1779) EVN: 484 005 RFI: 270 015
FI 1390	SNCB 8066	ELETTRI-FER, Rignano sull'Arno			
FI 1409	ÖBB 2062 048	D'Adetta	BA 4370	DB 211 017	GCF EVN: 484 006 RFI: 270 069
FI 1418	SNCB 9160	Della Buona			
RM 1524	DB 216 xxx	Ge.Fer	BA 4481	FS 235.6006	Cosfer, Tagliacozzo (ex T 5753)
VE 1758	DB 332 009	Il.VE.COS, Vittorio Veneto EVN: 481 030 RFI: 270 112	MI 5129	DB 323 206	Icefe-Due Cividate Camuno
VE 1759	DB 332 103	EVN: 481 033 RFI: 270 113	MI 5423	ÖBB 2062.09	Notari RFI: 270 300
VE 1781	SNCB 9154	Sedico			
RM 1826	ÖBB 2064 006	Ceprini	MI 5444	SBB Tm 9583	Recuperi
VE 2001	DB 323 011	Semenzato (T 2007)	MI 5485	DB 323 235	Recuperi, Malegno
VE 2002	DB 260 030	Segeco (ex T 2097)			

MI 5515	ÖBB 2062 015	Gaetano
MI 5519	DB 335 183	Icefe Due
MI 7018	DB 323 194	Recuperi, Malegno
MI 7063	SNCB 9110	ICEFE Due
MI 7072	FS 235.3009	Valsecchi (ex TX 507)
MI 7097	DB 323 468	Valsecchi (ex T 664)
MI 7170	SNCB 8065	Notari
MI 7239	DB 211 346	De Aloe
		RFI: 270 208
RM 9077	DB 212 182	Valditerra Ex BA 4218
		RFI: 150 692
RM 9083	DB 323 785	De Aloe (ex T 7213)
RM 9092	DB 212 190	Cenedese, Roncade
		EVN: 484 001
		RFI: 150 130
RM 9131	DB 332 151	Settembre, Todi
T 02	DB 323 612	Ventura §
T 03	DB 323 345	Ventura §
T 06	DB 322 638	Ventura §
		(ex T 7004)
T 09	FS 142 2002	Ventura
T 070	DB 323 857	AVE, Ceggia
T 158	FS 213.921?	Cariboni
T 184	FS 235.3011	Ar.Fer
T 291	SNCB 6089	CLB
T 708	DB 265 004	IPE
T 885	FS 225 2002	Bertinoro
T 1590	DB 211 003	Ar.Fer
Tk 1661	DB 211 094	Acciai Speciali, Terni
T 1742	SNCB 80xx	Impresa d'Alessio, Pignataro
T 1788	SNCB 80xx	A.Ba-Fer, Napoli
T 1801	SNCB 80xx	Co.Ge.Mar, Napoli
T 1804	SNCB 80xx	Co.Ge.Mar, Napoli
T 1812	SNCB 8029	Gemmo, Vicenza
T 1829	DB 216 033	CLF (rebuilt with centre cab. No 23)
T 1848	SNCB 8023	MI.COS, Roma
T 1878	SNCB 80xx	Co.Ge.Mar, Napoli
T 1904	DB 211 265	Ge.Fer
T 1939	DB 216 141	CLF (rebuilt with off-centre cab. No. 7)
		EVN: 484 020
T 1965	FS 235.3001	Masfer
T 2209	DB 331 003	Agip, Livorno
		Ex Ser.Fer K 178
T 3009	DB 323 431	Railoc
T 3665	DB 323 947	Ge.Fer
T 3673	DB 322 608	De Aloe (metre gauge)
T 3686	SNCB 8005	RIC
T 3687	SNCB 8048	RIC
T 3694	DB 323 807	CLF No. 19
T 3714	DB 260 228	IPE
T 3738	DB 261 003	GCF
T 3757	DB 323 213	Salcef
T 4018	DB 323 435	Ceprini
T 4109	FS 225.7068	Cooperativa di Lavoro Rigutino
T 4416	DB 323 605	??
T 4572	DB 323 993	CEMES, Pisa (No. 1)
C 5205	FS 216.0023	Sveco, Latina
C 5206	FS 216.0054	Sveco, Latina
T 5220	DB 323 211	Salcef

T 5503	DB 280 003	Arvedi Tubi Acciaio, Cremona
T 5505	FS 235.3013	Salcef
T 5714	DB 260 381	RIC
T 5754	FS 235.6009?	Esposito
T 5773	FS 234.xxxx	Cosfer, Tagliacozzo
Tk 5817	FS 235.6005	Edilrogen, Roma
Tk 5965	FS 225.6012	Falck
T 6029	DB 332 184	Del Monte, Portici §
NT 6089	DB 260 003	Ventura
T 6092	DB 323 057	?
T 6100	FS 213.913	Esposito
T 6156	DB 260 218	Logyca
T 6265	DB 323 959	COMES, Villaricca
T 6317	DB 323 755	Edil.ge.ma, Cerami
T 6561	DB 260 xxx	Fersalento
T 6646	DB 323 180	Fersalento
T 6647	DB 260 103	Fersalento
NT 6649	DB 216 126	Fersalento
TR 6826	DB 323 076	Salcef
N 7000	DB 216 206	Fersalento Named "Ercole"
Tk 7009	ÖBB 2060 063	Ventura
Tk 7029	DB 323 673	Ventura
T 7106	DB 323 204	Ventura
T 7121	SNCB 6016	Ar.Fer (ex T 898)
T 7131	DB 323 283	Raffaele Gangemi
T 7140	DB 211 292	Ventura
T 7152	DB 252 901	Ventura (metre g.)
T 7183	DB 323 671	Ventura
T 7187	DB 323 836	Cogetir
T 7191	DB 323 645	Ventura
T 7192	DB 323 791	Ventura
T 7194	DB 323 243	Fersalento
T 7223	DB 323 623	Ventura
T 7224	DB 323 695	Ventura
T 7519	DB 323 938	?
T 12025	DB 323 921	T-Rail, Trecate
T 14070	DB 323 285	?
T 16173	DB 323 310	Siette, Firenze
M 17239	DB 211 346	De Aloe
AC 20081	FS 234.2008	OMTE
DB 211 049		Taranto Container Terminal "61"
DB 211 063		Taranto Container Terminal "62"
DB 211 118		GCF, for spares
DB 211 347		Autoporto di Fernetti, Trieste
DB 212 082		Railoc, hired to Oceanogate
DB 212 295		Quadrante Servizi, Verona "1"
DB 213 906		Globalfer
DB 216 160		Fersalento
DB 260 224		IPE
DB 323 080		OMM, Moretta "46" (ex Ser.Fer. K 127)
DB 323 679		Cava di Nuova Bartolina, Castellaccia
DB 324 060		Cioce, Bari
DB 332 219		Railoc
DB 333 008		Tecnofer, Mantova RFI: 270 464
DB 333 043		Railoc
DB 333 534		Railoc
DB 333 680		Railoc

DB 333 681	Feroni, Napoli
DB 335 088	DRF, Firenze
DB 362 924	Railoc
DB 363 045	TS Traction, Buja "5273"
DB 365 102	Notari (ex Ser.Fer K 241)
DB 365 828	Railoc "30117"
FS 142 2001	Zanolla, Cagliari.
FS 209.001	Martini
FS 209.002	Martini
FS 213.913	Esposito
FS 215.004	Masfer
FS 216.0015	Magliola
FS 225.6009	Porto Carrara
FS 225.6013	Tecnofer
FS 225.7034	T-Rail, Trecate
FS 225.7052	Coop Lavoro Rigutino
FS 234.3005	Masfer
FS 234.3012	Masfer
FS 235.3018	Casalpusterlengo
FS 245.1012	Cargo Docks, Modena
FS D.343.1010	Transminter, Frosinone
NS 2500	Bonciani "317"
ÖBB 2060 019	Railoc
ÖBB 2062 035	Migos
ÖBB 2062 065	Railoc
ÖBB 2043 030	IPE
ÖBB 2143 007	GCF

ÖBB 2143 012	GCF
SNCB 5111	Globalfer
SNCB 5121	Ventura
SNCB 5170	Ventura
SNCB 5174	Ventura
SNCB 6060	Abibes, Cremona
SNCB 6302	Ventura (in Venezuela)
SNCB 7336	Interporto, Ronco Scrivia
SNCB 7363	Logyca, Foggia
SNCB 7365	Borsari, Poggio Rusco
SNCB 7374	Logyca
SNCB 7376	Interporto, Ronco Scrivia
SNCB 7377	Interporto, Ronco Scrivia
SNCB 7392	Lotras
SNCB 8012	Gleisfrei
SNCB 8030	IPE
SNCB 8032	Gleisfrei
SNCB 8037	Gleisfrei
SNCB 8043	Cariboni
SNCB 8045	Gleisfrei
SNCB 8067	Logyca
SNCB 8068	Gleisfrei
SNCB 8069	Gleisfrei
SNCB 8206	Lotras
SNCB 8207	Lotras
SNCB 8208	Lotras
SNCB 9125	Geocom

Major loco owners

Ar.Fer	AR.FER, Alessandria
Armafer	ARMAFER, Lecce
Bonaventura	Luigi Bonaventura, Preganziol
Bonciani	Impresa Bonciani, Ravenna
Cariboni	Cariboni, Colico
CEMES	CEMES SpA, Pisa
Ceprini	Ceprini Construzioni, Orvieto
CLF	Costruzioni Linee Ferroviarie, Bologna
Co.Rac.Fer	CO.RAC.FER, Casale sul Sile
De Aloe	De Aloe Construzioni, Brescia
Fersalento	FERSALENTO, Lecce
GCF	GCF, Grottaglie
Gefer	Ge.fer, Roma
Gleisfrei	Gleisfrei Construzioni Ferroviarie, Castel d'Ario (dealer)
Gleismac	Gleismac Italiana, Gazzo di Bigarello (dealer)
Globalfer	Globalfer, Roccapalumba
IPE	IPE, Pradelle di Nogarole Rocca (dealer/refurbisher)
Logyca	Logyca, Verona (loco hire company)

Lotras	Lotras, Incoronata
Magliola	Magliola, Santhià (workshops)
Martini	Martini, Villaverla-Montecchio
Masfer	MCF Masfer, Trecate
Notari	Luigi Notari, Milano
Paggetti	Luigi Paggetti, Arezzo
Paroldi	Paroldi, Ponti
Pasolini	Pasolini, Bertinoro
Railoc	Railoc, Trasaghis (leasing company)
RIC	RIC, Bologna
SALCEF	SALCEF, Roma
Scala	Scala, Montevarchi
SEGI	SEGI, Avezzano
Semenzato	Luciano Semenzato, Mestre
Valditerra	Valditerra, Novi Ligure
Valsecchi	Valsecchi Armamento Ferroviario, Eupilio
Ventura	Francesco Ventura, Paola

GCF and Gefer are now part of the Rossi group.

5. MUSEUMS AND MUSEUM LINES

Italy is unusual in having very few preserved lines, most stock preserved in working order being used over the RFI network. In August 2017, a new law was passed to allow disused lines to be converted to tourist railways and this opens up great potential for new services. Trenitalia itself set up the foundation FFSI in 2013 and this has led to the enlargement of an already large historic fleet, including steam locomotives, many operational. The foundation also took over responsibility for the national rail museum in Pietrarsa, near Napoli, and the museum in Trieste which will reopen in 2020. FFSI has a small number of technical staff but also works with several associations which "look after" specific items of stock. It can therefore be difficult to determine who owns what, and also means that items of stock move around more than before. There are a few museums with static exhibits across Italy plus several preservation centres, but most are not open regularly to the public. As for preserved lines, several lines with no public service were declared as "preserved" in 2018 and these are now shown in yellow on the maps in this book.

Associazione Culturale Amatori Ferrovie/Museo del Treno   ACAF

http://www.acaf-montesilvano.com/

An association based at Montesilvano with one steam, one diesel and one electric loco. The "museum" is an annexe to the south-west of Montesilvano station.

Adriavapore (Associazione Treni Storici Emilia Romagne)   ATSER

http://www.adriavapore.it/

A club based in Emilia Romagna whose locos are based at Bologna Centrale. The former base at Rimini has closed.

GRUPPO ALe 883   ALe 883

www.ale883.it

A club based in the old FS depot at Tirano, north of Milano, on the border with Switzerland. The group started up to save an ALe 883 electric railcar but is now involved with several locos owned by FFSI. In 2018 most of the stock was moved to Milano Smistamento. The group regularly runs special trains in the Milano area.

Associazione Rotabili Storici Milano Smistamento   ARSMS

www.milanosmistamento.com/

A group of railway staff working on FFSI stock at Milano Smistamento depot.

Associazione "Turno C"   TURNO C

www.turnoc.it

A group which looks after FFSI locomotives in the old depot (*rimessa* – not the workshops) in Foligno.

Associazione Veneta Treni Storici   AVTS

www.avts.it

An association of railway staff looking after preserved trains at Verona depot. Trains are owned by FFSI.

Associazione Società Veneta Ferrovie   SVF

www.societavenetaferrovie.it

Maintains steam loco 880.001, ex SV diesel E.424.04 and former FCV diesel shunter L.914 plus some stock, with a small depot at Primolano on the Trento–Venezia line.

Centrale Montemartini

www.centralemontemartini.org

This art museum in an old factory in Roma houses three coaches from very old trains used by the Pope.

Feralp Team

www.feralpteam.com

An association which is creating a "trans alpine" railway museum known as *Museo del Trasporto Ferroviario Attraverso le Alpi* in the old FS depot at Bussoleno on the Fréjus line. Most stock, belonging to FFSI, has been moved to Torino Smistamento depot.

Ferrovia del Basso Sebino   FBS

www.ferrovieturistiche.it/it/trenoblu

A group operating Treno Blu tourist trains on the line from Palazzolo sull'Oglio to Paratico-Sarnico on Lago d'Iseo. There is some stock at Palazzolo.

The Ferrovie Turistiche website also hosts *Ferrovia Val d'Orcia* which operates heritage trains from Siena with FFSI stock and *Ferrovia Turistica Camuno* which operates tourist trains on the Brescia–Edolo line with Trenord (FNM) stock.

Fondazione FS Italiane   FFSI

www.fondazionefs.it

A foundation set up in 2013 by FS to administer historic locos and stock owned by the company. Since its creation the foundation has "saved" a great deal more than the initial fleet, has taken over responsibility for MNF and MFT (see below) and has launched new tourist services. Some of the stock is based at Pistoia depot (PT) also known as *Deposito Rotabili Storici* (DRS), while other major bases are Milano Smistamento (MS), Milano Squadra Rialzo (SR) and La Spezia Magliarina (LS). The last site has a few items stored at Santo Stefano di Magra (SSM). Other stock is based at Trenitalia depots and "looked after" by various associations. DRS can now be visited by appointment – by individuals on Sundays and by groups on Tuesdays and Thursdays. Other sites occasionally hold open days.

Gruppo Romano Amici della Ferrovia   GRAF

www.graftreni.it

An enthusiast group which is involved in saving former ATAC train, tram and trolleybus plus ex ACT railcar ALn 2451 from the scrap heap. The club's two ex FS railcars have now been taken over by FFSI.

Italvapore (Associazione Toscana Treni Storici)   ATTS

www.italvapore.it

This club organises special trains, usually hauled by steam, in the Toscana region. Locos, which are jointly managed by FFSI and Italvapore, are mainly at Pistoia.

Museo Europeo dei Trasporte Ogliari

volandia.it/collezione-ogliari

This collection, including some railway exhibits, was created by a Mr Ogliari at Ranco but was moved recently to the site of the Volandia air museum at Somma Lombardo, near Milano's Malpensa airport.

Museo Ferroviario di Porta Vescova   MFPV

A minor museum a short distance from Verona Porta Vescovo station. Currently closed for rebuilding.

▲ 940.008 and 835.088 are seen at the FFSI depot at Pistoia on 8 April 2018. **David Haydock**

▼ Mini shunter 207.023 is seen inside the Museo Ferriviario della Puglia at Lecce on 8 April 2013.
David Haydock

Museo Ferroviario Piemontese · MFP

www.museoferroviariopiemontese.com

After many years of being stored outside at Torino Ponte Mosca (also known as Porta Milano), part of MFP's collection moved to a permanent site at Savigliano (home of Alstom's main plant in Italy, formerly Fiat). However, many other items are still stored at Torino Ponte Mosca or at Santhià. The Savigliano museum is south of the station in the fork of the Fossano and Saluzzo lines. It contains many interesting items, particularly linked to three-phase electrification.

Museo Ferroviario della Puglia · MP

ferromuseopuglia.altervista.org

A small museum hidden away to the south-west of Lecce station. *Associazione Ionico-Salentina Amici Ferrovie* (AISAF) is the association which runs the museum and organises occasional specials with former FSE locos and railcars. The collection contains former FS and FSE items.

Museo Ferroviario di Trieste Campo Marzio · MFT

This railway museum is mainly outside at the closed Trieste Campo Marzio station. Currently closed for renovation, it will reopen, under FFSI management, in 2020.

Museo Ferroviario del Verbano · MFV

www.verbanoexpress.it

Museum at Luino run by the association Verbano Express with both Italian and Swiss items.

Museo Nazionale Ferroviario di Pietrarsa · MNF

www.museopietrarsa.it

This is Italy's national railway museum, situated at Pietrarsa, just south of Napoli. FFSI now runs the *"Pietrarsa Express"* from Napoli Centrale to the museum with heritage trains two Sundays each month.

Museo Nazionale della Scienza e della Tecnologia · MNST

www.museoscienza.org

As the title suggests, this is Italy's national museum of science and technology which houses several railway exhibits in Milano as well as a collection of other transport and science exhibits.

Museo Nazionale dei Trasporti La Spezia · MNT

www.museonazionaletrasporti.it

A small museum (with a big name!) covering all forms of transport west of the station in La Spezia. Linked to the Associazione Treni Storici Liguria (ATSL). Only open on Sundays, except public holidays! The most interesting exhibit is Franco-Crosti-boilered 743.301. Not to be confused with the much bigger former FS depot at La Spezia Magliarina which is run by FFSI!

Roma Treno Vapore Team · RTVT

rtvt.it/web/

A group based in Roma which, with FFSI, jointly manages two steam and one electric loco at Roma Smistamento depot.

Sardegnavapore (Associazione Sarda Treni Storici)   ASTS

A group based in Cagliari (Sardinia) dedicated to the maintenance of and operation of trains using 2-8-0 740.423, as well as the restoration of diesel railcar ALn 772.3263. The museum next to Cagliari station is rarely open to the public.

TRENO D.O.C.

www.trenodoc.com

A group based at Palermo depot which jointly manages preserved traction with FFSI.

VOLANDIA

Also known as Museo Europeo dei Trasporte Ogliari: see above.

▲ Diesel shunter 214.7013 is seen outside the grandly-named "National Transport Museum" in La Spezia on 9 April 2013.   **David Haydock**

6. PRESERVED LOCOMOTIVES AND ROLLING STOCK

This list covers only motive power formerly with FS or one of its constituent companies. A number of other items from local and industrial railways are also preserved in Italy. The list uses the following codes for the current status of motive power:

M	Museum, on display but not active	P	Plinthed
MA	Museum, active	S	Stored
MR	Museum, being restored		

For museum abbreviations, see Section 5.

Items of stock which are passed for main line operation carry 12-figure EVNs. Examples include:

880.051	90 83 2880 051-5
D.141.1011	98 83 2141 111-4
E.626.443	91 83 2626 443-2

6.1. STEAM LOCOMOTIVES

Locos with a prefix P or R are narrow gauge. Others are standard gauge. The Whyte notation is used for steam locomotive wheel arrangement. The number of leading wheels are given, followed by the number of driving wheels and then the trailing wheels. Suffixes are used to denote tank locomotives as follows: T – side tank, PT – pannier tank, ST – saddle tank, WT – well tank. For example 2-6-2T.

Number	Details	Built	Status	Location
P 7	0-8-2T	1922	M	MNST
R 301.2	2-6-0T	1912	M	MNST
R 301.027	2-6-0T	1914	P	Marsala, seafront
R 302.19	2-6-0T	1922	M	MNF
R 302.038	2-6-0T	1927	P	Marcon, ASI SpA
R 370.002	0-6-0T	1908	P	Monterotondo, private owner
R 370.012	0-6-0T	1914	P	Catania Centrale station
R 370.018	0-6-0T	1914	P	Città di Castello-Garavelle, Museo Gioacchino Capelletti
R 370.023	0-6-0T	1921	M	MNF
R 370.024	0-6-0T	1921	P	Canove di Asiago, near Museo della Guerra
R 410.004	0-8-0T	1916	P	Ortisei
"BAYARD"	2-2-2	1839*	M	MNF (* replica, built by FS, 1939)
290.319	0-6-0	1913	M	MNF
422.009	0-8-0	1911	S	MFP. Savigliano (Ex KPEV G8 4813 "LUCIA")
422.022	0-8-0	1913	S	MFP. Favria
470.092	0-10-0	1907	M	MNST
476.073	0-10-0	1911	M	MFT (ex JŽ 28.023 and kkStB 80.100)
477.011	0-10-0	1904	M	MNF (ex kkStB 180.56)
480.017	2-10-0	1923	M	MNF
552.036	4-4-0	1900	M	MNST
625.011	2-6-0	1910	P	Trento station
625.012	2-6-0	1910	P	Rimini Fiabilandia theme park
625.017	2-6-0	1910	MA	FFSI. RTVT. RS
625.027	2-6-0	1911	M	Moretta (spares)
625.030	2-6-0	1911	M	MNF
625.050	2-6-0	1912	S	SSM. For MNF
625.054	2-6-0	1912	MR	FFSI. PT
625.055	2-6-0	1912	M	ATTS. PT
625.076	2-6-0	1913	P	Desenzano del Garda, lakeside
625.077	2-6-0	1913	M	RTVT. RS
625.089	2-6-0	1913	M	PT
625.091	2-6-0	1914	P	Castelfranco Veneto, Dotto, near Giocattoli
625.100	2-6-0	1914	MA	FFSI. ALe 883. SR
625.101	2-6-0	1914	MR	FFSI. PT
625.102	2-6-0	1914	P	Miradolo Terme, park
625.107	2-6-0	1914	M	Smartno ob Paki, Slovenia
625.116	2-6-0	1922	M	MFV. Luino
625.123	2-6-0	1922	P	Verona Porta Vescovo

625.131	2-6-0	1922	P	Vicenza depot
625.142	2-6-0	1922	S	FFSI. ATTS. PT
625.144	2-6-0	1922	P	Catanzaro Lido depot
625.152	2-6-0	1922	P	Ascoli Satriano, Strada Provinciali 87
625.153	2-6-0	1922	P	Museo Storico Ansaldo. Genova Sampierdarena (wrong works plate)
625.161	2-6-0	1922	P	San Giovanni Lupatoto, Pastificio ditta Rana
625.164	2-6-0	1922	M	MFP. Savigliano
625.177	2-6-0	1922	MA	FFSI. ALe 883. SR
625.308	2-6-0	1904	MR	Italvapore. PT
640.003	2-6-0	1907	M	FFSI. ATTS. PT
640.004	2-6-0	1907	S	SSM. For MNF
640.008	2-6-0	1907	M	FFSI. TC
640.019	2-6-0	1907	P	Museo Piana delle Orme, Borgo Faiti
640.021	2-6-0	1907	P	Abandoned Fréjus tunnel, near Modane, France
640.064	2-6-0	1908	M	MFT
640.071	2-6-0	1908	M	MFP, stored Torino Ponte Mosca
640.088	2-6-0	1910	M	MNF
640.091	2-6-0	1910	MA	Arezzo Pescaiola TFT depot, owner Nettunia Sud
640.095	2-6-0	1910	MR	Arezzo Pescaiola TFT depot, owner Nettunia Sud
640.105	2-6-0	1910	MR	Officine Magliola Santhià
640.115	2-6-0	1910	M	Villa del Conte
640.121	2-6-0	1910	MA	FFSI. ATSER. PT
640.122	2-6-0	1910	MR	MFP, Torino Ponte Mosca (numbered 640.2)
640.143	2-6-0	1911	MA	FFSI. LS
640.148	2-6-0	1911	P	FFSI. ATTS. SR
680.037	2-6-2	1908	M	MNF
683.015	2-6-2	1918	M	MFT (ex JŽ 22.069, ex MÁV 324 736)
685.068	2-6-2	1914	M	MNF
685.089	2-6-2	1915	MA	FFSI. ATTS. PT
685.196	2-6-2	1920	MA	FFSI. AVTS. VR
685.222	2-6-2	1926	S	PT. Private owner
S.685.600	2-6-2	1908	M	MNST
691.022	4-6-2	1914	M	MNST
728.008	2-8-0	1920	P	Crnomelj, Slovenia (ex JŽ 25.018, ex kkStB 270.215)
728.014	2-8-0	1920	P	Novo Mesto, Slovenia (ex JŽ 25.019, ex kkStB 270.150)
728.022	2-8-0	1920	MA	FFSI. TS (ex JŽ 25.022 ex kkStB 270.158)
728.028	2-8-0	1920	MA	Ljubljana museum (ex JŽ 25.026, ex kkStB 270.164)
735.128	2-8-0	1919	M	MNF
735.155	2-8-0	1919	S	MFP, Stored Torino Ponte Mosca
736.073	2-8-0	1944	MR	Tyseley depot, UK (USATC Type S160 3278)
736.083	2-8-0	1944	S	MFP. Stored Torino Ponte Mosca (USATC 3292)
736.090	2-8-0	1944	S	Tithorea, Greece
736.114	2-8-0	1944	M	MNF, (USATC 3324, restored as 3671)
740.002	2-8-0	1911	M	ATSER. BC ?
740.003	2-8-0	1911	M	ASTS. CG
740.009	2-8-0	1911	S	FFSI. FI
740.017	2-8-0	1911	P	Sassari, Piazza Largo di Baratz
740.019	2-8-0	1911	P	Rimini works
740.038	2-8-0	1911	MA	FFSI. AVTS. VR
740.045	2-8-0	1911	P	Vicenza, Beltrame steel works
740.054	2-8-0	1912	P	Bova Superiore, park Via 4 Novembre
740.072	2-8-0	1912	P	Acireale station
740.074	2-8-0	1912	MR	ALe 883, MS
740.095	2-8-0	1913	M	MFT
740.097	2-8-0	1913	P	Verona, private works
740.103	2-8-0	1913	P	Tecnofreno, S. Pietro in Cariano
740.108	2-8-0	1914	M	MFT
740.113	2-8-0	1914	P	Caserno Genio Ferroviario, Torino
740.115	2-8-0	1914	M	PT (ex 741.115)
740.117	2-8-0	1914	S	Falconara Marittima
740.121	2-8-0	1914	P	Postojna, Slovenia
740.130	2-8-0	1914	S	FFSI. ALe 883. CR
740.135	2-8-0	1914	P	Roma San Lorenzo depot

740.143	2-8-0	1914	P		Outside Hitachi plant, Pistoia
740.144	2-8-0	1915	S		Fabriano
740.151	2-8-0	1915	S		Cagliari yard
740.160	2-8-0	1915	S		FA
740.161	2-8-0	1915	P		Casale Monferrato, ditta Gaiero
740.171	2-8-0	1915	P		Zagarolo, Guazzolini Mobili, Viale Stazione
740.192	2-8-0	1915	P		Camerano di Poggio Berni
740.244	2-8-0	1919	MA		FFSI. PT
740.254	2-8-0	1919	M		FFSI. PT
740.267	2-8-0	1919	P		Museo delle Comunicazioni, Cormano
740.278	2-8-0	1922	MA		FFSI. ATSL. LS
740.282	2-8-0	1920	M		MFP.
740.284	2-8-0	1920	S		Civitanova Marche
740.286	2-8-0	1920	MA		FFSI. PT
740.287	2-8-0	1920	P		Lamezia Terme, market place
740.293	2-8-0	1922	MA		FFSI. AVTS. MT
740.296	2-8-0	1919	M		FFSI. RTVT. RS
740.299	2-8-0	1919	P		Pioltello, Voiture Café bar
740.300	2-8-0	1919	MR		PA. To be plinthed at Porto Empedocle Centrale
740.303	2-8-0	1919	S		Cagliari yard
740.311	2-8-0	1919	MR		FFSI. ALe 883. CR
740.329	2-8-0	1920	MA		Arezzo Pescaiola TFT depot, owner Nettunia Sud
740.351	2-8-0	1921	P		near Pescara Centrale station
740.397	2-8-0	1920	P		Cerea
740.409	2-8-0	1920	MR		FFSI. ATSER. FO
740.423	2-8-0	1923	MA		FFSI. ASTS. CG
740.436	2-8-0	1923	P		Roma, Istituto Sperimentale RFI
740.439	2-8-0	1923	P		Cornuda, Trattoria "Alla Beccaccia"
740.451	2-8-0	1922	P		MFPV. ATTS
740.452	2-8-0	1922	S		Siracusa goods yard
740.462	2-8-0	1922	S		S. Guiliano d'Arezzo TFT station, owner Nettunia Sud
741.120	2-8-0	1914	MA		FFSI. ATTS. PT
741.137	2-8-0	1914	M		MNF
743.283	2-8-0	1920	M		FFSI. TC
743.301	2-8-0	1920	M		FFSI. MNT
744.003	2-8-0	1928	P		Cagliari station

▲ 2-8-0 740.143 is seen plinthed outside the Hitachi factory in Pistoia on 9 February 2018. **Robert Pritchard**

744.118	2-8-0	1928	M	FFSI. PT
746.031	2-8-2	1922	M	MNST
746.038	2-8-2	1923	M	FFSI. ATTS. PT
800.008	0-4-0T	1907	M	MNF
814.002	0-4-2T	1881	M	MNST
813.011	0-6-0T	1923	M	Museo dei Trasporti, Bologna (TBPM 11 in disguise)
817.004	0-6-0T	1907	P	Utensileria Foppoli, Piamborno
829.001	0-6-0T	1900	P	Alpignano, private house
830.001	0-6-0T	1902	P	Cokitalia, San Giuseppe di Cairo "1"
830.006	0-6-0T	1902	P	Via Muzza Sud 969, Crevalcore
830.008	0-6-0T	1902	P	Savona docks "7"
830.010	0-6-0T	1902	M	Castelletto Monferrato (ex CSFT Bologna)
830.011	0-6-0T	1902	P	Acqui Terme
830.017	0-6-0T	1906	P	Parco Archelogico Industriale, ex Breda, Sesto S. Giovanni
830.022	0-6-0T	1906	P	Savona Marittima (EMP 10)
830.035	0-6-0T	1906	P	Autodromo, Pergusa (Sicily)
835.001	0-6-0T	1906	M	MNF
835.008	0-6-0T	1906	P	Savona docks "7"
835.009	0-6-0T	1906	P	Cave di Botticino, near Brescia
835.012	0-6-0T	1906	P	Marradi, park
835.015	0-6-0T	1906	P	Ospedaletto di Pescantina, near Casa del Bambù
835.029	0-6-0T	1907	P	Cecina, park
835.040	0-6-0T	1908	P	Pula station, Croatia
835.043	0-6-0T	1908	P	Viadana Bresciana, Calvisano steel works
835.046	0-6-0T	1908	P	San Zenone al Lambro
835.047	0-6-0T	1908	MR	ARSMS. MS
835.051	0-6-0T	1908	P	Musea Storico Piana delle Orme, Borgo Faiti
835.053	0-6-0T	1906	M	LS, for MNF
835.062	0-6-0T	1908	P	Campiglia Marittima, near Museo della Civiltà del Lavoro
835.067	0-6-0T	1908	S	Falconara Marittima
835.069	0-6-0T	1908	P	Hotel Willy, Gemona del Friuli (disguised as 835.034)
835.073	0-6-0T	1908	P	Castelletto Ticino, Museo Gottard Park
835.084	0-6-0T	1908	P	Livorno, G Micheli school, Piazza Undici Maggio
835.088	0-6-0T	1908	M	ATTS. PT
835.092	0-6-0T	1908	P	Sulmona station
835.106	0-6-0T	1908	P	Brescello, near Museo Peppone e Don Camillo
835.114	0-6-0T	1908	P	Salerno FS Dopolavoro, park, via Dalmatia
835.127	0-6-0T	1909	P	Arquata Scrivia
835.136	0-6-0T	1909	P	ditto Fausti, Passo di Treia, Strada 361
835.149	0-6-0T	1909	P	Savona docks "10"
835.156	0-6-0T	1910	S	Feralp, Bussoleno
835.157	0-6-0T	1910	P	Vallecrosia, Museo della Canzone
835.159	0-6-0T	1910	P	Museo dei Tramways, Altavilla Monferrato
835.160	0-6-0T	1910	P	Castel Maggiore, Caserma del Genio Ferrovieri (as 835.244)
835.163	0-6-0T	1910	P	Vanzaghello, via Foscolo, gardens
835.166	0-6-0T	1910	M	Falconara Marittima
835.168	0-6-0T	1910	P	Museo Memoriale della Libertà, Bologna
835.186	0-6-0T	1910	M	MNST
835.203	0-6-0T	1911	P	Genova Bolzaneto
835.205	0-6-0T	1911	P	Polla station
835.213	0-6-0T	1906	P	LS
835.222	0-6-0T	1911	M	Volandia, Somma Lombardo
835.226	0-6-0T	1911	MR	FFSI. ARSMS. MS
835.231	0-6-0T	1911	M	MFT (wrong works plate)
835.234	0-6-0T	1911	P	Camposampiero station
835.240	0-6-0T	1911	M	MFP
835.241	0-6-0T	1911	P	Carpignano Sesia, gardens
835.244	0-6-0T	1911	M	MP, Lecce
835.255	0-6-0T	1912	P	Dopolavoro park via Serlio, Bologna
835.257	0-6-0T	1912	P	Landriano, private owner
835.260	0-6-0T	1912	P	Ancona, Verbena park, via Giuseppe Ungaresti
835 262	0-6-0T	1912	P	Viadana, private owner (as 835 234)
835.271	0-6-0T	1912	P	Affi, old station

835.274	0-6-0T	1912	P	S. Donà di Piave, near Europa garden
835.275	0-6-0T	1912	P	Taino, park
835.276	0-6-0T	1912	P	San Zeno Naviglio, near Duferdofin plant
835.291	0-6-0T	1915	P	Campo San Martino, A&O supermarket
835.295	0-6-0T	1915	P	Caserma Gamberini, Ozzano del'Emilia
835.322	0-6-0T	1921	P	Caldaro
835.323	0-6-0T	1921	P	LV
835.327	0-6-0T	1921	P	TA
835.348	0-6-0T	1921	P	Sequals, private owner
850.022	4-4-0T	1896	M	MNF (numbered N 22, ex MMO)
851.036	0-6-0T	1905	P	Laghi di Sibari park
851.043	0-6-0T	1907	P	San Benedetto Po station
851.057	0-6-0T	1907	P	ALe 883, Tirano
851.066	0-6-0T	1906	P	Fossalta di Portogruaro
851.074	0-6-0T	1906	S	ATSER. BC ?
851.097	0-6-0T	1900	P	Ponton di Domegliara, Istituto Casa Nazareth
851.103	0-6-0T	1900	P	Museo Bersano, Nizza Monferrato
851.105	0-6-0T	1900	P	Faenza, Parco Roberto Bucci, via Oberdan
851.110	0-6-0T	1904	M	MNF
851.112	0-6-0T	1900	P	Mestre, Via Olimpia
851.113	0-6-0T	1900	P	Palagianello
851.130	0-6-0T	1908	P	Rapallo, Parco Comunale Luigi Casale
851.186	0-6-0T	1909	P	Como, Giardino Zoologica (zoo)
851.203	0-6-0T	1910	P	Sulphur (museum), Perticara di Novafeltria (Rimini)
875.019	2-6-0T	1912	P	Asti, school, via Galvani
875.039	2-6-0T	1913	M	MNF
875.083	2-6-0T	1914	M	Sartid steelworks, Smedorovo, Serbia (ex JŽ 154-008)
875.090	2-6-0T	1915	P	Castelletto Ticino, near Museo Gottard Park
880.001	2-6-0T	1916	MA	SVF, Museo Ferroviario (old depot), Primolano
880.002	2-6-0T	1916	P	Carmignano di Brenta, scuola media statale
880.004	2-6-0T	1916	P	Romagnano Sesia station
880.006	2-6-0T	1916	P	Palazzo del Te, Mantova
880.008	2-6-0T	1916	M	MFP, Magliola Santhià
880.009	2-6-0T	1916	P	Foggia, Parco Karol Wojtyla
880.010	2-6-0T	1916	P	Castelnuovo di Sotto, Ristorante Poli alla Stazione, in old station
880.012	2-6-0T	1916	P	Senago, ditta Tosi
880.016	2-6-0T	1922	P	Rive d'Arcano, school
880.023	2-6-0T	1922	M	MFT
880.038	2-6-0T	1922	P	Bologna Centrale FS depot
880.045	2-6-0T	1922	MR	MFP, Torino Ponte Mosca (MFP 880.1)
880.051	2-6-0T	1922	MA	FFSI. ALe 883. MS
880.054	2-6-0T	1922	P	Treviso FS depot
880.108	2-6-0T	1922	P	Villa Santina old station
880.157	2-6-0T	1922	S	CFTB, Ste Foy l'Argentière, France
880.159	2-6-0T	1922	M	MNST
895.014	0-8-0T	1909	P	Perugia, Città della Domenica theme park
895.024	0-8-0T	1909	P	Cava Museo, Miseglia Massa-Carrara
895.115	0-8-0T	1913	M	MFT
895.159	0-8-0T	1916	M	MFP, Savigliano
896.030	0-8-0T	1922	M	MNF
899.006	0-6-0T	1882	M	MNF
905.032	2-6-0T	1910	M	MNF
905.043	2-6-0T	1911	M	MP, Lecce
910.001	2-6-2T	1905	M	MNF
940.001	2-8-2T	1921	M	MNST
940.002	2-8-2T	1921	P	Piazza al Serchio station
940.003	2-8-2T	1921	M	ATSER. BC ?
940.006	2-8-2T	1922	M	FFSI. Foligno
940.008	2-8-2T	1922	M	FFSI. PT
940.014	2-8-2T	1922	MR	Voghera, Politechnico Milano, viale Carlo Marx
940.015	2-8-2T	1922	P	Nova Gorica, Slovenia (JŽ 118-005)
940.019	2-8-2T	1922	P	Ronco Briantino, park, via Don Biago Rossetti
940.022	2-8-2T	1922	MA	FFSI. AVTS. MT

940.026	2-8-2T	1922	S	Italvapore, Firenze Romito.
940.030	2-8-2T	1922	M	MFP, Savigliano
940.033	2-8-2T	1922	M	MNF
940.036	2-8-2T	1922	M	FFSI. ATSL. PT, for Pietrarsa museum
940.038	2-8-2T	1922	M	PT
940.041	2-8-2T	1922	MA	FFSI. TC
940.044	2-8-2T	1922	S	FFSI. Foligno
940.047	2-8-2T	1922	P	Casarsa della Delizia, near station
940.050	2-8-2T	1922	M	LS, for MNF
940.052	2-8-2T	1924	P	ACAF, Montesilvano station
980.002	0-6-0T	1908	M	MNF
981.001	0-6-0T	1922	R	MFP, Savigliano
981.004	0-6-0T	1922	M	Paola. FS Dopolavoro, Strada E1
981.005	0-6-0T	1922	S	FFSI. RS
981.006	0-6-0T	1922	S	Cosenza depot
981.007	0-6-0T	1922	M	Corinaldo, private owner
981.008	0-6-0T	1922	M	ATTS. PT

6.2. DIESEL LOCOMOTIVES

Number	Details	Built	Status	Location
D.141.1011	Bo-Bo de	1963	MA	FFSI. ALe 883. SR
D.143.3021	Bo-Bo de	1943	MA	FFSI. Treno DOC. LS
D.143.3045	Bo-Bo de	1942	M	FFSI. Treno DOC. PA ?
207.002	B dm	1935	P	Verona Quadrante Europa
207.020	B dm	1935	M	MNF
207.023	B dm	1935	M	MP. Lecce
207.040	B dm	1934	M	MFT
208.003	B dm	1938	M	FBS
209.005	B dm	1968	M	ARSMS (ex industrial, dressed up in FS livery)
210.006	B m	1940	MA	FFSI. PT
210.010	B m	1940	S	FFSI. PT
211.050	B dm	1949	MR	ARSMS. MS
211.063	B dm	1951	MA	FFSI. ATSER. PT
214.7013	B dh	1965	M	MNT
215.005	B dh	1956	MR	MFP. Torino Ponte Mosca
215.006	B dh	1956	M	MNF
216.0015	B dh	1967	M	MFP. Officine Magliola Santhià
216.0016	B dh	1967	M	TA
216.0022	B dh	1967	M	BC ?
216.0042	B dh	1967	M	MP. Lecce
225.6011	B dh	1960	M	ACAF. Montesilvano
234.2012	C dh	1962	P	MFP. Magliola Santhià
235.0003	C dh	1957	M	MNT. for MNF
235.3005	C dh	1961	M	MNF
245.0001	C dh	1964	P	ACAF. Montesilvano
250.2001	C dh	1966	MR	FFSI. LS
D.341.1016	Bo-Bo de	1958	M	MNF
D.341.1022	Bo-Bo de	1961	S	FFSI. Foligno (ex FCU)
D.341.1029	Bo-Bo de	1961	S	FFSI. Foligno (ex FCU)
D.341.1066	Bo-Bo de	1963	S	FFSI. Foligno (ex FCU)
D.341.2016	Bo-Bo de	1958	S	MFP
D.341.2020	Bo-Bo de	1958	P	Aeroporto Militare, Rieti
D.341.2026	Bo-Bo de	1958	S	MFP
D.341.2028	Bo-Bo de	1958	S	MFP
D.342.4004	B-B dh	1959	M	MFP Torino Ponte Mosca
D.342.4010	B-B dh	1960	MA	FFSI. PT
D.342.4011	B-B dh	1961	M	MNF
D.343.1001	B-B de	1967	MR	FFSI. Treno D.O.C., PA
D.343.1030	B-B de	1968	MA	FFSI. ALe 883. MC
D.343.1039	B-B de	1968	MA	MP. Lecce (as FSE BB 169)
D.343.1055	B-B de	1968	MA	FFSI. TS
D.343.2026	B-B de	1969	MA	FFSI.

D.345.1118	B-B de	1977	MA	FFSI. ATSL. LS
D.345.1121	B-B de	1977	MA	FFSI. Treno DOC. PA
D.345.1142	B-B de	1979	MA	FFSI. TC
372.002	1A-A1	1942	M	TPER. As Ld 372 FP. Ferrara PR
D.443.1030	B-B de	1968	MA	FFSI. ATSP. TA ?
D.443.2002	B-B de	1967	M	FFSI. PT
D.443.2018	B-B de	1967	M	FFSI. CG
D.445.1006	B-B de	1974	MA	FFSI. PT
D.445.1011	B-B de	1974	MA	FFSI. PT
D.445.1034	B-B de	1975	MA	FFSI. Treno DOC. PA
D.461.1001	Co-Co de	1961	M	MFP. Savigliano
Ne 700.001	C	1941	S	MFP. Torino Ponte Mosca

6.3. DIESEL RAILCARS

Number	Details	Built	Status	Location
ALn 40.1001	1A-A1	1943	M	FFSI, ex GTT. TC
ALn 40.1008	1A-A1	1943	MA	FFSI. TC (as GTT ALn 40.004)
ALn 56.136	1A-A1	1935	MR	Migliaro. Associazione Amici della FSF
ALn 56.1903	B-B	1937	M	Rahmi M. Koc museum, Istanbul, on loan from Wolfsonian Museum, Miami Beach, Florida, USA
ALn 448.2008	B-2	1958	S	Officine Magliola, Santhià
ALn 460.2008	2-B	1958	S	Officine Magliola, Santhià
ALn 556.1236	1A-A1	1937	S	FFSI. MS
ALn 556.1277	1A-A1	1937	S	FFSI. MS
ALn 556.1202	1A-A1	1937	M	MNF
ALn 556.2312	1A-A1	1939	M	MNF
ALn 556.2331	1A-A1	1940	MA	FFSI. PT
ALn 668.1220	1A-A1	1979	MA	FFSI. CR
ALn 668.1224	1A-A1	1979	MA	FFSI. CR
ALn 668.1401	1A-A1	1956	MA	FFSI. PT
ALn 668.1452	1A-A1	1960	MA	FFSI. PT
ALn 668.1462	1A-A1	1960	S	FFSI. SSM
ALn 668.1478	1A-A1	1960	S	FFSI. SSM
ALn 668.1615	1A-A1	1970	MA	FFSI. Treno DOC. CT
ALn 668.1616	1A-A1	1970	MA	FFSI. Treno DOC. CT
ALn 668.1870	1A-A1	1972	MA	FFSI. BE
ALn 668.1882	1A-A1	1973	MA	FFSI. BE
ALn 668.1904	1A-A1	1975	MA	FFSI. SR
ALn 668.1908	1A-A1	1975	MA	FFSI. SR
ALn 668.1936	1A-A1	1976	MA	FFSI. Treno DOC. SR
ALn 772.1005	1A-A1	1940	S	FFSI. Foligno
ALn 772.1033	1A-A1	1940	S	MFP. TC
ALn 772.3263	1A-A1	1942	S	FFSI. ASTS. FO
ALn 772.3265	1A-A1	1942	MA	FFSI. PT
ALn 772.3375	1A-A1	1956	M	MNF
ALn 773.3504	1A-A1	1957	MA	FFSI. Foligno
ALn 773.3505	1A-A1	1957	MA	FFSI. Foligno
ALn 773.3516	1A-A1	1957	M	FFSI. Foligno
ALn 773.3538	1A-A1	1958	S	FFSI. SSM
ALn 773.3542	1A-A1	1962	MA	EAV (FA). Piedimonte Matese (as ALn 773.012)
ALn 773.3558	1A-A1	1958	S	FFSI. SSM
ALn 776.1001	1A-A1	1940	M	MFP. Savigliano
ALn 873.3505	1A-A1	1962	M	FFSI. AVTS. VR
ALn 873.3511	1A-A1	1962	M	FFSI. AVTS. VR
ALn 880.2018	B-2	1951	MA	MNF
ALn 990.1005	B-2	1951	S	FFSI. Treno DOC. PA
ATR.410	-	-	-	MFP
RALn 60.09	B-B	1950	S	Castelvetrano depot
RALn 60.10	B-B	1950	S	Castelvetrano depot
RALn 60.11	B-B	1950	S	Castelvetrano depot
RALn 60.12	B-B	1950	P	Villarosa

▲ Diesel railcars ALn 668.1452 and 1401 are seen outside the FFSI depot at Pistoia on 8 April 2018. **David Haydock**

▼ Former three-phase five-axle electric loco E.554.174 is plinthed at Bombardier's plant at Vado Ligure. **David Haydock**

6.4. ELECTRIC LOCOMOTIVES

Number	Details	Built	Status	Location
E.321.003	C	1960	M	ALe 883. Lecco Maggianico
E.321.012	C	1927	P	MNST
E.321.016	C	1927	M	MFPV
E.323.004	C	1966	S	Foligno works
E.323.010	C	1966	S	Rimini depot
E.323.105	C	1966	M	MP, Lecce
E.324.105	C	1966	M	MP, Lecce
E.326.004	2-Co-2	1932	M	MNF
E.330.008	1-C-1	1914	M	MNST
E.333.026	1-C-1	1923	M	MNF
E.400.001	Bo-Bo	1929	M	MNF (ex FCV L.903)
E.404.000	Bo-Bo	1988	M	FFSI. FI
E.424.005	Bo-Bo	1944	MA	FFSI. PT
E.424.049	Bo-Bo	1949	M	FFSI. LS (E.424.249)
E.424.075	Bo-Bo	1949	MA	FFSI. Feralp. Bussoleno
E.424.296	Bo-Bo	1949	MA	CR
E.428.014	2-Bo-Bo-2	1935	MA	FFSI. ATTS. LS
E.428.033	2-Bo-Bo-2	1936	P	Bari depot
E.428.058	2-Bo-Bo-2	1937	MA	Feralp. Bussoleno
E.428.131	2-Bo-Bo-2	1932	M	MFP. Savigliano
E.428.174	2-Bo-Bo-2	1939	M	MFV. Luino
E.428.202	2-Bo-Bo-2	1940	MA	FFSI. ATSL. LS
E.428.208	2-Bo-Bo-2	1940	M	MFV. Luino
E.428.209	2-Bo-Bo-2	1940	M	MNF
E.428.226	2-Bo-Bo-2	1941	MA	FFSI. LS
E.430.001	Bo-Bo	1902	M	MNST
E.431.027	1-D-1	1924	M	MFP. Savigliano
E.431.037	1-D-1	1924	M	Technik Museum, Speyer, Germany (loan from Luzern)
E.432.001	1-D-1	1928	M	MNF
E.432.031	1-D-1	1928	M	MFP. Savigliano
E.444.001	Bo-Bo	1965	M	MNF
E.454.001	Bo-Bo	1989	M	FFSI. LS
E.491.011	Bo-Bo	1988	M	FFSI. Turno C. Foligno
E.550.022	E	1910	M	FFSI. PT (ex Vnx 806.211)
E.550.025	E	1910	M	Museum, St Louis, USA (to move to MFP Savigliano)
E.550.030	E	1927	M	MNST
E.550.086	E	1916	M	Feralp. Bussoleno (as snow plough Vnx 806.200)
E.550.115	E	1916	M	MFT (as snow plough Vnx 806.201)
E.550.173	E	1916	S	MFP. Savigliano (as snow plough Vnx 806.221)
E.551.001	E	1939	M	MNF
E.554.078	E	1929	M	Volandia, Somma Lombarda
E.554.174	E	1930	P	MFP. Bombardier plant. Vado Ligure
E.626.001	Bo-Bo-Bo	1928	MA	FFSI. ATSER. BC
E.626.005 [II]	Bo-Bo-Bo	1927	M	MNF (ex E.625.006)
E.626.015	Bo-Bo-Bo	1931	MA	FFSI. AVTS. MT
E.626.023	Bo-Bo-Bo	1931	P	Ljubljana, Slovenia
E.626.033	Bo-Bo-Bo	1932	M	MP, Lecce
E.626.045	Bo-Bo-Bo	1931	MA	FFSI. Treno DOC. LS
E.626.059	Bo-Bo-Bo	1932	M	MFT. Falsely restored as E.626.027
E.626.074	Bo-Bo-Bo	1932	M	MFPV
E.626.077	Bo-Bo-Bo	1931	M	Ljubljana, Slovenia
E.626.084	Bo-Bo-Bo	1932	S	LS
E.626.089	Bo-Bo-Bo	1932	M	MNT
E.626.093	Bo-Bo-Bo	1932	M	Zagreb, Croatia
E.626.128	Bo-Bo-Bo	1935	MA	PT
E.626.150	Bo-Bo-Bo	1934	M	MFP
E.626.156	Bo-Bo-Bo	1934	P	Foligno works
E.626.183	Bo-Bo-Bo	1935	M	MNT ??
E.626.185	Bo-Bo-Bo	1935	MA	FFSI. ATSP. LS

E.626.188	Bo-Bo-Bo	1935	P	Hotel Willy, Gemona del Friuli (as E.626.384)
E.626.193	Bo-Bo-Bo	1935	M	LS
E.626.194	Bo-Bo-Bo	1934	MA	FFSI. RTVT. RS
E.626.215	Bo-Bo-Bo	1934	M	MFP
E.626.220	Bo-Bo-Bo	1935	M	MFP. Ponte Mosca
E.626.225	Bo-Bo-Bo	1935	MR	FFSI. ALe 883. MS
E.626.231	Bo-Bo-Bo	1935	MA	FFSI. AVTS. VR
E.626.238	Bo-Bo-Bo	1935	MA	FFSI. MFT. LS
E.626.248	Bo-Bo-Bo	1936	M	MFP. Torino Porta Milano
E.626.249	Bo-Bo-Bo	1936	M	Volandia. Somma Lombarda
E.626.266	Bo-Bo-Bo	1936	MA	FFSI. LS
E.626.287	Bo-Bo-Bo	1937	MA	FFSI. Feralp Team. TC
E.626.294	Bo-Bo-Bo	1937	MA	FFSI. LS
E.626.386	Bo-Bo-Bo	1937	M	MFP
E.626.428	Bo-Bo-Bo	1939	MA	FFSI. Treno DOC. LS
E.626.443	Bo-Bo-Bo	1939	MA	FFSI. ALe 883. Tirano
E.632.030	B-B-B	1986	MA	FFSI. SR
E.636.002	Bo-Bo-Bo	1942	M	Feralp Team. TC
E.636.065	Bo-Bo-Bo	1942	MA	FFSI. LS
E.636.117	Bo-Bo-Bo	1953	S	FFSI. ALe 883. MS
E.636.128	Bo-Bo-Bo	1955	MA	FFSI. Treno DOC. PA
E.636.147	Bo-Bo-Bo	1955	M	ARSMS. Bahnpark, Augsburg, Germany
E.636.161	Bo-Bo-Bo	1956	MA	FFSI. LS
E.636.164	Bo-Bo-Bo	1956	MA	FFSI. ALe 883. MS
E.636.243	Bo-Bo-Bo	1956	MA	FFSI. ALe 883. LS
E.636.265	Bo-Bo-Bo	1961	MA	FFSI. ATSL. LS
E.636.284	Bo-Bo-Bo	1961	MA	FFSI. ALe 883. MS
E.636.318	Bo-Bo-Bo	1960	MA	FFSI. ATSP. LS
E.636.356	Bo-Bo-Bo	1960	M	ACAF. Montesilvano
E.636.365	Bo-Bo-Bo	1960	M	FFSI. LS
E.636.385	Bo-Bo-Bo	1961	MA	FFSI. LS

▲ E.636.065 and 740.278 are seen outside FFSI's depot at La Spezia on 9 April 2018.

David Haydock

E.636.454	Bo-Bo-Bo	1962	M	MFT. LS
E.645.021	Bo-Bo-Bo	1952	P	MS
E.645.022	Bo-Bo-Bo	1952	S	ARSMS. MS
E.645.023	Bo-Bo-Bo	1959	MA	FFSI. ATSL. LS
E.645.063	Bo-Bo-Bo	1965	M	MFT
E.645.084	Bo-Bo-Bo	1965	M	FFSI. ARSMS. PT
E.645.090	Bo-Bo-Bo	1963	M	MS. ALe 883
E.645.104	Bo-Bo-Bo	1958	MA	MS. ALe 883 (as E.646.004)
E.646.028	Bo-Bo-Bo	1962	MA	FFSI. ATSP. LS
E.646.085	Bo-Bo-Bo	1963	MA	FFSI. ATSL. LS
E.646.158	Bo-Bo-Bo	1964	MA	FFSI. ALe 883. SR
E.646.190	Bo-Bo-Bo	1966	M	FFSI. Treno DOC. PA
E.646.196	Bo-Bo-Bo	1966	MA	FFSI. Treno DOC. PA
E.656.001	Bo-Bo-Bo	1976	MA	FFSI. ALe 883. SR
E.656.023	Bo-Bo-Bo	1975	MA	FFSI. PT
E.656.031	Bo-Bo-Bo	1976	M	MFT
E.655.079	Bo-Bo-Bo	1977	S	FFSI. ARSMS. MS?
E.656.454	Bo-Bo-Bo	1987	M	FFSI. LS
E.656.590	Bo-Bo-Bo	1989	MA	FFSI. LS

6.5. ELECTRIC MULTIPLE UNITS / RAILCARS

Number	Details	Built	Status	Location
ALe 540.010	Bo-Bo	1959	MA	MFT
ALe 540.030	Bo-Bo	1960	MA	MFT
ALe 601.003	Bo-Bo	1961	M	FFSI. ALe 883. SSM
ALe 601.017	Bo-Bo	1962	M	FFSI. ALe 883. SSM
ALe 601.031	Bo-Bo	1965	M	FFSI. ALe 883. SSM
ALe 601.039	Bo-Bo	1965	M	FFSI. ALe 883. SSM
ALe 781.005	Bo-Bo	1939	M	MFP. Savigliano
ALe 790.030	Bo-Bo	1944	M	MFP
ALe 792.004	Bo-Bo	1937	M	MNF
ALe 840.012	Bo-Bo	1951	M	FFSI. AVTS. CR
ALe 840.046	Bo-Bo	1950	MA	Feralp. Bussoleno
ALe 880.045	Bo-Bo	1940	MA	FFSI. FO
ALe 880.085	Bo-Bo	1939	MA	FFSI. FO
ALe 883.007	Bo-Bo	1942	MA	FFSI. ALe 883. SR
E.623.100	Bo-Bo	1932	MA	TFT. Arezzo
E.623.106	Bo-Bo	1932	M	MNF
E.623.601	Bo-Bo	1932	M	MFP. Ponte Mosca
E.623.612	Bo-Bo	1932	MA	FFSI. ALe 883. MS
E.623.629	Bo-Bo	1932	MA	FFSI. ALe 883. MS

6.5. HIGH-SPEED ELECTRIC MULTIPLE UNITS

Number	Details	Built	Status	Location
ETR.232	Bo-2-2-Bo+Bo-2	1939	MA	FFSI. Roma Termini
ETR.252	Bo-2-Bo+2-2-Bo	1960	MR	FFSI. Porrena
ETR.302	Bo-2-Bo+Bo-2-2-Bo+Bo-2-Bo	1953	MR	FFSI. Voghera
ETR.401	1A-A1-1A-A1+1A-A1-1A-A1	1976	M	FFSI. CR/Falconara Marittima
ETR.450.03	-	1988	M	FFSI. ??

6.6. FOREIGN LOCOMOTIVES (from State railways)

Number	Details	Built	Status	Location
DR 50 3673	2-10-0	1961	MA	MFV. Luino
DB 323 495	B	1935	M	MNT as Kö 4641
JZ 33.107	2-10-0	1943	M	MFT. (DRB 52 4752)
SBB 12339	1-B-B-1	1922	M	MFV. Luino

See also JZ steam locos above.

▲ Electric railcars E.623.629 and 612, with two trailers between them are seen at Salsomaggiore Terma on 23 April 2017.   **Marco Cacozza**

▼ Former DB "Köf" shunter 323 495 is seen inside the "National Railway Museum" in La Spezia on 9 April 2018.   **David Haydock**

APPENDIX I. BUILDERS

The following abbreviations for traction and rolling stock builders are used in this book. In general, modern construction contracts are split between several companies so the same sort of loco is built by different countries at the same time.

ABB	Asea Brown Boveri, Milano & Vado Ligure.
ABB Tecnomasio	ABB Tecnomasio, Vado Ligure. Formerly TIBB. Later ADtranz.
ABR	Ateliers Belges Réunis, Belgium.
ACEC	Ateliers de Constructions Électriques, Charleroi, Belgium.
ADtranz Italia	Adtranz Italia, Vado Ligure. Formerly ABB Tecnomasio. Now Bombardier.
AEG	Allgemeine Elektricitäts Gesellshaft, Berlin-Hennigsdorf, Germany.
AERFER	Societa Anonima Industrie Meccaniche Aeronautiche Meridionali "Aerfer", Pomigliano & Pozzuoli.
Aerosicula	Aerosicula Metalmeccanica, Palermo & Carini.
Alce	Azionaria Laziale Costruzioni Elletromecchaniche, Roma & Pomezia.
Alco	American Locomotive Works, Schenectady, New York, USA.
Alioth	Elektrizitätsgesellshaft Alioth, Münchenstein, Switzerland. Later BBC.
Alstom	Alstom Ferroviaria, Savigliano and Colleferro. Formerly Fiat.
AMT	Consorzio Ansaldo-Marelli-Tibb.
Ansaldo	Ansaldo Trasporti, Napoli.
AnsaldoBreda	AnsaldoBreda, Napoli and Pistoia. Formerly Ansaldo and Breda.
ASGEN	Ansaldo S. Giorgio Compagnia Generale Stabilimenti Elettromeccanici Riuniti, Genova
Badoni (ABL)	Antonio Badoni, Lecco.
Baldwin	Baldwin Locomotive Works, Philadelphia, Pennsylvania, USA.
Beilhack	Martin Beilhack Maschinenfabrik, Rosenheim, Germany.
B&M	Baume et Marpent, Morlanwetz, Belgium.
BN	La Brugeoise et Nivelles, Brugge, Belgium.
Bombardier	Bombardier Transportation, Vado Ligure. Formerly Adtranz Italia.
Borsig	Borsig, Berlin Tegal.
Breda	Breda Eletromeccanica & Locomotive, Milano & Sesto San Giovanni.
Breda Pt	Breda Construzioni Ferroviairie, Pistoia.
BRIF	Fabbrica Automobili Isotta Fraschini & Motori Breda, Saronno.
Casaralta	Officine di Casaralta, Bologna.
Casertane	Officine Meccaniche Casertane SpA, Caserta.
Caterpillar	Caterpillar, Peoria, Illinois, USA.
CaTo	Carminati & Toselli, Milano.
CEMSA	Construzioni Elletromeccaniche di Saronno SpA, Saronno.
Cesa	Construzioni Elettromeccaniche SpA, Sesto San Giovanni.
CGE	Compagnia Generale di Elletricità, Milano.
Citadella	Officine di Cittadella, Cittadella, Padova.
CKD	CKD, Praha, Czech Republic.
CNR	Cantieri Navali Riuniti, Pelermo.
Costaferroviaria	Costaferroviaria, Costa Masnaga.
Couillet	Couillet, Belgium.
Daimler	Daimler Benz, Stuttgart, Germany.
Deutz	Deutz, Köln, Germany.
DPA	DPA, Catania.
Drewry	Drewry Car Company.
Düwag	Düsseldorfer Waggonfabrik, Düsseldorf, Germany.
Electroputere	Electroputere, Craiova, Romania.
Esslingen	Maschinenfabrik Esslingen, Esslingen am Neckar, Germany.
Fer	Galileo Ferraris.
Ferrosud	Ferrosud, Matera.
FERVET	Fervet, Castelfranco Veneto.
Fiat	Fiat Ferroviairia, Colleferro, Torino & Savigliano.
Fiore	Officine Fiore, Ercolano.
Fipem	Fabbrica Italiana Prodotti Elettrici e Meccanici spA, Regello.
FIREMA	Firema Trasporti, Sesto San Giovanni.
GEC-Alsthom	GEC-Alsthom, Belfort, France.
GE	General Electric, Erie, Pennsylvania, USA.
Gmeinder	Gmeinder & Co., Mosbach, Germany.
GM	General Motors, USA.

Graz	Johann Weitzer Waggonfabrik, Graz, Austria (Grazerr Waggon).
Greco	Ing. Greco & Com, Reggio Emilia.
Henschel	Henschel und Sohn, Kassel, Germany.
IMAM	IMAM, Napoli.
IMER	Industrie Metalmeccaniche Riunite, Palermo & Carini.
IMESI	Industrie Meccaniche Siciliane, Carini.
IMPA	IMPA, Catania.
Isotta Fraschini	Isotta Fraschini, Saronno.
Italtrafo	Italtrafo SpA, Napoli, Milano & Pomezia.
ITIN	Italimprese Industrie, Catania.
Jenbach	Jenbacher Werke, Jenbach, Austria.
Jung	Jung Lokomotivfabrik, Jungenthal bei Kirchberg an der Sieg, Germany.
KM	Krauss Maffei, München Germany.
Krupp	Friedrich Krupp Maschinenfabrik, Essen, Germany.
La Meuse	Société Anonyme des Atliers de la Meuse, Liège, Belgium.
LHB	Linke Hoffmann Werke, Breslau, Germany.
Liaz	Liaz, Liberec, Czech Republic.
LMS	London, Midland & Scottish Railway, Derby Locomotive Works, England.
Lucana	Metalmeccanica Lucana, Napoli & Tito Scalo.
Macchi	Fratelli Macchi, Varese.
Maffei	Maffei, München, Germany.
MaK	Maschinenbau Kiel, Kiel, Germany.
MAN	Maschinenfabrik Augsburg-Nürnberg, Germany.
Marelli	Ercole Marelli Trazione, Milano & Sesto San Giovanni.
MATER	Motori Alternatori Trasformatori Elettrici Roma, Roma.
Maybach	Maybach Motorenbau, Friedrichshafen, Germany.
MR	Mercedes Benz, Berlin Marienfeld, Germany.
MeRo	Meccanica Romana, Roma.
Moyse	Etablissements Gaston Moyse, La Courneuve, France.
MTU	Motoren und Turbinen Union, Friedrichshafen, Germany.
Navali	Officine Meccaniche e Navali, Napoli.
Ness	Nesselsdorfer Wagenbau Fabriks Gesellschaft.
OCREN	Officine Costruzioni Riparazioni Elettromeccaniche Napoletane, Napoli.
OEFT	Tallero, Milano.
OFM	Officine Meriodionali Ferroviaire, Napoli.
O&K	Orenstein & Koppel, Berlin Drewitz, Germany.
OMECA	Officine Meccaniche Calabresi, Reggio di Calabria.
OM	Officine Meccaniche, Milano & Brescia.
OP	Onofri e Paganelli, Granarolo Emilia.
OTO	Odero Terni Orlando Stabilimenti Meccanichi, La Spezia.
Parizzi	Elettromeccanica Parizzi, Bresso. Now Alstom.
Pistoiesi	Officine Meccaniche Ferroviarie Pistoiesi, Pistoia.
Pozzuoli	Stabilimento Meccanico di Pozzuoli.
Ranieri	Ranieri, Roma.
Reggiane	"Reggiane" Officine Meccaniche Italiane, Reggio Emilia.
Reggio E	Officine Meccaniche Italiane, Reggio Emilia.
RETAM	Retam Elettrofin Industria Elettromeccanica ed Elettronica, Bresso
Rolba	Rolba Zürich, Switzerland.
Romeo	S.A. Ital. Ing. Nicola Romeo & C., Saronno.
San Giorgio	Officine San Giorgio, San Giorgio delle Pertiche.
Saronno	Costruzioni Meccaniche, Saronno.
Saurer	Saurer, Arbon, Switzerland.
Savigliano	Soc. Nazionale delle Officine di Savigliano, Savigliano & Torino.
Schwarzkopff	Schwarzkopff, Berlin, Germany.
Siemens	Siemens Transportation, Munchen Allach, Germany.
SIMM	Soc. Sicula Metalmeccanica, Carini.
Škoda	Škoda, Plzen, Czech Republic.
SLM	Schweizerische Lokomotiv und Maschinenfabrik, Winterthur, Switzerland.
Socimi	Soc. Costruzioni Industriali Milano, Binasco & Sassari.
SOFER	Officine Ferroviarie, Pozzuoli.
Stadler	Stadler Rail, Bussnang, Switzerland.
Stanga	Officina Meccanica della Stanga, Padova.
Sulzer	Gebrüder Sulzer, Winterthur, Switzerland.
TIBB	Tecnomasio Italiano Brown Boveri, Milano & Vado Ligure, later ABB Tecnomasio.

Tosi	Tosi, Legnano.
VM	Stabilimenti Meccanici VM, Cento & Trieste.
Voith	J.M. Voith, Heidenheim, Germany.
Vossloh	Vossloh, Kiel, Germany.
Werkspoor	Werkspoor, Utrecht, Netherlands.
Whitcomb	Whitcomb Locomotove Company, Rochelle, Illinois, USA
Windhoff	Windhoff, Rheine, Germany.
Zephir	Zephir Lok, Modena.

APPENDIX II. COMMON TERMS IN ITALIAN AND ENGLISH

(Note: In Italian c is pronounced like ch in chocolate and ch like k in kite).

Assegnazione – allocation
Automotrici termiche – diesel multiple unit
Automotori da manovre – shunting tractor
Biglietto – ticket
Binario –track/platform
Cambio – change – train or money
Carozza letti – sleeping coach
Caroza cuchette – couchette coach
Deposito Locomotive (D.L.) – loco depot
Elettromotrici – electric multiple unit
Gruppi – class
In arrive – arriving
In partenza – departing
In Ritardo – late (now not so common as in past)
Locomotive: da manovra – shunter
              : a vapour – steam loco
Officine – workshops or garage
Orario – timetable
Prenotazione – seat reservation
Rimessa – Stabling point
Rimorchi – trailer car
Scalo – goods yard
Scartmento – gauge : normale – standard : ridotto – narrow
Sciopero – strike (all too common)
Smistamento – marshalling yard
Stazione – station
Supplemento – supplement
Treno merci – freight train

APPENDIX III. DEPOTS & WORKSHOPS

DEPOTS

Many FSI depots now specialising in maintenance for one division of Trenitalia. Depots maintaining trains for *Regionale* almost all work for just one region, which is noted under Activity.

All locomotives in the book are shown with a code to indicate sector allocation – C for *Mercitilia Rail* (formerly Trenitalia Cargo), I for RFI (infrastructure), M for *Mercitia Shunting and Terminals*, P for *Passeggeri*, R for *Regionale* and TR for *Trenord*. All DMUs and EMUs are allocated to *Regionale* or *Trenord*. All ETR high speed trains are allocated to *Passeggeri* (*Alta Velocità*).

Since the third edition, Cuneo and Pescara depots have been closed. La Spezia and Pistoia are now only used for historic stock. The former FS depot at Udine closed and was taken over by InRail. A newer depot north of Udine is used by *Mercitalia Shunting & Terminals*. We have added Novate Milanese Trenord (FNM) and Sermide (TPER) depots.

Several other operators have their own depots. These are mentioned in Section 2.

Code	Depot	Status	Activity
AL	Alessandria	OML	Regionale (+ OMV). Piemonte.
AN	Ancona	OMR	Regionale (+ OMV). Marche.
BA	Bari	OMR	Passeggeri.
BC	Bologna Centrale	OML	Regionale. Emilia Romagna. RFI has separate depot.
BE	Benevento	OML	Regionale. Campania.
BR	Bologna Ravone	OMV	Regionale. Emilia Romagna.
BS	Bologna San Donato	OMR	Cargo (to close).
BZ	Bolzano	OMR	Regionale. Alto Adige.
CG	Cagliari	OMR	Regionale. Sardegna.
CR	Cremona	OMR	Trenord. Lombardia.
CT	Catania	OMR	Regionale. Sicilia.
CV	Cervignano Smistamento	OMR	Cargo.
CZ	Catanzaro Lido	OML	Regionale. Calabria.
FA	Fabriano	OML	Regionale. Marche.
FG	Foggia	OMR	Regionale. Puglia.
FI	Firenze Osmannaro	OML	Regionale (+ OMV). Toscana.
GB	Genova Brignole	OML	Regionale. Liguria.
GR	Genova Rivarolo	OML	Cargo (to close)
GT	Genova Trasta	OMV	Regionale. Liguria.
IS	Iseo	-	Trenord (FNM). Lombardia.
LC	Lecco	OML	Trenord. Lombardia.
LE	Lecce	OMR	Passeggeri.
LV	Livorno	OMR	Cargo.
MA	Marcianise	-	Cargo.
MC	Milano Centrale	OMV	Passeggeri.
MG	Milano Greco	OML	Passeggeri.
ME	Messina	OMR	Cargo.
MF	Milano Fiorenza	IDP	Trenord. Lombardia.
MI	Milano Farini	OMV	Trenord. Lombardia.
MM	Milano Martesana	OMAV	Passeggeri (+OMV).
MS	Milano Smistamento	OML	Cargo.
MT	Mestre	OMR	Passeggeri.
NC	Napoli Centrale	OMV	Passeggeri.
NF	Napoli Campi Flegrei	OML	Regionale. Campania.
NO	Novara	OML	Regionale. Piemonte.
NS	Napoli Smistamento	OML	Passeggeri.
NV	Novate Milanese		Trenord (FNM). Lombardia.
PA	Palermo	OML	Regionale (+OMV). Sicilia.
PD	Padova	-	Historic.
PE	Pescara	OMR	Regionale. Abruzzo.
PI	Pisa	IMR	Regionale (+OMV). Toscana.

PO	Paola	OMV	Regionale. Calabria.
RC	Reggio di Calabria	OML	Regionale (+OMV). Calabria.
RI	Rimini	-	Historic.
RP	Roma Prenestina	OMV	Passeggeri.
RL	Roma San Lorenzo	OMAV	Passeggeri (+OML).
RS	Roma Smistamento	OMR	Regionale. Lazio.
SI	Siena	OML	Regionale. Toscana.
SL	Salerno	DL	Regionale. Campania.
SM	Sermide		TPER depot.
SR	Siracusa	OMR	Passeggeri.
SS	Sassari	OMR	Regionale. Sardegna.
SU	Sulmona	OMR	Regionale. Abruzzo.
SV	Savona	OMR	Cargo.
TA	Taranto	OMR	Regionale. Puglia.
TC	Torino Smistamento	OML	Regionale. Piemonte.
TE	Terni	OMV	Regionale. Umbria.
TO	Torino Orbassano	OML	Cargo.
TP	Torino RN	OMV	Passeggeri.
TR	Trento	DL	Regionale. Trentino.
TS	Trieste	OMR	Regionale. Friuli-Venezia-Giulia.
TV	Treviso	OML	Regionale. Veneto.
VE	Venezia	-	-
VR	Verona	OML	Regionale (+IMC). Veneto.

DL	Deposito Locomotive.
IDP	Impianto Dinamico Polifunzionale (ETR and EMU depot).
IMC	Impianto di Manutenzione Corrente.
OMAV	Officina Manutenzione Alta Velocita (Pendolino depot).
OML	Officina Manutenzione Locomotive (Loco depot).
OMR	Officina Manutenzione Rotabile (Loco & carriage depot).
OMV	Officina Manutenzione Veicoli (Carriage depot).

FSI WORKSHOPS

FSI has several locomotive and rolling stock workshops but often farms out work to private contractors. Since the last edition, Bologna and Messina works have closed.

Code	Workshop	Activity
FO	Foligno	Electric locos.
FP	Firenze Osmannoro	Carriages.
FW	Foggia	Diesel railcars & EMUs.
	Napoli Santa Maria la Bruna	Carriages.
RW	Rimini	Diesel locos, DMUs, coaching stock.
VW	Verona Porta Vescova	Electric locos, coaching stock.
VI	Vicenza	High speed sets.
VO	Voghera	Carriages.

ACKNOWLEDGEMENTS

We should like to thank Francesco Bloisi, Marco Cacozza, David Campione, Brian Garvin, Gerhard Kernstock, Sylvain Meillasson, Lorenzo Pantani and Stefano Paolini.

The following references were consulted during preparation: Today's Railways Europe, I Treni, Tutto Treno and En Lignes.

Also websites: www.ferrovie.info.it, www.photorail.com, www.trenomania.it